THE LANGUAGE
OF MODERN POETRY

THE LANGUAGE LIBRARY

EDITED BY ERIC PARTRIDGE AND SIMEON POTTER

A. C. Partridge

𝕊𝕊𝕊𝕊𝕊𝕊𝕊𝕊𝕊𝕊𝕊𝕊𝕊𝕊𝕊𝕊𝕊𝕊𝕊𝕊𝕊𝕊𝕊𝕊𝕊

THE LANGUAGE OF MODERN POETRY
Yeats, Eliot, Auden

𝕊𝕊𝕊𝕊𝕊𝕊𝕊𝕊𝕊𝕊𝕊𝕊𝕊𝕊𝕊𝕊𝕊𝕊𝕊𝕊𝕊𝕊𝕊𝕊𝕊

ANDRE DEUTSCH

BASILIO BLACKWELL
ARMIGERO
SOCIO ATQUE AMICO

First Published 1976 by
André Deutsch Limited
105 Great Russell Street London WC1

Copyright © 1976 by A. C. Partridge
All rights reserved

Printed in Great Britain by
W & J Mackay Limited, Chatham

ISBN 0 233 96642 0

Contents

𖦹𖦹𖦹𖦹𖦹𖦹

Acknowledgements

🐍🐍🐍🐍🐍

The author and publishers gratefully acknowledge the permission given by the copyright-holders and publishers to quote poems and prose extracts from the works of the following Authors.

W. H. AUDEN

Faber & Faber Limited: Extracts and poems from *Collected Shorter Poems 1930–1944*, *Collected Shorter Poems 1927–1957*, *Collected Longer Poems 1968*, 'The Shield of Achilles', 'Homage to Clio', 'Epistle to a Godson', 'City Without Walls'.
Random House Inc: For permission to quote from the copyrighted works of W. H. Auden.
Curtis Brown Limited: Extract from 'Letter To Lord Byron' from *Letters From Iceland*.

W. E. BAKER

The Regents of the University of California: Extract from *Syntax In English Poetry* originally published by the University of California Press, 1967.

D. DAVIE

Routledge & Kegan Paul: Extracts from *Articulate Energy*.

C. DAY-LEWIS

Jonathan Cape Limited and The Executors of the Estate of C. Day Lewis: 'The Ecstatic', 'How They Would Jeer At Us', from *Transitional Poem* from *The Collected Poems (1954)*. Originally published by The Hogarth Press Limited.

T. S. ELIOT

Faber & Faber Limited: Extracts from *Poems Written In Early Youth*, *Collected Poems 1909–1962*, *Selected Essays, On Poetry and Poets, Knowledge And Experience, To Criticise The Critic*.
Farrar Straus & Giroux: *Knowledge And Experience (1964)*, *To Criticise The Critic (1965)*.

7

Acknowledgements

Harcourt Brace Jovanovich Inc: Excerpts from the Poetry of T. S. Eliot, 'Tradition and the Individual Talent', and 'Dante'; copyright © 1943, 1963, 1964 by T. S. Eliot; copyright © 1971 by Esme Valerie Eliot.

Routledge & Kegan Paul: 'Introduction to Valery's Art of Poetry' from *The Collected Works of Paul Valery, Vol 7.*

Princeton University Press: *The Collected Works of Paul Valery*, edited by Jackson Mathews, Bollingen Series XLV, vol 7, 'The Art of Poetry', from the Introduction by T. S. Eliot; copyright © 1958 by Bollingen Foundation.

THOMAS HARDY

Macmillan London & Basingstoke; The Macmillan Company of Canada Limited and The Trustees of the Hardy Estate: 'Tolerance' and 'The Monument-Maker' from *Collected Poems.*

Macmillan Publishing Co Inc: 'Tolerance' copyright © 1925 by Macmillan Publishing Co Inc; 'The Monument-Maker' copyright © 1925 by Macmillan Publishing Co Inc, renewed 1953 by Lloyds Bank Limited.

D. H. LAWRENCE

Laurence Pollinger Limited: 'The Song of A Man Who Has Come Through' from *The Complete Poems.* Excerpt from *Introduction to New Poems.* Originally published by William Heinemann Publishers Limited.

Viking Press Inc: From *The Complete Poems of D. H. Lawrence* edited by Vivian de Sola Pinto and F. Warrne Roberts. Copyright © 1964, 1971 by Angelo Ravagli and C. M. Weekley, Executors of the Estate of Frieda Lawrence Ravagli. All rights reserved. Reprinted by permission of The Viking Press, Inc.

LOUIS MACNEICE

Faber & Faber Limited: 'The Creditor' from *The Collected Poems.*

Oxford University Press, New York: 'The Creditor' from *The Collected Poems* edited by E. R. Dodds. Copyright © The Estate of Louis MacNeice 1966.

MARIANNE MOORE

Faber & Faber Limited: 'To A Snail' from *The Complete Poems.*

Macmillan Publishing Co Inc: 'To A Snail' from *Collected Poems* copyright © 1953 by Marianne Moore, renewed 1963 by Marianne Moore and T. S. Eliot.

EZRA POUND

Faber & Faber Limited: Extracts from *Hugh Selwyn Mauberley* and 'The Age Demanded' from *Collected Shorter Poems.*

Acknowledgements

New Directions Publishing Corporation: PERSONAE. Copyright
© 1926 by Ezra Pound.

MICHAEL ROBERTS

Faber & Faber Limited: 'The Child' from *Collected Poems*.

STEPHEN SPENDER

Faber & Faber Limited: 'Prelude 8' from *Collected Poems*.
Random House Inc: 'Prelude 8' from *Collected Poems 1928–1953* copyright © 1934 and renewed 1962 by Stephen Spender.

DYLAN THOMAS

New Directions Publishing Corporation: *The Poems of Dylan Thomas*;
copyright © 1938, 1939, 1946.
J. M. Dent & Sons Ltd and The Trustees for the Copyrights of the late
Dylan Thomas: Extracts from 'In Memory of Ann Jones', 'From
Love's First Fever', 'Poem in October' from *Collected Poems*.
David Higham Associates Ltd: Extract from 'Notes on the Art of
Poetry' from *Modern Poets on Modern Poetry* by James Scully; originally
published by Fontana Literature 1973.
Harold Ober Associates: Extract from 'Notes on the Art of Poetry';
originally published in the *Texas Quarterly*. Copyright © 1961 by the
Trustees for the Estate of Dylan Thomas.

D. WARD

Routledge & Kegan Paul Ltd: Extract from *T. S. Eliot, Between Two
Worlds*.

CHARLES WILLIAMS

Clarendon Press: Extract from *Poetry At Present, 1930*.

G. T. WRIGHT

The Regents of the University of California: Extract from *The Poet in
the Poem*; originally published by the University of California Press
1960.

W. B. YEATS

A. P. Watt & Son; M. B. Yeats; Miss Anne Yeats; Macmillan London
and Basingstoke and the Macmillan Co of Canada: Extracts from
Collected Poems and extracts from the following prose works: *A Vision,
Essays and Introductions, Journal, A Packet for Ezra Pound, On the Boiler*,
Introduction *To Michael Robartes and The Dancer*.
Macmillan Publishing Co Inc: 'An Acre of Grass' and 'The Municipal
Gallery Revisited' (Copyright © 1940 by Georgie Yeats, renewed

1968 by Bertha Georgie Yeats, Michael Butler Yeats and Anne Yeats); 'A Dialogue of Self and Soul' (Copyright © 1933 by Macmillan Publishing Co, Inc, renewed 1961 by Bertha Georgie Yeats); 'Sailing to Byzantium' (Copyright © 1928 by Macmillan Publishing Co, Inc, renewed 1956 by Georgie Yeats); 'The Second Coming' (Copyright © 1924 by Macmillan Publishing Co, Inc, renewed 1952 by Bertha Georgie Yeats); 'In Memory of Major Robert Gregory' (Copyright © 1919 by Macmillan Publishing Co, Inc, renewed 1947 by Bertha Georgie Yeats); 'Ego Dominus Tuus' (Copyright © 1918 by Macmillan Publishing Co, Inc, renewed 1946 by Bertha Georgie Yeats); 'A Coat' (Copyright © 1916 by Macmillan Publishing Co, Inc, renewed 1944 by Bertha Georgie Yeats); 'To Ireland in the Coming Times', 'Ephemera', 'The Sorrow of Love', 'When You are Old', 'He Bids His Beloved Be at Peace', 'He Wishes for the Cloths of Heaven' (Copyright © 1906 by Macmillan Publishing Co, Inc, renewed 1934 by William Butler Yeats); 'The Folly of Being Comforted' (1903); *A Vision* (Copyright © 1937 by William Butler Yeats, renewed 1965 by Bertha Georgie Yeats and Anne Butler Yeats); *Essays and Introductions* (Copyright © Mrs. W. B. Yeats, 1961); *Autobiography* (selection from the Journal); (Copyright © 1916, 1932 by Macmillan Publishing Co, Inc, renewed 1944, 1963 by Bertha Georgie Yeats); Introduction to *Michael Robartes and the Dancer* (Copyright © 1924 by Macmillan Publishing Co, Inc, renewed 1955 by Bertha Georgie Yeats).

Preface

🙚🙚🙚🙚🙚🙚

IN the last chapter, but one, of *Articulate Energy*, Donald Davie suggests that 'modern poetry, as we usually understand it, is something that appears aggressively and consciously different' (p. 147). While the views expressed in this book do not necessarily subscribe to this dictum, there is much to be said for it. The most characteristic poetry of the twentieth century connotes, in the minds of many readers, irregular, rhymeless and obscure verse.

So many worthy poets have contributed to the chequered literary annals of the last eighty years that selection has been essential, and the choice fell on Yeats, Eliot and Auden, as the dominant figures in language and technical accomplishment. The first three chapters and the last, however, afford opportunities for extending the source of modern concepts, and sampling poets whose lustre has been dimmed only by the massive achievement of three writers mentioned. Yeats, Eliot and Auden are acknowledged as leaders, and are as diverse in thought and practice as any three representatives of a period could be.

Free verse, which is neither a genre nor a specific technique, is characteristic of poetry since 1919, and has far from exhausted itself; nor were its origins solely in Britain. The American contribution to modern poetry has been considerable, and the debt has not been overlooked in these pages. The truth is that a separate book is required for it, and another should be written on the language of poetic drama, in which Yeats, Eliot and Auden made significant advances. Poets and critics in Europe, particularly France, were so noteworthy and closely allied that a niche had to be found for them in Chapter II, which provides the historical background. Perhaps the rationalizing instinct of the French language accounts for the impact of such writers as Mallarmé and Valéry; it goes far to explain why the successful poet in France generally becomes a public figure.

Preface

In this, as in other studies for The Language Library, the view is promoted that the disciplines of language and literature are diplomatically inseparable. They are interdependent activities, and to isolate them denies some benefits to students with catholic interests. The enduring adaptation of rhetoric to the principles of poetry raises considerations that are linguistic as well as stylistic. Rhythm, stress, pause and sound values (divisions of language study) contribute as much to the structural complexities of poetry as do tropes and schemes. From feelings and sense perceptions, as much as from thoughts, poems are made.

In the following pages *paragraph* or *section* is used for a division of verse that is *blank* in the sense of 'unrhymed'. I use *strophe* for sections of rhymed verse, even where the pattern is somewhat irregular and the rhymes approximate. The term *stanza* is confined to a repeated pattern of lines, usually with a recognizable rhyme scheme.

I have been generously helped by three librarians in obtaining texts and bibliographies: Mr J. Perry, of the University of the Witwatersrand, Johannesburg, and Misses E. Day and J. H. Ogilvie, of the Reference section of the Johannesburg City Library. My wife has earned my gratitude for typing the text and helping with proof-reading and the Index. Professor Simeon Potter leaves me deeply in his debt for impartial advice and scrupulous editing, and I am very grateful to Mr Eric Partridge for some suggestions about Hardy and Meredith.

Johannesburg, November 1974   A. C. PARTRIDGE

CHAPTER I

Free Verse

🙚🙚🙚🙚🙚🙚

FREE verse has dominated English poetry, and that of Europe and America, since 1919. It should be admitted, however, that the genres here considered have no agreed limits in chronology. He would be a bold literary historian who would venture to say how far back the ancestry can be traced. Yeats, Eliot and Auden, the subjects of this study, had no expressed bias towards free verse, and were capable of poems within the three-century Renaissance tradition of Spenser and Shakespeare. The trio have been selected, and may safely be regarded as 'moderns' (a vague term) because their work shows signs of enduring, and because the major part of it is typical of the now recognized method of poetic writing.

Anyone who has studied the theory of prosody, as reflected in the actual composition of poems, knows how controversial the subject can be. But it is an essential preliminary to characterize, if not to define, 'free verse', and to show what kind of liberation it achieved for poets born under the moribund influence of the Renaissance metrical tradition, as were Yeats, Eliot and Auden. The text-book dichotomy of 'metred poetry' and 'free verse' is an awkward thesis to maintain, unless one assents to Shapiro and Beum's dictum (*A Prosody Handbook*, 1965, p. 7) that 'all *free verse* is unmetered'. Free verse can undoubtedly be scanned, but little value is likely to accrue from the exercise; patterns are indeterminate, because creative principles are differently conceived.

As soon as one attempts to define free verse by reference to studied examples, it becomes obvious that the style is *free* only in its eclectic use of established techniques. It employs sporadically most of the devices of metrical poetry, such as assonance and alliteration, and more rarely rhyme; it may indulge in spells of regular metre. Freedom lies in the disposition and count of stresses,

13

and the frequency of other syllables within the line. The retention of lines, often uneven in length, is indeed a verse-signal, and accounts for the importance in free verse of the visual aspect on the printed page. Lineation seems to depend on the phrasal syntax, which in turn determines the sequence of rhythm. The method has the merit of dispensing with unnecessary punctuation, especially that which indicates pauses, and is therefore relevant to interpretation.

In free verse, phrasal groupings, lineally displayed, make a rhythmical impact that readers of stanzaic metres and rhyme find it difficult to explain. Bridges segmented blank verse from Milton differently, and produced free verse with a completely different rhythmical progression. Not only is the bulk of free verse anomalous in structure, but yardsticks have changed in the attitudes to language deemed proper for poetry. Prosaic locutions, as well as expressive sounds, are employed to impress the sensibility of the reader favourably or antipathetically. It is not always intended that they should convey logical meaning. What the poem, as a whole, suggests to a perceptive mind is its only proper significance. While the poem still retains a vestige of form, rhythmical impetus replaces the traditional pleasure that was once derived from a recurring pattern of stresses and count of syllables. The range of variation is more abundant than could formerly be achieved by modulation of stress positions, which is one source of rhythmical flexibility in orthodox metrics. Exponents of free verse claim that liberation of method materially reinforces the meaning, by its accord with living utterance, and modern poetry is therefore less 'artful' in performance. They argue that overworked conventions tend to literary contrivance, and this is out of harmony with the spirit of the times. They have made their point that rhythmic organization has powerful psychological effects on both the reader and the listener.

It is not necessary, however, to traverse the barren ground of prosody, or to maintain that metre is essentially an abstraction. The plan is to treat poems empirically, and to discover the modernity of poets in their technique, in the range of their experiments rather than the theories that they have followed less successfully. Experiments vary, from invoking the nuances of everyday speech to simulating scientific prose, as in the opening lines of D. H. Lawrence's *God is born*:

The hístory of the cósmos
is the hístory of the strúggle of becóming.
When the dìm flúx of ùnfòrmed lífe
strúggled, convúlsed bàck and fòrth upon itsélf
and bróke at lást into líght and dárk.

Shapiro would probably have described this as prose 'imposed upon by arithmetic'. The verse segments are inadequate to distinguish the writing as poetry. Lines 1, 2 and 5 have perceptible rhythm; but 3 and 4, with more than four stresses each, lack rhythmical organization. Indeterminate stresses fall on the ear like flat prose; and with such deviations metre can hardly be said to exist. One is reminded of T. S. Eliot's observation in 'Reflections on Vers libre' (*New Statesman*, March 3, 1917): 'There is no escape from metre; there is only mastery'.

This essay by Eliot provides an unrivalled starting point for a discussion of modernist poetry. He declared that *vers libre* is a 'preposterous fiction', because there can be 'no freedom in art'; the life of verse is found in 'the contrast between fixity and flux', and the 'unperceived evasion of monotony'. To dispense with rhyme is not a facility; for this imposes more strain on the poet's language; and any deficiencies in word-choice, syntax or order at once become apparent, when the poetry is compared with good prose.

Francis Brett Young once observed that 'modern poetry' is a misnomer; there is only good poetry and bad poetry; to which Eliot added a *tertium quid* – chaos. To this formless category belong the effusions of many undisciplined contributors to the poetry magazines, who have been taught to cultivate the art of self-expression. Although Eliot discredited *verslibrists* as a school, and their zeal to 'revolutionize or demoralize poetry', he was able to cite examples of what he meant by the free-verse method; they include now familiar lines from Webster, Middleton and Matthew Arnold. Three examples from contemporary verse are conservative by modern standards. The first employs rhyme and near-rhyme; the second has the rhetorical abruptness of Websterian blank verse. Only the third quotation is characteristic of the type of freedom Eliot had in mind:

The boughs of the trees
Are twisted

By many bafflings;
Twisted are
The small-leafed boughs.
But the shádow of thèm
Is nòt the shádow of the mást héad
Nòr of the tórn sáils.

These lines have a charm that is enhanced by the grouping of
phrases in short verse lines. The absence of rhyme and the simple
iambic-anapaestic rhythm at once invites comparison with competent descriptive prose. The orthodox technical devices of the verse
are then exposed: repetition in lines 1 and 5, 2 and 4, 6 and 7;
pervasive alliteration; an uncolloquial inversion in line 4. Written
out as prose, these lines (especially 4) would not please. What
poetic quality they have resides (a) in the choice of the word
bafflings and the compound epithet *small-leaved*; and (b) in the skilful
modulation of the stresses in the last three lines.

No one now uses the word *diction* for a poet's word-choice, and
many modern practitioners of verse would agree with John Press
(*The Chequered Shade*) that 'a poet's syntax is almost more important
than his vocabulary'. In what way a poet can fragment or invert
the normal order of words depends on the grammatical nature of
the medium in use. There is nothing novel in omitting articles,
conjunctions and punctuation; for in the English language syntactical completeness is not essential to meaning. Inverting the
normal order, as in lines 4 and 5 above (*Twisted* are / *The small-
leafed boughs*) may be a sign of weakness. One reason for it in this
poem is the trochaic substitution in line 4, to vary the rhythm. In
orthodox metrics, inversions are usually designed to modulate the
metrical pattern or to prop the rhyme scheme. A common method
of fragmentation is to substitute phrases for complete sentences, a
device frequently employed by Whitman, Eliot and Pound.

The principal aim of the modernist poet is to secure naturalness
of speech, and Eliot recommended by his practice the cultivation
of the rhythmical effects of prose, using line-division to replace
punctuation. As modern poetry frequently favours subjective
monologue, this technique has become increasingly handy, often
to the point of spinelessness.

What Eliot esteemed in the arresting dramatic rhythms of
Webster was seemingly a combination of dislocation and elliptical

Free Verse

phrasing, which are common in present-day speech. Webster may
have been in revolt against baroque writing, which utilized the
stylistic extreme of elaboration by subordinate clauses. When a
poet resorts to devices for modifying language he is usually in
quest of a particular rhythm. There is little old or new in such
practices.

The distaste for Victorian poetry, which sparked the modern
reaction, was primarily a dislike of its content, artifice and
vocabulary. The real service of consulting poets such as Pound
and Eliot was to school others in the arts of concentration,
tautness and economy. Eliot was self-critical, and therefore less to
be faulted in technical accomplishment.

The notion that a poem is *endowed* with a style is for most
modernist poets untenable. The form is subsumed in the theme;
the form is identified with the content. If the rhythm and the line
arrangement are right, punctuation becomes a supererogation. In
surrealist poems of the post-war generation, reality is manifest in
the words as they enact themselves on the page; taking a lead from
the plastic arts, typography and the visualization of ideas are
allowed to enter into the spirit of the poetry. The writers believe
that poetry is a good deal more than the word-surface suggests.

Much modern poetry is observed to be impressionist in
technique, the effects being achieved through juxtapositions and
tensions that reveal how deeply psychology enters into creation.
Technique, in the rhetorical sense of schemes of thought and
phrase, is not regarded in *avant-garde* circles as a valid criterion of a
poem's merit. The writer aims to be a sensitive interpreter of his
environment. A poem, he thinks, promises success if he can keep
what the American, John Berryman, calls a steady tone.

Modern poets with a sensory intelligence do not vie with
philosophers in attempting to give meaning to the universe
through art; they assume that the world *has* an obscure meaning,
which gropingly they try to discern and articulate. They are in
sympathy with trends in philosophy that seek clarification in the
logic of concepts; and a poem should therefore be regarded as
an exploration, whose ultimate form is likely to be unpredictable.
The urgency of poetry resides in the transmitted life of the words.

Although an appreciable gap exists between the withdrawn
writer and his public, modernist poets shrink from explanation of
what they write. They rely on the cumulative impact of words,

which succeeds when the assault is made by a disciplined mind, with emotions under control. A poem may be as personal as a jotting in a writer's diary; and its experience should be communicated with minimal description.

Paul Valéry said of modern poetry-writing that 'there is no recognized means of prescribing or forbidding anything to anyone'. Poetry is for every man, and has been completely democratized. It claims neither a privileged subject nor a special social tone. In a disorderly world a poet should have no prejudice for cultural preciosity. Training himself as a sensitive observer, a poet *becomes*; he does not necessarily belong to a class that is personally gifted or inspired. No poet of substance but responds critically to the needs of his time; and as a result, one must expect more thinking than feeling in a modern poem.

Ideologies expressed in programmes, whether inspired by Sartre, Ginsberg or Picasso, seldom work out in practice. The so-called 'revolution' in English and American poetry was inspired before 1920 by Pound and Eliot. But the time has come when innovation no longer surprises, and the liberation proclaimed by Valéry attracts little critical notice, except (as Howard Nemerov reminds us) when it is accompanied by a manifesto. His poem *Lion and Honeycomb* is about an aspiring poet who is disillusioned by critical maunderings about 'technical virtuosity' (see his 'Attentiveness and Obedience' in *Contemporary American Poetry*).

He didn't want to do it with skill,
He'd had enough of skill. If he never saw
Another villanelle, it would be too soon;
And the same went for sonnets. If it had been
Hard work learning to rime, it would be much   5
Harder learning not to. The time came
He had to ask himself, what did he want?
What did he want when he began
That idiot fiddling with the sounds of things?
He asked himself, poor moron, because he had   10

Nobody else to ask. The others went right on
Talking about form, talking about myth
And the (so help us) need for a modern idiom;
The verseballs among them kept counting syllables.

So there he was, this forty-year-old teen-ager   15
Dreaming preposterous merger and divisions
Of vowels like water, consonants like rock
(While everybody kept discussing values
And the need for values), for words that would
Enter the silence and be there as a light.   20
So much coffee and so many cigarettes
Gone down the drain, gone up in smoke,
Just for the sake of getting something right.

This is a fair example of free verse that fails as poetry. Bridges might have said that its fault is 'indetermination of subsidiary accent'. Although cast in unrhymed iambic pentameter form and colloquial language, using the dialectic method of T.S. Eliot, the poem is shapeless. What holds it together is the meaning, not the pattern. The lines usually have five stresses, varying in syllables from 8 to 12; but the redundancies produce a rather unstable rhythm. Trisyllabic feet and metrical inversions appear casual, and the syntax, especially in the first four lines, is at odds with the deliberately prosaic movement. *Verseballs* has a characteristically American debunking tone, and the only sign of figurative grace is in the imaginative lines

> Dreaming preposterous merger and divisions
> Of vowels like water, consonants like rock.

It is difficult for a young modern poet to achieve an individual style amid tentative schools and the flux of fashion. He looks to models and judicious experimentation to guide his daily decisions; and it was not unexpected that Yeats should become a 'cult' and Eliot an 'international literary hero'. Ezra Pound, Yeats and Eliot put a brake on ill-conceived projects, and dispelled many misconceptions about what poetry can be supposed to do in an urbanized society. Compressed and purged of magical elements, at what stage does language begin to be sterile as a poetic medium?

No critical reasoning can obscure the justice of Bridges's contention that 'diction, rhythm and sonority are carried by the versification ... Deprived of that resource (he continues) free verse must be full of disconsolate patches' (see 'Humdrum and Harum-Scarum', *Collected Essays II*, Oxford University Press, 1922). In free verse, and especially in longer compositions, the poet is forever adapting his form to new matter, instead of adjusting the matter to aesthetic needs. In the first ten lines of *Lion and Honeycomb*, Nemerov seems to have adjusted the line structure to grammatical units, and thus to have limited its rhythmical mobility. The truth, according to Bridges, is that the English language is restricted and therefore repetitive in its grammatical constructions, each of which has a familiar intonation pattern. The tension of intonation schemes against the metrical pattern constitutes a principal charm of reading poetry. 'One of the difficulties in writing good verse of any kind', adds Bridges, 'is to escape from the tyranny of . . . recurrent speech-forms'.

When critics acclaim natural speech rhythms as the cause to which free verse is dedicated, it is necessary to remind them how tediously recurrent these may be. The terms 'organic' and 'exact' are bandied about, as though they were not relative in rhythm, whether the medium is verse or prose. A rhythm can easily be sensed only when a complete utterance is apprehended – intonation, pause, cadence and content. In verse there are added the spatial conventions of lines, which, as we have seen, are not arbitrary. The segments or phrasal groups are deliberate signals of interpretation, because in reading (even though silent) the eye and the ear co-operate. Yeats, Eliot and Auden learnt from, and compromised with, the traditional metrics of their youth; and what they did was to enrich the successful experiments from the diversified rhythms of attractive prose.

Ezra Pound, publishing his Imagist manifesto in 1912, jotted down under the heading 'rhythm' this reminder: 'compose in the sequence of the musical phrase, not the metronome'. But the adequacy of the result he cautiously left to the reader's decision. He advised the modern poet to *present*, rather than *describe*, and to attend to the rhythmical enjambement of his lines, while not destroying the shape of the words. He believed in free verse, because, though symmetrical forms had their uses, many subjects could not be precisely rendered in them.

Among the obstinate questionings of this study, one will be to establish free verse, like any other kind, as a rigorous discipline for the genuine poet; but also to suggest that such poets do not commit themselves to this style, except for special kinds of thematic invention. Pound's search in 1917 for the musical phrase, the concrete and adequate symbol and the rhythm which links line to line, has had an immense influence for good on modern poetry.

Graham Hough expressed the view that the poetry-reading public have always treated free verse with 'dubiety and reserve', because it seems to be 'an evasion of the real difficulty of writing verse' (*Image and Experience*, Duckworth, 1960, Chap. II). His list of the characteristics of free verse is quite commonplace: *absence* of comfortable line-length and pattern, *lack* of any scheme of metrical feet, and *abandonment* of the normal uses of rhyme; these indicate that his attitude to free verse tends to be negative. Positive principles are so tenuous that Hough doubts whether free verse is a 'uniform phenomenon'. What the French called *vers libre*, he thinks, is simply an adaptation of prose rhythms, arbitrarily arranged in typographical lengths, its true aims being fluid rhythms and 'psychological spontaneity'.

Hough's conclusion is that free verse, as in Eliot's *Prufrock*, invariably has a conventional pattern, the iambic pentameter, behind it, from which the poet may recede without departing rhythmically from the norm to a substantial degree. The *form* of free verse does not therefore differ radically from the tradition, and this makes it 'extremely difficult to develop a new poetic idiom'. The practitioner of free verse inevitably resorts to what Donne taught poetic libertarians – dislocation of thought and syntax, to create the illusion of a rhythm that resembles natural speech.

Hough is of the opinion that Eliot, though a *liberated* metrist who stretches and modifies, is more in the tradition of English poetry than Lawrence or Pound; but his conclusion results from an analysis of early and occasionally inadequate samples. What Lawrence achieves in *Snake*, he says, is a predominantly prose rhythm, conditioned by his experience, and alternated with snatches of virtually blank verse. Pound appeared to him the most resourceful of the experimenters, but he was foiled in the attempt to adapt quantitative measures in *Homage to Propertius* by the English language's strongly accentual character.

What flows from Hough's analysis is that metrical usage has been liberated by practitioners of free verse since 1919 in the following ways:

1) Avoidance, where possible, of the natural iambic-anapaestic rhythm and countering it by a falling rhythm.

2) Modifying the accentual rhythm of English by using some quantitative effects.
3) Organizing form through verbal repetition and rhythmical or other uses of parallelism, which abound in English biblical translation.

Hough's sensitive approach to his inquiry is, however, troubled by a two-fold suspicion, first that the term 'free verse' is unsatisfactory in its inability to cover miscellaneous phenomena; and secondly that the thing it describes, although often impressive, is not poetry, but prose masquerading as verse. He argues that the 'stylistic divisions' of prose are necessarily syntactical, for the 'figure of grammar' alone supplies its rhythmic unity. Free verse approximates to prose because sense and syntax unify its rhythm, and determine the lineation. Traditional verse has the better claim to be regarded as the medium of poetry, because in its greater possibilities of enjambement it can counterpoint the metrical against the sense rhythm more successfully. In free verse 'almost every line is a sentence, or a grammatical subdivision of a sentence, or a self-contained descriptive phrase' (p. 104). The weakness of free verse, he concludes, is the absence of a metrical norm, and hence its 'tenuity' of rhythm.

Here the critique of Hough's opposition is open to question. Syntax is important to prose rhythm, but its capacity for variant constructions shows that judgement and sensitivity are equally significant factors in securing a pleasing shape. Succeeding chapters aim to show that the rhythm of competent free verse is not tenuous, but the major force in stabilizing its structure. Every discipline *unrealized* makes for fugitive verse, and the linguistic problem whether free verse (or imaginative prose) should be classed as mono-rhythmic has not yet been settled. In an age when prose has been largely relegated to utilitarian needs, no one need disagree with the observation of Mallarmé and Hough that poetry is primarily 'language organized for an aesthetic purpose'.

The most sensible attitude to free verse is to accept it as an inevitable development, an extension to literature not unlike that which overtook the plastic arts. 'Significant form' is not abandoned: discipline is not relaxed, but is only different, and in a sense more fluent. W. H. Auden puts the difference well in his essay on 'D. H. Lawrence' (*The Dyer's Hand*, Faber, 1963, p. 287):

The difference between formal and free verse may be likened to
the difference between carving and modelling; the formal poet,
that is to say, thinks of the poem he is writing as something
already latent in the language which he has to reveal, while the
free verse poet thinks of language as a plastic passive medium
upon which he imposes his artistic conception. One might also
say that, in their attitude towards art, the formal verse writer
is a catholic, the free verse writer a protestant.

This plastic quality suggests the justification for free verse. It
enlarges both the technical possibilities and the range of experience
that the language of poetry is capable of comprehending. Today
the expression of authentic experience, through which the poet is
fulfilled, is made more difficult by the pressures of his professional
contacts and public labels. The writer is compelled simultaneously
to protect and project himself by using *personae* or masks, enabling
the poem, in Eliot's ideal, to enjoy 'a life of its own'. *Personae*
and prose rhythms help him to escape from the strait-jacket of
romantic subjectivism into another spatial dimension, where the
highest self-discipline is required. The exercise of this freedom is
demonstrated in Sylvia Plath's poem *Lady Lazarus*, with its dual
personae, Lazarus risen from the dead and the Nazi doctor of the
concentration camps, the poem's symbols of good and evil. (See
Alvarez, *The New Poetry*, Penguin, 1966, p. 61). The subjective
elements of the first *persona* tend to exhibitionism. But through the
objectifying symbols and metaphors of the less congenial *persona*,
'Herr Lucifer', an ironic balance emerges.

CHAPTER II

The Forebears of Modern Poetry

🙚🙚🙚🙚🙚🙚

'You seem to have no conception of the extent to which poetry has become estranged from the springs of contemporary sensibility', (B. Higgins, 'Ancients and Moderns', *Scrutinies*, ed. E. Rickword, 1928). 'The success of a poem depends almost entirely on its execution, on the organic structure of its language, . . . the only thing a poet cannot beg, borrow or steal'. (Roy Campbell, 'Contemporary Poetry', in the same volume). Dogmatically, Campbell concluded that it is the inferior poet who bursts 'the bounds of ordinary poetic form' in order to express himself.

Robert Browning was an innovator who overstepped the bounds deliberately. What modern poets have learnt from him is the method of dramatic monologue. The Victorian poet was skilled in twisting a character to display its oddities, in creating a *persona*, through which he could express personal conflicts, reflections and beliefs. Browning's thought is contorted by what Thomas Blackburn called his 'gymnastic exuberance' (*Robert Browning*, Eyre and Spottiswoode, 1967, p. 176). His philosophy shows no complexity in the psychological sense. The original contribution of his poetry is the dialectical organization of ideas.

John Donne's gift of objectifying thought and sensation in ironic contrast, was the earlier, but paradoxically the more modern innovation. Browning learnt from him the confidential note, the ability to actualize poems in the naturalistic style of familiar speech. The muscular persuasiveness, the word-play, the elliptical phrasing, the figurative concentration, were derived from Donne; yet the result, for poetry, was entirely different. Ezra Pound thought the most exciting poems in Victorian English were Browning's *Men and Women*.

The irregular metres of Browning were cunningly adapted to the monologues of his mature style. The earlier and longer poems had been either in orthodox blank verse or couplets, surprisingly free from intellectual comment. But in *Men and Women* and *Dramatis Personae* he devised a verse, free but not unlicensed, which is marked by disruptions of syntax, parentheses and abrupt transitions of thought. The halting rhythm is partly caused by disregard of the orthodox positions of metrical pauses; they are often within the first and last three syllables of the pentameter line. There are six examples (marked |) in the following fifteen lines from *One Word More*:

What of Rafael's sonnets, Dante's picture?
This: | no artist lives and loves that longs not
Once, | and only once, and for One only,
(Ah, the prize!) to find his love a language
Fit and fair and simple and sufficient –   5
Using nature that's an art to others,
Not, | this one time, art that's turned his nature.
Ay, | of all the artists living, | loving,
None but would forego his proper dowry, –
Does he paint? he fain would write a poem, –   10
Does he write? he fain would paint a picture,
Put to proof art alien to the artist's,
Once, | and only once, and for One only,
So to be the man and leave the artist,
Gain the man's joy, miss the artist's sorrow.   15

Browning was a skilful inventor of rhymes, falling rhythms and complex stanzas. These gifts found an outlet in some of his finest poems: *Two in Campagna*, *A Toccata of Galuppi's*, *Abt Vogler* and *Rabbi Ben Ezra*. His blank verse reaches most dignified expression in his longest poem, *The Ring and the Book*.

Mrs Sutherland Orr, who knew and consulted the poet, described Browning's personal style as a 'determination never to sacrifice sense to sound'. In the *Handbook to Robert Browning* (Bell, 1886, pp. 12–14) she sets out ten technical rules that the poet thought he observed in composition. Some of them are as follows: minimal use of words consonant with meaning; sparing employment of adjectives; preference for picturesque Anglo-Saxon monosyllables; colloquial contraction of prepositions, with occasional omission of pronouns, articles and conjunctions. He regarded consonants as 'the backbone of the language', and specially important in rhyme. He tried to restrict double rhymes

to verse of comic or satirical intention. He declared he was strict
in observance of unusual metres, but took liberties with usual ones
to escape monotony. In poems expressive of a poetic mood, he
shunned prosaic tricks of language.

Caliban upon Setebos is representative of the style here described.
Archaic poeticisms do not here sound incongruous in the context
of colloquial speech and Darwinian ideas, perhaps because of the
Renaissance background of the poem. Except in the employment
of scientific and aesthetic terms, Browning's influence upon poetic
vocabulary was not enduring.

When Ruskin adversely criticized the obscurity of *Men and
Women*, Browning replied:

> I cannot begin writing poetry till my imaginary reader has con-
> ceded licences to me . . . I know that I don't make out my con-
> ception by my language: all poetry being a putting the infinite
> within the finite. You would have me paint it all plain out,
> which can't be; but by various artifices I try to make shift with
> touches and bits of outlines which *succeed* if they bear the
> conception from me to you.

Ruskin, an art critic who was also a master of prose, confronted
with a passage like this in *Fra Lippo Lippi*, would have had understandable compunctions:

> The Prior and the learned pulled a face
> And stopped all that in no time. 'How? what's here?
> Quite from the mark of painting, bless us all!
> Faces, arms, legs and bodies like the true
> As much as pea and pea! it's devil's game!
> Your business is not to catch men with show,
> With homage to the perishable clay,
> But lift them over it, ignore it all,
> Make them forget there's such a thing as flesh.
> Your business is to paint the souls of men—
> Man's soul, and it's a fire, smoke . . . no it's not . . .
> It's vapour done up like a new-born babe—
> (In that shape when you die it leaves your mouth)
> It's . . . well, what matters talking, it's the soul!'

Modern poetry, in spite of its prosaic rhythms, is seldom given to
colloquial oddities of this kind. Browning has not what Eliot

called 'an innate sense of form', nor the craftsman's wish to perfect the single line as a construct in a well-conceived whole. He was a perverse metrist, rugged in rhythm (even in some lyrical forms) and an impulsive thinker. The characters of the monologues are dramatized in special situations, and the rhythm reflects the conversational tone of presentation. It encourages emphatic or rhetorical stresses, cutting across the musical beat of the verse, which metrical form invites.

Browning disturbed the foundations of poetry's Renaissance conventions by showing that what many regarded as laws were, in truth, fashions or conveniences. Those bounds of poetic form, which he broke in dramatizing ideas, with deprecated freedom of language, now appear to critics to have been inevitable.

There were many factors at work in Europe, and in America, where a contemporary, Walt Whitman (1819–92), published *Leaves of Grass* in 1855. Visualizing the 'great American poet' in abstract, Whitman forecast that poetic expression would become 'transcendent and new, indirect and not . . . descriptive . . . The great poet never stagnates . . . He is a seer – he is an individual – . . . he does not stop for any regulation . . . The poetic quality is not marshal'd in rhyme or uniformity'.

Whitman became the master of a declamatory, prophetic style, who claimed the poet as a 'channel of thoughts and things'; one whose literary personality was concealed by no 'curtains' of elegance, effect or originality. In his revelatory poem *Song of Myself* he seems to be a vitalist, with unquenchable faith in Nature (though he was a town poet like Eliot) and Democracy. His untutored poetry abounds in invocations, apostrophes and emphasizing capitals. The shape of the poems is as unruly as his trust in the shape of things to come. The dramatization of emotions and national events has parallels with Browning's promotion of personal philosophy. In Whitman's case, however, the pronouncements were the products not of nurture but of nature; for the poet lacked formal teaching, except in the domestic tenets of Quakerism. His self-education included much reading of Carlyle and Emerson, both sharing his transcendental love of liberty.

The majority of Whitman's output in verse is without stanza form or metrical pattern. (*The Love that is Hereafter* and *O Captain! My Captain* are notable exceptions). As the herald of modern free verse, he relies on cadences, on the sentence rhythm of orotund lyrical phrases, not on the modulations of a well-formed line. *A Clear Midnight*, written in 1881, is an example:

> This is my hour O Soul, ‖ thy free flight into the wordless,
> Away from books, away from art, ‖ the day erased, the lesson done,
> Thée fùlly fòrth emérging, sílent gázing, ‖ póndering the thémes thou lóvest bést,
> Night, sleep, death and the stars.

A poet of this century would probably have divided these four lines into seven, as indicated by the evocative caesuras. But Whitman imposed no limits on the length of his units, with the result that the third line has no less than ten stresses. As free verse would have it, this has the nuance of the speaking voice; it has no absolute rules, except to complete the strophe, the so-called unit of *organic* rhythm. The function of the accusative *Thee* (line 3) is not clear, and one supposes that it is a grammatical solecism.

Whitman's attempts at imagist poetry, as in *The Dalliance of the Eagles*, are not, in pictorial immediacy, altogether successful. His favourite themes are his own experience, and *Leaves of Grass* (to which he added throughout his life) is sometimes regarded as the autobiography of an egoist. He is at his characteristic best in the *Song of Myself*:

> The spotted hawk swoops by and accuses me, he complains of my gab and my loitering.
> I too am not a bit tamed, I too am untranslatable,
> I sound my barbaric jawp over the roofs of the world.
> The last scud of day holds back for me,
> It flings my likeness after the rest and true as any on the shadow'd wilds,
> It coaxes me to the vapour and the dusk.
> I depart as air, I shake my white locks at the runaway sun,
> I effuse my flesh in eddies, and drift it in lacy jags.
> I bequeath myself to the dirt to grow from the grass I love,
> If you want me again look for me under your boot-soles.

It was the technique of poems like this that attracted the nineteenth-century symbolists, and gave occasion to unconscious, as well as deliberate, echoes of Whitman in T. S. Eliot. If poetic language, as Paul Valéry demanded, should 'preserve itself, through itself', Whitman's will endure; it is not only in phrases like *gab*, *barbaric yawp*, *scud* and *lacy jags* that he gives the reader the illusion of power.

According to Enid Starkie (*From Gautier to Eliot*, 1960, p. 99), Jules Laforgue borrowed the idea of free verse from Whitman, when he made translations from *Leaves of Grass* for the journal *La Vogue* in 1886. In a period of great political upheaval, when poets like Chateaubriand, Lamartine and Victor Hugo became public figures, the 'decadent' French symbolists led a notable reaction against the rhetoric and exuberance of the waning nineteenth-century romantic tradition. Few symbolist poets used free verse: word-painting or word-music was their forte, and the majority of poems were in rhyme and stanza form, including sonnets.

The symbolist proponents of Art for Art's sake, such as Théophile Gautier and Charles Baudelaire, became an effective literary force in the Second Empire of 1851. The movement began with the preface to Gautier's novel *Mademoiselle de Maupin* in 1835, and was aided by Baudelaire's enthusiasm for Edgar Allan Poe's aesthetic theories: some of Poe's tales he translated in 1852. But symbolism's immediate effect was upon the content of poetry, its moral and religious ideas, rather than on the words and metrical concept of French verse. Laforgue's perceptive 'Notes on Baudelaire' are a brilliant evocation of the kind of poetry this symbolist wrote:

Baudelaire has a series of litanies in which he lists the physical attributes of his *Most Adored Queen*.

Her skin sparkles, her walk is like a serpent at the end of a stick, her hair is an ocean, her head sways with the gentleness of a young elephant, her body leans like a frail vessel plunging its yardarms into the water, her saliva mounts to her mouth like a wave swollen by the melting of rumbling glaciers, her neck is a tower of ivory, her teeth are sheep suspended on the edge of the Hebron ... This is Americanism superimposed on the metaphorical language of the *Song of Songs*.

Extolling the virtues of perfect form in poetry, the Symbolists demonstrated the relevance of the plastic arts to their writing.

Their counterpart in England was Dante Gabriel Rossetti and the Pre-Raphaelite group.

Mallarmé became the high priest of Symbolism in the next generation. He was a teacher of English, who received literary guests in his Paris apartment on Tuesday evenings, among them Valéry, Laforgue, Wilde, Symons and Yeats. His aim 'to give poetry a purer sense' limited its effective scope by linking it abstractly to music, and making it more private.

Most revolutionary of the French symbolists were the poets Arthur Rimbaud and Jules Laforgue. Rimbaud was the energetic but disdainful vagabond on whom Roy Campbell modelled the splendours of his phrasing and cosmic imagery. Much is to be learnt about him from the autobiographical poem in quatrains entitled *The Frenzied Ship* (1886). In free verse the extravagance and metrical virtuosity are better displayed in the short poem *Movement*. The translation is from Dorothy Martin's *Sextette* (Scholartis Press, 1928):

MOVEMENT
(Mouvement)

The sinuous play of water upon the vessel's sides,
The surge about the stern,
The headlong drop,
The immeasurable streaming of the current
Lead on the voyagers by miracles of light   5
And strange new chemistries
Through wreaths of spray from ebbing wave
And whirling pool.

These are the conquerors of the world
Who would explore the science of their fate.   10
Beside them sport and comfort travel too.
Theirs is the voice
To whose tones race, class, prejudice must yield.
Quiet and ecstasy
Of deluged light,   15
Of racking studious nights.

And from their talk, mid tackle, blood, flowers, fire, jewels,
From sayings flung to the flying ship,

Emerges, like a monstrous sea-wall in the pathway of
    hydraulic motion,
Steadfastly shining, their philosophic store;   20
They, driving onwards to the harmonies and raptures
And heroisms of discovery.
Thus, mid bewildering atmospheric chances,
The two, with youth aflame, remain apart,
– Is it some ancient, innocent, untamed shyness in them? –   25
Motionless, singing.

Each stanza contains bold symbolic gestures: *miracles of light,
deluged light, hydraulic motion, atmospheric chances, untamed shyness.*
Even in translation the polysyllabic adjectives are vigorous and
arresting. Each line is composed as a separate metrical entity.

Laforgue was the melancholy, lonely intellectual, who in 1881
became reader to the Empress Augusta at the German Court in
Berlin. Some poems reflect the tragic ironies of Shakespeare's
Hamlet and other plays, in which he was well read; but Laforgue
was also influenced by the philosophy of Schopenhauer and
Edouard Hartmann's *Philosophy of the Unconscious.* The *Last Poems,*
which Eliot studied for juxtaposed images and recurrent, rever-
berating phrases, were the most advanced technically. The surrealist element was probably a novelty initiated by Laforgue. In the
free verse influenced by Whitman, he abandoned stanza form,
rhyme and the time-honoured French count of syllables. The
following is from *The Coming of Winter* (W. J. Smith's translation,
Selected Writings of Jules Laforgue, Evergreen Books, New York,
1956):

Now is the time when rust invades the masses,
When rust gnaws into the kilometric spleen
Of telegraph wires on roads where no one passes.

The horns, the horns, – the sad,
Sad horns! . . .
They go on and on now changing their tone,
Changing their tone and changing their tune,
Ton-ton, ton-ton, ton-tone! . . .
Away on the north wind now is borne
The sound of the horns, the sad, sad horns.

French writers had long interested themselves in the role of expressive art, and Charles Mauron (*Aesthetics and Psychology*, Hogarth, 1935) describes the quest as a means of transmitting 'states of mind'. According to this critic, when sensations link up with past impressions, feelings and desires, the poets endeavour to illumine the association through symbols. One physiological result is to be found in *rhythm*, whose effect is to release emotion. Without symbols, language fails to transmit 'states of mind', because symbols provide a common ground between the speaker and the listener. Using an in-built 'dictionary of sentiment', says Mauron, each experiencer finds his own meaning for symbols. Art is not the transmission of a point of view, but the spontaneous expression of 'accumulated energy'; its object is to 'savour existence instead of letting it escape'. A writer, then, 'speaks for the pleasure of speaking' but does not necessarily aim at being understood – which is one of the 'ironies of symbolic art'. The artist has to be 'double-minded', in that he is impelled by emotions on the one hand, and pauses to savour his experience on the other. Art therefore tends to be a condition of 'unstable equilibrium'.

Mauron's study of the psychology of aesthetics is a valuable contribution to the understanding of the Symbolist movement. The diverse poets were a subjective group, who wanted words to convey states of mind rather than objects of intellectual perception. In a manifesto that appeared in *Figaro* in 1886, the 'Decadents' spoke of 'sensory appearances', 'esoteric affinities' and 'primordial Ideas', as would an idealistic and mystical group, whose origin was Neo-Platonism. But their symbolism was, as J. T. Shipley suggests in *World Literary Terms* (Allen and Unwin, 1955, p. 409) not religious; it may have come from the Illuminati of the eighteenth century, through Blake's inspirer Swedenborg. Baudelaire's sonnet on 'Correspondences' involved a private symbolism, which licensed the artist to convert all objects into symbols of personal significance, to replace the old myths and allegories. Baudelaire's lyrical poetry is therefore anti-romantic in character, obliquely based on his life-experiences, without temporal, spatial or logical connections.

Other influences upon French Symbolism were Wagner's music, Maeterlinck, Impressionist painting, and Sigmund Freud, the last of whom claimed that clinical investigation was actually suggested to him by the works of European literary men. The Celtic spirit was always peculiarly liable to symbolism, and the

Irish poets Yeats and Synge took easily to the new symbolic methods.

A. C. Swinburne, who was of French descent, interpreted Baudelaire and the Symbolists in England, and wrote tributes to several French poets, with whom he kept in contact on frequent visits to Paris. He became in 1862 the first of the English 'decadents', whose number later included Arthur Symons, Ernest Dowson, Oscar Wilde and Lionel Johnson, all literary friends of Yeats. Swinburne should be regarded as one of several English neo-Romantics, who based their work on intelligent use of the classics. He excelled in the diversity of his metrical rhythms, enriched with the sound effects of words. Both he and Tennyson had much to teach twentieth-century poets about the musical properties of verse, but the impact of *Poems and Ballads* and *Atalanta in Calydon* on modern poetry is negligible. The languorous imagery is overwrought, and the elaborate syntax creates the impression of verbal facility without associated depth of meaning.

Although most of the verse of Meredith and Hardy was in stanza and rhyme, their experiments in form and rhythm were richer in influence. In prose fiction Meredith's lyrical energy is known to be immensely original; of his ten publications in verse only *Modern Love* (1862), and the shorter poems *Love in the Valley* and *The Lark Ascending* are appreciated. Yet the nature poems are extremely sensitive in image and rhythm. Meredith also produced one dramatic monologue, which is the nineteenth-century counterpart to Shakespeare's *Sonnets*; it has the same appeal of psychological insight and capacity for self-revelation. As in the novel, Meredith in *Modern Love* looked into the 'cerebral cortex', as well as the heart. The expanded sonnets are unique in the expertise with which each poem is fitted to a narrative episode.

The elliptical method of expressing thought Meredith displays with virtuosity in the first two sections of *In the Woods* (1870).

I
Hill-sides are dark,
And hill-tops reach the star,
And down is the lark,
And I from my mark
Am far.   5

Unlighted I foot the ways.
I know that a dawn is before me,
And behind me many days;
    Not what is o'er me.

II
    I am in deep woods,   10
      Between the two twilights.

Whatsoever I am and may be,
Write it down to the light in me;
I am I, and it is my deed;
For I know that paths are dark   15
      Between the two twilights:

My foot on the nodding weed,
My hand on the wrinkled bark,
I have made my choice to proceed
By the light I have within;   20
And the issue rests with me,
Who might sleep in a chrysalis,
In the fold of a simple prayer,
      Between the two twilights:

Flying safe from even to morn: 25
Not stumbling abroad in air
That shudders to touch and to kiss,
And is unfraternal and thin:
Self-hunted in it, forlorn,
Unloved, unresting, bare,   30
      Between the two twilights:

Having nought but the light in me,
Which I take for my soul in arms,
Resolved to go unto the wells
For water, rejecting spells,   35
And mouthings of magic for charms,
And the cup that does not flow.

    I am in deep woods
      Between the two twilights:

Over valley and hill   40

> I hear the woodland wave,
> Like the voice of Time, as slow,
> The voice of Life, as grave,
> The voice of Death, as still.

The language of this is concentrated and suggestive, and the poem is chosen because it is very different in style from *Modern Love*, with its fifty pseudo-sonnets, each consisting of four quatrains. In this poem's preference for monosyllabic words and short lines, there is nevertheless a kind of opacity of meaning, resulting perhaps from the writer's inability to realize completely the thought in the expression. But note the economy in the use of attributive adjectives; conventional poeticisms are confined to *deep* and *forlorn* in lines 10 and 29.

Meredith cheerfully accepted the theory of evolution, and the line 'Having nought but the light in me' has undoubted symbolic significance. The poet's joy in nature obviously has not the same healing and steeling power as Wordsworth's. The 'two twilights' (evening and morning), stand for 'the voice of Life' and 'the voice of Death'; the suggestion in 'which I take for my soul in arms' is that self-determination should not be mistaken for a confession of spiritual solipsism.

One reason for Meredith's lack of reader-popularity is his wish to avoid the familiar rhythms of poetry; he seems here to be reluctantly escaping from the conventions of rhyme. The result is a poem more like free verse than his other paean of nature, *The Woods of Westermain*. It is always difficult to extract passages from his poems without hurt to the meaning as a whole. The nine sections of *In the Woods* invite the sort of exploration that poetry needs. Whatever Meredith's themes, there is a certain chastity in the choice of imagery, as in the simile that opens poem VIII, 'The lover of life holds life in his hands, / *Like a ring for the bride*'.

To think of Meredith is to recall that other undervalued transitional poet, who was also a novelist, though less optimistic in his portrayal of nature and humanity. Hardy's verse, beginning with *Wessex Poems* in 1898, covers a period of twenty-seven years, and the best of it, in four volumes, appeared after 1910, when 'modern' poetry unmistakably begins. Charles Williams in *Poetry at Present* (Oxford University Press, 1930) is kindly-harsh in his

appraisement of Hardy's language in poetry; but now that readers
are used to it, the countryman's crudeness of word-choice is seen
to be characteristic of the poet's inwardness, and does not inhibit
re-appraisal of Hardy as one of England's major modern poets. He
has a less ponderous touch than the philosophic Wordsworth, but
like him is a poet of the affections, with little use for the blandish-
ments of rhetoric. Williams neatly describes the style as 'deliberate
meiosis'.

As in his novels, Hardy tells the truth about life without
blinking its disappointed emotions. Most remarkable is the
spareness of the words with which he transmits his experience.
The rhythms are so natural that no dividing line, except in the
versatility of stanza forms, is apparent between the poetry and the
prose. A fair example is the poem *Tolerance*.

> 'It is a foolish thing,' said I,
> 'To bear with such, and pass it by;
> Yet so I do, I know not why!'
>
> And at each cross I would surmise
> That if I had willed not in that wise   5
> I might have spared me many sighs.
>
> But now the only happiness
> In looking back that I possess –
> Whose lack would leave me comfortless –
>
> Is to remember I refrained   10
> From masteries I might have gained,
> And for my tolerance was disdained;
>
> For see, a tomb. And if it were
> I had bent and broke, I should not dare
> To linger in the shadows there.   15

Few would regard this confidential self-examination as the proper
stuff of poetry. Hardy's invariable practice is to deflate the *ego*.
Yet how much these fifteen lines communicate of the speaker's
state of mind – a mood, not of stoical, but of nearly apathetical
acquiescence. The middle word *happiness* is the fulcrum of the
poem; but note with what an array of epithets it is counter-
balanced: *foolish, cross, sighs, comfortless, disdained, tomb, bent and
broke, shadows*. There are only two poeticisms in a passage almost

entirely in colloquial speech; these are the inversion *said I* (line 1), and the rhyme word *surmise* (line 4). Rhyme is important to Hardy; the simplicity of the language needs some rhythmical recurrence to give the sparsely punctuated stanzas the desired metrical form. The poem returns upon itself with the resonant word *tomb* in line 13; and with what finality it is placed before the long caesural pause.

Hardy's ability to find themes for poetry in the drab and dispiriting experiences of everyday life is a rare gift, but explicable in the light of his late-coming to the profession of poet, when close on sixty years of age. It enables him to blend ideas and feelings, often antithetically, and to cajole stanzas of his own invention to take their shape from the rhythm of the language he wants to use. He splendidly exemplifies the grafting of free verse upon the stock of established metrical laws, as in *The Monument-Maker*:

> I chíselled her mónumènt
> To my mínd's contént,
> Tóok it to the chúrch by níght,
> When her plánet was at its héight,
> And sét it whère I had fígured the pláce in the dáytìme.   5
> Having níched it thére
> I stépped bàck, | chéered, | and thòught its oútlines fáir,
> And its márbles ráre.
>
> Then laúghed shè over my shóulder | as in our Máytìme:
> 'It spélls not mé!' | she sáid: 10
> 'Télls nòthing about my béauty, | wít, or gáy tìme
> With àll those, | quíck and déad,
> Of hígh or lówlihèad,
> That hóvered neár,
> Inclùding yóu, | who cárve thère your devótion;   15
> But yòu félt nòne, | my déar!'
>
> And thèn she vánished. | Chéckless spráng my emótion
> And fórced a téar
> At seéing I'd nòt been trúly knówn by hér,
> And néver prízed! – | that my memórial hére,   20
> To cónsecràte her sépulchrè,
> Was scórned, | álmòst,
> By hèr swèet ghóst:
> Yet I hóped nòt quíte, | in her vèry ínnermòst!

Oddities of order, diction and grammar, of which Hardy is accused, are a part of his method, and are not often determined by the necessities of rhyme. Though he uses the monologue style constantly, the speech-rhythms have not so many jolting turns of movement as Browning's. In *The Monument-Maker* the only inversion of word-order is *laughed she* (9). The choice of *niched* (verb 6), *lowlihead* (13) and *innermost* (noun 24), two of them involving vicarious use of parts of speech (*enallage*), is entirely happy in context. Although *lowlihead* was already archaic by the nineteenth century, one finds it revived by Tennyson, Rossetti and Browning.

To appreciate the rhythmical and metrical structure of this poem, one should consider the primary and secondary stresses, and the internal pauses that a sensitive interpreter might observe. Metrically, the long lines 5, 7, 9, 11, 15, 17, 19, 20 and 24 are complex, but their prosaic rhythm enacts the inflexions of the speaking (and thinking) voice. Each stanza has eight lines, but is unique in its strophic rhythm and internal structure, being diversified by the length of its lines, the position of pauses and the scheme of rhyme, which includes five polysyllabic ones (*daytime / Maytime / gaytime* and *devotion / emotion*) that link the stanzas naturally together. When the rhyme falls on syllables of secondary (metrical) stress, as in lines 1, 13, 21, 22 and 24, the effect of the modulation upon the rhythm is impressive. There are nine rhyming groups, but in two instances, where rhyme is given to a metrical syllable bearing secondary stress (lines 1 and 21), the phonetic quality of the sound is a poetic licence. Here is a line by line analysis of the technical effects:

First Stanza	*Rhyme*	*Phonetic Sound*
Line 1, seven syllables, 3 stresses (2 primary)	a	[ɛ] metrical, [ə] natural
Line 2, five syllables, 2 primary stresses	a	[ɛ]
Line 3, seven syllables, 3 primary stresses	b	[aɪ]
Line 4, eight syllables, 2 primary stresses	b	[aɪ]
Line 5, fourteen syllables, 6 stresses (4 primary)	c (double)	[eɪ] [aɪ]
Line 6, five syllables, 2 primary stresses	d	[ɛə]
Line 7, ten syllables, 6 stresses (4 primary)	d	[ɛə]
Line 8, five syllables, 2 primary stresses	d	[ɛə]
Second Stanza		
Line 1, thirteen syllables, 5 stresses (3 primary)	c (double)	[eɪ] [aɪ]

Second Stanza	Rhyme	Phonetic Sound
Line 2, six syllables, 3 primary stresses	e	[ɛ]
Line 3, twelve syllables, 6 stresses (4 primary)	c (double)	[eɪ] [aɪ]
Line 4, six syllables, 3 stresses (2 primary)	e	[ɛ]
Line 5, six syllables, 3 stresses (2 primary)	e	[ɛ]
Line 6, four syllables, 2 primary stresses	f	[ɪə]
Line 7, eleven syllables, 5 stresses (3 primary)	g (triple)	[ɪ] [ou] [ə]
Line 8, six syllables, 4 stresses (2 primary)	f	[ɪə]

Third Stanza		
Line 1, twelve syllables, 5 stresses (4 primary)	g (triple)	[ɪ] [ou] [ə]
Line 2, four syllables, 2 primary stresses	f	[ɪə]
Line 3, eleven syllables, 5 stresses (4 primary)	h	[ɜ]
Line 4, ten syllables, 4 primary stresses	h	[ɜ]
Line 5, eight syllables, 4 stresses (2 primary)	h	[ɜ] metrical, [ə] natural
Line 6, four syllables, 3 stresses (2 primary)	i	[ou]
Line 7, four syllables, 3 stresses (1 primary)	i	[ou]
Line 8, twelve syllables, 6 stresses (3 primary)	i	[ou]

It can be seen at a glance that there is no correspondence of respective lines in these stanzas, whether in syllable count, number and disposition of primary and secondary stresses, or the location of medial pauses. There are masculine, feminine and weak line-endings, and the rhymes occasionally introduce imperfection in phonetic accord. The *Monument-Maker* is thus written in free verse, despite its conventional garb of rhyme and stanza form. Here, as in *Tolerance*, we have a poem complete in itself, centred in disciplined emotion, and expressed with satisfying artlessness. As used by Hardy, rhyme is not the 'bondage' Milton thought it was; it exists as evolutionary nick-points in the terrain the poem covers.

Gerard Manley Hopkins (1844–89) belonged to the same generation as Hardy, but died comparatively young, and had been writing verse as early as the eighteen-sixties. A convert to Catholicism and a Jesuit priest, he published practically nothing during his lifetime; and Robert Bridges, his literary executor, offered only a selection of his poems to the public in 1918, thinking them too unorthodox for contemporary taste. In the Victorian milieu, Hopkins was indeed a literary phenomenon; his revolutionary style was a novelty with which Bridges, an acknowledged metrist, could hardly be expected to agree. Just before Bridges's death, a fuller second edition of the *Poems*, edited by Charles Williams with a sympathetic introduction, appeared in 1930. Only then did the poet, who had been dead for forty-one years, make any impact.

Williams and T. S. Eliot both observed that Hopkins had some resemblance to Meredith, and that he came as a salutary corrective to Victorian orthodoxy in technical matters. Adept as a craftsman with the pencil, and a lover of music, Hopkins wanted to be a poet–painter, and was at first touched by the aesthetic influence of the Pre-Raphaelites and Swinburne. At Oxford he proved to be a first-class classical scholar, and an admirer of Greek poetry, Plato and Duns Scotus. Throughout his life there was, however, conflict between what he conceived to be his religious duty and the poet's sense of vocation. The latter suffered, and the tension had psychological effects upon the style, texture and pattern of his poems, when he found time to write them. It was only at the theological Rector's request that he composed his first experimental and best esteemed poem *The Wreck of the Deutschland*. This was while he was studying for the priesthood in North Wales, where he discovered the haunting effects of internal rhyme from Welsh poetry. He outdid the models in the ingenuity with which he introduced rhythmical novelty, as in poem 57:

> Stones *ring*; like each tucked *string tells*, each *hung bell's*
> Bow *swung* finds *tongue* to *fling* out broad its name.

This is unusual poetry from two aspects: its adjacent strong accents, which make the rhythm difficult to sense; and the meaning, which the syntax makes it equally hard to communicate.

Bridges's criticisms of the Hopkins technique were numerous, and though much reproved on the score of prejudice by later critics, they cannot be altogether ignored. Besides noting that Hopkins tended to force emotion into sectarian channels, he complained of 'occasional affectation in metaphor'. But the major charges were 'oddity and obscurity', 'liberties and ellipses in grammar' (*eg*, the omission of relative pronouns), and confusion in the parts of speech, which leaves an interpreter groping. He felt that Hopkins sacrificed the toneless structural elements of syntax for more colourful poetic expressions. The poet, we now realize, offers considerable compensations; but it should be remarked that a recent research-worker, W. E. Baker, finds Hopkins almost unique among moderns in the number of his syntactical dislocations. From the writing of *The Wreck of the Deutschland* in 1875, ambiguities frequently prove insoluble; and a further disadvantage arises from fragmented phrases, in which others are interposed for rhythmical effect, *eg,*

> No mouth had, *no nor mind,* expressed   (*Spring and Fall,* 12)
> Somewhere elsewhere there is *ah well where!* one   (*The Golden Echo,* 6)
> Your *round me roaming* end, and under be my boughs   (*Peace,* 2)

Though he seldom abandoned stanzaic form, Hopkins achieved within it a different kind of rhythmic flexibility from Hardy's. The metres of the many experiments in the *Collected Poems* (fourth edition, 1967) are often more complex than the poet's inconclusive theory of sprung rhythm envisages. Before this theory is outlined, it should be made clear that the appeal of Hopkins surely lies in the use he made of Keatsian pictorial imagery and Miltonic harmony of phrase, qualities that survived the unfamiliar rhythms of the verse, which he partially owed to the Welsh tradition. Hopkins wrote in a letter to R. W. Dixon in 1878 that in his later poetry he wanted, like Milton, to do 'something necessary and eternal' (perhaps like the Parthenon frieze). Hebrew poetry of the Old Testament, and Milton's *Paradise Regained* and *Samson Agonistes* were his models.

In the free verse of eight-line stanzas in *The Wreck of the Deutschland,* Hopkins said that he scanned 'by accents or stresses alone'. A disciplined use of assonance and alliteration inspires the daring word-choice and surprising compound expressions:

4
I am sóft síft
In an hóurglàss – at the wáll
Fást, but míned with a mótion, a dríft,
And it crówds and it cómbs to the fáll;
Í steàdy as a wáter in a wéll, to a póise, to a páne,   5
But róped with, álways, áll the way dòwn from the táll
Félls or flánks of the vóel, a véin
Of the góspel próffer, a préssure, a prínciple, Chríst's gíft.

5

I kíss my hánd
To the stárs, lóvely-asúnder   10
Stárlìght, wáfting him óut of it; and
Glów, glóry in thúnder;
Kíss my hánd to the dáppled-with-dámson wést:
Sínce, tho' he is únder the wòrld's spléndour and wónder,
His mýstery mùst be instréssed, stréssed;   15
For I gréet him the dàys I méet him, and bléss when I ùnder-
stánd.

There is much variation in the disposition of stresses, but the
number in each of the corresponding lines is the same, the only
exceptions being lines 5 and 13, where there are six and five beats
respectively. In line 7, double alliteration is made possible by the
use of the Welsh word *voel* (mountain) pronounced [vɔil], which
echoes the sound in *poise* (line 5). Compound phrases *lovely-
asunder* (10) and *dappled-with-damson* (13) are evidence of Hopkins's
quest for arresting epithets.

Hopkins was a pleader for the intensifying power of rhetoric
in poetry; Bridges said that 'emphasis seemed to oust euphony'.
Two examples will suffice to illustrate his different uses:

Not, I'll *not*, carrion comfort, Despair, *not* feast on thee;
Not untwist – slack they may be – these last strands of man
In me *ór*, most weary, cry I can no more. I can;
Can something, hope, wish day come, *not* choose *not* to be.
(*Carrion Comfort*, 1–4)

The defiant negative adverb *not*, repeated six times, is a characteristic use of rhetorical emphasis. So is accented *or*, to rhyme with
more, in line 3. Several words marked with an acute accent in the
poet's manuscripts, indicate likewise a strong *metrical* stress, as in
these lines from *The Leaden and the Golden Echo* (A Maiden's song
from St Winefred's Well):

Ó is there no frowning of these wrinkles, rankèd wrinkles deep,
Dówn? no waving off of these most mournful messengers.

The Elizabethan licence of sounded past-participle inflexions, as
in *rankèd*, Hopkins admitted freely.

The Leaden and the Golden Echo was discussed in some detail with

Bridges, whose comments drew attention to the poet's meticulous search for the right word. Hopkins wrote: 'The things must come from the *mundus muliebris* (feminine world) . . . they must not be markedly oldfashioned' . . . 'I have marked the stronger stresses, but *with the degree of stress so constantly varying no marking is satisfactory* (my italics). Do you think that all had best be left to the reader?' Bridges answered the latter question in the affirmative; but he quotes Hopkins's desire that his poetry should always be read 'with ears'.

In Hopkins's elucidation, sprung rhythm begins with juxtaposition of two stresses, thereby inhibiting smooth 'running' (or Common English) rhythm; there are plenty of examples in natural speech. On the analogy of a bar of music, where the chief accent always comes first, he favoured trochaic and dactylic (or falling) rhythms. He knew that poets modulate by inversion of stress, which in orthodox metrical systems is permissible in the first foot and after a medial pause. In Hopkins's theory, counterpoint, sometimes marked with a twirl, is the mounting of a new rhythm on the ground-pattern, and is realized when inversion is introduced in successive feet of a verse line. If the poet does not acquaint the reader with the ground-pattern, as in the choruses of *Samson Agonistes*, the counter-rhythm virtually supersedes it, and gives rise to sprung rhythm. But Hopkins maintained that the strict sprung rhythm postulated 'cannot be counterpointed'.

The system Hopkins advocates admits feet of four and (when the occasion demands) even more syllables; the slack syllables should therefore out-number the stressed ones. For practical purposes, his extremes are the stressed monosyllable and the first paeon ($/xxx$). Like Coventry Patmore in his 'Essay on English Metrical Law' (1856), he believed in *isochronism*; he held that 'the feet are assumed to be equally long or strong, and their seeming inequality is made up by pause (which he often indicated) or stressing'. Sprung rhythm resembles Greek 'logaoedic' rhythm (*eg*, in alcaics and sapphics), where dactyls may be combined with trochees or iambs. There are good imitations of the latter in English versions of Tennyson and Swinburne. The important consideration is that Hopkins, rightly or wrongly, intended his verse to be scanned by metrical conventions.

Sprung rhythm is not only that of common speech and prose, but also of music and old nursey rhymes, whose irregular rhythms

43

may be the result of deteriorated word-inflexions. In the stanzas of Hopkins, the rhythm runs on without a break to the end of each grouping. His system admits enjambement, even to separating the syllables of a word; however, he avoids confusion with conventional metrics by using the term *rove over* ('spliced') lines. Among his licences (which include 'pauses') are *hangers* and *outrides*, or supernumerary unstressed syllables. He says that they 'hang below the line or ride forward or backward from it in another dimension'. *Felix Randal* illustrates the employment of these licences. In spite of the seeming irregularity of the poem, each line of *Felix Randal* has six stresses:

> Síckness bróke him. Impátient, he cúrsed at fírst, but ménded
>
> Béing anoínted and áll; though a heávenlier héart begán some
>
> Mónths eárlier, since Í had our swéet repríeve and ránsom
>
> Téndered to him. Áh well, God rést him áll roád éver he
> offénded!

One should notice that these licences tend to efface the binding purpose of the feminine rhymes, and that prosaic texture makes the value of stresses somewhat arbitrary, especially in line 4. In the manuscripts of this poem the hangers and outrides are marked with a loop below. The slur in line 3 has a loop *over* the syllables; such slurs effect the uniting of syllables in time, and make an acceptable metrical unit. In other poems, a loop at the end of a line occasionally indicates 'that the rhyme goes on to the first letter of the next line'. Fortunately, these complicated devices have not been emulated by other poets.

In a letter to Bridges dated June 22, 1879, Hopkins says that *The Windhover* 'is the best thing I ever wrote'; it is in 'falling paeonic rhythm, sprung and outriding'. The paeonic feet of this sonnet are the first two in line 5:

> Hígh thĕre, hŏw hĕ | rúng ŭpŏn thĕ | réin ŏf ă wímplĭng wíng

Hopkins knew well that Whitman had improvised along similar lines by instinct; he wished to better the example by rational design. He was conscious of licence, and had it pointed out to him by his advisers; but he restrained the freedom by his own strict laws. Many of his poems have majestic form, and the best do not lack Whitman's creative energy. He was as skilful as Pope in counterpoising parallel phrases, and he regarded parallelism as the basis of all artifice in poetry. The poems, he told his friends, were intended for *performance*, not for reading. But it is rarely possible in delivery to make meaningful such a line as

His mýstery mùst be instréssed, stréssed

with the disruptive pause between the final syllables. Elizabeth Schneider regrets his 'arbitrary wrenchings of sense for the sake of a desired pattern' (*The Dragon in the Gate*, University of California Press, 1968, p. 86).

In its recognition that rhythm and rhetoric live in sensitive relation, the practice of Hopkins has not received the attention it deserves. Verse was for him speech that partakes of the nature of music. Hence his admiration for the composer, Purcell. *Spelt from Sybil's Leaves* he says is a sonnet 'timed in *tempo rubato*'. He writes what Patmore characterized as dipodic verse, resembling the strongly stressed metre of *Piers Plowman*, in which the unit of rhythm covers two adjacent feet. But Hopkins extends this technique to the compass of his quatrains or other stanza groupings. He has in mind the strophic movement of alliterative poetry in the Middle Ages, where rhythm is linked, if not infallibly, by identical initial consonants. In the poetry of Hopkins, however, rhyme, assonance and word repetition co-operate; the technical resources make a combined assault on eye, ear and the emotions. Rhetoric powerfully reinforces the structural principle. Reading between the lines, one can appreciate the point he tries to make in a fragment from *Floris in Italy*:

> Beauty it may be is the meet of lines,
> Or careful-spacèd sequences of sound,
> These rather are the arc where beauty shines,
> The temper'd soil where only her flower is found.
> Allow at least it has one term and part
> Beyond, and one within the looker's eye;
> And I must have the centre in my heart
> To spread the compass on the all-starr'd sky:

Ezra Pound (1885–1972), an American from the Middle West, is one of the most difficult modern poets to assess. There is no denying the importance of the impact he and T. S. Eliot made upon the future of poetry in English, during the period from 1908 to 1920, when Pound was resident in London. He was a nephew of the New England poet Longfellow, whose links with Europe and its Latin and Germanic languages were strong. Though Pound became an international figure, he carried the stamp of Americanism wherever he lived, and his pedagogic zeal, founded upon a disinterested love of letters, was responsible for forging many durable bonds between writers in England and America. It is doubtful whether Poe, Emerson, Henry James and Frost made a more dynamic contribution. By the time he left London to live in Paris and Italy, he had given a direction to modern English poetry so devious that no historian can disentangle the indigenous from the American elements in its development.

Pound was a reputable linguist, who had specialized at the University of Pennsylvania in Romance Languages, and had afterwards lectured on the earlier literatures of south-western Europe. He often said that his studies in ancient and alien traditions of poetry (including Chinese, Greek and Latin) were undertaken to discover why some forms and styles had survived, while others failed or became exhausted. His 'yawp' was not that of a 'barbarian let loose in a Museum', but the voice of a delighted enthusiast who became willy-nilly a cultural propagandist. His major life-work, the *Cantos*, was a widely-ranging poetical commentary, often with satirical intention, on the evolution of European culture. The satire was directed largely at developments he had witnessed in the twentieth century. This was an incredible theme for a modern epic, and most critics have done no more than point to isolated beauties and condemn the rambling poem's lack of form. Pound is primarily an explorer of the aesthetic and moral *ethos*, not of Browningesque personalities.

Pound's preoccupation with eclectic 'culture', as necessary for a man of letters, is characteristically American; but it was not of the people, like Whitman's. He is an aesthete, like Berenson, an expatriate living permanently in Europe to be nearer to the sources of his inspiration; and his internationalism was fruitful at a time when Georgian poetry in England tended to become provincial. Pound's poetry, in its vocabulary and ideas, is designed to show that 'all ages are contemporaneous'. The universal praise given to his translation of the Old English poem *The Seafarer* is proof of the success which attended his efforts to refresh the rhythms of modern poetry from ancient sources. Most of his earlier books of verse, such as *Cathay*, *Canzoni* and *Homage to Sextus Propertius*, were paraphrases rather than translations; he did not aim at verbal fidelity to the originals, and was unjustly criticized for failing to do what was not his intention.

When Pound arrived in London in 1908, he claimed to be a disciple of Catullus and the Provençal troubadours, a confession most unlikely to impress a leader of thought like T. E. Hulme, who was a reactionary realist and a pupil of Bergson. Yet within four years of his arrival, Pound was the centre of a group of young writers whom he was the first to call Imagists in 1912, in reference to a handful of poems by Hulme, which he appended to his own volume *Ripostes*. The Imagists had, since 1909, been dining at a club in Soho, founded by F. S. Flint, the protagonists being Ford Madox Hueffer (who afterwards changed his surname to Ford), T. E. Hulme, W. B. Yeats, Edward Storer, Richard Aldington and Hilda Doolittle, another American, whom Aldington married in 1913. Their dissatisfaction with contemporary English poetry led them to imitate Japanese and Hebrew, as well as French symbolist verse. Their reaction was not against any of the widely differing Georgian poets, sponsored by their patron Edward Marsh, among whom Rupert Brooke and Walter de la Mare were the most admired examples; indeed, many *avant-garde* poets, such as D. H. Lawrence, published their work in both the Georgian and the Imagist anthologies. There was rather a generalized dislike of enfeebled rural themes and conventionalizing theories of prosody, encouraged by treatises from the pens of Robert Bridges and Lascelles Abercrombie, who happened to be aligned with the Georgians.

Pound's brief Imagist manifesto was 'A Few Don'ts', published in the American journal *Poetry* in March 1913. Here he defined an *Image* as something that presents an intellectual and emotional complex in an instant of time, giving a sense of liberation and of 'sudden growth'. A more subjective account could hardly be found, and Pound amplified it in 1914, when he published *Des Imagistes*, an anthology of English and American poetry written by his friends, including James Joyce, Amy Lowell and William Carlos Williams.

At the beginning of the First World War, Pound withdrew from leadership of the Imagist movement, chiefly because his personal vanity and occasional arrogance had lost him friends. He was an individualist who refused to be stereotyped; his instinct for usefully appraising new writing was invaluable in a transitional literary society, but Eliot was among the few who loyally appreciated Pound's guidance. Pound described his dilemma and demise in the very first poem of *Hugh Selwyn Mauberley*:

> For three years, out of key with his time,
> He strove to resuscitate the dead art
> Of poetry; to maintain 'the sublime'
> In the old sense. Wrong from the start—
>
> . . .
>
> His true Penelope was Flaubert,
> He fished by obstinate isles;
> Observed the elegance of Circe's hair
> Rather than the mottoes on sundials.
>
> Unaffected by 'the march of events',
> He passed from men's memory in *l'an trentiesme*,
> *De son eage*; the case presents
> No adjunct to the Muses' diadem.

The wealth of allusions shows that this free verse in quatrains is coterie or learned poetry. The rhythm unfolds the reflection so naturally that anyone might be excused in mistaking it for the work of Eliot or Laforgue. It fulfils the aims of modernist poetry, and should not be dismissed, in Frank Swinnerton's terms, as 'the poetry of a critic... restricted in range of emotion' (see *The Georgian Literary Scene*, Dent, 1938, p. 363).

Richard Aldington and Amy Lowell, upon whom the Imagist mantle had fallen, sought in *Some Imagist Poems* (1915) to enlarge the aims of the movement by proclaiming their passionate belief in 'the artistic values of modern life', not as painters, but as writers who thought that poetry 'should render particulars exactly'. This implied greater concentration, but 'absolute freedom in the choice of subject'. The only technical contribution Aldington made in the Preface was to suggest that the cadence of free verse 'is more marked, more definite, and closer knit than that of prose'; but it is 'not so violently nor so obviously accented' as regular verse.

The Imagist movement played an indispensable role in the development of modernist poetry, and was important because its new concept of style had been even more manifest in America than in England. Amy Lowell was the spokesman of poets across the Atlantic in 1916, and Yeats of the middle period was the new voice of the Celtic reformation in Ireland. The term *vers libre* was being bandied about by writers who had no clear conception of its meaning or purpose. Amy Lowell described it as 'verse-form based upon cadence', written to be read aloud; 'the unit is the strophe, which may be the whole poem, or . . . only a part'. Amid the confusion, the voice of Hopkins was, unfortunately, not yet heard.

T. S. Eliot's logical mind was, however, able to perceive a distinction between *vers libre* and English/American free verse, that was not apparent to Imagists in the period 1912–17, nor indeed to Yeats in the Introduction to his *Oxford Book of Modern Verse* (1936). In the Introduction to *Selected Poems of Ezra Pound* (Faber, 1935) Eliot explained *vers libre* as a development peculiar to France, beginning with the liberation of the French alexandrine by Victor Hugo, whose ideas were later advanced by Rimbaud, Corbière and Laforgue. He observed that English blank verse underwent a comparable but earlier development in the hands of Marlowe, Shakespeare and the Jacobean dramatists.

D. H. Lawrence followed Yeats in believing that *vers libre* and free verse were one and the same; this becomes clear from his Introduction to *New Poems* (New York, 1920):

> All that can be said, first and last, is that free verse is, or should be, direct utterance from the instant, whole man. . . . It is no use inventing fancy laws for free verse, no use drawing a melodic line which all the feet must toe. . . . Whitman pruned away his clichés – perhaps his clichés of rhythm as well as of phrase. And this is about all we can do, deliberately, with free verse. We can get rid of the stereotyped movements and the old hackneyed associations of sound or sense. We can break down those artificial conduits and canals through which we do so love to force out utterance. We can break the stiff neck of habit. We can be in ourselves spontaneous and flexible as flame, we can see that utterance rushes out without artificial form or artificial smoothness. But we cannot positively prescribe any motion, any rhythm. . . .
>
> To break the lovely form of metrical verse, and to dish up

the fragments as a new substance, called *vers libre*, this is what most of the free-versifiers accomplish. They do not know that free verse has its own *nature*, that it is neither star nor pearl, but instantaneous like plasm. . . .

For such utterance any externally applied law would be mere shackles and death. The law must come new each time from within.

This plea accounts for Lawrence's sometimes invertebrate rhythms in the poems of *Pansies*; but it also explains the silent disaffection of Pound and Eliot with the Imagist group. In the free verse of the American-born pair, the rhythm is not always that of common speech, nor does it reject rhyme and stanza form. Pound admitted that he learnt less about free verse from his countryman Whitman than from Browning and Yeats. His adoption of *personae* (or what Yeats called *masks*) to express a point of view in a moment of time, as in *Near Perigord* and *Hugh Selwyn Mauberley*, unmistakably marks his dependence on Browning. The reciprocal influence of Yeats upon Pound and Pound upon Yeats after 1919, would provide a very instructive study. In 1913 Yeats had written to Lady Gregory that Pound helped him 'to get back to the definite and the concrete, and away from modern abstractions'; but that unfortunately he had 'more sound principles than taste'.

Pound's persistent experiments in verse were prompted by a typically American belief in progress, and unwillingness to be content with a style which uninformed critics thought he had perfected. The Poems in *Hugh Selwyn Mauberley* (1920) are the neatest exemplars of his varied techniques, and they are at the same time lively evidence of his disappointed contacts with English literary movements. The central figure or *persona* is a cultured impressionist reflecting ironically on the distressing times that came in the wake of a disastrous war.

POEM II

The age demanded an image
Of its accelerated grimace,
Something for the modern stage,
Not, at any rate, an Attic grace;

Not, not certainly, the obscure reveries 5
Of the inward gaze;

Better mendacities
Than the classics in paraphrase!

The 'age demanded' chiefly a mould in plaster,
Made with no loss of time,   10
A prose kinema, not, not assuredly, alabaster
Or the 'sculpture' of rhyme.

The metrical plan of this poem is relatively simple; it consists of
quatrains in a rising rhythm and lines of irregular length. They
have plentiful trisyllabic modulation, occasional prosaic lines (2
and 11) and numerous inversions of stress at the beginning of the
line (3, 4, 5, 7, 10), often arising from the colloquial emphasis of
the speaker (as the repetitions of *not* in lines 4 and 5). The latter are
rhetorical devices known as *epizeuxis*, which conversationalists
often employ unconsciously (cf line 11). The natural speech
rhythm is aided by rhymes that are off-beat (*ímăge / stáge*), or
dependent on secondary stresses for metrical licence (*révĕriès /
mĕndáčitiès* and *gáze / párăphràse*).

The meaning is not readily derived, because the allusions
require a considerable intellectual background. Pound is an
historian to whom cultural disorders since 1850 have come with
something of an emotional shock, despite his mask of detachment.
The speaker is seen to be detached, because Pound records events
through the eyes of Mauberley, not his own. We know this because the speaker thinks that 'classics in paraphrase' (Pound's
forte) are worse than lies. A progressive vulgarization of art forms
is referred to in lines 2 and 4, and more specifically in lines 9, 11
and 12. The word 'sculpture' in inverted commas reverts to a
concept of Théophile Gautier about the uses of rhyme.

This poem is closely related to a later one in Part II entitled *The
Age Demanded*, in which Pound continues his ironic analysis in the
same querulous tone. The poem is replete with polysyllabic
critical terms familiar to literary disputants:

Incapable of the least utterance or composition,
Emendation, conservation of the 'better tradition',
Refinement of medium, elimination of superfluities,
August attraction or concentration.

Nothing, in brief, but maudlin confession,   5
Irresponse to human aggression,

Amid the precipitation, down-float
Of insubstantial manna,
Lifting the faint susurrus
Of his subjective hosannah.   10

Ultimate affronts to
Human redundancies;

Non-esteem of self-styled 'his betters'
Leading, as he well knew,
To his final   15
Exclusion from the world of letters.

This is free verse with multiple rhymes, though lines 3, 4, 7, 9 and
15 are blank. An obscure passage in lines 7 to 12 has the uncommon expression *susurrus* signifying 'murmur', and the
Hebrew rhyme-word *hosannah*, meaning 'save us'; these are 'subjective' means of suggesting the poet's spiritual deterioration. It
is obvious that Pound in Europe had become conscious of his
growing isolation in a world unsympathetic to his literary interests.

Poem IV of Part I, in which he looks back to the First World
War, begins with an analysis of the motives of those who partici-
pated; then follow the tragic disillusionments:

walked *eye-deep* in hell
believing in old men's *lies*, then un*believing*
came *home, home* to a *lie*,
home to many deceits,
home to *old lies* and new infamy;   5
usury *age-old* and *age-thick*
and *liars* in public places.

Daring *as never before*, wastage *as never before*.
Young *blood* and high *blood*,
fair cheeks, and *fine* bodies;   10

fortitude as never before

frankness as never before,
disillusions as never told in the old days,
hysterias, trench confessions
laughter out of dead bellies.   15

No rhyme is needed here, because the binding force is the complex
of rhetorical usages. The principle figures involve repetition of

various kinds. Notice the structural use of repetition in the words *lie* and *liars* of lines 1 to 7; also the compounds *eye-deep, age-old* and *age-thick*, the last two subtly balanced against each other in line 6. *Anaphora* is found in the repetition of *home* at the beginning of lines 4 and 5. *Epanalepsis* occurs in 2, with the use of *believing* at the beginning and end of the line. Antithesis and *ploce* are employed pervasively, especially in lines 5 and 6, 8 and 9, 11 and 12. It would be hard to find, even in Elizabethan literature, a passage in which rhetoric, in the commendable sense, is so functional.

Baker (*op. cit.*, p. 54–60) complains that Pound uses more fragments than regular sentences, a truth borne out by the above citations. But in this colloquial, and therefore elliptical, method the modern poet is an impressionist; and Baker shows the linking effect secured by repetition of key words, also exploited by Eliot. The technique calls, he says, for 'a new way of reading poetry', based on 'the principle of allowing nouns, and the extensive substructures they generate, to replace sentences'.

In retrospect, the innovators of the two generations 1850–1910 do not seem to have been conscious of a break with the past more radical than the expansion of ideas and themes; yet step by step, this led to a less romantic poetic treatment. The changed intellectual content of poems came largely from science and psychology, and it enabled the poet to invent new images, as well as to extend his vocabulary to unfamiliar frontiers of ideas. There was no rational intention in Browning, Hopkins and Hardy to cut adrift from tradition, rather the revese; but there was a desire to recall the virtues of classical strength and lucidity, and to play down the expression of emotion in the febrile sentiments of neo-romanticism. In *The Death of a Hero* Aldington suggests that *fin-de-siècle* poetry had become 'turgid and boresome and sloppy and wordy', which he ascribed to the backward-looking tastes of the English middle class.

By the end of the First World War the position was radically changed. The accelerated progress of science and new directions in philosophy gave to critics a different orientation. The optimistic humanism of Browning and Whitman, and the aesthetic doctrine of Art for Art's sake came under serious scrutiny, as did the determinist scepticism of Hardy. In 'The Possibility of a Poetic Drama' (*The Sacred Wood,* 1920), T. S. Eliot maintained that 'every work of imagination must have a philosophy', but warned of the dangers of embodying it in a work of art, as Goethe does. Thought should subserve and be consecrated to the creative principle, not aggrandize the *ego* of the poet. Writers like Yeats and Eliot sought rather to extend the boundaries of consciousness by sensitive use of the auditory imagination. They studied each other's work and aimed at a greater concentration of language. No attentive reader can fail to discern in Pound and Eliot a disciplined return to the advantages of rhetoric: this helped stanzaless verse to achieve concentration of form.

Form and technique were closely associated in the new poetry, but the advances were at first cautious and tentative. The strophe or paragraph of free-verse was slow in liberating rhythms from the domination of stanza, rhyme and formal metre. Pound, Yeats and Eliot proved to be more restrained in experiment than Hopkins. As Eliot observed in 'The Music of Poetry' (*On Poetry and Poets*, p. 28), 'it may be possible that the beauty of some English poetry is due to the presence of more than one metrical structure in it'.

The principal strength of the new poetry is its coalescence of meaning and rhythm. Powerful effects may result from the nuances of phonetic variation, such as vowel quality and length, consonant combination, and the many durations of pause of which colloquial speech is capable. The activating principle behind the lines of Lawrence's verse – length rather than stress – was stoutly defended in a letter to Edward Marsh in November 1913. He describes the rhythm as 'movements in space', rather than 'footsteps hitting the earth'; and he adds: 'It all depends on the *pause* – the natural pause, the natural *lingering* of the voice according to the feeling – it is the hidden *emotional* pattern that makes poetry, not the obvious form'.

About this time a new word *texture* entered the critical vocabulary of poetry. This comprehends both the sound values of syllables and the associations of words; it cannot be entirely separated from metrical design. It is the verbal texture of lines that disappears when a poem is paraphrased or translated. The emotional impact of a poem rests on a sensitive appreciation of tone or verbal texture; and the psychological explanation seems to be that this tone sets up sympathetic vibrations in the mind's ear.

CHAPTER III

Form and Rhythm;
Meaning and Rhetoric

〰〰〰〰〰〰

In 'Humdrum and Harum-Scarum' (*Collected Essays* II, Oxford University Press, 1930) Robert Bridges illustrated the futility of separating poetry from prose, especially imaginative prose, whose rhythm resembles that of free verse. W. B. Yeats lent colour to the view by placing first in his *Oxford Book of Modern Verse* Walter Pater's eulogy of Mona Lisa from his essay on Leonardo da Vinci. In free verse, Bridges went on to suggest, the form is more significant than the content. This dichotomy is now considered to be fallacious, if Bridges meant by form 'the general movement of the rhythm', rather than the unified impression the poem makes.

In the following passage from 'The Music of Poetry' (W. P. Ker Memorial Lecture, Glasgow, 1942) T. S. Eliot employs the word 'form' in different senses:

> It is sometimes assumed that modern poetry has done away with [stanza] forms. . . . I believe that the tendency to return to set, and even elaborate patterns [stanzas] is permanent. . . . Only a bad poet could welcome free verse as a liberation from form [rhythmical shape]. It was a revolt against dead form, and a preparation for new form or for renewal of the old; it was an insistence upon the inner unity which is unique to every poem, against the outer unity which is typical. The poem comes before the form [general design], in the sense that a form [intention of language] grows out of the attempt of somebody to say something . . . I know that a poem, or a passage of a poem, may tend to realize itself first as a particular rhythm before it reaches expression in words, and that this rhythm may bring to birth the idea and the image.

The term *form* is thus variously conceived by poets themselves, and the precise intention has to be gleaned from the context.

What kind of formal pattern can *free* (or *irregular*) verse be said to possess? One answer is organic completeness. The impression of unity is created, if sense, sound and feeling co-operate. Since Coleridge, it has been customary to refer to this unity as *'organic form'*, suggesting that vitality arises from a matching of structure to content. There is, however, another form which Coleridge called 'mechanical', and modern critics designate as *abstract*, because it does not appear to be inherent in 'the dynamic invention'. This is the metrical pattern, representing a poet's subsidiary desire to adapt content to a preconceived structure, not necessarily that of stanzaic verse.

The above distinction is to some extent metaphysical; and this should be so, seeing that a poet works by intuitive impulse. In his quest for organic completeness, he makes adjustments of language to ensure the texture appropriate to his idea of unity. His conception, in taking shape, is invariably modified as the theme develops. By constant adjustment of means to ends, form and content are induced to complement each other. Verbal texture is sincere when meaning, movement and the sound associations of the words appear to a sensitive reader to be happily correlated; though this unity is unlikely to be achieved, unless the construct embodies pleasing elements of variety.

In stanzaic and blank verse, metrical form once played a significant role; the liberation claimed for modern free verse is lesser dependence on that system's licences of modulation. A considerable amount of hybrid free verse of distinction was, however, composed by the 1930 poets Spender, Day Lewis and Auden, as it had been by Hardy and others before them; in Spender's *Prelude 8*, stanzaic groupings of lines are designedly preserved.

> An 'I' can never be a great man.
> This known great one has weakness,
> To friends is most remarkable for weakness:
> His ill-temper at meals, dislike of being contradicted,
> His only real pleasure fishing in ponds,　　　　　5
> His only real wish – forgetting.
>
> To advance from friends to the composite self,
> Central 'I' is surrounded by 'I eating',
> 'I loving', 'I angry', 'I excreting',

And the great 'I' planted in him   10
Has nothing to do with all these,

Can never claim *its* true place
Resting in the forehead, and calm in *his* gaze.
The great 'I' is an unfortunate intruder
Quarrelling with 'I tiring' and 'I sleeping'   15
And all those other 'I's' who long for 'We dying'.

The poem divides itself naturally into three parts, corresponding
to switches in the point of view; the starting point is the premise
that 'no man can appear "great" to himself'. In stanza 1 the poet
takes an objective view of the 'ego' – the man as his friends see
him. Stanza 2 proceeds to self-examination; the poet sees himself
as a diversity of biological 'ego's', with which the real self (his
personal ideal) has nothing to do. Stanza 3 returns to objective
analysis, a significant grammatical change being the replacement of
his by *its* in line 12. The 'great I' is an intellectual myth, not at all
philosophical in outlook. The words *true place* / *Resting in the forehead* seem to refer to intellectual identity, the ideal the poet vainly
aspires to attain, which can never be realized because of internal
conflicts. The meaning of the poem, unfolded as the thought is
externalized in words, suggests itself rhythmically, and justifies
the stanza division (2 leading naturally into 3) on other than
metrical grounds. The poem can be said to have 'meaningful'
shape.

In free verse, form belongs more to the unified conception, and
less to elements of composition, such as patterned stanzas, paragraphs or syllabic lines. Rhythm is important to it, and no other
conception of form is likely to have much critical value. In poems
of length, such as Bridge's *Testament of Beauty* and Pound's *Cantos,*
the aim of rhythmical continuity in the parts presents difficulties.
But the general practice is to match homogeneously a number of
related poems in different rhythms, as does Eliot in *Four Quartets,*
using stanza and rhyme for lyric sections. Form in longer poems
is not alone the planning of the thematic content; cohesion comes
from the chosen language (the texture), through which the conception unfolds itself.

Because free verse is the mode of expression of many poets with
radical ideas, it is sometimes misconceived as an arbitrary medium,

whereas the reverse should be the case. It needs to be highly disciplined in rhythm, and undoubtedly enjoys fewer licences of modulation than metrical poetry. In orthodox metrical verse the poet varies the pattern as much as he wishes, but stops short of defeating expectancy. In free verse, as in poetic prose, an anticipatory pattern is not postulated.

The interplay of sounds of varying magnitude with silences (or pauses) constitutes the rhythm, and it is nominally measured in time. As D. H. Lawrence realized, it would be unwise to underestimate the quantitative value of rhythm in English free verse, despite an understood contrast between stressed and unstressed syllables. The force of stress is necessarily flexible in poetry, because context and grammatical order, through meaning, express logical or rhetorical shades of emphasis. Free verse is said to be 'cadenced', because speech rhythm dominates its structure.

Natural speech rhythm, in the creation of all verse, has a tendency to group units of articulation round determinable primary stresses. In Yeats's poem *A Coat,* which follows, I indicate the units of speech rhythm, and find that they are less in number than foot divisions:

A COAT

I máde | my sóng | a cóat
Cóvered | with embróideries
Oút of | óld | mythólogies
From héel | to thróat;
But the fóols | caúght it,   5
Wóre it | in the wórld's | eýes
As thóugh | they'd | wroúght it.
Sóng, | let them táke it,
For thére's | móre | énterprise
In wálking | náked.   10

Scanned in the feet of metrical verse, only lines 1, 4 and 5 coincide with the natural units of delivery. More feet are required because of the theoretical secondary stresses in several lines:

2. Cóvĕred wĭth | ĕmbrói | dĕrìes |
3. | Oŭt ŏf óld | mўthó | lŏgiès |
6. | Wóre ĭt | iň thě | wórld's éyes |
7. Aš thóugh | thèy'd wroúght ĭt |

58

8. Sóng lĕt | thĕm táke ĭt |
9. | Fŏr thére's | mòre én | tĕrprìse |
10. | Iň wál | kiňg nákĕd |

Difficulty in determining the weight of secondary stresses relative to primary ones suggests the artificiality of metrical scansion, when adapted to irregular cadenced verse. It follows that foot scansion should be reserved for verse that establishes a pattern of regularity. Yeats's poem does not, although it is not entirely free. In free verse, rhythms are measured from stress to stress, and the units are not scientifically isochronous. Although Hopkins believed that units of verse rhythm ought to be isochronous, they can only be of approximately equal duration. Phonetically measured by instruments, they derive from an individual *performance*, not the objective poem embodied in a printed text. The concept of equivalence in verse is inevitably impressionistic.

Fifty years ago, Egerton Smith pointed out in *The Principles of English Metre* that 'it is not sufficient to define rhythm merely as a succession of equal periods of time' (p. 7); what impresses a listener (and a reader in his mind's ear) is 'regularly recurrent difference' in the organic continuity of the rhythm. Modern English speech is full of borrowed polysyllables, and these can be juxtaposed, or used as rhyme words, in free verse, though difficult to handle in scanned measures. The use of *embroideries* and *mythologies* in Yeats's poem should be noted. The rhythm that is organic to form and understanding, Egerton Smith called *primary*; abstract or metrical rhythm, he called *secondary*. He thought there was an undoubted tension between the two.

Seymour Chatman's contribution to the study of rhythm in *A Theory of Meter* (Mouton, 1965) demonstrated that stress has the different characteristics of loudness, length and pitch, all important to interpretation. The most subjective is length; and he reminds us that stressed syllables may be shorter than unstressed ones, as in the word *mythólŏgies*. There is a definite connection between stress and meaning, which it is necessary to perceive, because vowels and diphthongs enjoy full phonetic values in stressed positions, but tend to be neutralized in unprominent ones. (Compare the sound in *coat* with that in the third syllable of *mythologies*). Stress is selective prominence and can be unmistakenly identified in three powers, emphasized stress, normal stress and absence of stress.

A heightening of pitch accompanies special emphasis, the reasons being lexical. Even a silent reader can recognize intonational pattern in contextual utterances; it is a *sine qua non* for appreciating personal poetry, like that of D. H. Lawrence:

SONG OF A MAN WHO HAS COME THROUGH

Not *Í*, not *Í*, but the wind that blows through me!
A fine wind is blowing the new direction of Time.
If only I let it bear me, carry me, if only it cárry me!
If only I am sensitive, subtle, *óh, délicate,* a *wínged* gift!
If only, most lovely of all, I yield myself and am
    bŏrrowed   5
By the *fíne, fíne* wind that takes its course through the
    chaos of the world
Like a fine, an exquisite chisel, a *wédge*-blade inserted;
If only I am keen and hard like the sheer tip of a wedge
Driven by invisible blows,
The rock will split, we shall come at the *wŏnder,* we
    shall find the Hesperides.   10

Oh, for the *wŏnder* that bubbles into my soul,
I would be a good fountain, a good well-head,
Would blur no whisper, spoil no expression.

What is the knocking?
What is the knocking at the door in the night?   15
It is somebody wants to do us harm.

Nŏ, nŏ, it is the three strange angels.
Admít them, *admít* them.

Rhetorical repetition and amplification are the keys, but interpretation would be inadequate without emphatic stress on the words in italics, to which other individualisms may be added. A metrical system is unable to do justice to this kind of poetry, because it is linguistically irrelevant.

It is worth noting that the length of Lawrence's lines is determined by syntax as well as vehement fullness of utterance. The only enjambement called for is in lines 5/6. Freedom of length need not, of course, inhibit the employment of run-on lines.

Though enjambement properly belongs to blank verse and pentameter couplets, the run-on line is fairly common in free

verse. With some American poets, eg, Marianne Moore and
E. E. Cummings, it tends to become a mannerism. Hyphenated
enjambement is also permissible, and was sportively used by
Byron in *Don Juan*. A phenomenon of particular interest, in
performance, is syntactical enjambement that aims to promote
continuity of linear rhythm, as in MacNeice's poem *The Creditor*:

> The quietude of a soft wind
> Will not rescind
> *My debts to God,* but gentle-skinned
> His finger probes. I lull myself
> In *quiet* in *diet* in *riot* in *dreams,*   5
> In dopes in *drams* in *drums* in *dreams*
> Till God retire and the door shut.
> But
> Now I am left in the *fire-blaze*
> The peacefulness of the *fire-blaze*   10
> Will not erase
> *My debts to God* for His mind strays
> Over and under and *all ways*
> *All days* and *always.*

Note that the punctuation is scant and unorthodox. Lines 1–5
and 10–13 are run-on, the solitary *But* in line 8 being used as the
poem's fulcrum.

In MacNeice's poem straddling of successive lines occurs in
several different situations: (*a*) between subject and predicate
(lines 1/2 and 10/11), (*b*) between predicate and object (lines 2/3
and 11/12), (*c*) between modifier (*gentle-skinned*) and subject
(lines 3/4), (*d*) between object and prepositional phrase (lines 4/5),
(*e*) between predicate and prepositional phrase (lines 12/13). The
pattern is thus intricate, the latter half of the poem trying to repeat
the structure of the first. The key phrase is *My debts to God*. The
identical rhyme *dreams* (5/6) matches the *fire-blaze* pair (9/10).
Triple assonance in line 5, is varied by triple alliteration in line 6.
All ways | All days and *always* provide simultaneously *ploce,*
assonance, and a rhyming semantic pun.

Perhaps the principal effect of run-on lines in free verse is to
discourage token pauses at the terminal juncture; this has always
been assumed in metrical verse, if syntactical punctuation is not
supplied.

The compression aimed at and achieved in modern verse lies at the root of difficulties in interpreting the meaning; but there is also the problem of ambiguity, recognized as inherent in all lexical language, and abetted in poetry by the employment of symbols that may be misunderstood or variously interpreted. Critics in the present century have made it abundantly clear that the meaning of a poem is more than the cognitive sum of its words. It is part of poetry's function to enrich meaning and extend consciousness by the overtones and associations of words, and especially their emotive connotations. A poem, then, has a 'total significance' beyond the logical senses of the words, which linguists call 'monosigns'. To some extent this invalidates poetic language as an object of linguistic investigation. Expression of feeling is notoriously subjective, but rhetoric rightly recognizes *hyperbole* and *litotes* as legitimate means of communication. In reading poetry one has constantly to be on one's guard against interpreting figurative language literally, and vice versa.

Modern verse is prone to represent states of mind, and in so doing to juxtapose situations and phrases that seem to want logical connection. Syntactical fragmentation is not always a cause of obscurity; it is ubiquitous in the poetry of T. S. Eliot and D. H. Lawrence, but different attitudes make the first obscure, while the second is readily intelligible. Eliot observed in *The Use of Poetry and the Use of Criticism* that many readers puzzle over meaning 'which is not there, and is not meant to be there'; there are poets, he adds, who 'perceive possibilities of intensity through its elimination'.

There has developed since 1950 a theory of composition that holds a poem to be a microcosm, generating through its unique experience an identity, which Philip Larkin claims should be independent of theory and tradition. This is a move towards primitivism, and away from the cultured substratum of Eliot and Pound. The ground lost is Pound's fragmented syntax and juxtaposed images, advances making for discontinuity in poetry and new possibilities of discourse. The liberation of poetic syntax was, in fact, a triumphant extension by Pound and Eliot of an art's technique (cf. Cézanne and the Impressionists), withdrawal from which may well prove retrograde. The technical revolution in poetry was to forge a syntax that short-circuits logical thought; its dislocation is said to reflect a lack of order and lucidity in society.

The road to originality in the modern world lies through technical experiment with language, and the boldest is through syntax and image. Originality is for Marianne Moore 'a by-product of sincerity; that is to say of feeling that is honest and accordingly rejects anything that might cloud the impression, such as unnecessary commas, modifying clauses, or delayed predicates' (*Predilections*, Faber, 1956, p. 13). In this essay she quotes with approval William Cowper's *The Snail*, as 'a thing of gusto', though the poem could be 'dismissed as mere description':

> Give but his horns the slightest touch,
> His self-collective power is such,
> He shrinks into his house with much
> > Displeasure.
>
> Where'er he dwells, he dwells alone.   5
> *Except himself,* has chattels none,
> Well satisfied to be his own
> > Whole treasure.
>
> Thus hermit-like his life he leads,
> Nor partner of his banquet needs,   10
> And if he meets one, only feeds
> > The faster.
>
> Who seeks him must be worse than blind,
> *He* and his house are so combined,
> If finding it, *he* fails to find   15
> > Its master.

The poem amuses by its quaintness, simplicity and symmetry. As a description of the creature, however, a naturalist would probably think it inaccurate. The words *Except himself* in line 6 are pleonastic, and the syntax is uncertain in lines 14 and 15, where *he* refers to different entities. Criticism tends to be confined to logical lapses, because the language is that of plain-statement, save for the slightly emotive use of *Displeasure* (4), *treasure* (8), *hermit-like* (9), and *banquet* (10).

The critic apparently liked Cowper's *jeu d'esprit,* for she afterwards composed a more concentrated poem on the same theme, in which the physical habits of the snail become analogues for good writing. The virtues were summarized in the title of her essay as 'humility, concentration and gusto':

TO A SNAIL

If '*compression* is the first grace of style',
you have it. *Contractility* is a virtue
as modesty is a virtue.
It is not the *acquisition* of any one thing
that is able to adorn,   5
or the *incidental* quality that occurs
as a *concomitant* of something well said,
that we value in style,
but the *principle* that is hid:
in the absence of feet, 'a method of *conclusions*';   10
'a knowledge of *principles*',
in the curious *phenomenon* of your *occipital* horn.

Such a poem, in the spirit of seventeenth-century metaphysical wit, could not have been written in the eighteenth century. Intellectual analysis of style occupies nine of the twelve prosaic lines, the whole being an extended metaphor, in which 'a snail' is the referent. What makes the rhythm pedestrian is the absence of imagery and the ten technical polysyllables. Wit is inherent in the comic pedantry, the ingenuity of the parallels and the tangential treatment of the theme, which slyly evades the title. Critical jargon, indicated by the three uses of quotation marks, finds an outlet only in free verse, because technical polysyllables cannot, without strain, be accommodated in an orthodox metrical system.

It can be said with confidence that the main causes of obscurity in modern poetry are ambiguity and dislocation of syntax. They have been the field of inquiry of William Empson and the structural linguists, who think of ambiguity in terms of 'plurisigns'. *Poetic* language is, for them, a thing apart from *logical* language, whose 'atomic ingredient', according to Philip Wheelwright, is the 'monosign' (see 'Literary Form and Meaning', *Essays on the Language of Literature*, Houghton Mifflin, 1969). The argument is inescapable that poetic ambiguity 'deliberately transcends the literal'; one type is found in Marianne Moore's reference to *absence of feet* and *occipital horn* in lines 10 and 12 of *A Snail*. Ambiguity in poetry invariably arises from the context, and the kind that is valuable does not spring from looseness of reference. Its significance is that it projects, in Wheelwright's words, 'a living insight' into a poet's 'connotative discourse' (p. 252). Not only the words, but the rhythm, images and allusions contribute to the evocative effect. What it evokes is a special enjoyment, not divorced from meaning, but extending possibilities by association.

Not only has modern poetry, through free verse, given greater scope to thematic content, but it has re-discovered schematic possibilities of words through rhetoric. As yet, the principal inquiry has been into the nature and varieties of metaphor; but definitions and the entire semantic employment of tropes, figures of speech and schemes of thought need to be overhauled, since the *manner* of presenting content is fundamental to style. Many Greek and Latin terms are still in use, though sometimes, as in *paronomasia* and *anaphora*, they are imperfectly understood. If alliteration and assonance are figurative devices, it is important that rhyme (of which the Greeks and Roman poets did not approve) should be seen to belong to a similar category. Rhetoric came into disrepute through the multiplication of unprofitable classifications, whose identification became a game unconnected with aesthetic utility. The practical use of tropes, figures and schemes is in poetic organization, which contributes to meaning, not to mention performance. What linguists see as *deviations* from the norms of speech are significant structural elements in poetry; and free verse can be understood only through perception of how much of it is free, and how much carefully disciplined.

In spite of the original dissociation of rhetoric and poetic, Greek teachers of oratory widened their subject to include, first the principles of prose composition, and then (through Longinus) the nobler utterances of poetry. Rhetoric still helps the poet to choose effective means of expression in a number of sentence situations. Of nearly a hundred tropes, schemes and figures found in Spenser, at least half are unconsciously employed by modern poets, including *metaplasms,* now regarded as colloquial contractions. Two questions therefore need to be answered: (1) How can the figures and schemes of rhetoric be grouped functionally? And (2) What manifestations continue to be practical for poetry under modern conditions? For the structural linguist the categories that matter are the phonological, the morphological and the semantic; but boundaries are not limited by definition and several kinds are hardly distinguishable. The pun, for instance, may be regarded as both phonological and semantic. Many linguists believe that metaphor is outside the province of language and belongs to psychology.

Phonological classes, including rhyme, alliteration and assonance, are all prosodic in application. The formal classes, *eg,* parallelism and the several figures of repetition, are important elements in patterning and grouping grammatical phrases and clauses, which gives discipline to the rhythm. The semantic classes, formerly called *tropes,* cover figurative meanings, and are most illuminating in context and reference; but there is often room for doubt whether a poet uses a word or phrase figuratively or literally. Under the heading semantic are included metaphor, simile, metonymy, synecdoche, paradox and hyperbole. There is no point in revising the un-Anglicized classical names; but a better understanding of the role of each figure in poetic organization is desirable.

Among the phonological deviations from normal practice, imperfect and half-rhymes are familiar in modern poetry. *Pararhyme,* often cited from Wilfred Owen's *Strange Meeting,* is that in which consonants agree, but not vowel-sounds, the object being to extend the lexical range of the poet who feels inhibited by the poor rhyming resources of certain words. The purpose of rhyme is rhythmical, marking the end of a line with a regular beat, thereby contributing to the structural progress of couplets or stanzas. But it also occurs within the line. An excellent illustration of the many uses of phonological devices is to be found in C. Day Lewis's poem *The Ecstatic*:

> *Lark,* sky*lark,* *spill*ing your rubbed and *round*
> Pebbles of *sound* in air's *still* lake,
> Whose widening circles *fill* the *noon*; yet *none*
> Is *known* so small beside the sun:
>
> Be *strong* your fervent soaring, your skyward *air*!
> Tremble *there,* a nerve of *song*!
> Float up *there where* voice and *wing* are one,
> A *sing*ing star, a note of light!
>
> *Buoyed,* em*bayed* in heaven's *noon*-wide reaches –
> For *soon light's tide* will turn – oh *stay*!
> *Cease* not till *day* streams to the west, then *down*
> That estuary drop *down* to *peace.*

The poem teems with internal rhyme, assonance and alliteration; the sibilant, liquid, nasal and trilled consonants ensure melody for the rhythm.

The rhyming ingenuity of Day Lewis was sometimes exercised in ways that were of pedagogical interest, without being valuable as verse experiments. *How They Would Jeer at Us* displays every tangential artifice, from off-rhyme and near-rhyme to good rhyme and no rhyme. Some of the oddities are italicized:

> How they would jeer *at us* –
> Ulysses, Hero*dotus,*
> The Hard-headed Phoe*nicians*
> Or, of later *nations,*
> Columbus, the Pilgrim F*athers*
> And a thousand *others*
> Who laboured only to *find*
> Some pittance of new *ground,*
> Merchandise or women.
> Those rude and bourgeois seamen
> Got glory thrown *in*
> As it were with every *ton*
> Of wave that swept their boat,
> And would have preferred a coat
> For keeping off the spray.
>
> Since the heroes *lie*
> Entombed with the reci*pe*
> Of epic in their heart,
> And have buried – it seems – that art
> Of minding one's own busi*ness*
> Magnanimously, for *us*
> There's nothing but to re*cant*
> Ambition, and be con*tent*
> Like the poor child at play
> To find a holiday
> In the sticks and *mud*
> Of a familiar *road.*

The truth is that rhythm and the dexterity of the run-on lines make precision of rhyme relatively unimportant; recurrence of similar sounds alone is needed to give to this reflective poem the semblance of formality.

Formal schemes in poetry turn largely on the principles and permutations of balance and repetition that give writing, of whatever kind, neatness and shape. The dominant forms of repetition still employed seem to be *anaphora* and *ploce*. An unorthodox unrhymed sonnet, *The Child,* by Michael Roberts, may serve to illustrate a few of the formal and semantic uses of rhetoric in modern poetry. The poem should also reveal how interlocked figurative language is, how profoundly imagery permeates it, and how subtly the interaction impinges on the mind.

> *How can I* teach, *how can I* save,
> This child *whose* features *are my own,*
> *Whose* feet run down the ways where I have walked?
>
> *How can I* name that vision past the corner,
> *How* ^ warn the *seed* that *grows to constant anger,*   5
> *How can I* draw the *map that tells no lies?*
>
> *His* world is a small world of *hours and minutes,*
> Hedgerows shut in the *horizons of his thought,*
> *His* loves are *uncritical* and deep,
> *His* anger innocent and sudden *like a minnow.*   10
>
> *His* eyes, acute and quick, are unprotected,
> *Unsandalled still,* his feet run *down* the lane,
> *Down* to that *lingering horror* in the brambles,
> The *limp crashed airman, in the splintered goggles.*

Line 1. *How can I* teach, *how can I* save. The device is parallelism, in which the correlative questions, separated by a medial pause, balance each other; the scheme of rhetoric is *amplification*. The three-word repetition comes under the general heading of *anaphora,* and the rhetorical questions are classed as *erotema.* A congeries of questions, as in the first six lines, was named by the rhetoricians *pysma*. The names of the figures are not important, but their effect on the structure of the sestet is.

Lines 2 and 3. The repetition of *whose,* with intervening words, is called *ploce* (cf *down* in lines 12/13). The clause, *whose features are my own,* contains a hidden *metaphor*; identity is not only implied, it is stated. Similar metaphorical utterances are *the seed that grows to constant anger* (5) and *the map that tells no lies* (6), the latter strictly a personal metaphor, since predicate and object involve *personification*.

Line 5. The omission of *can I* (understood) after *How* is known as *eclipsis*, and is here a syntactical and rhythmical convenience.

Lines 6–10. Repetition of *His* at the beginning of lines 7, 9 and 10 is named *epanaphora*. The *simile* in line 10 *like a minnow* is a telescoping device that causes solecism, since it is not *anger* that resembles a minnow's agility, but the epithet *sudden* (quick in movement). The phrases *world of hours and minutes* (7), *horizons of his thought* (8) and *uncritical* (9), all have metaphorical connotations.

Lines 11–14. *Unsandalled still* (12) exemplifies metrical inversion, to give the polysyllabic word rhythmical prominence in the line.

The poem, as a whole, is a convincing example of extended metaphor. The words *corner* (4), *sudden* (10), *eyes, acute* (11), *lingering horror* (13) and *splintered goggles* (14), indeed the entire last line, have imagist overtones, and suggest the shock of cruel reality to an unsophisticated mind. Imagery cannot be isolated in a systematic way, because the language of poetry is holistic as well as aesthetic in tendency, and will continue to defy linguistic analysis.

Dorothy Wordsworth has an ingenuous entry in her *Journals,* which reads: 'William tired himself with seeking an epithet for the cuckoo'. This, for a poet, is not a unique experience. Though words in common currency are the coin of all post-Wordsworth writers, there are times when inspiration delayed is less fallible than deliberate choice. Creative prompting springs largely from the subconscious mind, and the poet is never entirely aware of what chosen words in rhythmic association portend for the reader. If what he produces is true poetry, no other form of words will have the same meaning. We need not doubt the sincerity of T. S. Eliot's view that 'in really creative writing the author is making something which he does not understand himself'. ('The Aims of Poetic Drama', *Adam,* 1951).

A reader may look in vain in a modernist poem for physical shape, metrical system, unambiguous meaning or beauty of phrase. Innovation means revolt against technical ingenuity, poured into traditional moulds. What art modern poetry possesses is usually of an impressionist kind: neglect of detail, control of feeling. Self-conscious style is replaced by a mood of activity in which thought is self-creative, and every word supplies a significant stroke. Rhythm evolves naturally in the process of gestation; and there would be no point in generalizing about constructive principles, because each poem is unique. In this reasoning, of which Robert Graves has been the prime mover, there is an obvious desire to keep in step with recent movements in painting and music.

CHAPTER IV

W. B. Yeats (1)

𝕤𝕤𝕤𝕤𝕤𝕤

THE literary life of William Butler Yeats, spanning a period of fifty years, begins with the transition from Symbolism to Imagism, and reflects his personal and politico-moral conflicts, faced with a sense of grave responsibility. The significance of his writing, both in verse and prose, is the use he found in the complexities of his time to make poetry of universal validity and appeal.

Born in Dublin in 1865, Yeats lived partly in London, but mainly in Ireland, until his twenty-second year. By then the Celtic past, despite a lack of Gaelic, had so captured his imagination that it permeated all he subsequently wrote. Few poets in English have been more sensitive to the spirit of place. Yeats was, moreover, well endowed with that double vision which enables the gifted Celt to combine human dignity with spiritual insight. During his vacations with his mother's family in Sligo, he learned in the legendary West country of the heroic Celtic myths, which were peopled with ghosts. The mythologies he cared for were more ancient than the peaceful era of the Irish Saints.

Though Yeats was conscious of his Yorkshire ancestry, and acknowledged English as his mother tongue, Irish nationalism was a constant stimulus to his creative talents; it gave him permanent roots in Celtic history, though throughout his life he was at variance with the bigotry and narrowness of Irish life under the orthodox church. There is no trace of propaganda in his early writing, because he mistrusted the hollowness of declamatory language. He so humanized his attitudes to nationalism, even when he became an Irish senator, that it never debased the art for which he lived. His father, J. B. Yeats, was a Pre-Raphaelite painter, and he himself entered an art school in preference to a university. It was not surprising, therefore, that the earliest influences on his writing were derived from the Rossettis and William Morris; the latter spoke approvingly of the mythological poetry that Yeats soon began to publish.

The poetry of the period before 1900 is characteristic of a romantic individualist; it is full of mystical speculation, tinged with melancholy. One of Yeats's earliest commissions was to collaborate with Ellis in editing the poetry of Blake. He rightly judged that the world of Irish legendary history, which he read in English translations, should be regarded as imaginative fiction. In 1892 he wrote to John O'Leary: 'The mystical life is the centre of all that I do and all that I think and all that I write'. The connections with theosophy and dabblings in the occult were part of Yeats's search for philosophic stability, outside of orthodox religion. His poetic identities were *personae*, or masks for different roles in which he imagined himself. In consequence the dramas are not peopled with characters in their own right; unsympathetic critics see them as masks of a poseur. Yeats has been universally acclaimed as a reflective and elegiac poet.

His intransigent philosophy has undoubted elements of determinism, which mingle strangely with mystic symbolism. A language study needs to take these into account, because they affected his developing style and the content of the poems. Yeats was a wide reader, taking particular pains to be informed in defence of doctrines contained in his prose writing. He gives lively and reasoned accounts of indebtedness to Spenser (last of the Anglo-Norman feudalists), Donne, Blake, Shelley, the French Symbolists, Henley, Dowson, Lionel Johnson and Ezra Pound. He was not uninfluenced, too, by Maeterlinck. But no account of the poet's psychological development would be complete without reference to the character-forming encouragement of his Victorian father, whose letters reveal a thinker and writer of ability. Yeats relied for intellectual stimulus on constant exchanges with those who were closest to him. The Autobiographies, Essays and Introductions enable the critical biographer to trace the growth of ideas motivating changes in his poetic diction.

Before the Yeats family moved to England in 1887, William had no decisive notions about the rhythms and syntax most suitable for the kind of poetry he wished to write. He describes his ambitions in *To Ireland in the Coming Times*, a poem published in *The Rose* (1893). There is not much challenge to the conventions in these couplets:

Know, that I would accounted be
True brother of a company
That sang, to sweeten Ireland's wrong,
Ballad and story, rann and song;
Nor be I any less of them,   5
Because the red-rose-bordered hem
Of her, whose history began
Before God made the angelic clan,
Trails all about the written page . . .

Nor may I less be counted one
With Davis, Mangan, Ferguson,   10
Because, to him who ponders well,
My rhymes more than their rhyming tell
Of things discovered in the deep,
Where only body's laid alseep . . .

In truth's consuming ecstasy,   15
No place for love and dream at all;
For God goes by with white footfall.
I cast my heart into my rhymes,
That you, in the dim coming times,
May know how my heart went with them   20
After the red-rose-bordered hem.

The red rose in the refrain is a symbol of spiritual beauty, and
in this group of poems represents both Maud Gonne, to whom the
song is dedicated, and the spirit of Ireland. The poems of Yeats
are full of similar ambivalent meanings. *Rann* (4) is a line of verse
in the Old Irish metrical system.

Between 1889, when his first poems appeared in book form,
and his marriage in 1917 to a young woman half his age, Yeats
published seven volumes of poems, and became a prominent
leader of the Irish literary Renaissance. He was also for six years
production manager of the Abbey Theatre in Dublin; the plays he
wrote for it were in either blank verse or prose. The non-dramatic
poetry in the *Collected Works* of 1908 was elaborate in pattern,
making only Victorian breaks with the Spenserian tradition.
From 1890, while he was a member of the Rhymers' Club,
meeting at the Cheshire Cheese in Fleet Street, he had become
familiar with the Symbolist movement through his friend Arthur
Symons.

The Rhymers were disciples of Pater and Rossetti, and vague adherents of Mallarmé, whom Yeats several times visited in Paris. One of their credos, to which Yeats half-heartedly subscribed, was the avoidance of schools, theories and manifestos, the aspiration being for 'pure' poetry. This meant repudiation of all rhetoric; but the die-hards merely echoed the denunciations of Verlaine. The Rhymers were aesthetic absolutists, like Wilde, turning a blind eye to the encroachments upon literature of science and sociology. Though Yeats was never happy with these ideas, it took him two decades to escape from their influence. The only durable impact of the Pre-Raphaelites upon him was that of William Morris, whose narrative poetry was never fired by Yeats's passion for form. He shared Morris's contempt for industrial civilization, and saw in George Eliot the mother of 'the Accusers of Sin'. Indeed, Yeats credited her with the founding of a women's liberation movement, of which he disapproved.

The later phase in Yeats's development began in 1909, after his introduction to Ezra Pound, with whom he later became associated through their marriages. In 1912 he submitted to Pound some verses intended for publication in the American magazine *Poetry*; the idea was that the critic should draw attention to tendencies of abstraction, of which Yeats was very conscious at this period. The younger poet persuaded him to strengthen his resources of metaphor with a more masculine rhythm, and a directly personal dialectical language. In matters of diction, Yeats was humble enough to profit from advice. He acknowledged in *Responsibilities* (1914) that his preoccupations with style had been too esoteric and 'embroidered'; this was, indeed, the confession behind the short poem *A Coat*, cited and analysed in the last chapter. By 1925 Yeats was able to report in *A Vision* a transformation in his attitude:

> I can now, if I have the energy, find the simplicity I have sought in vain. I need no longer write poems like 'The Phases of the Moon' nor 'Ego Dominus Tuus', nor spend barren years, as I have done some three or four times, striving with abstractions ... I would forget the wisdom of the East and remember its grossness and its romance. Yet when I wander upon the cliffs where Augustus and Tiberius wandered, I know that the new intensity that seems to have come into all

visible and tangible things is not a reaction from that wisdom
but its very self . . .

I think that in early Byzantium, maybe never before or since
in recorded history, religious, aesthetic and practical life were
one, that architects and artificers . . . spoke to the multitude
and the few alike. The painter, the mosaic worker, the worker
in gold and silver, the illuminator of sacred books, were almost
impersonal, almost perhaps without the consciousness of individual design, absorbed in their subject-matter and that the
vision of a whole people.

The importance of Yeats's poetic history is its comprehensive
account of a cycle of development. His conflicts, as a 'solitary'
artist, were internal, and made him metaphysically restless; he
was conscious of isolation in his thinking from other men. This
may have been due to his interest in psychic phenomena; it is
not mere coincidence that his uneasy relations with society were
being scientifically adumbrated in the psychology of Carl Jung,
with whom he had certain affinities. No sooner had he abandoned
the mask of the mythical hero than he adopted others reflecting
his incongruous personality; his theory of the *anti-self* describes
stages and symptoms of polarity in all human conduct. He was
firmly convinced of man's re-birth in lunar phases, and of cyclic
re-incarnation in what the neo-Platonists once called the *Great
Year*. Many of the later poems embody *gyres* of cyclic history, not
unlike the theories propounded by Arnold Toynbee; Yeats admitted that they were poems to be treated as 'texts for exposition'.
The spiral or antithetical movement of history has a family likeness to the system of dialectical materialism, derived from Hegel.

In his earlier poetry Yeats showed a preference for slow iambic
rhythms, rather than for dynamic ones. In the enervated, featureless blank verse of the plays, he seems to have experienced similar
difficulties to Eliot, until he abandoned the measure. His procedure in composing poetry was to jot down images and ideas in
prose, afterwards to be shaped into verse; the entire poem was
then recast before publication. When the poem appeared in book
form, it was frequently revised. Composition was thus a laborious,
line-by-line process, with the same respect for craftsmanship as
was exercised by Horace and Vergil. Yeats was content if the lines
came, as he wished them, at the rate of four or five a day. When the

content became autobiographical, the imagery appears to be more centralized; it was here that he seems to have found his rhythmic power. What he called 'pure experience' was expressed fearlessly, in such a way as to mirror, not alone *his* personality, but the universal human condition. In letters to his father, written in 1910 and 1913, he said: 'the antithesis to personality is not so much will as an evergrowing burden of noble attitudes and literary words'. When Yeats wrote at his best he fulfilled the hope 'that the hearer would feel the presence of a man thinking and feeling'. Among the shaping forces in Yeats's reflective poetry was a vibrant mastery of adjectives and verbs; his real achievement was to free lyric poetry from rhythmical monotony.

In practice, Yeats had closer links with the tradition of English poetry than T. S. Eliot; he did not need irregular verse to secure the organic rhythms of his maturity. Pound's free verse he spoke of as 'devil's metres'. He had as sensitive an ear as Eliot for the rhythmic appeal of incantation in contemplative poetry. Without the benefit of university training, Yeats offered a ripe individualistic wisdom that casts doubt upon the justice of Eliot's deprecation of personality in creative work. Eliot's was a classical, sophisticated and cultured mind; but he was ill at ease when appraising Yeats's romantic attitudes. It would be difficult to discover among contemporaries two poets more opposed in beliefs, education and accomplishments. Eliot found in Yeats's early poetry a want of 'particularity' in providing 'the material for general truth' (*On Poetry and Poets*, p. 256). This may be true of the poetry before *The Wind Among the Reeds* (1899). But Yeats learned by patient experiment to discipline emotion to the service of thought, and once pictured himself in the role of a Creator 'who toils in rounding the delicate spiral of a shell'.

An enduring legacy of Yeats's poetry is the gift for gnomic expression, through which he communicated his delicate perceptions of form and unity. Every good poem seems to have, besides some philosophic significance, a metaphor or symbol central to the grand design of Yeats's artistic life, which was truth through vision, rather than through reason. Re-writing, and re-arranging poems in order, had holistic ends; kinship of poems one with another he illuminated in autobiographies and letters, penned with the care of a writer whose salvation depends upon exactitude. In a broadcast talk three years before his death, Yeats defined a poem as 'an elaboration of the rhythms of common speech and their association with profound feeling'. Among the first principles enunciated in the projected Introduction to his complete works towards the end of his life, is the following:

> A poet writes always of his personal life . . . there is always a phantasmagoria . . . he is never the bundle of accident and incoherence that sits down to breakfast; he has been reborn as an idea, something intended complete (*Essays and Introductions*, Macmillan, 1961, p. 509).

Yeats's account of his poetic development, under 'Style and Attitude' in the same *Introduction* is a document of some importance:

> I planned to write short lyrics or poetic drama where every speech would be short and concentrated, knit by dramatic tension . . . I tried to make the language of poetry coincide with that of passionate, normal speech. I wanted to write in whatever language comes most naturally when we soliloquise, as I do all day long, upon the events of our own lives or of any life where we can see ourselves for the moment . . .
>
> It was a long time before I had made a language to my liking; I began to make it when I discovered some twenty years ago that I must seek, not as Wordsworth thought, words in common use, but a powerful and passionate syntax, and a complete coincidence between period and stanza. Because I need a passionate syntax for passionate subject-matter I compel myself to accept those traditional metres that have developed with the language. Ezra Pound, Turner, Lawrence wrote admirable free verse; I could not. I would lose myself, become joyless . . . If I wrote of personal love or sorrow in free verse, or in any rhythm that left it unchanged, amid all its accidence, I would be full of self-contempt because of my egotism and indiscretion, and foresee the boredom of my reader. I must choose a traditional stanza, even what I alter must seem traditional. . . . Talk to me of originality and I will turn on you with rage. I am a crowd, I am a lonely man, I am nothing. Ancient salt is best packing.
>
> When I wrote in blank verse, I was dissatisfied; my vaguely mediaeval *Countess Cathleen* fitted the measure, but our Heroic

Age went better, or so I fancied, in the ballad metre of *The Green Helmet*. There was something in what I felt about Deirdre, about Cuchulain, that rejected the Renaissance and its characteristic metres, and this was a principal reason why I created in dance plays the form that varies blank verse with lyric metres. . . . The folk song is still there, but a ghostly voice, an unvariable possibility, an unconscious norm. What moves me and my hearer is a vivid speech that has no laws except that it must not exorcise the ghostly voice. I am awake and asleep, at my moment of revelation, self-possessed in self-surrender; there is no rhyme, no echo of the beaten drum, the dancing foot, that would overset my balance (pp. 521–4).

In 'An Introduction for my Plays' (*ibid*, pp. 529–30), Yeats explains, with the same individualism, the language he sought to create in them:

I have spent my life in clearing out of poetry every phrase written for the eye, and bringing all back to syntax that is for ear alone . . .

As I altered my syntax I altered my intellect . . . I would have poetry turn its back upon all that modish curiosity, psychology . . .

Disapproval of rhetoric was, in Yeats, to some degree an uncritical prejudice of the later Symbolists. On this score he had a quarrel with his father about the merits of Victorian writers, and another with his political friend J. F. Taylor, who by Yeats's own account was a considerable orator. Rhetoric as 'the analytical study of the arts of composition' (including metaphor and other tropes) he did not apparently distinguish from its pejorative alternative, 'oratory as an instrument of propaganda'. That this is so can be deduced from this typical statement in *Per Amica Silentia Lunae* (1917):

We make out of the quarrel with others, rhetoric, but of the quarrel with ourselves, poetry. Unlike the rhetoricians, who get a confident voice from remembering the crowd they have won or may win, we sing amid our uncertainty: and, smitten even in the presence of the most high beauty by the knowledge of our solitude, our rhythm shudders.

Yeats's poems will be found, however, to employ nearly as many figures of rhetoric as those of his contemporaries. Rhetoric is not avoided, as he seems to have thought, by writing verse first as prose; he advocated this remedy again in the nineteen-thirties, when Pound criticized *The King of the Great Clock Tower* for what he called its 'nobody' language.

One of Yeats's unconscious employments of rhetoric is to be observed in the recurrence of balanced structures, common in the deliberative poetry. This is not surprising in view of his knowledge of the antithetical principle, in the self and in history. The familiar device of balance and repetition was part of his Renaissance inheritance, and Rosemund Tuve draws attention to it constantly in *Elizabethan and Metaphysical Imagery* (University of Chicago Press, 1947).

POEMS OF THE LONDON–SLIGO PERIOD, 1889–1914

The twenty-five years ending with the publication of *Responsibilities* in 1914 were productive of many fruitful experiments, and the poems scrutinized have been chosen to demonstrate Yeats's development and technical practice. Wherever practicable, the analysis uses the fourfold division indicated in Chapter III.

EPHEMERA
(from *Crossways*, 1889)

The wóods were róund them, | and the *yéllow* léaves
Féll like *faint* méteors in the glóom, | and ónce
A rábbit *óld* and *láme* límped down the páth;
Aútumn was óver him: | and nów they stóod
On the *lóne* bórder of the láke once móre: 5
Túrning, | he sáw that she had thrúst *déad* leáves
Gáthered in sílence, | *déwy* as her éyes,
In bósom and háir. |
           'Áh, do not móurn,' | he sáid,
'That wé are tíred, | for óther lóves awáit us;
Háte on and lóve through *unrepíning* hóurs.   10
Befóre us liés etérnity; | our sóuls
Are lóve, | and a *contínual* fàrewéll.'

This passage is part of a dialogue between two lovers who have agreed to separate; of particular interest is the description in lines 1–8. *Ephemera* was written in 1884, when Yeats was nineteen, and one critic has suggested that the style owes something to Verlaine's *Colloque Sentimental*. The poem is a revision of one published in *The Wanderings of Oisin* (1889), and is linked with a group of four Indian compositions that precede it, depicting the Golden Age. The first of these was *Anashuya and Vijaya*, also in dialogue form.

Narrative poetry in blank verse is a difficult form to handle; but the nineteenth-century poets Wordsworth, Keats, Shelley, Tennyson, Browning and Arnold regarded it as a challenge, and gave it characteristic nuances of their own. The difficulty lies in predetermining the complex rhythm of the verse unit or paragraph. Milton alone mastered the art, while Shakespeare and Marlowe seem deliberately to have avoided blank verse, except in drama; here situation and the interaction of character enable the poet to concentrate power in shorter rhythmical spans. The movement of blank verse is conditioned by the thought, and the choice of words in which it is expressed. Poets like to master the measure, because it is an extraordinarily plastic medium, capable of much rhythmic momentum.

Yeats's practice in this poem is without the creative feeling that invariably supplies diversity of cadence. Metrically, he is skilful, for he modulates by enjambing four of the twelve lines, and varies the location of the medial pauses in nine of them, lines 1, 2, 4, 6, 7, 8, 9, 11 and 12. In eight of the verses, he respects the English pentameter tradition of only four primary stresses, modulating with an additional beat in lines 3, 6, 8, 9. There is inversion of stress (trochaic substitution) in the first foot of lines 2, 4, 6, 7 and 10. These are conventional devices to achieve smoothness, while avoiding monotony, and it is worth observing that the most musical lines are the last three, in which Yeats introduces the latinized polysyllables *unrepining, eternity* and *continual*.

In blank verse there is an unavoidable tendency of syntax to overrun the line, and to squander the energy of the rhythm in subordinate clauses. Milton overcame this difficulty by placing strong, emphatic words in key positions; he contrived to project the rhythm by the impetus of the feelings they arouse. To this end he favoured periodic structures, which keep the meaning of sentences in suspense until the climactic word. Yeats's syntax in *Ephemera* is simple and predicative, the only subordinate noun and adverbial clauses being in lines 6, 8 and 9. The figures of speech are simile (lines 2 and 7), personification (10, *unrepining* hours), and metaphor in *our souls | Are love, and a continual farewell* (11–12); but there are no schemes of rhetoric.

Meaning is not in doubt in these lines, partly because of the undistinguished nature of the diction; this can be seen in the choice of such conventional adjectives as *yellow, faint, old, lame, lone* (poetical overtones), *dead, dewy*. The melancholy substantives *gloom, Autumn, silence, souls, eternity, farewell*, were the stock-in-trade of elegiac poets in the nineteenth century. The verbs *thrust* (6), *mourn* (8) and *Hate* (10) are the ones that give impetus to the rhythm. In this early ceremonious style Yeats was unquestionably 'picture-making', in order to avoid abstraction. The beginning of his verbal concentration is seen in the omission of the possessive pronoun before *bosom* in line 8.

THE SORROW OF LOVE
(from *The Rose*, 1893)

In an unpublished manuscript, cited by A. N. Jeffares in his Yeats Commentary (1968), the poet states that the collection called *The Rose* had a mystical purpose, 'to reunite the perception of the spirit, of the divine with natural beauty . . . Commerce and manufacture have made the world ugly. The death of pagan nature worship [in early Ireland] had robbed visible beauty of its inviolable sanctity'. The woman Yeats celebrates in most of the poems is Maud Gonne, who stimulated his nationalism and shared his visions. He identifies her with Helen of Troy. The writing and revision of the poems took place in 1891–2, when Yeats was a member of the Rosicrucian Order of the Golden Dawn. Several versions of *The Sorrow of Love* are extant; the poem was revised in 1892, 1895, 1899 and 1922.

(*a*) From the manuscript of October 1891:

> The quarrel of the sparrows in the *eaves*,
> The full round moon and the star-laden *sky*,
> The song of the ever-singing *leaves*,
> Had hushed away earth's old and weary *cry*.

And then you came with those red mournful lips, 5
And with you came the whole of the world's tears,
And all the sorrows of her labouring ships,
And all the burden of her million years.

And now the angry sparrows in the *eaves*,
The withered moon, the white stars in the *sky*, 10
The wearisome loud chanting of the *leaves*,
Are shaken with earth's old and weary *cry*.

(*b*) As Yeats revised it for *The Countess Kathleen and Various Legends and Lyrics*, 1892:

The quarrel of the sparrows in the eaves,
The full round moon and the star-laden sky,
And the *loud* song of the ever-singing leaves
Had *hid* away earth's old and weary cry.

And then you came with those red mournful lips, 5
And with you came the whole of the world's tears,
And all the sorrows[1] of her labouring ships
And all the burden[1] of her *myriad* years.

And now the *sparrows warring* in the eaves,
The *crumbling*[2] moon, the white stars in the sky, 10
And the loud chanting of the *unquiet* leaves,
Are shaken with earth's old and weary cry.

(*c*) As Yeats revised it in *Early Poems and Stories*, 1925:

The *bráwling* of *a* spárrow in the eáves,
The *brílliant* móon and *áll the mílky* ský,
And *áll that fámous hármony of* léaves,
Had *blótted óut mán's ímage and his* crý.

A gírl aróse that had réd móurnful líps 5
And seémed the gréatness of the wórld *in* teárs,
Doómed like Odýsseus and the lábouring shíps
And próud as Príam múrdered with his peérs;

Aróse, and on the ínstant clámorous eáves,
A clímbing móon *upon an émpty* ský, 10
And *áll that lámentátion of the* leáves,
Coúld but compóse mán's ímage and crý.

[1] *trouble* (1899)
[2] *curd-pale* (1895)

The first revision for the *Countess Kathleen* collection made few changes that would be considered as improvements. The extra foot in 3, to introduce the epithet *loud*, seems pointless, especially as the same adjective appears in line 11; while the past participle *hid* for *hushed* (4) is less appropriate in the context of sounds. The substitution *myriad* for *million* (8) has romantic vagueness, and offers a trisyllabic rhythmic variation. *Crumbling* for *withered* 'moon' (10) is possibly a more vigorous adjective, but it sacrifices alliteration and the happy connection with *leaves* in the next line. Yeats apparently wanted to get rid of *wearisome* in line 11, because of '*weary* cry' in 12; but the unfortunate insertion of *unquiet* before *leaves* (already 'loud chanting') suggests want of decision in the choice of epithets.

The poem, finally revised when Yeats was nearly sixty, represents a radical re-handling of the theme, one object being to depersonalize the private tragedy and give the poem universal appeal. While Maud Gonne, disturber of the poet's peace, is still the protagonist, she has become, like Helen of Troy, a symbol of Man's disquietude. The definitive version of *The Sorrow of Love* therefore deserves closer scrutiny; T. Parkinson in *W. B. Yeats, Self-Critic* (University of California Press, 1951) justifiably describes the poem as 'a literal translation from one idiom into the other' (p. 165). Yeats had good reason to be dissatisfied with the diction of the earlier versions, because there was neither pictorial firmness nor consistency.

In the formal presentation of the final version there is little change, but the second stanza was altered in content and strengthened. First, Yeats eliminated the anomalous line (3) of the manuscript poem, and recast it as a pentameter. He took pains to diversify the organic rhythm of the whole, which is skilful in manipulation of vowels and consonants; the judicious employment of alliteration tends to disarm critical judgement in the last stanza. The meaning of the poem is seldom uncertain, once the reader realizes that each stanza is a microcosm of man's life cycle: first, early joy in nature; then adult awareness of the sexual struggle; and, finally, the grief of maturity, bred in frustration.

Yeats's idea was to preserve the mood of each stanza and breathe new life into the language, through the rhythmic structure of each part. *Brawling* is a rather aggressive activity for a single

sparrow; '*brilliant* moon' and '*famous* harmony' contain un-
inspiring adjectives, tending to hyperbole. Extravagance in the
second stanza is toned down by the use of *seemed* in line 6. In order
to make plausible the likeness between the poet's lady and Helen
of Troy, the style is elevated to classical sublimity in lines 6 and 7,
where *Doomed, Odysseus, proud, Priam* and *peers* introduce a noble
resonance. These lines link the tragedy of stanza two with the
singularly loaded word *lamentation* in line 11. The adjectives in
'*clamorous* eaves' (9) '*climbing* moon' (10) are appropriate as well as
alliterative; but the verb *compose* is contextually remote and
insignificant.

The conventional figures of rhetoric should not be overlooked:
personification, 1 *brawling*, 6 *world in tears*, 9 *clamorous leaves*, 10
climbing moon, 11 *lamentation of the leaves*; metonymy, 3 *harmony of
leaves*; metaphor, 2 *milky sky*, 4 *blotted out*; paronomasia (pun)
5 and 9 *arose* (= a *Rose*, symbol for Maud Gonne). The most
important of the schemes of rhetoric is *anaphora,* one aspect being
the repetition of identical rhyme words in the first and last
stanza, together with the refrain *man's image and his cry* (4 and 12).
Arose, at the beginning of line 9, which echoes the verb in 5, is a
heavily emphasized word, linking stanzas two and three. *Polysyndeton* is employed in the repetition of the conjunction *And* at the
beginning of lines 5 to 9 of the manuscript poem; but this is
reduced to three instances in the revision. Yeats was habituated to
the pronominal adjective *all*, followed by a demonstrative or
definite article, as in lines 2, 3 and 11.

Louis MacNeice in *The Poetry of W. B. Yeats* (Oxford University
Press, 1941) is among a minority of critics who deplored the poet's
final revision. He wrote:

> The poem is no longer languid, but it no longer rings true.
> Yeats, with a different poem in his mind's eye, has distorted
> it ... The new version as a whole is both ill-digested and
> obscure (p. 71).

Later critics have been able to correct this harsh judgement.

WHEN YOU ARE OLD
(from *The Rose*, 1893)

When you are old *and* grey *and* full of sleep,
And nodding by the fire, | take down this book,

And slowly read, | *and* dream of the soft look
Your eyes had once, | *and* of their *shadows deep*;

How many *loved* your moments of glad grace,   5
And loved your beauty | with *love false or true*;
But one man *loved* the pilgrim soul in you,
And loved the sorrows of your changing face.

And bending down beside the glowing bars,
Murmur, | a little sadly, | how *love* fled   10
And paced upon the mountains overhead
And hid his face amid a crowd of stars.

This poem was written on October 21, 1891. At this period Yeats
was fond of the twelve-line lyric of sentiment in three iambic
pentameter quatrains. *When you are Old* has the form of a Shakespearian sonnet, without the final couplet; it has also Shakespeare's monosyllabic simplicity. The first stanza has but three
words of more than one syllable, the second five, the third eight
in the initial three lines, but only one in the last, which closes the
stanza with a splendid cadence.

Yeats laboured with care to perfect his rhythms, and this poem,
Jeffares suggests, was modelled on Ronsard's *Sonnets pour Hélène*
(1578). The movement emulates the dreamy ease aimed at by
French Symbolist craftsmen. In Yeats's poem smoothness results
from the dominance of long vowels and diphthongs, liquid nasal
and sibilant consonants, well-defined monosyllabic rhymes to
mark end-stopped lines (line 3 has the only enjambement), skilful
disposition of internal pauses, and judicious use of *polysyndeton* and
ploce (*and* is repeated 11 times, *love* 6 times). In each stanza the
opening line is a conventional pentameter, with five stresses; but
the second is gracefully modulated. The rhythm is 'paced' by a
succession of three polysyllables in the penultimate line, then
gently retarded by the weight of long-vowelled monosyllables
(*face, crowd, stars*) in line 12.

Yeats's respected orthodoxy in lyrics of this kind established
his early reputation. The perspicuity of his 'common' syntax,
one which prefers co-ordinated structures to subordination,
counted in his favour. In *When you are Old* the meaning is un-
complicated by much figurative use of words. The personal metaphor in *pilgrim soul* (7) is a probable reference to Maud Gonne's

good works, especially among the poor in Donegal. The next line shows sympathy with the complex psycho-pathology of her earlier life in France. The personified flight of love (10) reflects the poet's endless frustration. He made fine poetry out of it, however, as Maud Gonne encouraged him to do. Lines 11 and 12, in which the personification is sustained, refer to Yeats's escape into the mystical life and the higher consolations of poetry. It should be realized that the introduction of rhetorical figures conceals the art with which the poet brings the poem to a triumphant conclusion.

Provided a young poet creates telling images out of his felt experience, the use of such conventional lyrical adjectives as *old*, *grey, deep, glad, false, true, changing* and *glowing*, need not limit his talents. There are only two instances of syntactical inversion in this poem, *shadows deep* (4) and *love false or true* (6); these instances of nouns followed by their modifying adjectives were no doubt due to the exigencies of rhyme.

HE BIDS HIS BELOVED BE AT PEACE
(from *The Wind Among the Reeds*, 1899)

In *The Wind Among the Reeds* Yeats made a deliberate break with the early tentative concepts of his art. He was still a poet in quest of a style that critics would recognize as individual. In works of the creative imagination, no change was possible, he thought, without much 'forethought and afterthought'. The result of such meditations was the finely-wrought essay on 'Symbolism of Poetry' (*Essays and Introductions*, p. 153). It contains some thoughts that are significant for the understanding of the poems in the 1899 volume:

> Metaphors are not profound enough to be moving, when they are not symbols, and when they are symbols they are the most perfect of all, because the most subtle, outside of pure sound . . .
>
> All sounds, all colours, all forms, either because of their preordained energies or because of long association, evoke indefinable and yet precise emotions . . . An emotion does not exist, or does not become perceptible and active among us, till it has found its expression, in colour or in sound or in form . . .
>
> I doubt indeed if the crude circumstance of the world, which seems to create all our emotions, does more than reflect, as in multiplying mirrors, the emotions that have come to

solitary men in moments of poetical contemplation; or that love itself would be more than an animal hunger but for the poet and his shadow the priest ... How can the arts overcome the slow dying of men's hearts that we call the progress of the world, and lay their hands upon men's heart-strings again, without becoming the garment of religion as in old times?

If people were to accept the theory that poetry moves us because of its symbolism, what change should one look for in the manner of our poetry? A return to the way of our fathers, a casting out of descriptions of nature for the sake of nature ... We would cast out of serious poetry those energetic rhythms, as of a man running, which are the invention of the will with its eyes always on something to be done or undone; and we would seek out those wavering, meditative, organic rhythms, which are the embodiment of the imagination ... You cannot give a body to something that moves beyond the senses, unless your words are as subtle, as complex, as full of mysterious life, as the body of a flower or of a woman.

The woman for whom *Michael Robartes bids his Beloved be at Peace* was written (24 September 1895) was Diana Vernon; so Yeats confides in his *Autobiography* (XXX, p. 86). The name was chosen from Scott's *Rob Roy* to conceal the identity of Mrs Olivia Shakespeare. The poem, a twelve-line lyric, belongs to an experimental group on the private passions of men and women, in this case through the *persona* of Michael Robartes in which anonymity is preserved. The idea seems to have been suggested to Yeats by his work on Blake's *Prophetic Books*. Four different *personae* are assumed, but Yeats explained that they represent principles of the mind, rather than 'actual personages':

I héar the Shádowy Hórses, | their lóng mánes a-sháke,
Their hóofs heávy with túmult, | their éyes glímmering whíte;
The Nórth unfólds abóve them | clínging, créeping, níght,
The Eást her hídden jóy | befóre the mórning bréak,
The Wést wéeps in pále déw | and síghs pássing awáy,   5
The Sóuth is póuring down róses of crímson fíre:
Ó vánity of Sléep, | Hópe, | Dréam, | éndless Desíre,
The Hórses of Disáster plúnge in the héavy cláy:
Belóved, | let your éyes hálf clóse, | and yòur héart beát
Óver mỳ héart, | and your háir fáll óver my bréast,   10

Drówning lóve's lónely hóur | in déep twílight of rést,
And híding their tóssing mánes | and thèir tumúltuous féet.

Yeats had been reading Lady Guest's version of the *Mabinogion*
and Sir James Frazer's *Golden Bough*; the mystical influence of the
elements in picturing apocalyptic visions is obvious from lines 1
to 8. Because intentionally vague in reference, the love poems are
difficult to interpret; the mood that prompted them was more
sensuous than anything Yeats had yet expressed. Of necessity, the
book was provided with notes, whose tenor confirms that the poet
not only drew the images from a scarcely known mythology, but
arbitrarily gave them personal interpretations. A year before the
appearance of *The Wind Among the Reeds*, Yeats said in an essay
entitled 'The Autumn of the Body', that he now 'took little
pleasure in a book unless it was *spiritual and unemphatic*'. This is the
kind of poetry he sought to write before the turn of the century.

Though this experimental poem resembles free verse, its
rhythm is disciplined; but it is never easy to determine the value
of secondary stresses in verse of this nature. The pattern consists
of iambic hexameter quatrains, with normally six stresses in the
end-stopped lines; but there is some modulation in lines 5, 7, 9 and
10 with seven beats, and in lines 6 and 8 with only five. The rhyme
scheme is abbacddceffe, and the rhyme words are firm monosyllables. The length of the lines makes an internal caesura desirable; it occurs naturally after the third primary stress in lines 1, 2,
3, 4, 5 and 10. Only line 6 is without a medial pause, and line 9
offers the single instance of enjambement.

The compulsion to 'hammer his thoughts into a unity' and
secure lasting indivisibility of form was the credo of Yeats's
artistic life. The mythology of lines 1 to 8 and the private passion
of lines 9 to 11 are admirably fused throughout the poem; but
there is a note of doom for illicit love in the final line, with the
impressive symbolic phrases *tossing manes* and *tumultuous feet*.
The adjective *tumultuous* is loaded with sensuous feeling, mingling
overtones with *tossing manes* in the happy collocation of consonants
t, *m*, and *s*.

Yeats's allusions are not altogether mysterious, if one re-
members that in Michael Robartes (a character taken from his
tales of *The Secret Rose*, 1897), the mask represents 'fire' (energy)
reflected in 'water' (stillness), and that Robartes, really, sym-

bolizes 'pride of the imagination'. It is significant that Yeats gives us a clue to the character of Diana Vernon in his *Autobiography*: 'Her beauty, *dark* and *still,* had the nobility of *defeated things.*'

The *Shadowy Horses* of the first line and the *Horses of Disaster* in line 8 call for some explanation. Yeats had in mind the horses of the mythical deity Mannannan, who ruled the land of the dead; they were associated with waves of the sea, with the cold and darkness of winter. According to the poet's notes, the North (Fomor) symbolized night and sleep; the East, sunrise and hope; the West, sunset and fading dreams; the South, midday and passion or desire. In each line, the choice of epithets and the phrasing bring out these characteristics. In 3 to 8, symbolism is subtly interwoven with suggestions of physical love; *eg, clinging, creeping night, hidden joy, weeps in pale dew, roses of crimson fire.* In line 2, 'hoofs *heavy* with tumult' anticipates 'plunge in the *heavy* clay' (line 8). The love poems of this book have recurring images of *hair, breast* and *lonely* hours in *deep twilight.* If the language is romantically vague, it is effective in creating the atmosphere of mystery and vanity which Yeats liked to associate with the passion of love. Line 7 with its opening rhetorical figure of *ecphonesis* seems to contain the core of the poem's meaning.

It is worth noting that Yeats is compelled by rhythm and rhyme to admit two archaisms: *a-shake* (1), and the subjunctive *break* (4) after *before* in the adverbial clause, the only subordination in the poem. Among the tropes, Yeats continued to favour personification: *clinging, creeping* night (3), The West *weeps* in pale dew (5), *Drowning* love's *lonely* hour in deep twilight (11).

HE WISHES FOR THE CLOTHS OF HEAVEN
(from *The Wind Among the Reeds,* 1899)

Had Í the heávens' embróidered *clóths,*
Enwróught with gólden *and* sílver *light,*
The blúe *and* the dím *and* the dárk *clóths*
Of níght *and* líght *and* the hálf *light,*
I would *spréad* the *clóths únder your féet*:   5
But Í, being poór, have ónly my *dréams*;
I have *spréad* my *dréams únder your féet*;
Treád sóftly because you *tréad* on my *dréams.*

This decorous complaint, addressed to Maud Gonne when the

liaison with Diana Vernon had ended sadly, is included because it marks an ambivalent point in Yeats's technical development. It is generally described as the last of the Pre-Raphaelite poems, and Yeats himself described the poem as defeatist, one likely to lose the lady rather than to win her. The mood of despair in which he found himself led him sometimes to doubt his sanity. From this hopelessness he was probably rescued by the kindness and common sense of Lady Gregory.

The mask assumed in this poem is that of Aedh, another character in *The Secret Rose* tales, who stands for 'fire burning by itself'. Yeats added in the notes that 'Aedh is the myrrh and frankincense that the imagination offers continually before all that it loves'. The prevailing feeling is pathos in the poet's self-abasement. But while the sentiment is sincere, the figure of metonymy in *the heavens' embroidered cloths | Enwrought,* which contains nearly all the polysyllables, tends to be archaic and decorative in the Rossetti manner; and the matching of adjectives in 'The *blue* and the *dim* and the *dark* cloths' with nouns in '*night* and *light* and the *half light*' is patterned and poetic, rather than realistic.

In this lyric, there are four strongly stressed syllables in the tetrameter lines, which are skilfully modulated by trisyllabic substitution in one or more of the iambic feet of every line but the first, designed to set the pattern. Pyrrhic feet in lines 3, 4 and 8, and trochaic substitutes in lines 5 and 7 provide further variation. The rhythm suggests a compromise between freedom and restraint, well illustrated in the movement of the last line. The eight-line poem is closely knit by assonance, alliteration and other repetitive devices, of which *ploce* is the most conspicuous rhetorical example. The internal rhyming of line 4 has a centripetal significance, apart from its ornamental value. Notice that it completes the long conditional clause (the *protasis*), to which the first half of the poem is devoted.

In an important sense, rhyme should be regarded as an aspect of rhetoric, since it often involves parallelism, as of thought and syntax, as well as repetition, involving likeness of sounds. Rhyme had, for Yeats, a structural value which he never neglected in the 370 poems where he employed it. *He Wishes for the Cloths of Heaven* deliberately contains a rhetorical scheme of words known as *epiphora,* seen in alternately rhyming pairs of identical words; and its functional aspect is well worth considering. It has a similar nuance to Eliot's incantational repetition of words at the beginning of *Ash Wednesday*. It achieves the decorative, weaving effect suggested by *embroidered cloths*, worked in silver and gold. It conveys, especially through the repeated vowel-sounds [i] of the last four rhymes, the claustrophobic sense of frustration in the poet's unrewarded passion.

With orthodox rhyme, in a chosen stanza form, Yeats's usual practice was to draw up a scheme of possible chiming words, before he composed the lines themselves. Incentives to meaning were therefore phonetically predetermined, though the rhyme-scheme was liable to subsequent adjustment. The semantic potentialities of rhyme in this procedure are obvious. Acoustic repetition, which may be too mechanical, is the danger to be avoided; and Yeats was conscious that the function of rhyme should rather be to reinforce all the sounds considered suitable for an organic rhythm in completion.

It will be observed, later, that in stanzaic verse, Yeats had no compunction in using approximate rhyme, if it seemed natural. Indeed, the frequency of his approximate rhymes increased with the development and maturation of his metrical art. When he acquired mastery of form, he grew impatient with the restraints of exact rhyme.

THE FOLLY OF BEING COMFORTED
(from *In the Seven Woods*, 1904)

The poems of this 1904 volume introduce Yeats's middle period, in which there is change both of theme and treatment. Maud Gonne married John MacBride in 1903, and Yeats became involved with the production and writing of plays for the Abbey Theatre. The dream-like quality of the romantic poetry gradually disappears through his preoccupation with men and affairs; and personal problems now provide him with fresh subject matter. The important factor in the development of a new conversational and prosaic style was, however, the compulsion to revise his earlier work for Bullen's edition of the *Collected Poems,* published in 1908.

The Folly of Being Comforted first appeared in January 1902, and recalls the rejection of his suit by Maud Gonne. The 'kind' person who tried to console the poet was apparently Lady Gregory, at

whose home, Coole Park, he was invited to spend the summer
months of each year. The 'seven woods' of the volume's title
were those situated on her large estate.

> Óne that is éver kínd said yésterdày:
> 'Your wéll-belóved's háir has thréads of gréy,
> And líttle shádows cóme about her éyes;
> Tíme can but máke it eásier to be wíse
> Though nów it *séem* impóssible, | and sò   5
> Áll that you néed is pátience.'
>   Heárt cries 'Nő'.
> I have *nót a crúmb* of cómfort, | *nót a gráin*,
> *Tíme* can but máke her béauty óver agáin:
> Becaúse of thàt gréat nóbleness of hérs
> The *fíre* that *stírs* abóut her, | when she *stírs*   10
> Búrns but móre cléarly. | Ó she had nót these wáys,
> When áll the *wíld súmmer* was in her *gáze*."
> Ó heárt! | Ó heárt! | if shé'd but túrn her héad,
> You'd knów the fólly of being cómfortèd.

Although it has fourteen iambic pentameter lines, the poem is not
a sonnet. The rhymed couplets have only one enjambed line (5),
and closely resemble epigrams in the same metre, written by Ben
Jonson in imitation of Horace. The colloquial language of the
first six lines is without a single image, and has few polysyllables.
Throughout the only traces of poetic language are: *well-beloved* (2),
the archaic subjunctive *seem* in the concessive clause of line 5, and
the rhyme-word *gaze* in line 12. The paucity of attributive adjectives (*little*, *great* and *wild*) demonstrates the classical restraint of
the diction.

The three parts of the poem (1–6a; 6b–12, 13 and 14) are dis-
creetly modelled for natural utterance. The first speech has only
one internal pause (5), the second three (7, 10 and 11), and the
final couplet two, in line 11. Note the declamatory and decisive
effect of *Heart cries 'No'* at the end of line 6. Lines 12–14 are
examples of the greater freedom of movement, through stress
variation, towards which Yeats was moving. The last syllable of
comforted carries a metrical half-stress, which satisfies the mind's
expectancy of rhyme.

The rhythm seems to gather momentum from line 6, when the

poet's emotion finds expression in a more vital, figurative language, embodying the following tropes:

Personification, *Heart cries 'No'*. (6), *Time can but make* (8)
Metonymy, *a crumb of comfort, not a grain* (7)
Metaphor, *The fire that stirs* (10), *wild summer was in her gaze* (12)

Among the rhetorical schemes of words and thought are:
Isocolon, the balanced repetition of the phrases *not a crumb | not a grain* in line 7
Ploce, 10 The fire that *stirs* about her, when she *stirs*
Ecphonesis, 11 O she had not these ways
Epizeuxis, 13 O heart! O heart!
Aphaeresis, the colloquial contractions *she'd* (13 = she would) and *You'd* (14 = you would)

The traditional classifications of these ten figures may not be important, but their effect upon rhythm, feeling and tempo is. The direct speech of this poem is dramatic, and illustrates the impact upon style of Yeats's experience inside the theatre.

THESE ARE THE CLOUDS
(from *The Green Helmet*, 1912)

This poem, in gratitude to Lady Gregory, was written in May 1910, shortly after Yeats had become a member of the Royal Society of Literature. He was by now a name in the world of theatre, and demands upon him as a lecturer made it incumbent to write more prose than lyric poetry. What non-dramatic verse he composed during the eight years after *In the Seven Woods* has a Jonsonian tautness of discipline, characteristic of the middle period. The following confirms the Yeatsian preference for twelve iambic pentameter lines:

> These are the clouds about the *fallen* sun,
> The *majesty that shuts his burning eye*:
> The weak lay hand on what the strong has *done*,
> Till that *be* tumbled that was lifted high
> *And* discord *follow* upon uni*son*,   5
> *And* all things at one common level lie.
> *And* therefore, friend, if your great race *were run*
> *And* these things *came*, so much the more thereby

> Have you made greatness your compan*ion*,
> Although it *be* for children that you sigh: 10
> These are the clouds about the fallen sun,
> The majesty that shuts his burning eye.

Yeats needed a personal stimulus to write his occasional lyrics. His conscientious regard for form enabled him to eliminate all detail irrelevant to the emotion, and to organize his ideas with great economy of words. In January to March 1909, he wrote in his *Journal*: 'Emotion is always justified by time, thought hardly ever. It can only bring us back to emotion . . . The artist has vulgarized himself the moment his systematized thought passes out of his passion *as from a fiery cloud* . . . I think all happiness depends on having the energy to assume the mask of some other self, that all joyous or creative life is a rebirth as something not onself' (pp. 154, 170, 191).

The occasion for this poem was the news that the Courts had instructed Lady Gregory to reduce the rentals paid by tenants on her estate. The future of a way of life, under which the poet shared the benefits of art and culture, was threatened; and Yeats's fears were subsequently realized, for the residence, which once housed treasures of all kinds, was not long after demolished to make room for a scheme of afforestation. The Gregorys had been wealthy rulers of men, patrons of the arts, and collectors of books, paintings and folklore. Yeats likened the Coole Park community to the Renaissance Dukedom of Urbino in Castiglione's *The Courtier*. He believed that Lady Gregory had achieved the selfless 'happiness' described in his *Journal*, and that natural aristocrats were alone able to enjoy the advantages of leisure.

The poet's theme is therefore the value of Lady Gregory's gracious and dignified contribution to Irish culture; hence the princely personal metaphors *fallen sun* and *majesty that shuts his burning eye* in the opening lines, and the personified *greatness* of line 9. By *children* (line 10) Yeats probably meant a 'new generation of young artists and writers'. A lofty tone is sustained throughout, and the impressive imagery of the first two lines repeated as a refrain. The second half of the poem is balanced against the first, and the rhythm, despite lack of enjambement, has an uninterrupted flow. Lines 4 and 7 are given no end punctuation, but a metrical pause is required by the syntax. The subjunctive forms of the verbs *be* (4 and 10), *follow* (5) and *run* (7) are characteristic of Yeats's structure in subordinate adverbial clauses.

Polysyndeton, the repeated employment of the conjunction *And* at the beginning of lines 5 to 8, is the single rhetorical scheme of words, and one of Yeats's favourite linking devices. Two approximate rhymes reflect his growing flexibility in this regard, one terminal being a monosyllabic Anglo-Saxon word, the other a polysyllabic latinism (see lines 4/6, *done | unisòn*; 7/9 *run | companiòn*). The rhythmic unity owes something to the employment of two vowel-sounds only ([ʌ] and [ai]) in ten of the rhyme words.

THE COLD HEAVEN
(from *Responsibilities,* 1914)

Several controversial issues and the death of two friends (Synge and Parnell) troubled Yeats's Dublin life during the years preceding the publication of *Responsibilities;* they are reflected in certain groups of poems, such as the angry ones on the rejection of the Hugh Lane bequest of modern French paintings. Yeats had met Ezra Pound in 1909, and spent an autumn and two winters with him at Stone Cottage in Sussex; the effects of this friendship upon his writing were not immediate in *Responsibilities,* which Pound reviewed favourably for its 'gaunter' note and 'greater hardness of outline'. 'Yeats', he wrote, 'is assuredly an immortal . . . there is no need for him to recast his style to suit our winds of doctrine'. Pound shrewdly observed that Yeats is not a poet whose quality can be assessed in 'partial quotation'; a 'curious nobility', he said, is 'the constant element of his writing'.

Pound's review mentions obscurity in *The Grey Rock* (for which Yeats was awarded a prize by the magazine *Poetry*), but not in *The Cold Heaven,* described by John Unterecker as 'a reservoir of possibilities' (*A Reader's Guide to W. B. Yeats,* p. 128). With the ambivalence of the poem, the symbolic imagery has much to do:

Súddenly I sáw the cóld and *róok-delíghting* héaven
That séemed as though *íce búrned and wàs but the móre íce,*
And théreupòn imáginàtion and héart were dríven
Só wíld that èvery cásual thóught of thát and thís
Vánished, | and léft but mémories, | that shóuld be oút of
    séason   5
With the *hót blóod* of yoúth, | of lóve cróssed lóng agó;

And Í took áll the bláme | oùt of áll sénse and réason,
Untíl I críed and trémbled | and rócked tó and fró,
Ríddled with líght. | Áh! | when the ghóst begíns to quícken,
Confúsion of the déath-béd óver, | ìs it sént   10
Out náked on the róads, | as the bóoks sáy, | and strícken
Bỳ the *injústice of the skíes* for púnishmènt?

This metaphysical poem is as near to free verse as Yeats permitted
his art to go. The twelve lines are pregnant with symbolic meaning,
which the poet does not submit to the bondage of metrical convention. Yeats's success with the hexameter is a tour-de-force in
creating an atmosphere of wonder, initiated by the anomalous
figure of *oxymoron* in *ice burned and was but the more ice* (2). Obscurity
arises from other key phrases, too, such as *Riddled with light* (9),
Confusion of the death-bed (10) and *injustice of the skies* (12), all metaphors of considerable power. The stimulus to these emotions, as
Yeats explained to Maud Gonne, was the sight of a cheerless
wintry sky, which he heralds by the compound epithet in '*rook-
delighting* heaven' (personification). *Ice burned* suggests a watery
sun, either at dawn or sunset; the impression is confirmed by the
image *Riddled with light* in line 9.

Yeats makes the association between a cold depressing day and
his own mood of frustration a natural one. The weather not only
drives commonplace thought from his mind, but induces dismal
reflections on the past, of disappointment in young love, for
which the poet irrationally blames himself. *Ice that burns* also
suggests passion frigidly responded to, the sort of analogy that
would occur spontaneously to the *imagination and heart* of a
rejected lover. The agony of longing over the years, without
return of affection, brought on a pathological condition (*I cried
and trembled and rocked to and fro*), perceived in moments of insight
and illumination (*Riddled with light*). The quickened *ghost* is surely
the spirit of dead love; and *Confusion of the death-bed over* may well
refer to the shock of Maud Gonne's marriage to MacBride. The
extended image of lines 9 to 12 is not intelligible without reference to doctrines of Spiritualism; that must be the significance of
the interpolation 'as the books say'. Yeats asks a question, not
himself knowing the answer. *Injustice of the skies* seems to imply
'dispensation of nature'. Phrased in simple prose sense, the
question put in lines 10 to 12 takes this form: Is the memory of a

love thought to be dead revived from time to time to torment the sufferer for his folly ? [Yeats continued to idolize the woman whose nature he knew to be antipathetic. According to Yeats's Autobiography, Maud Gonne confessed that she was sexually frigid, and he disapproved of her violently fanatical politics. Her attraction for the poet seems to have been largely physical.]

The poem reveals Yeats's well-known skill in fusing thought and feeling; his slow, meditative rhythm suggests different nuances of primary and secondary stress to different readers. The long lines have several enjambements in the first half of the poem, but no internal pause occurs until the fifth line. By contrast, the imagepacked second half employs syntactical modulation, to heighten the tone and match the complexity of the language. The alternately-rhymed quatrains are not self-contained; they achieve a deliberately prosaic rhythm through occasional use of approximate rhymes: 1/3 *heaven / driven*; 2/4 *ice / this*; 10/12 *sent / punishmènt*. Yeats found weak rhymes like the last rhythmically satisfying, especially when a poem ends with a Latin polysyllable. The use of *ecphonesis* (*Ah!*), to begin the incomplete first line (9) of the final quatrain, is most effective, especially in the length of the medial pauses entailed by the pensive exclamation.

In twenty-five years of literary life, Yeats had become preeminent, to the world outside Ireland, through a number of shorter lyrics, such as those analysed in this chapter. Some are among the most perfect examples of his craft at this stage. The period 1889 to 1914 was a tentative, though serious one in which he developed fresh rhythms for poetry, especially in the use of the dignified iambic line, without challenging its conventional framework. His procedure was self-critical and laborious, an endless search for the *mot juste*, accompanied by ruthless retrenchment of words. In consequence, Yeats admitted, he was easily drawn from his craft by other interests. Compact, rhymed poems, stanzaic in form, represent the early Yeats at his best, because they are conceived holistically, as rhythms in completion.

When each volume was about to appear, Yeats re-arranged the themes, often neglecting chronology, to reflect the emerging pattern of his life and personality. His end was to depersonalize the biographical substratum, and give the poetry universality. The splendidly proportioned lyrics are not those of a dilettante, but satisfying demonstrations that personality in poetry is not an undesirable intrusion, provided the poet is at the same time a profound thinker and a conscientious craftsman.

Three women played a significant role in Yeats's intellectual growth, by giving him different measures of sympathy and encouragement. Diana Vernon (Mrs Olivia Shakespeare), herself a writer of novels, remained on terms of intimate friendship for forty years. Lady Gregory helped him first to collect folklore, then to establish the Irish theatre movement; the comfortable, but down-to-earth stability of her household afforded the poet the restful atmosphere necessary for his work. Maud Gonne aroused in Yeats the national spirit, and became the theme of some of the most moving, if unorthodox, love poems in the language. Without the influence of these personalities, Yeats might have been a very different poet. His tribute to them is paid in *Friends*, the poem immediately preceding *The Cold Heaven* in *Responsibilities*:

> Now must I these three praise –
> Three women that have wrought
> What *joy* is in my days;
> One that no passing thought,
> Nor those *unpassing cares,*
> No, not in these fifteen
> Many times troubled years,
> Could ever come between
> *Mind and delighted mind*;
> And one because her hand
> Had *strength that could unbind*
> *What none can understand,*
> What none can have and thrive,
> *Youth's dreamy load,* till she
> So changed me that I live
> *Labouring in ecstasy.*
> And what of her that took
> All till my youth was gone
> With *scarce a pitying look*?
> How should I praise that one?
> When day begins to break
> I count my good and bad,

> Being wakeful for her sake,
> Remembering what she had,
> What *eagle look* still shows,
> While up *from my heart's root*
> *So great a sweetness flows*
> I shake from head to foot.

There is no rancour in the final acknowledgement to Maud Gonne, the only woman of the three to outlive him. The essential dignity of the phrasing italicized was early achieved through a philosophical serenity of mind; the *Journal* abounds in candid self-critical analysis.

By 1914, Yeats had succeeded in simplifying his vocabulary and eliminating most poeticisms and archaisms; but not all of the latter, as his use of *thereupon* in line 3 of *The Cold Heaven* testifies. In his essay on 'Popular Poetry' he came to the conclusion that the kind of simplicity valuable to art does not come from 'the people'; rather it is the product of a written tradition, using material gleaned from an unwritten inheritance, sometimes notable for its 'clear rhetoric'. There is a significant comment in *Letter 343* of A. Wade's edition, 1954:

> I avoid every kind of word that seems to me either 'poetical' or 'modern' and above all I avoid suggesting the ghostly (the vague) idea about a god, for it is a modern conception. All ancient vision was definite and precise.

The 'common syntax' that Yeats wished to attain was not assured by avoiding 'rhetoric'. 'The natural order of words' he sought differs from traditional poetic syntax chiefly in the rejection of inversions. Even in this Yeats was not altogether successful; modulation and rhyme compelled him to admit syntactical inversion on occasion, as in the first line of *Friends*: Now *must I these three praise* (showing two inversions in one simple statement). It has been shown that Yeats retains some archaic relics in subordinate clauses, for instance in preferring the Irish use of subjunctives in adverbial clauses. Modern English still has this practice in the hypothetical past of the verb *to be*, as in 'if your great race *were* run' (*These are the Clouds*, line 5). Yeats's abundant relative clauses, especially those beginning with the defining connective *that*, as in line 4 of *The Cold Heaven* and line 2 of *Friends*, have a learned rather than a natural look.

A recognized gift of Yeats was his ability to animate or retard rhythm through his sensitive command of expression. Whatever the subject or form of a poem, he had an instinctive feeling for the rhythm proper to its self-determining pattern. He used rhyme both to excite and to sustain the movement, and he was never satisfied with isolated distinction of phrase. There must be inter-action of key words throughout the poem if the impetus that gave it birth was not prematurely to exhaust its influence. The popular lyric *Innisfree*, he maintained, was the 'first lyric with anything in its rhythm of my own music' (*Autobiographies*, p. 153). In 1915, when Yeats wrote *Ego Dominus Tuus*, he was moving towards art as 'a vision of reality', based on the sincere belief that a senti-mentalist was one who deceived himself.

CHAPTER V

W. B. Yeats (2):
The Ballylee Period 1915–39

🐟🐟🐟🐟🐟🐟

IN our last chapter the poems of Yeats most worthy of study proved to be a homogeneous group on the theme of love, not as the lyrical impulse of the Elizabethans or Victorians, but as a complex relationship between a man and a woman. In this relationship, which Yeats valued and dignified, he could confront the anti-self creatively; and, consequently, these poems have a unified technical, as well as spiritual interest, which is fitfully illuminated by the admirable prose *Autobiographies*, begun in 1914. Here Yeats described himself as 'a gregarious man going hither and thither looking for conversation'.

Yeats's marriage in 1917 to Georgina Hyde-Lees was both a stabilizing and transforming event in his life. He said that she made his days 'serene and full of order'. She was sympathetic to his preoccupation with the supernatural, and it was discovered through what started as a pleasant distraction, that she was a medium with a gift for automatic writing, which Yeats encouraged. The communications of the spirit world were interpreted and enlarged by Yeats into a philosophical system, which he preserved in the prose work, *A Vision*, published in January 1926. The methodical care and the quality of the writing in this book alone justify its perusal; the ideas contained in its rhythmical prose throw much light on the meaning and purpose of Yeats's later poems.

Many English commentators, of whom W. H. Auden is sufficient example, regard *A Vision* as an aberration slightly embarrassing to a critic, and harmful to the poet's reputation as a thinker. (See 'Yeats as an example', *Kenyon Review*, Spring 1948, pp. 187–95). Yeats did not write this book to oppose Imagination to Reason; the foundation of his cosmology is seen to be a belief in antitheses or opposites: for example, Will and Desire, Creativity and a Determinist Environment. In his system, human beings are not psychologically subjective or objective, introvert or extrovert, but *primary* and *antithetical*, complex creatures adumbrated in the studies of Carl Jung. Not magic fascinates Yeats, so much as the disturbing tensions, and the irrational forces of the modern world. He is anti-scientific, because science makes little of the opposing pairs of faculties in man's nature; and he rejects naturalism as a fruitful source of inspiration in literature.

There is as yet no means of judging whether Yeats's philosophy is true or false; it would be manifestly unfair to assess it by rationalist criteria. But demonstrably it contains valuable material for poetry, and the interpretation of profound poems after 1917 is hampered by lack of understanding of Yeats's actuating principles. The bearing of *A Vision* on Yeats's later poetry has been persuasively explained by three American critics: Edmund Wilson, R. P. Blackmur and Cleanth Brooks, whose essays stand at the head of the contents of *The Permanence of Yeats* (Macmillan, 1950), edited by J. Hall and M. Steinmann.

The changes made in the 1937 edition of *A Vision* were fairly substantial, and necessitated by Yeats's subsequent readings in philosophy; but he never tampered with fundamental ideas or symbols. His great poetry would not have been realizable without the pseudo-philosophy that occupied the mature years of his life. As Wilson remarked in *Axel's Castle* (1931), 'Yeats's sense of reality . . . is inferior to that of no man alive'. He thought that the integrity of his poetry had its origin in the images which, he claimed, were of supernatural validity. This statement about his beliefs, in *A Packet for Ezra Pound* (1929), is worth noting:

> Does the word belief . . . belong to our age, can I think of the world as there and I here judging it? I will never think any thoughts but these; when I write prose or verse they must be somewhere present, though it may not be in the words; they must affect my judgement of friends and events; but then there are many symbolisms and none exactly resembles mine . . . He has best imagined reality who has best imagined justice.

The supernatural part of Yeats's system is concerned with the life of the soul after death, and the miraculous certainty of reincarnation.

Among the symbols that occur pervasively after 1917 are *sun*, *moon*, *blood*, *tower*, *fire*, *gyre*, *Spiritus Mundi* and *Byzantium*. All the symbols have a place in his private mythology, which does not exclude images from Christianity, especially in the Byzantine period. Varied, yet unified by the 'passionate intensity' of his imagination, the images of Yeats's poetry never employ the abstruser elements of the system, which give to the philosophical prose a professional obscurity. The prose technicalities are derived from the particular occult learning he favoured from time to time. It is often found that Yeats's language in the poems is clarified, less by a rational than by a rhetorical discipline.

Of the origins of *A Vision,* Yeats gives plentiful circumstantial evidence in the 1926 edition:

> I had made a new religion, almost an infallible church of poetic tradition, of a fardel of stories and of personages, and of *emotions, inseparable from their first expression* . . . I wished for a system of thought that would leave my imagination free to create as it chose and yet make all it created, or could create, part of one history, and that the soul's.

An attentive reading of the poems makes it certain that Yeats did not formulate his system to make a tragic drama of masks and faces. He wanted creative integration of his reflections through words that could express the *individual* strength of convictions. He believed this was a power the *fin-de-siècle* poets had squandered in an eclecticism that was anaemic, and an a-morality that was theatrical.

A lover of discourse and the company of men and women of taste and intellect, Yeats nevertheless composed his most esteemed poems in the solitude of his West Country retreat, Thoor Ballylee, which he purchased soon after his marriage in 1917. He had known the square Norman tower, near the village of Gort in Galway, since 1896, when he toured western Ireland with Arthur Symons, and called at Coole Park to see Lady Gregory. It was among the villagers of the neighbourhood that they collected many of their treasured examples of folklore. Ballylee was the Yeats's place of summer residence from 1919, when *The Wild Swans at Coole* appeared, until 1929, when the poet's health began to fail. Here he wrote many of the poems in *Michael Robartes and the Dancer* (1921) *The Tower* (1928) and *The Winding Stair* (1933). The work of this period reveals a considerable extension of vision, and a finer distinction of language.

Yeats gave much thought to new conceptions of metaphor and symbol. He wrote and re-wrote, convinced that the first draft of a poem was bound to be crude, and strike the ear as artificial. Always, he tested the words aloud as he composed. Open as he was to experiment, he realized that free verse was not for him; he told Dorothy Wellesley in 1935 that he disliked 'the constant uncertainty as to where the accent falls'. But he was not indifferent to the occasional need for 'a sublte hesitating rhythm'. The spontaneity of his enormous correspondence abounds in unexpected lapses of spelling, and so does the initial drafting of his poems. Of the younger generation of post-war poets he wrote: 'These new men are goldsmiths working with a glass screwed in one eye, whereas we stride ahead of the crowd, its swordsmen'. Yeats's idea of the tradition was very different from Eliot's.

IN MEMORY OF MAJOR ROBERT GREGORY
(from *The Wild Swans at Coole*, 1919)

This poem, in twelve stanzas, was written in June 1918, and published in the *English Review* the following August; it commemorates the death in the same year of Major Gregory, of the Royal Flying Corps, only son of Lady Gregory, killed in action on the Italian front. Four stanzas (2, 5, 8 and 9) have been omitted, including a tribute to Yeats's maternal uncle, George Pollexfen of Sligo. Two of the introductory memories concern Lionel Johnson, the poet-friend of his youth (1867–1902), who was a member of the Rhymers' Club; and John Millington Synge (1871–1909), the dramatist whom Yeats met in Paris in 1896. Like the promising painter, Gregory, both writers were cut down in their prime.

> Nów that *we're* álmost séttled in our *hóuse*
> *I'll* náme the fríends that cánnot súp with *ús*
> Besíde a fíre of túrf in *th'* áncient tówer,
> And hàving tálked to sòme láte hóur
> Clímb up the nárrow wínding stáir to béd: 5
> Discóverers of forgótten trúth
> Or mére compánions of my yóuth,
> *Áll,* | *áll* are in my thóughts to-níght | being déad.
>
> Líonel Jóhnson còmes the fírst to mínd,
> *That* lóved his léarning bétter than mankínd,   10

Though cóurteous to the wórst; | mùch fálling *hé*
Bróoded upòn sánctit*ỳ*
Till *áll* his Gréek and Látin léarning séemed
A lóng blást upon the hórn | that broúght
A líttle néarer to his thóught   15
A méasureless cònsummátion that he dréamed.

And that enquiring man John Synge comes next,
That dying chose the living world for text
And never could have rested in the *tomb*
But that, *long travelling,* he had *come*   20
Towards nightfall upon certain‸set apart
In a most desolate stony place,
Towards nightfall upon a race
Passionate and simple like his heart.

They were my close companions many a year   25
A portion of my mind and life, as it were,
And now their *breathless faces* seem to look
Out of some old picture-book;
I am accustomed to their lack of breath,
But not that my *dear* friend's *dear son,*   30
Our Sidney and our perfect *man,*
Could share in that *discourtesy of death.*

For *all* things the *delighted eye* now sees
Were loved by him; the old storm-broken trees
That cast their shadows upon road and *bridge;*   35
The tower set on the stream's *edge;*
The ford where drinking cattle make a *stir*
Nightly, and startled by that sound
The water-hen must change her ground;
He might have been your heartiest welco*mer.*   40

What other could so well have counselled *us*
In *all* lovely intricacies of a *house*
As he that practised or that understood
All work in metal or in wood,
In moulded plaster or in *carven* stone?   45
Soldier, scholar, horseman, he,
And *all* he did done perfect*ly*
As though he had but that one trade alone.

Some burn damp faggots, others may consume
The *entire combustible world* in one small room   50
As though dried straw, and if we turn about
The bare chimney is gone *black out*
Because the work had finished in that flare.
Soldier, scholar, horseman, he,
As 'twere *all* life's epito*me*.   55
What made us dream that he could *comb grey hair*?

I had thought, seeing how bitter is that *wind*
That shakes the shutter, to have brought to *mind*
All those that manhood tried, or childhood *loved,*
Or boyish intellect appr*oved,*   60
With some appropriate commentary on each;
Until *imagination brought*
A *fitter welcome*; but *a thought*
Of that late death took all my heart for speech.

Frank Kermode has shown in *Romantic Image* (Routledge and Kegan Paul, 1957) that the eight-line stanza was used by Cowley in his *Ode on the Death of Mr William Harvey,* a much longer poem of nineteen stanzas. The rhyme scheme is aabbcddc, in which 4, 6 and 7 have only four feet; the pattern of the five remaining lines is the iambic pentameter. As in the best wit-poetry of the seventeenth century, Cowley's verses are usually end-stopped; and the rhythm is less flexible than that of Yeats, whose tribute cannot be likened to the swelling movement of an ode. Nor has it Cowley's mingled strands of wit and gravity. The poem to Gregory is conversational in tone, yet dignified and sincere; it exemplifies Yeats's plea for the common syntax of speech, and, with few exceptions, it preserves the natural order of words. By comparing Gregory with Sir Philip Sidney, Yeats suggested that there is a bond between humanist courtesy and civility. The word *courtesy* recurs in the later poems, and is twice used in this one.

Though Cowley was not a seventeenth-century mystic, the terms of poet-philosophers and theologians, such as Henry More, were in the air. Many phrases and lines in the *Ode on the Death of Mr William Harvey* would have appealed to the questing spirit of Yeats:

3 Sleep, *Deaths Image,* left my troubled brest
13 Thy *Soul and Body* when Deaths Agonie / Besieg'd

22 As *sullen Ghosts stalk* speechless by
26 A Strong and mighty *Influence joyn'd our Birth*
35 Till the *Ledaean Stars so fam'd for Love* | Wondred at us
73–4 Large was his Soul; *as large a Soul as ere* | *Submitted to inform a Body*
99 His Judgement like *the heav'nly Moon* did show
119–20 Just like *the First and Highest Sphere* | *Which wheels about,* and turns all Heav'n one way
134–6 *Infectious Death* | Malitiously *seiz'd on that Breath* | *Where Life, Spirit, Pleasure always us'd to dwell*
137–8 But happy Thou, ta'ne from *this frantick age,* | *Where Igno'rance and Hypocrisie does rage*!

This ode is bound to have struck a sympathetic chord, when Yeats was pondering the loss of three practitioners of the arts, for whom his affection was as deep as Cowley's for Harvey. Moreover, Harvey's scientific knowledge was not incompatible with his religion.

Yeats's conversational note is apparent, not only in colloquial contractions, such as *I'll* and *we're*, but in the choice of familiar words; there is a marked preference for monosyllables in the last line of each stanza. The tone of homely strength is accompanied by a deliberate rejection of classical and mythological allusions; but more important is the loosening of the rhythm the reader experiences in the unorthodox juxtaposition of stressed and unstressed syllables of lines like the following:

25 Ă pór | tiŏn ŏf | mỹ mínd, | ănd lĭfe, | aš ĭt wére
42 Iň áll | lóvelỹ, iňtríc | ăciĕs ŏf | ă hóuse
52 Thĕ báre | chímnĕy | iš góne | bláck óut

The supple rhythm, it should be observed, is aided by judicious employment of approximate rhymes:

1/2 *house* | *us*, 11/12 *he* | sanctit*ỳ*, 19/20, *tomb* | *come*, 30/31 *son* | *man*, 35/6 *bridge* | *edge*, 37/40 *stir* | welcom*è*, 41/42 *us* | *house*, 46/7 *he* | perfect*lỳ*, 54/5 *he* | epito*mè*, 57/8 *wind* | *mind*, 59/60 *loved* | *approved*.

The second stanza is a model of polysyllabic modulation, achieved through the longer words *Brooded, sanctity, measureless* and *consummation* in lines 12 and 16.

There can be few memorial poems in the language where

figures of rhetoric play so minimal a role. In Yeats's first stanza the language of Cowley is yet implanted in his mind, and so is the formality of the prototype's movement. Notice the use of *metaplasm* in the elision of line 3, *th'ancient tower*; a similar contraction (*aphaeresis*) occurs in line 55, *As 'twere*, for reasons of rhythm. The archaism *carven* is introduced in line 45 for a similar reason. Among the schemes of words, *ploce* occurs only once, in line 30: my *dear* friend's *dear* son. There are rhythmically emphatic uses of repetition, too, such as *epizeuxis* in line 8: *All, all* are in my thoughts; and more telling is the use of *anaphora* in the repeated phrase *Towards nightfall,* at the beginning of lines 21 and 23, and of *Soldier, scholar, horseman, he* in lines 46 and 54. The latter refrain effectively modulates the rhythm by disjunction, after long final pauses. The introduction of *erotema* (rhetorical question) in lines 41 to 45 is conventional in odes, but is only twice employed by Yeats.

The tropes are inventive in this poem, but not numerous.

Personification: 27 *breathless* faces, 32 *discourtesy* of death, 33 the *delighted* eye, 62/3 *imagination brought | A fitter welcome*, 64 *a thought | Of that late death took all my heart* for speech.

Metonymy and hyperbole: *The entire combustible world in one small room.*

Synecdoche and erotema: *What made us dream that he could comb grey hair?* (*ie*, How could we think that he would ever grow old?).

Syntactical habits in Yeats are difficult to isolate, but two are ubiquitous: (1) The persistent use of the pronoun of totality (or pronominal adjective) *all* (it is used nine times in eight stanzas); (2) a strong preference for the relative pronoun *that,* and avoidance of *which*, even in non-restrictive clauses, *eg*, in lines 10, 18 and 58. The third stanza of the poem reveals other characteristics. In line 20 the absolute participial phrase *long travelling* is more compact than an adverbial clause, but the literary touch is at odds with the common speech Yeats desired. So is the substantival use of *certain* in the next line, in the sense of 'certain people'. This, in classical rhetoric, would be regarded as an instance of *eclipsis*, one of the schemes of words to secure a particular nuance of rhythm.

The interest of Yeats in Cowley could not have been a passing one, for he used the stanza of the Harvey ode again in *A Prayer for my Daughter*; and for the form of a later poem, *The Mother of*

God, he was further indebted to the seventeenth-century poet's ode on *Solitude*, which ends the essay of that title.

THE SECOND COMING
(from *Michael Robartes and the Dancer*, 1921)

This poem, written in January 1919, owes its conception to the *Prophetic Books* of Blake (*eg, the First Book of Urizen*), and to the New Testament, especially the *Book of Revelation* VI.12–17 and XIII, and *Matthew* XXIV. There are also recollections of Shelley's *Prometheus Unbound* and *Ozymandias*, and of Dante's *Divina Commedia*. In the gospel, Christ prophesies, for the benefit of his disciples, the destruction of the Temple, and the end of the world. *Matthew* XXIV, 29 reads:

> Immediately after the tribulation of those dayes, shall the Sunne be darkened, and the Moone shall not give her light, and the starres shall fall from heaven, and the powers of the heavens shall be shaken.

This passage may have suggested lines 3 and 4 of *The Second Coming*:

> Things fall apart; the centre cannot hold;
> Mere anarchy is loosed upon the world.

The Second Coming foretells the end of the Christian cycle of two thousand years, and the birth of an age of violence. On this subject Yeats provided a lengthy note (quoted below) in the Cuala limited edition of *Michael Robartes and the Dancer*, explaining that the nature of a new age is invariably revealed at the end of the preceding one.

> Túrning and túrning in the wídening gýre
> The *fálcon* cànnot héar the *fálcon*er;
> Thíngs fáll apárt; | the céntre cánnot hóld;
> *Mére* ánarchy is *lóosed* upòn the wórld,
> The blóod-dímmed tíde is *lóosed*, | and éverywhère   5
> The céremony of ínnocence is drówned;
> *The bést láck* áll convíction, | while the *wórst*
> Are fúll of pássionate inténsity.

Súrely some révelàtion *is at hánd*;
Súrely the Sécond Cóming is at hánd.   10
The Sécond Cóming! ‖ Hárdly are thóse wórds óut
When a *vást* image out of *Spíritus Múndi*
Tróubles my síght: | sómewhere in sánds of the désert
A shápe with líon bódy and the héad of a mán,
A gáze blánk and pítiless as the sún,   15
Is móving its slów *thíghs*, | while áll aboút it
Réel shádows of the indígnant désert bírds.
The dárkness dróps agáin; | but nów I knów
That twénty cénturies of stóny sléep
Were véxed to níghtmare by a rócking crádle,   20
And whát róugh béast, its hóur come róund at lást,
Slóuches towards Béthlehem to be bórn?

The evolution of the poem's form and powerful wording may be
traced in Jon Stallworthy's reconstruction from Yeats's manuscripts, in chapter I of *Between the Lines* (Clarendon, 1963). Several
preliminary drafts exist, indicating imaginative revisions, the most
important 'second' or 'third' thoughts being the following:

2 *falcon* replaced *hawk*
3 *Things fall apart* replaced *All things break up*
4 *Mere* replaced *Vile*
7 *lack* replaced *lose*
12 *vast* replaced *stark*
15 *A gaze* replaced *An eye*
16 *thighs* replaced *feet*
17 *Reel* replaced *fall*
22 *Slouches* replaced *has set out*

These are suggestive changes, and illustrate the meticulous
handling by which the poem took shape.

The twenty-two lines of blank verse are in paragraphs of eight
and fourteen verses; but the structural break is properly in the
middle of line 11. The transitional two-and-a-half lines (9–11a)
link the subjective first half, and the objective second half, of the
poet's thinking. The form of the whole is an ingeniously realized
mathematical figure of interpenetrating cones, to which Yeats
refers in the *widening gyre* of line 1.

The slow, deliberate rhythmical movement admirably suggests

the dire note of prophecy. Primary stresses in the iambic pentameter lines vary from three to six; though the rhythm is harmed by
conceiving the lines in terms of metrical feet. The impressive-
sounding lines are splendidly weighted by the spondaic use of
stressed monosyllables, *eg*, 3 *Things fall apart*, 5 *The blood-dimmed
tide*, 7 *The best lack all*, 11 *Hardly are those words out*, 21 And *what
rough beast*. In the absence of rhyme, the movement is made coherent by skilful employment of assonance, alliteration, word-
repetition and the satisfying disposition of the eight internal pauses.

The importance Yeats here attached to attributive adjectives
is as remarkable for economy as for aptness: 4 *Mere* anarchy, 5
blood-dimmed tide, 8 *passionate* intensity, 12 *vast* image, 15 gaze
blank and *pitiless*, 16 *slow* thighs, 17 *indignant* desert birds, 19 *stony*
sleep, 21 *rough* beast. Read in context, even such common epithets
as *mere, vast, slow* and *rough* seem to be not only right, but inevitable.

Meaning presents few difficulties, once the significance of the
symbols *gyre, falcon, Spiritus Mundi* and *rough beast* is understood,
and the historical origin of the poem recognized. The inspiration
for Yeats's *gyre* seems to have come from Swedenborg's *Principia*
and other occult literature, though the word had been employed in
various senses by Spenser in *The Faerie Queene*, by Jonson, Drayton,
Massinger, Cary in translating Dante's *Inferno*, Southey, Mrs. E. B.
Browning, Rossetti and W. E. Henley, the last an undoubted
influence on Yeats's early writing. As the *gyre* image recurs in
several of the later poems, extracts from the poet's explanatory
note in *Michael Robartes and the Dancer* are worth recording:

All living mind has . . . a fundamental mathematical movement;
. . . when you have found this movement and calculated its
relations, you can foretell the entire future of that mind. . . .
The mathematical figure is an expression of the mind's desire,
and the more rapid the development of the figure the greater
the freedom of the soul. The figure, while the soul is in the
body, or suffering from the consequences of that life, is frequently drawn as a double cone, the narrow end of each cone
being in the centre of the broad end of the other. . . . It is
marked out by two gyres which represent the conflicts, as it
were, of plane and line, by two movements, which circle about
a centre . . . The circling is always narrowing or spreading,

because one movement or other is always the stronger. In other words, the human soul is always moving outward into the objective world or inward into itself; & this movement is double because the human soul would not be conscious were it not suspended between contraries, the greater the contrast the more intense the consciousness. The man, in whom the movement inward is stronger than the movement outward, the man who sees all reflected within himself, the subjective man, reaches the narrow end of a gyre at death; death is always . . . preceded by an intensification of the subjective life; and has a moment of revelation immediately after death . . . The objective man on the other hand, whose gyre moves outward, receives at this moment the revelation, not of himself seen from within, for that is impossible to objective man, but of himself as if he were somebody else. This figure is true also of history, for the end of an age, which always receives the revelation of the character of the next age, is represented by the coming of one gyre to its place of greatest expansion, and of the other to that of its greatest contraction. At the present moment the life gyre is sweeping outward, unlike that before the birth of Christ which was narrowing, and has almost reached its greatest expansion. The revelation which approaches will however take its character from the contrary movement of the interior gyre. All our scientific, democratic, fact-accumulating, heterogeneous civilisation belongs to the outward gyre and prepares not the continuance of itself, but the revelation as in a lightning flash, though in a flash that will not strike only in one place, and will for a time be constantly repeated, of the civilization that must slowly take its place.

According to Stallworthy, the *falcon* represents 'pride of the intellect'; its upward flight is in gyres. A. N. Jeffares observes that the *falcon* also represents civilized man, 'out of touch with Christ' (the falconer), whose birth initiated the Christian era. *Spiritus Mundi* (elsewhere *Anima Mundi*) stands for the world of imagination, of universal symbols, but not those that are invented by individual minds. The *rough beast* is a purposely vague monster, partly human, which Yeats revived in the Introduction to his play, *The Resurrection*, as 'a brazen winged beast . . . associated with laughing, ecstatic destruction'.

When Yeats wrote the poem he was distressed by events in and after the First World War. Many Irish patriots had lost their lives in the Easter revolution of 1916. The sentence *Mere anarchy is loosed upon the world* is thought to refer to the Bolshevik Revolution in Russia in October 1917, followed by the murder of the Tsar and his family. Lenin surrendered large Baltic territories to the Germans in March 1918. Yeats believed that civilized peoples were losing their power to fanatics, the *worst* elements of society, 'full of passionate intensity'. Belief in historical cycles, each with a presiding Deity, was one of the doctrines of Theosophy; and Yeats feared the impending changes as a *nightmare*, with the ruling power vested in the representatives of Antichrist. In the fine line (6) 'The ceremony of innocence is drowned', he had in mind the extinction of aristocratic and cultured ways of life he respected. The background of the cataclysm and of the new era is once more Palestine and the desert regions of the Middle East.

The rhetorical schemes and figures of *The Second Coming* are important to its structural vigour. The repetitions of *turning* and *falcon* in lines 1 and 2, and of *loosed* in lines 4 and 5, are effective use of *ploce*; while a note of incantational ritual is struck in lines 9–11, in the recurring words *Surely, Second Coming,* and *is at hand,* all schemes of rhetoric classified as *anaphora*. The antithesis of *The best* and *the worst* in line 7 should not be overlooked.

The use of metaphor and other tropes pervades the poem's symbolism. In *The blood-dimmed tide is loosed* (5) and *The ceremony of innocence is drowned* there are strong leanings to personification, which is continued in the second half of the prophecy through the images in lines 15, 17 and 19–21.

Donald Davie in *An Honoured Guest* (Arnold, 1965, pp. 76–80) argues that Yeats misled readers by supplying the long explanatory note in the Cuala edition; he holds, with some justice, that the poem is inconsistent with the philosophy. *The Second Coming* undoubtedly presents an historical situation resembling that in the Apocalypse, rather than in the Gospel of St Matthew; but the poem arouses emotional convictions independent of the annotations. These should be read solely as aids to understanding the symbolism, not as an argument to the poem. Davie shows that the 'ceremony of innocence' (which Yeats feared would be eclipsed by sub-human forces) survives with characteristic approval in the next poem, *A Prayer for my Daughter*.

SAILING TO BYZANTIUM
(from *The Tower*, 1928)

This poem, originally entitled 'Towards Byzantium', was written in September 1926, when Yeats was sixty-one; it served as an introduction to *The Tower*, published two years later. The theme is the symbolic voyage of an ageing man in search of a congenial spiritual climate. The manuscript fragments and typescripts that survive show that the gestation of *Sailing to Byzantium* was complicated and arduous. The poet followed the usual discipline of removing traces of personal experience, to give the poem universal application.

Yeats was awarded the Nobel Prize for Literature in 1923, a year after he had become a Senator of the Irish Free State. At no time did he take his responsibilities lightly. He was then engaged in writing *A Vision*, to clarify and consolidate his beliefs in spiritualism and extrasensory perception. In 1924 his health failed, and in November he travelled, on medical advice, to Sicily, Rome and other places in Italy. Forbidden to write poetry, he occupied his mind studying the cultural history of the Eastern Mediterranean.

Yeats had no regrets at leaving Ireland, being disgusted with the rancour of its political life, and depressed through consciousness of his declining physical powers. He never visited Constantinople, but was steeped in Byzantine history and art. In Italy he was captivated by the mosaics of Palermo and Ravenna, having visited the latter city with Lady Gregory in 1907. The particulars he used in this poem were from Gibbon's *Decline and Fall of the Roman Empire*, W. G. Holmes's *The Age of Justinian and Theodora* and G. Finlay's *History of the Byzantine Empire*. The period of perfect integration of Byzantium's culture, through art, religion and government, is not specified; but from *A Vision* (p. 279–80) it becomes clear that Yeats thought of the first half of the 6th century AD; for he refers to Justinian's foundation of St Sophia and the closing of Plato's Academy. The companion poem *Byzantium,* in *The Winding Stair* (1930), chronicles the city 'towards the end of the first Christian millennium' (*ie,* some three hundred years later – see the prose draft of the poem in Yeats's *Diary,* 1930). The quality of Byzantine civilization in these centuries was substantially advanced, and the absolute sovereignty remained

elective. Gradually Byzantine art, which owed as much to the
East as to the West, became less stylized and two-dimensional.
Yeats liked the earlier mosaics because they were more im-
personal, and emphasized the antithesis between Nature and Art.

Thát is nò cóuntry for óld mén. | The *yóung*
In óne anóther's árms, | bírds in the trées,
– Thóse *dýing* gènerátions – | at their *sóng*,
The sálmon-fálls, | the máckerel-crówded séas,
Físh, | flésh, | or fówl, | comménd *áll* súmmer lóng   5
Whatéver is begótten, | bórn, | and díes.
Caúght in that sénsual músic | *àll* negléct
Mónuments of un*ágeing* íntellèct.

An *áged* mán is *but* a páltry thíng,
A *táttere*d cóat upòn a stíck, | unléss   10
ˌSóul cláp its hánds and *síng*, | and lóuder *síng*
For évery *tátter* in its mórtal dréss,
Nór is there *sínging* schóol | *but* stúdy*ìng*
Mónuments of its ówn magnéficènce;
And thérefore I have sáiled the séas and *cóme*   15
To the *hóly* cíty of Byzántiùm.

Ó ságes stánding in Gód's *hóly fíre*
As in the *góld* mosáic of a *wáll*,
Cóme from the *hóly fíre*, | pérne in a gýre,
And bé the *sínging* másters of my *sóul*   20
Consúme my héart awáy; | síck with desíre
And fástened to a *dýing* ánimàl
It knóws not whát it ís; and gáther mé
Ínto the ártifice of etérni*tỳ*.

Ónce out of *nature* | I shall néver táke   25
My bódily *fórm* from àny *nátural thíng*,
But súch a *fórm* as Grécian *góld*smìths máke
Of hámmered *góld* | and *góld* enámellìng
To kéep a drówsy émperor awáke;
Or sét upòn a *góld*en bóugh to *síng*   30
To lórds and ládies of Byzántiùm
Of whàt is *pást*, | or *pássing*, | or to *cóme*.

This is possibly the best rounded product of Yeats's struggle to
'hammer [his] thoughts into a unity'. The first impulse was to

compare judicially modern Ireland with ancient Byzantium, as physical ambiences for the sensual man. The poem opens with an appraisal of the fertility *motif* in his native land, and the earliest drafts had *Here* or *This* as the initial word, not *That*, which the poet chose finally for the sake of greater objectivity. The opposition of body and soul was, however, uppermost in his mind, and Yeats said that he wrote the poem 'to recover his spirits'. Neither for the elderly lover nor the creative artist did Ireland seem a wholesome place to live in.

Sailing to Byzantium was eventually completed in four stanzas of eight iambic pentameter lines, with the rhyme-scheme ababab(?) cc. The rhythmical modulation has deceptively short-looking sixth and eighth lines, preferring polysyllables, except in the normative last stanza; here, for the first time, line 6 admits perfect rhyme. The significance of approximate rhyme for the poem's organic movement is carefully calculated, *eg,* 1/3 *young | song,* 4/6 *seas | dies,* 15/16 *come |* Byzan*tiùm,* 18/20/22 *wall | soul |* anim*àl,* 31/32 Byzan*tiùm | come.* In line 14, *magnificence* offers only unstressed *e* to match the rhyme-word *dress.* In every stanza there are terminal polysyllables with rhetorical secondary stress for rhyme in the ultimate syllable, *eg,* 7/8 *neglect |* inte*llèct,* 11/13 *sing |* study*ìng,* 20/22 *soul |* anim*àl,* 23/24 *me |* eterni*tỳ,* 26/28 *thing |* enamel*lìng.*

Yeats often said that he liked a rhythm in which the accents are unequivocally determined. The singing tone of *Sailing to Byzantium* rests upon heavy beats, more numerous and measured than usual, and a discreet modulation of internal pauses. In stanza one, the ten internal breaks occur after different metrical feet.

Most skilfully the language is adapted to the germinal ideas of each stanza. Ostensibly, the first stanza describes Ireland and Irish youth; but it is actually concerned with procreative tendencies of nature, admirably suggested by *isocolon* in the balanced phrases *Fish, flesh or fowl* and *begotten, born, and dies* in lines 5 and 6. The seminal images are *Those dying generations, salmon-falls, mackerel-crowded seas* and *sensual music,* all hinting at the reproductive cycle observed by the poet in Galway and Sligo Bay. The rhythm of nature is deterministic, since each generation makes way for the next. The dilemma of the poet is that preoccupation with sex prejudices the life of the mind, and disfigures the enduring monuments of man's spiritual nature.

The second stanza concerns the ageing poet himself, featureless as the scarecrow (*A tattered coat upon a stick*) were it not that the *Soul* may rejoice (*clap its hands*) and sing. Even though unlettered, a poet may learn from the *magnificence* of his past. Byzantium was such a haven of aesthetic contemplation.

The third stanza invokes the saints and sages of history, to instil the fervour of dedication; Yeats here recalls the martyrs in golden splendour on the mosaic frieze of Santo Apollinare Nuovo in Ravenna. The ascetic became 'God's Athlete', he wrote in *A Vision*. The sentence *perne in a gyre* suggests a 'descending downward, circular movement'; the verb is from the Irish dialect noun *pern* 'spool', on which peasant women wind their thread. The poet prays to be instructed in spiritual wisdom, to be divested of his body with its animal pangs of ignorant desire, and to be fired with zeal for the life of the imagination, through art (*gather me / Into the artifice of eternity*). Perhaps he had in mind the Latin proverb *Ars longa vita brevis*.

Stanza four is a plea, not for re-incarnation, but for inanimate existence. The artifact (a mechanical bird) of the goldsmiths (lines 27/8) may have been suggested to Yeats by memories of Hans Andersen's *The Emperor's Nightingale*. (This is substantiated in line 29 *To keep a drowsy Emperor awake*). The *golden bough* of line 30 comes from Vergil's *aureus . . . ramus* of *Aeneid* VI.137. The poet's determinism is suggested by the imitation bird's singing of past, present and future.

Yeats in this poem is caught in the 'sensual music' of his own verse, and perhaps he had in mind Shakespeare's magnificent line about the bees in *Henry V*, I.ii.198: *The singing Masons building roofes of Gold*. *Sing* (or *song*) occurs six times in the poem, and the present participle termination *-ing* is pervasive: *dying* (3, 22), *unageing* (8), *studying* (13), *standing* (17), *enamelling* (28), *passing* (32); twice the ending is used to rhyme with *thing*. These *-ing* inflexions, indeed, provide the memorable assonances; but there are other impressive echoes, such as *fire* and *gyre* in line 19.

Repetitive words are used to relate one stanza of the poem to another; eg, *age* links the first and second, *holy* the second and third, *gold* and *come* the third and fourth. The rhetorical device of *ploce* is so deliberate that the following examples seldom escape notice: *all* (5, 7), *Monuments* (8, 14), *tatter* (10, 12), *soul* (11, 20), *Byzantium* (16, 31), *fire* (17, 19), *nature* (25, 26), *form* (26, 27), *pass* (twice in 32). *Holy* dominates stanza 3, as *gold* (four times) dominates stanza 4. Even unobtrusive relation words *but, of* and *or* are repetitive (see lines 8, 12, 28, 30, 32), as if part of the pattern of argument.

By the time of writing *Sailing to Byzantium*, Yeats had mastered the intricacies of the iambic pentameter line in stanzaic form. The perfection of the music in this poem is largely owing to his phonetic sensibility, in which he is not surpassed by other romantics, such as Shelley, Keats and Tennyson. Modulation of the vowel sounds may be easily sampled by examining the phonemes in consecutive verses; there are ten in lines 1 and 2. But the interplay of consonants, voiced and unvoiced, should not be overlooked. The following is a list of some occurrences:

nasals, *n, m* – 101 times
sibilants *s, z* – 74 times
lateral *l* – 37 times
fricative *th* – 19 times
trilled *r* – 14 times (the numerous unsounded instances in received Standard English are omitted).

Sequences of liquid, nasal and sibilant consonants contribute largely to the smoothness of the versification.

Resonant polysyllables are freely indulged in *The Tower* and contribute to the obliquity of this poem. But most of the arcane meanings are due to the pregnant imagery, which is sometimes difficult to classify. In the first stanza *Those dying generations* (3) indicates metonymy, *commend* (5) and *unageing intellect* (8) suggest personification, while *sensual music* (7) has the stamp of metaphor. The second stanza employs metonymy in line 10 and personification in 11 and 12. Every line of the third stanza is metaphorical; the sense is not contingent on a knowledge of Yeats's system in *A Vision*. But this cannot be said of the symbols in stanza 4, partly because the allusions are puzzling. The role of the poet in lines 25–7 is hardly a flattering one, but not out of harmony with Yeats's philosophical determinism, and his taste for impersonality in Byzantine art.

In this complete specimen of his art, it is not surprising to find that the poet subconsciously employed several technical devices of rhetoric. C. M. Bowra shrewdly observed that Yeats's 'style is not rhetoric, but it is rhetorical. It is meant to be declaimed' (*The Heritage of Symbolism*, Macmillan, 1947, p. 196). *Ploce* and *isocolon* are the schemes of word and thought already mentioned. In lines 2 to 5 *asyndeton* is conspicuous in the avoidance of co-ordinating conjunctions. *Parenthesis* is used with good effect in line 3. *Eclipsis* helps occasionally to secure a compression of phrase required by the rhythm, as in the definite article omitted before *Soul* in line 11. *Ecphonesis* (*O sages standing in God's holy fire*) is among the oldest of poetry's figures, and introduces a sublime note in the latter half of the poem, by raising the emotional level. Stanza 3 is necessarily rhetorical, because it employs the language of invocation. A lowered tone is called for in the final stanza, and the rhythm is steadily retarded after the word *drowsy* (29). The rhetorical figure *polyptoton*, in line 32, is apt to be overlooked; the same verb is used, but with different functional terminations. The only indication of Yeats's Irish archaism is the subjunctive *sing*, after *unless*, in line 11.

The poet's taste for orientalism in Byzantine art, at a time of declining physical potency, is best explained by a passage from *On the Boiler* (1939):

> There are moments when I am certain that art must once again accept those Greek proportions which carry into plastic art the Pythagorean numbers, those faces which are divine because all there is empty and measured. Europe was not born when Greek galleys defeated the Persian hordes at Salamis, but when the Doric studios sent out those broad-backed marble statues against the multiform, vague, expressive Asiatic sea, they gave to the sexual instinct of Europe its goal, its fixed type (p. 27).

The personal irony of *Sailing to Byzantium* does not affect its poetic relevance. The poem captivates a passing mood, in which a sensualist adopts the mask of an aesthete, by opposing art to nature. The creative awareness resembles that of Keats in the *Letters*. Yeats's 'passionate intensity' in *The Tower* marks a gradual rejection of the language of common speech, and there is no better account of this change than John Holloway's essay on 'Style and World' in *An Honoured Guest* (Arnold, 1965):

> All the important words of his sentence take their meanings from a progressive charging, which they receive from the developing poem ... Yeats's nodal objects ... arrive starkly and as it seems arbitrarily ... 'Intensity of pattern' is created

for him by . . . his all-pervading energy: energy of argument
(pp. 95–99).

A DIALOGUE OF SELF AND SOUL
(from *The Winding Stair,* 1933)

Originally entitled 'Sword and Tower', this poem was written
late in 1927 and early in 1928, and first published in America in
the following year. When *The Winding Stair* appeared in 1933, it
was dedicated to the theme of re-birth, and was intended to be
antithetical in mood and outlook to *The Tower*; for Yeats had now
come to oppose stoical resignation to 'escape'. Some poems celebrate friendships he remembered with gratitude. In America, a
Japanese friend, Sato, had presented him with a sword and with
part of a court-lady's silk dress to cover it; and this sword became
an heroic symbol of Yeats's resurgent life after illness. Another
symbol was the winding staircase of Thoor Ballylee, which Yeats
associated with the *gyre* of the theosophical system.

Part I of the *Dialogue* dramatizes the conflict between the poet's
dominant passions. The sword represents the worldly self, and its
fulfilment through creative energy. The soul's symbol is the
winding stair, leading by successive incarnations to the Buddhist's
nirvana, 'extinction (of passion)'. Yeats in part II rejects the latter,
because personality requires commitment to the genetic character
of a man's nature. This extract from the *Dialogue* contains only
the poet's annunciation of *self*:

> A líving mán is *blínd* and drínks his *dróp.*
> *Whàt mátter if* the *dítches* are *impúre*?
> *Whàt mátter if* I líve it *áll* ònce *móre*?
> Endúre that tóil of grówing *úp*;
> The ígnomìny of *bóyhoòd*; | the distréss   5
> Of *bóyhoòd* chánging ìnto *mán*;
> The un*fínished mán* and his *páin*
> Broùght *fáce* to *fáce* with his òwn clúmsin*èss*;
>
> The *fínished mán* amòng his énem*iès*? –
> Hów in the náme of Héaven can hé *escápe*   10
> Thát defíling and disfígured *shápe*
> The mírror of malícious *éyes*
> Cásts upòn his *éyes* | untìl at lást

He thínks thàt *shápe* must bè hís *shápe*?
And whát*'s* the góod of an *escápe*   15
If hónour fínd him in the wíntry blást?

Í *am contént to* líve it *áll* agaín
And yét agaín, | if it be lífe to pítch
Ínto the fróg-spáwn of a *blínd mán's dítch*,
A *blínd màn* báttering *blínd mén*;   20
Or ìnto that móst fécund *dítch* of *áll*,
The fólly that *mán dóes*
Or mùst súffer, | if he *wóos*
A proúd wóman not kíndred of his *sóul*.

Í *am contént to* fóllow to its *sóurce*   25
Évery evént in áction or in *thóught*;
Méasure *the lót*; | forgíve mysélf *the lót*!
When sùch as Í cást oùt remórse
So gréat a swéetness flóws ìnto the bréast
Wè must laúgh | and *wé mùst* síng,   30
Wè are *blést* by *éverythìng*,
Éverythìng we loók upòn is *blést*.

In the eight-line stanzas the rhyme-scheme is abba, cddc, in
which only lines 1, 2, 3, 5 and 8 are pentameters. Most other lines
have four feet, but 7 and 22 have only three. The dominant metre
in the first quatrain is iambic; but in the second there is much
trochaic substitution to provide rhythmic variation. This touch of
informality gives the movement the flexibility the thought requires. The majority of the lines are end-stopped, there being only
six internal pauses in thirty-two lines. Half the lines have one or
more secondary stresses, which gives naturalness to the dialogue.

This manipulation provides the loosening of metrical pattern
that the speech requires, and the effect is heightened by the fre-
quent approximate rhymes: 1/4 *drop | up*, 2/3 *impure | more*, 6/7
man | pain, 9/12 *enemies | eyes*, 21/24 *all | soul*, 22/3 *does | woos*,
26/7 *thought | lot*; and to these should be added two polysyllabic
rhymes, in which the secondary stress is metrical, 5/8 dis*tress* /
clumsin*èss*, 30/1 *sing* / every*thìng*. In *Rhyme and Meaning in the
Poetry of Yeats* (Mouton, 1970, p. 113), Marjorie Perloff has the
following comment:

The Winding Stair ... is ... the volume which contains the greatest variety of types of approximate rhyme ... as well as the volume in which pun-rhyme and symbolic association-rhyme become most prominent ... It represents, in short, the culmination of Yeats's rhyming technique with respect both to the phonetic and the semantic aspect of rhyme ... The distribution of approximate rhyme in Yeats's poetry is similar to the distribution of rhymes that involve semantic relationships. As Yeats becomes more aware of the phonetic possibilities of rhyme, he also begins to exploit its semantic properties.

The esoteric symbolism of *A Dialogue of Self and Soul* is resolved in the second part of this poem, where Yeats reviews, and absolves himself from, the frustration and tragedy of his past life. Cumulative uses of metaphor and metonymy are observable in stanza 1 in the key words *blind* ('foolish'), *ditch* ('source of life'), *impure* ('sinful'), *toil* ('dreariness'), and *clumsiness* ('ineptitude'). Adolescence (*unfinished man*), from the vantage point of age, is seen as *the ignominy of boyhood.*

If youth is distressful, adulthood is filled with calumny and distortion of the truth. The significant phrases of stanza 2 are the metaphors *The mirror of malicious eyes* (12) and *wintry blast* (15). Yeats implies that there was no escape from the passions of his fellow countrymen, because honourable neutrality left one out in the cold. He seems here to universalize the hatred of contemporary Irish patriots.

Stanza 3 argues that a reasonable man must accept his mistakes. The poet finds no consolation in religious remorse, and prefers uncompromising acceptance of the world's evil. Heroic resolution is doubly important, because of the probability of re-incarnation, hinted at in line 18. The significant metaphorical words here are: *if it be life to pitch | Into the frog-spawn of a blind man's ditch* (19/20). The association of *frog-spawn* ('breeding-place') and *blind man's ditch* ('life of the sensual man') with the powerful qualifier *fecund* in line 21, exemplifies the poet's skill in mounting image upon image. The supreme folly of man's antithetical destiny is to bestow love unwisely.

In stanza 4 the poet's conviction is that self-analysis should trace mistakes, whether of action or thought, to their source. It becomes evident that man has complementary existences, the actual and the symbolic; he is therefore invariably at odds with his destiny. Three years before his death Yeats wrote to Dorothy Wellesley that he thought of his sick soul only 'from ambition and vanity'; his new resolution was 'to avoid deep places and die blaspheming'. This would explain the poet's decision to 'cast out remorse'. An old man, preparing for the grave, could attain to Yeats's final euphoria only through a feeling of resignation.

The semantic linking of stanza to stanza is important to Yeats's technique, which late in his career employs numerous devices of rhetoric. *Finished man,* in line 9, looks back to *unfinished man* in 7; *pitch* (18), though used as a verb, has a metonymic relation to *defiling* in line 11; while *I am content* (17/25) introduces both of the last two stanzas. There are five rhetorical questions (*erotemata*) in the first two stanzas. But the dominating verbal scheme is *ploce*, in the following employments: *live* (1, 3, 17), *blind* (1, 19, 20), *What matter if* (2, 3), *ditch* (2, 19, 21), *all* (3, 17, 21), *boyhood* (5, 6), *man* (1, 6, 7, 8, 19, 22), *face* (twice in 8), *escape* (10, 15), *shape* (11, 14 twice), *eyes* (12, 13), *again* (17, 18), *the lot* (twice in 27), *we must* (twice in 30), *blest* (31, 32), *everything* (31, 32), *we* (31, 32).

The student of Yeats's style should not overlook:

(*a*) the semantic antithesis of *ignominy* and *distress* (5), *unfinished man* (7) and *finished man* (9), of *blind* (1) and *eyes* (12);
(*b*) the grammatical antithesis of A *blind man* battering *blind men* (20);
(*c*) the rhythmical antithesis of *Measure the lot*; *forgive myself the lot* (27) and *We must laugh and we must sing* (30). With so much repetition and word insistence, alliteration and assonance abound, as in lines 11–13.

Yeats described his regeneration as 'heroic ecstasy'; it was in accord with his idealistic quest for a surrogate for religion. In his antithetical philosophy, universal love replaced the disappointments of individual love, benevolence replaced hatred, and contentment made tolerable the ubiquity of corruption. Whether this resignation is different from 'escape' depends upon one's approach to the Yeatsian allegory of existence.

AN ACRE OF GRASS
(from *Last Poems*, 1939)

Last Poems and Two Plays was published by the Cuala Press in 1939, the year of Yeats's death; but *An Acre of Grass*, written in

November 1936, had already appeared in *Atlantic Monthly* and in the *New Poems* of 1938. The title refers to Yeats's home Riversdale, in which he spent the last seven years of his life. It was a 'creeper-covered farm-house' in Rathfarnham, whose proximity to Dublin offered facilities for the education of his children.

At the time of writing *An Acre of Grass* Yeats had been reading Nietzsche's *The Dawn of Day* (1881), and pondering the philosopher's thoughts on the declining powers of writers in old age. The closing stanzas suggest that though 'quiet' is necessary to reflect upon life, truth remains sterile until a poet can recapture the creative energy that actuated artists like Shakespeare, Michelangelo and Blake.

> Pícture and bóok remáin,
> An ácre of gréen *gráss*
> For aír and éxercìse,
> Now stréngth of bódy *goés*;
> Mídnìght, an óld hóuse   5
> Where nóthing stírs but a móuse.
>
> Mý temptátion is quíet.
> Hére at lífe's *énd*
> Néither lóose imáginàtion,
> Nór the míll of the *mind*   10
> Consúming its rág and bóne,
> Can máke the trúth knówn.
>
> Gránt me an óld màn's *frénzy*,
> Mysélf mùst Í remáke
> *Till* Í am Tímon and Léar   15
> *Or* thát William Bláke
> Who béat upón the wáll
> *Till* Trúth obéyed his cáll;
>
> A mínd Mìchael Ángelo knéw
> Thát can piérce the clóuds,   20
> Ór inspíred by *frénzy*
> Sháke the déad in their shróuds;
> Forgótten *élse* by mànkínd,
> An óld màn's eágle *mínd*.

Manuscripts and typed versions of this poem illuminate not only Yeats's tentative jottings, but his craftsmanlike revisions. The earlier drafts show the following:

1–4 My picture and books remain / For acre of hills and grass, / Good for sufficient exercise / Now that health goes

7–9 Meditation is my temptation / Now the last chill draws near / Yet by loose reverie

10–11 Nor those thoughts that hear / Dry bone grind dry bone

14 Till I myself remake

The improvements in the final poem reveal Yeats's awareness that first thoughts are likely to be casual and personal. The first step in his revisions was to remove the subjective phrasing.

The poem is in four stanzas of six lines each, rhyming abcbdd. In the first two stanzas there are notable uses of approximate rhyme: 2/4 *grass / goes*, 8/10 *end / mind*. The metrical pattern is iambic trimeter, but there is much stress variation; and trochaic substitution in the first foot occurs in nearly half the lines, *eg*, 1, 5, 7, 8, 9, 10, 13, 20, 21 and 22. The rhythm of these short verses is secured by stress modulation, rather than internal pause, all the lines being end-stopped. The form of the poem is thus unique, its language being both economical and incisive. Lines 14 and 23 have inversion of the normal order of words, but the position of *Myself must* (14) and *else* (23) has rhythmic and semantic significance.

As usual, with Yeats, the balance of the parts (stanzas 1 and 2, against stanzas 3 and 4) is skilfully managed. The first half of the poem is an objective account of the ageing poet's physical and spiritual condition; the second is a prayer for restoration of his poetic powers. Perhaps Yeats recalled Shakespeare's lines in *A Midsummer Night's Dream* V.i.12–13: The poet's eye in a fine *frenzy* rolling, / Doth glance from heaven to earth, from earth to heaven.

Meaning calls for only figurative exposition. In *Picture and book remain* (1), the metonymy symbolizes the continuance of the poet's aesthetic and intellectual interests. *Midnight* (5) is a reference to insomnia, from which Yeats suffered at the time. In *My temptation is quiet*, the final word is a noun; the 'peace' implied is, for the poet, a seduction from the testing life of conflict that he and Nietzsche believed engendered creative work. Two effective metaphors *loose imagination* (9) and *mill of the mind* (10) have many suggestive overtones; *loose* might mean 'inconsequential' or 'unconcentrated' or leave room for further individual interpretations. *Mill of the mind* is an echo of Blake; the image extends to the next line (11) *Consuming its rag and bone*, giving to *mill* the mechanical significance the poet intends. *Rag and bone* suggests the husks of an old man's life.

In the third stanza *frenzy* (13) and *Truth* (18) are the key words. The latter is deliberately capitalized, and *obeyed his call* is therefore an excellent instance of personification. *Frenzy* (13 = 'madness') should be regarded as a dead metaphor signifying 'poetic energy'; and so is the verb *remake* (14), in the sense of the 're-shaping' of personality. Note that Yeats prefers metaphor to simile, in offering the comparison with Timon, Lear and Blake. A *mind . . . | That can pierce the clouds* (19/20) is another example of personification. Nietzsche in *The Dawn of the Day* called great minds 'Aeronauts of the Intellect', and said it was their fate 'to be wrecked on the infinite'. Yeats undoubtedly had this philosopher's work in mind when he used the metaphors *Shake the dead in their shrouds* (22) and *An old man's eagle mind* (24). The attributive use of *eagle* has the sense of 'detached' in this context.

There is much alliteration in this poem, and dexterous use of the liquid, nasal and sibilant consonants helps the fluidity of the movement. As always, Yeats is meticulous in choosing connectives. Among the schemes of words, conjunctions supply a few instances of *ploce*: 15/18 *Till*, 16/21 *Or*. The only other uses of this figure of rhetoric are *mind* in lines 10 and 24 and *frenzy* in lines 13 and 21; the former helps to link the parts of the poem semantically.

The intensity and compactness of *An Acre of Grass* are due to the technique employed. As he grew older, Yeats became more sparing in the use of adjectives; indeed, after studying Donne, he tried to eschew meaningless epithets. Critics who have thought *Last Poems* didactic or egocentric, probably missed the redeeming qualities of clarity and ardour, rare in poets as dedicated as Yeats in their seventies.

THE MUNICIPAL GALLERY REVISITED
(from *Last Poems*, 1939)

This poem Yeats completed in September 1937, and considered to be among the best in his last published volume. There are seven

stanzas, but only III–VII are cited here. The poetical sketches
on Ireland's notables, whose portaits hang in the Dublin Municipal Gallery, were prompted by a speech Yeats delivered to the
Irish Academy of Letters in August of the same year. The omitted
stanzas deal with a few acknowledged Irish patriots and martyrs.

III

Héart-smítten with emótion | Í sínk *dówn*,
My héart recóvering with *cóv*ered *éyes*;
Wheréver I *had lóoked* | I *had lóoked upón*
My *pérmanent* or *impèrmanent ímages*:
Augústa Grégory's són; | her síster's són,   5
Húgh Láne, | 'ónlie begétter' of *áll thése*;
Házel Lávery | *líving* and *dýing*, | *thát tále*
As thoùgh some bállad-*sínger* had *súng* it *áll*;

IV

Mancíni's *pórtrait* of *Augústa Grégorỳ*,
'*Gréa*test since Rémbràndt,' | accórding to *Jóhn Sýnge*;   10
A *gréat* ebúllient *pórtrait* | cértainly;
But whére is the brúsh *that* cóuld shów ánythìng
Of *áll that* príde and *thát* humílitỳ?
And Í am in despáir *that* tíme may bríng
Appróved pátterns of wómen or of mén   15
But nót *that* sélfsàme éxellence *agaín*.

V

My médiaéval knées làck héalth untìl they *bénd*,
But in *thát* wóman, | in *thát* hoúsehòld *whére*
Hónour had líved so lóng, | *áll* lácking *fóund*.
Chíldless I *thóught*, | 'Mý chíldren may fínd *hére*   20
Deép-*róoted* thíngs,' | but néver fòresáw its *énd*,
And nów *thàt énd* has cóme | I hàve not wépt;
No fóx can fóul the láir the bádger swépt –

VI

(An *ímage* out of Spénser and the cómmon *tóngue*).
Jóhn Sýnge, | Í and Augústa Grégory, | *thóught*   25
Áll that we díd, | *áll that* we sáid or *sáng*
Mùst cóme from *cóntact* with the sóil, | from *thát*

Cóntact éverything Antáeus-like gréw stróng.
Wé thrée alóne in módern tímes had bróught
Éverything dówn to thàt sóle tést agáin,   30
Dréam of the nóble and the béggar-mán.

VII

And hére's *Jóhn Sýnge* himsélf, | *that roóted mán*,
'Forgétting húman wórds,' | a gráve déep fáce.
Yóu *that* would *júdge* me, | dó not *júdge alóne*
Thís bóok or *thàt*, | cóme to thìs hállowed pláce   35
Where mỳ *friends' pórtraits* háng | and lóok thereòn;
Íreland's hístory in their líneaments tráce;
Thínk where *mán's glóry* móst begíns and énds,
And sáy my *glóry* was I hád súch *friénds*.

The stanza form is *ottava rima,* the same as that Yeats used in *Sailing to Byzantium,* except in stanza V, where the sixth line (the last of the *b*-rhymes) is missing from the pattern of eight iambic pentameters. The line deleted from the original manuscript reads: *Of all that scholarly generations had held dear*; its sacrifice is evidence of the poet's good taste. Approximate rhyme occurs throughout stanza III, and frequently in the last three stanzas: 1/3/5 *down* | *upon* | *son,* 2/4/6 *eyes* | *images* | *these,* 7/8 *tale* | *all,* 17/19 *bend* | *found,* 18/20 *where* | *here,* 24/26/28 *tongue* | *sang* | *strong,* 30/31 *again* | *man,* 32/34/36 *man* | *alone* | *thereon.* There are rhymes on half-stressed syllables in lines 4, 9, 11, 12, 13 and 36, the rhyme-words all being polysyllabic.

The rhythm is slow, measured and solemn, intended to stress the dignity of Yeats's civic utterance; some nine of the 39 lines have six primary stresses. In poetry of such eloquence the location of secondary stresses is often one of individual interpretation. Internal pauses accord with the syntax of common speech, from which there is a striking poetical departure in the absolute participial phrase *all lacking found* (19). Ten run-on lines (4, 7, 12, 14, 18, 20, 26, 27, 29 and 34) reveal a higher proportion than Yeats usually allows in metrical discourses.

It is proper in reminiscential poetry that meaning should be perspicuous as well as personal. Yeats pays the highest honour to the two friends who moulded the course of his poetic career: Lady Gregory and John Synge. Only a few images and allusions call for explanation. Hazel Lavery, who died in 1935, was an American by birth, the second wife of Sir John Lavery, and herself an artist; the *living* portrait therefore shows her at her easel; the other is a death-bed scene. The attributive adjective *ebullient* (11), meaning 'exuberant' (literally 'boiling over') is a distinctive metaphor. The epithet in *mediaeval knees* (17) is metonymy, but at the same time a reference to Yeats's courtesy and reverence for aristocracy; the secondary meaning adverts to the poet's old age and state of health, as does *My heart recovering* in line 2.

The parenthesis concerning Spenser (24) looks back to the last line of the preceding stanza, *No fox can foul the lair the badger swept* (23). This is a reminiscence of lines 222–4 of Spenser's elegy, *The Ruins of Time,* where the poet writes of the contemptible successors of the Earl of Leicester:

> Spite bites the dead, that living never bayed.
> He now is gone, the whiles the *fox* is crept
> Into the hole, the which the *badger swept.*

Implicitly, Yeats likens Lady Gregory to the Earl of Leicester, as renowned 'householders' and patrons of letters. In an essay on 'Edmund Spenser' (1902), he referred to this passage from Spenser's so-called 'Ode' (see *Essays and Introductions* pp. 359–60). There is, in the collected works, no Ode on Leicester's death, to which Yeats's annotators repeatedly refer.

The impact of Spenser may be responsible for the simile *Antaeus-like* (28). There are few classical allusions in Yeats's poetry, but this one is appropriate, the giant Antaeus being the son of Poseidon and Ge ('*Earth*'). Wrestling with Heracles, whenever thrown to the ground, Antaeus recovered strength from contact with his mother. The hero was finally compelled to crush him, while holding him up in the air. In the *sole test* (30), *Dream of the noble and the beggar-man* (31) Yeats recalled Aristotle's dictum, 'Think like a wise man, but express yourself like the common people', to which Lady Gregory constantly drew his attention (see *Explorations* p. 371).

The description of John Synge (whose portrait was painted by Yeats's father) as *that rooted man* (32) is an impressive metaphor. Synge was a 'rootless' wanderer among the poor in Europe, until Yeats persuaded him to live and write in the primitive Aran Islands (see *Essays and Introductions,* p. 325). There the playwright settled to study the social equality and language of the Gaelic-speaking islanders. The quoted phrase *'Forgetting human words'* (33) is probably from Synge himself. Of his life on Inishmaan, Yeats wrote in the Preface of Synge's *Poems and Translations*:

> Here above all was silence from all our great orator took delight in, from formidable men, from moral indignation, from the 'sciolist' who 'is never sad', from all in modern life that would destroy the arts.

It is also becoming to reminiscential poetry that there should be echoes of word and phrase to imprint the portraits indelibly on the mind. Yeats had by 1937 abandoned pretence at eschewing the devices of rhetoric; for his public voice, as well as verbal mastery, demanded the use of balance and repetition. In the five selected stanzas there are no less than nine different figures of rhetoric; among these, the poem abounds in *ploce,* some 64 or more of the words being repetitious: *cover* (2), *I had looked* (3), *permanent* (4), *that* (7, 12, 13 twice, 14, 16, 18, 22, 26 twice, 27, 32, 34, 35), *image* (4, 24), *son* (5), *all* (8, 13, 19, 26 twice), *portrait* (9, 11, 36), *great* (10, 11), *again* (16, 30), *thought* (20, 25), *rooted* (21, 32), *end* (21, 22), *contact* (22, 23), *everything* (28, 30), *man* (31, 32, 38), *friends* (36, 39), *glory* (38, 39). To these should be added the proper names *Augusta Gregory* (5, 9, 25) and John *Synge* (10, 25, 32).

A word-count of the uses of *all* and *that* in Yeats's poetry would show how indispensable they are to his technical effects. Demonstrative *that* has an integral part in the rhythm of the poem, whose thought-structure is designedly antithetic and dramatic. Other rhetorical devices are:

Antithesis – *living* and *dying* (7)
Polyptoton – *sing, sung* (8), *sang* (26)
Erotema – the rhetorical question in 12 and 13.

Yeats is a more controversial figure than Eliot in the hierarchy of modern writers. Formally, he upholds the tradition of English Renaissance poetry of a lyrical and discursive kind. His language is vigorous and chiefly memorable in iambic measures, disciplined by stanza forms. Within that framework, he became a master of modulation, and his contribution to the modernist movement lay in the rhythmic flexibility and common syntax he was able, after 1915, to command. A line by line, painstaking writer, his com-

position was unorthodox, because he thought in prose, and
tentatively versified afterwards by means of a skeletal rhyme-
stanza pattern. Rhyme never became an enslavement, however,
since he extended the experimental possibilities of approximate
rhyme further than any other poet. Numb and prosaic relief
enabled him to be modern, without loss of character as a tradi-
tionalist.

The lexical vigour of Yeats's poetry owes something to his
verbal economy. In no rhythmic pattern that he evolved was he
burdened by syllable count or multiple stress contiguity. Secondary stress he indulged, and it enabled him to use terminal polysyllables with the naturalness of a cultivated speaker. His poems
avoid syntactical inversions, and are not excessively figurative in
style; but few in the great period are without Elizabethan schemes
of word and thought, the principal devices employed being *ploce*
and *antithesis*. The splendid ear for resonant and impressive words
is without idiosyncrasy, except for his unconscious reliance on the
pronoun of totality *all*, and relative or demonstrative *that,* where he
might have chosen alternative forms. Because the best poems are
short, with a syntax relatively simple, these mannerisms do not
obtrude. His meditations became less vague and more complex as
he mastered the language of predication, and struck a happy
balance in the use of nouns, verbs and adjectives. He is sparing in
epithets and avoids the straddled adjectives of Milton. After
studying Donne and Jonson, there came a more athletic and
classic resilience of style. A striking passage in 'Poetry and
Tradition' (1907) announced his artistic *credo*:

> In life courtesy and self-possession, and in the arts style, are
> the sensible impressions of the free mind, for both arise out of
> a deliberate shaping of all things, and from never being swept
> away, whatever the emotion, into confusion or dullness.
>
> *(Essays and Introductions*, p. 253)

As the leading symbolist poet in Britain, Yeats was in a favourable
position to influence poets after the First World War, but seldom
did so because of their antipathy to his eclectic philosophy. What
attracted the new generation was the *personal* element in his
poetry, which was full of conflict between masks (like that of
Michael Robartes) and faces, between man's primary and antithetical nature. In the middle period, the most personal of the

poems, whose title was taken from Dante, was *Ego Dominus Tuus* (1915); though Yeats afterwards rejected the style in which it was written, it marked a turning point in his career. Out of this dialogue between *Hic* and *Ille* arose the dissociation of Body and Soul, the objective and subjective life, which he developed in *Per Amica Silentia Lunae* (1918) and *A Vision* seven years later. The poem is a valuable confession of the artist on his social role, and the sources of his creation; it resembles medieval debates on the merits of the active and the contemplative life. Yeats's sympathies are undoubtedly on the side of *Ille*, for which Pound skittishly substituted 'Willie':

Hic On the grey sand beside the shallow stream
    Under your old wind-beaten tower, where still
    A lamp burns on beside the open book
    That Michael Robartes left, you walk in the moon,
    And, though you have passed the best of life, still trace,
    Enthralled by the unconquerable delusion,
    Magical shapes.

Ille   By the help of an image
    I call to my own opposite, summon all
    That I have handled least, least looked upon.

Hic And I would find myself and not an image.

Ille That is our modern hope, and by its light
    We have lit upon the gentle, sensitive mind
    And lost the old nonchalance of the hand;
    Whether we have chosen chisel, pen or brush,
    We are but critics, or but half create,
    Timid, entangled, empty and abashed,
    Lacking the countenance of our friends.

Hic   And yet
    The chief imagination of Christendom,
    Dante Alighieri, so utterly found himself
    That he has made that hollow face of his
    More plain to the mind's eye than any face
    But that of Christ. . . .

Hic Yet surely there are men who have made their art
    Out of no tragic war, lovers of life,

Impulsive men that look for happiness
And sing when they have found it.

Ille   No, not sing,
  For those that love the world serve it in action,
  Grow rich, popular and full of influence,
  And should they paint or write, still it is action:
  The struggle of the fly in marmalade.
  The rhetorician would deceive his neighbours,
  The sentimentalist himself; while art
  Is but a vision of reality.
  What portion in the world can the artist have
  Who has awakened from the common dream
  But dissipation and despair?

Hic   And yet
  No one denies to Keats love of the world;
  Remember his deliberate happiness.

Ille His art is happy, but who knows his mind?
  I see a schoolboy when I think of him,
  With face and nose pressed to a sweet-shop window,
  For certainly he sank into his grave
  His senses and his heart unsatisfied,
  And made – being poor, ailing and ignorant,
  Shut out from all the luxury of the world,
  The coarse-bred son of a livery-stable keeper –
  Luxuriant song.

Hic   Why should you leave the lamp
  Burning alone beside an open book,
  And trace these characters upon the sands?
  A style is found by sedentary toil
  And by the imitation of great masters.

Ille Because I seek an image, not a book.
  Those men that in their writings are most wise
  Own nothing but their blind, stupefied hearts.
  I call to the mysterious one who yet
  Shall walk the wet sands by the edge of the stream
  And look most like me, being indeed my double,

And prove of all imaginable things
The most unlike, being my anti-self,
And, standing by these characters, disclose
All that I seek; and whisper it as though
He were afraid the birds, who cry aloud
Their momentary cries before it is dawn,
Would carry it away to blasphemous men.

While this is poetry readily to be understood by the educated common man, it has not the pregnant strength or memorial quality Yeats achieved, when romantic and classic distinction fell away. The more self-conscious Yeats's art became, the more zealously did he apply himself to a sinewy diction. He grew in stature as a craftsman, whose sense of form was different from, but complementary to, that of Eliot.

Keats, Tennyson and Yeats were similar in not being natural poets, but self-made and deliberate artists. Two objective mentors, Lady Gregory and Ezra Pound, warned Yeats against 'literaryism'; as the latter observed, it undermines a reader's patience and trust in a writer's sincerity. The 'common syntax' at which Yeats aimed is what most persons might naturally use, given the circumstance and emotion of the poem. The conversational tone preferred accounts for occasional fragmentation in Yeats's syntax. His life as an artist seems to have been a perpetual struggle between the imaginative life and a will to technical perfection; he could not have agreed with Eliot that art implies the extinction of personality, or with Pound that it will cease to attract the modern mind, unless liberated from formal theory.

Both these critics discredited Yeats's supernatural world. Eliot wrote in *After Strange Gods* (1934):

> It was not a world of spiritual significance, not a world of real Good and Evil, of holiness and sin, but a highly sophisticated lower mythology summoned, like a physician, to *supply the fading pulse of poetry with some transient stimulant* (p. 46).

The phrases in italics were among the prejudicial judgements Eliot later regretted; they were grounded in religious orthodoxy, not on the intrinsic merit of work that is full of intangible truths. Yeats was of the same mind as Pound in believing that the contemporary artist lived in a hostile world. The mundane American advised the serious Irishman to treat his artistic isolation with astringent irony.

Because of the secure esteem Yeats enjoyed in the world of letters, his politically inspired poems, though full of indignation, are not undignified. As a member of the minority Anglo-Irish, and a Protestant, Yeats was a moderate nationalist, drawn to politics, even before he met Maud Gonne, by admiration for the noble-looking John O'Leary. He became disenchanted with events after Easter 1916, because counsels of change had passed to demagogues with a passion for sudden violence. His mature aim was 'to oppose the new ill-breeding of Ireland, which may in a few years destroy all that has given Ireland a distinguished name' (*Journal,* January 22, 1909). In the same *Journal* he continued: 'I had to subdue a kind of Jacobin rage. I escaped from it all as a writer through my sense of style' (January 31, 1909).

Like Eliot, Yeats was the product of that modern urban culture, which began in poetry with Baudelaire. Urbanity is a quality his poetry possesses to a high degree. The literary renaissance, of which he was a central figure, was not essentially Celtic in spirit. As Kenneth Jackson has pointed out, he and his collaborators knew little of Irish Gaelic, and less of the Celtic attitude to life and to poetry, which goes back to the seventh century. The translations they read were couched in what Jackson calls 'an artificial semi-biblical English', which claimed to 'render "the spirit" rather than the word' (Preface to *A Celtic Miscellany*, Penguin, 1971). The spirit of Yeats's *Celtic Twilight* (1893), and of the Celtic revival in general, was a Pre-Raphaelite dream, too often imagined as mysterious, magical, melancholy and brooding. One has only to study the adjective-noun relationship in *The Wanderings of Oisin* (1889) to appreciate that this is true of the early Yeats. Jackson quotes Whitley Stokes (*Celtic Review* VI, 72, 1909) as responding that Irish literature was actually 'strong, manly, purposeful . . . realistic, and pitiless in logic'. No more appropriate attributes than these last could be found for Yeats's later poetry; but it is doubtful whether he inherited the more masculine qualities from readings in Irish literature.

By the time of his correspondence with Lady Dorothy Wellesley, beginning in 1935, Yeats's direction in verse was firmly established. About his new play *The King of the Great Clock Tower,* he wrote on 21 December:

I am writing in short lines but think I shall not use 'sprung verse' . . . it seems to make the verse vague and weak. I like a strong driving force . . . I shall write 'sprung verse' only if I find it comes spontaneously – if a foot of four syllables seems natural I shall know I am in for it.

After fifty years of composition, Yeats was satisfied that his practice was in 'the main road' of the European tradition of poetry. The letters to Dorothy Wellesley are scattered with the ripest of judgements: 'the pen confounds us with its sluggish deliberation'; 'metaphors must be such things as come to mind in the midst of speech' (3/5/36); 'no artesian well of the intellect can find the poetic theme' (24/5/38).

Lady Wellesley came to believe that Yeats was 'a frustrated man of action'. From his comments on her poems, she considered that poor eyesight was responsible for a lack of visual observation; the objects of nature seemed to interest him only as symbols or stimuli to philosophical reflection. After years of comment on the order of words in poetry, it is said that he was unable to define *syntax*, and had to clarify his mind by consulting a dictionary. Thought, dialogue and vision were his obsessions, and up to his last poem, *Under Ben Bulben,* he was dedicated to technical experiment. In her final judgement of his personality, Dorothy Wellesley concluded: 'Yeats alive or dead brought dignity and distinction wherever he came' (p. 215).

CHAPTER VI

T. S. Eliot (1):
The Poems 1909–25

೫೫೫೫೫೫

THOMAS STEARNS ELIOT, known to his friends as 'the gay American', was born in St Louis, Missouri, in 1888, but became a naturalized British subject after thirteen years' residence in England, in 1927. His family had emigrated to New England from Devon in the seventeenth century and became firm believers in the value of tradition and the Puritan way of life. The first Eliot to set foot in America became town clerk of Beverly, Massachusetts; the family, for generations, were respected merchants in Boston. In the eighteenth century Dr Andrew Eliot entered the ministry of the Congregational Church and was so busy that he had to decline the Presidency of Harvard University. In public life, the greatest figure of the nineteenth century was William Greenleaf Eliot, the poet's grandfather, a well-educated Unitarian minister, who chose the frontier town of St Louis for his mission; he was an untiring social worker, who opposed slavery, and founded Washington University, of which he became President, in 1872.

The poet's father, Henry Ware Eliot, was probably the first member of the family to rebel against the strict religious up-bringing of the home. He became a well-to-do brick manufacturer and public-spirited man, who owned a large summer home at Gloucester on the Massachusetts coast. Here his son acquired his love of the sea and sailing, of which there are reminiscences in *Ash Wednesday* VI, *Marina* and *The Dry Salvages*. Thomas's mother, Charlotte Eliot, was a writer of liberal opinions and a devotional poet, whose *Savonarola* was published, with a preface by her son, in 1926. Her tastes were conservative, and her technique shows how much she was steeped in the nineteenth-century New England tradition of Longfellow. It was family loyalty that led her to approve of *The Waste Land* when it appeared in 1922; for Eliot had told her that he had put much of his life into the poem.

The American background to his literary education is of immense importance in any evaluation of Eliot's writing; he acknowledged this when, years later, he lectured at Washington University. After a couple of years at Milton Academy, he entered Harvard University in 1906, where he felt the influence of two distinguished dons: George Santayana and Irving Babbitt. Among the 'Poems Written in Early Youth' (published by Faber in the Complete Works of 1969) are several contributed to the *Harvard Advocate* during Eliot's undergraduate years. He followed elementary courses in English and Comparative Literature, but his main interests were in ancient and modern philosophy, the Greek and Latin classics, Dante, and the French and German languages. His love of the past and European cultural traditions was a legacy of his mentors at Harvard, then at its prime; many epigraphs to his mature poems were drawn from the authors he then read. In 1908 he discovered Arthur Symons's *The Symbolist Movement in Literature* and became acquainted with the poems of Laforgue, Verlaine and Corbière. He says that he sensed an immediate affinity with the first, and aimed at achieving a similar interaction of feeling, rhythm and thought.

Up to this time Eliot had given little indication of his desire to innovate. Opinions were favourable on his self-critical attention to metrical effects, but there was scarcely more than a delicate vagueness in the earliest verses. Here is the first stanza of *Lyric*, as it appeared in the *Smith Academy Record*, 1905 (*Complete Poems and Plays*, 1969, p. 590):

> If Time and Space, as Sages say,
>   Are things *which* cannot be,
> The sun *which does not feel decay*
>   No greater is than we.
> So why, Love, should we ever pray   5
>   To live a century?
> The butterfly that lives a day
>   Has lived eternity.

On the opposite page is Eliot's revision, with the less pretentious title *Song*:

> If *space and time,* as sages say,
>   Are things *that* cannot be,
> The fly that lives a single day

138

Has lived as long as we.
But let us live while yet we may,   5
While love and life are free,
For time is time, and runs away,
Though sages disagree.

After removing the non-significant capitals in the first line, Eliot transposed *space* and *time,* which did not disturb the alliteration, but improved the sound modulation by separating the identical diphthongs [ei] in *Space, Sages* and *say*. In line 2 he correctly substituted the restrictive relative *that* for non-restrictive *which,* thus securing a smoother rhythm. In a poem about the transience and intensity of love, he was soon unhappy about the image in line 3: 'The sun which *does not feel decay*'. In scrapping the line and replacing the ethereal *butterfly* of line 7 by a mundane *fly,* he expressed the transience of love and life more earthly. From this change, the notion of *carpe diem* flows naturally in line 5. In lines 6 to 8, however, substantial improvement was necessary to rid the stanza of the infelicitous chiming of cent*ury* / eterni*ty,* where the rhyme is on the weak terminations of polysyllabic words. Transferring the rhyme to the stressed syllables of *free* / dis*agree* (6/8) materially strengthened the rhythm; and it turned the thought back on itself by recalling the words *time* and *sages,* to round off the stanza.

The satirical note (but not the ennui) of Laforgue's poetry is captured in *Humouresque* and *Spleen* (pp. 602–3), in such lines as: '(The kind of face that we forget) / *Pinched in a comic, dull grimace*'; 'His *who-the-devil-are-you stare*; / *Translated,* maybe, to the *moon*'; 'And Life, *a little bald and gray* / *Languid, fastidious, and bland*'; '*Punctilious of tie and suit* / (Somewhat impatient of delay) / *On the doorstep of the Absolute*'. This phrasing suggests the style of *Prufrock,* and there are clearer anticipations of *The Waste Land* (25–9) in *The Death of Saint Narcissus,* which opens:

Come under the shadow of this gray rock –
Come in under the shadow of this gray rock,
And I will show you something different from either
Your shadow sprawling over the sand at daybreak, or
Your shadow leaping behind the fire against the red rock: (p. 605)

In a modest way the juvenilia achieve the symbolist care for technique, through compression and search for the precise word that stamp the best of French poetry.

In a review headed 'The Education of Taste' (*Athenaeum*, June 27, 1919), Eliot wrote:

> Taste begins and ends in feeling. Sometimes it is thought that taste is a weak derivative of enthusiasm. What taste is, I suppose, is an organization of immediate experiences obtained in literature, which is individually modified in its shape by the points of concentration of our strongest feelings.

Eliot felt strongly that English and American poets, at the turn of the century, were living in a cultural desert. He had read, and sometimes in his writing recalled, Whitman, but he could not overcome a revulsion for his untutored exuberance, his themes and his methods. French symbolist poetry filled a need, which he was to satisfy by spending a year studying at the Sorbonne in Paris.

Eliot was in pursuit of the 'authentic speech' of which Symons wrote as one aspect of the Symbolist movement. In this he was assisted by Ezra Pound, whom he first met in London in September 1914, when Eliot was researching on F. H. Bradley at Merton College, Oxford. Pound recognized the merits of his work, introduced him to other writers, and to the editors of journals, such as the *Egoist*, of which he later became Assistant Editor. Eliot was sceptical, and therefore more cautious, than Pound about innovations that could contribute anything of value to modern poetry; he thought the improvements must be chiefly technical.

Much can be learnt from Eliot's essay on Pound's 'Metric and Poetry', published in 1917. The technical advance both poets sought was relaxation from the restraints of form and metre, including rhyme. Pound and Eliot did not sponsor free verse in England, but they developed its capacity to express thoughts and feelings vigorously, through prior experiment with stanza forms. Moreover, they persuaded publishers to print what they wrote. The aim was to retrench 'resonant abstractions' and favour 'definite and concrete' phrasing. What Eliot also learnt from Pound was the arbitrary image, for instance in *Hysteria*: 'her teeth were only *accidental stars* with a *talent for squad-drill*.' There is an American slickness about this, which Eliot later eliminated.

The images of Eliot are not intended to suggest Pre-Raphaelite or Keatsian 'beauty', but to fuse his real, commonplace and fantastic impressions. One idea behind tradition was to get 'as much as possible of the whole weight of the history of the language' behind the word ('The Three Provincialities', *Tyro*, 1922, p. 13). Few poets have provided more personal accounts of preferences and procedures in composition. Among terms over which Eliot's memory faltered were 'the names of feet and metres'; and he claimed in 'The Music of Poetry' (1942) that he never paid much respect to the rules of scansion, because they failed to distinguish for him a good from a bad line. In writing he believed in the method of 'assimilation and imitation', and the former he regarded as a matter of training the ear. A poet one imitates is the kind that invades, for a time, the personality of the imitator.

The true poetic instinct, for Eliot, is the 'auditory imagination', or sensitivity to syllable and rhythm, 'penetrating far below the conscious levels of thought and feeling' (*The Use of Poetry and the Use of Criticism*, 1933, p. 118). Musical verse is not likely to endure, unless meaning is deeply associated with the words used. Choice of words may be inspired, and their order in an effective line may need to be manipulated; but the organization of the poem, as a whole, is what chiefly matters.

rhythm

Yet the language in most of Eliot's poems is not only audacious, but lacking in intelligible connections. As a verbal impressionist, he flouts traditional syntax by introducing phrases that appear to have no grammatical function. The fragmentary style results from terse, conversational sentences, in the manner of Browning; it is very noticeable in the experimental poems, such as *Gerontion*:

1) I was neither at the hot gates / Nor fought in the warm rain / Nor knee deep in the salt marsh, heaving a cutlass, / Bitten by flies, *fought*.
2) In the juvescence of the year / Came Christ the tiger / In depraved May, *dogwood and chestnut, flowering judas,* / To be eaten, to be divided, to be drunk / Among whispers; by Mr Silvero / *With caressing hands,* at Limoges / *Who walked all night in the next room.*

This apparently chaotic style, in which the associations are psychological, arises from mosaic patterns that create the impression of unrelated vignettes. It is the style of evocation, fusing dialogue, statement, allusion and the poet's reflection. In some passages of incantation, for example in *Ash Wednesday*, syntactical ambivalence is without even punctuational signals.

In 'Poetry and Drama' (1951) Eliot offered important hints for the interpretation of his non-dramatic verse:

> I think that one is writing . . . in terms of one's own voice: the way it sounds when you read it to yourself is the test . . . The question of communication, of what the reader will get from it, is not paramount.

In dramatic monologue the poet, he says, is addressing other persons through a mask; and this he maintains in 'The Three Voices of Poetry' (1953), is the style frequently employed in poems with a social purpose, including narrative, didactic verse and satire. In Eliot's case, the difficulty is that the three voices – lyric, monologue and dramatic – may be embodied in one poem, as for instance in *The Waste Land*. In this lecture to the National Book League, Eliot ends with an observation relevant to his own methods:

> If you complain that a poet is obscure, and apparently ignoring you, the reader, or that he is speaking only to a limited circle of initiates from which you are excluded – remember that what he may have been trying to do, was to put something into words which could not be said in any other way, and therefore in a language which may be worth the trouble of learning.
>
> (On *Poetry and Poets*, pp. 101–2)

As a moral poet of the anthropological past of man, Eliot is concerned with 'amalgamating disparate experience'. He has as fine an integrity as Yeats, but a profounder philosophy, though sometimes it is obscured by inscrutability in the motivation. Eliot's championship of impersonality in literature encourages the practice in academic circles of evaluating poems as literary artifacts. Yet he seems to have been unsympathetic to 'words-on-the-page' exegesis of poems, not because he distrusted scientific method, but because these rigorous tutorials might stultify creativity, which springs from emotional life and the experience of the individual. *A Note on War Poetry* (1942) shows the prosaic style he developed in his later non-dramatic verse:

> Mostly the individual
> Experience is too large, or too small. Our emotions
> Are only 'incidents'
>
> In the effort to keep day and night together.
>
> . . . But the abstract conception
> Of private experience at its greatest intensity,
> Becoming universal, which we call 'poetry',
> May be affirmed in verse.
>
> (Complete Poems and Plays, p. 202)

The critical prose of Eliot should not be divorced from the poems on which he was engaged at the time, or from the reading known to have prompted many of the thoughts they express. Important poems in the period 1915 to 1925 were born of personal suffering, which his gay exterior in society belied. *Gerontion, The Waste Land* and *Ash Wednesday* were not only reflections of attitudes to life; what depth of feeling they conceal the reader will not know until further biographical evidence is available, which may explain the genesis of the poems.

In an essay of 1950 'What Dante means to Me' (*To Criticize the Critic,* Faber, 1965), Eliot demonstrates the impact upon his art made first by Laforgue, Baudelaire and others, and then by the author of the *Divina Commedia.* Laforgue first taught him 'the possibilities of [his] own idiom of speech'. From Baudelaire he learnt that 'the business of the poet was to make poetry out of the unexplored resources of the unpoetical'. Through Villon he came to appreciate the value of poetic honesty; from Sappho he studied how to fix 'a particular emotion in the right and the minimum number of words'. But these, in retrospect, were transient influences, compared with the enduring benefits conferred by Dante, the universal, as Eliot illustrates by passages from *The Waste Land* and *Little Gidding.* On page 128 there is a valuable description of the emphatic effect of rhyme in English verse, which modern poets have found it necessary to circumvent. In translation, observes Eliot, 'a different metre is a different mode of thought; it is a different kind of *punctuation*, for the emphases and the breath pauses do not come in the same place' (p. 129). Dante was the most 'painstaking and *conscious* practitioner of the *craft*' of poetry. He realized that 'the poet should be the servant of his language rather than the master of it'; and this realization is in essence the classical ideal. It is the universal poets, like Dante and Shakespeare, who 'give body to the soul of the language'. Eliot continues:

> To pass on to posterity one's own language, more highly developed, more refined, and more precise than it was before one wrote it, that is the highest possible achievement of the poet as poet ... The task of the poet, in making people comprehend the incomprehensible, demands immense resources of language; and in developing the language, enriching the meaning of words and showing how much words can do, he is making possible a much greater range of emotion and perception for other men, because he gives them the speech in which more can be expressed (pp. 133–4)

Eliot never completed his academic career, but secretly married an Englishwoman in 1915, and taught outside London for a year, when his disgruntled father reduced his allowance. In 1917 he joined the Colonial and Foreign Department of Lloyd's Bank, and remained there for the next nine years. To meet his writing commitments, he rose at five in the morning and would often work fourteen hours a day; he was no less burdened when he became Editor of the newly founded quarterly *Criterion* in 1922, under the financial patronage of Lady Rothermere. His health suffered, until he was invited to become a director of the publishing house of Faber and Gwyer, in November 1925. Geoffrey Faber's attempt to secure a Research Fellowship for him at All Souls College, Oxford, unfortunately failed.

THE LOVE SONG OF J. ALFRED PRUFROCK
(from *Prufrock and Other Observations*, 1917)

This mock-heroic poem was first published in the American magazine, *Poetry* VI. 3, in June 1915, and in *Catholic Anthology* in November of the same year. The slender volume of 1917, to which it gave the title, contained eleven other poems, all confirming Eliot as an iconoclast with original ideas. The dedication to Eliot's Parisian friend, Jean Verdenal, and the epigraph borrowed to set the stage, are from Dante's *Purgatorio* and *Inferno* respectively.

The 'Love Song' is not about London psuedo-intellectuals, but the Boston middle-class, at a time when American society seemed to the poet static. A New Englander, whose outlook was coloured by the symbolist poets, and who had recently read the novels of Dostoevsky in French, could be expected to have mixed reactions. Such an introvert as Prufrock, Eliot may have been after his return to Harvard from Paris in 1911.

The style of this tragicomedy of inertia is characteristic of the Imagists, whom Eliot consciously or unconsciously parodies. In *Prufrock* he was in a mood to ridicule his own feelings; the figure and dress of the 'cadaverous humorist' (E. M. Stephenson's phrase) suggest satirical self-portraiture. What could be more natural in the feelings of a young academic who was about to study the writings of F. H. Bradley on the relationship between appearance and reality?

<blockquote>

In the róom the wómen cóme and gó   35
Tálking of Mìchelángelò.

And indéed *there will be time*
To wónder, '*Dò I dáre?*' and, '*Dò I dáre?*'
Time to túrn báck and descénd the stáir,
With a báld spót in the míddle of *my* háir —   40
[*Thèy will sáy*: '*Hòw* his háir is gròwing *thín*!']
My mórning cóat, my cóllar móunting fírmly to the chín,
My nécktìe rích and módest, but assérted by a símple pín —
[*Thèy will sáy*: 'But *hów* his árms and légs are *thín*!']
Dò I dáre   45
Distúrb the únivèrse?
In a *mínute* there is *tíme*
For *decísions* and *revísions* which a *mínute* will revérse.

For I *have known them all already, known them all* —
Have known the *evenings, mornings*, afternoons,   50
I have measured out *my* life with coffee spoons;
I know the voices *dying* with a *dying* fall
Beneath the music from a farther room.
    So *how should I presume*?   54

       · · ·

And *would it have been worth* it, *after all,*   99
Would it have been worth while,

</blockquote>

After the sunsets and the dooryards and the sprinkled
    streets,
After the novels, *after* the teacups, *after* the skirts that
    trail along the floor —
And this, and so much more? —
It is impossible to say just what I mean!
But as if a magic lantern threw the nerves in patterns on a
    screen: 105
Would it have been worth while
If one, settling a pillow or throwing off a shawl,
And turning toward the window, should say:
  '*That is not* it *at all*,
   That is not what I meant, *at all*.'   110
    . . .

I grow old . . . I grow old . . .   120
I shall wear the bottoms of my *trousers* rolled.
Shall *I* part my hair behind? *Do I dare* to eat a peach?
I shall wear white flannel *trousers*, and walk upon the beach.
I have heard the mermaids *singing, each* to *each*.

I do not think that they will *sing* to me.   125

I have seen them riding *sea*ward on the *waves*
Combing the *white* hair of the *waves* blown back
When the wind blows the water *white* and black.
We have lingered in the chambers of the *sea*
By *sea*-girls wreathed with *sea*weed red and brown   130
Till human voices wake us, and we drown.

The technique of the 'Love Song' is typical of Eliot's earliest method of presentation; it is a mosaic of ideas and feelings, in which emotion is fathered by thought, and thought transformed into sensation. Eliot was concerned not only to imitate, but to extend, the conceits of metaphysical poets; their Jacobean irony is cunningly interwoven with Pope's Augustan objectivity.

Prufrock, meditating upon the fatuity of existence, is recognized as a self-conscious misfit of middle-age, about to pop the 'overwhelming question' to a lady with whom he probably had little affinity. The situation is Jamesian, and Grover Smith believes it was suggested by Henry James's 'Crapy Cornelia', published in *Harper's Magazine* in 1909. But Prufrock's tragedy goes deeper, and is more like the self-laceration of Hamlet; his

monologue reveals a private hell from which there is no escape
through the fantasies, to which he is all too prone. The first half
of the poem (lines 1–69) recounts the victim's fearful anticipation
of his proposal, the second (70–131) offers retrospective excuses
for his failure.

The poem opens with an exhortation:

> Let us go then, *you and I,*
> When the evening is spread out against the sky
> *Like a patient etherised upon a table*

The much-quoted image (3) is more relevant to Prufrock than to
the vesperal setting. *You and I,* and the final *we* of line 129, hint
that the pronouns represent the tragic figure's two selves, the
amorous and the timid, whose turpitude is at the root of his
indecision. Notice how cleverly Eliot exploits assonance, as
well as hesitant vagueness, in *indecisions, visions* and *revisions* (32–3).
In the complex image of the 'yellow fog', conveyed in two passages
(15–25 and 75–8) by analogy with a cat, there are suggestions of the
shabby quarter of Prufrock's residence; while the reference to
Michelangelo (13–14, 35–36) supplies the pseudo-cultural am-
bience of his destination. Among Renaissance rhetoricians, the
descriptions of place and time in the opening paragraphs of
Prufrock were known as *pragmatographia* and *chronographia*.

The dramatic monologue contains 131 lines, in eighteen free-
verse paragraphs, varying from one to thirteen lines, determined
by the semantic connections. The lines themselves are of unequal
length, and usually end-stopped; there appear to be only nine
instances of enjambement. It is a feature of Eliot's verse that
metrical pauses should be strongly felt; they help to secure the
rhythmical interpretation he requires. Rhyme predominates, but
there is no evidence of a stanzaic pattern. Sometimes Eliot favours
couplets, sometimes alternate rhyme; and there are sporadic unrhymed lines, to achieve the uninhibited movement of the verse.
The effect is that of natural speech, and the rhythm is unimpaired
by prosaic elements in the language. The result is a frequency of
syllables with secondary stress, and there are numerous extra unstressed syllables. The modifying influence upon rhythm of such
juxtapositions as *go* / Michelang*elo* is as cleverly managed by
Eliot as by Yeats. He is judicious in the use of polysyllables, a
good example being line 116 *Politic, cautious and meticulous.*

The word-choice, in general, is impeccably lucid, and the syntax of the common order, except for occasional archaisms, as in 107-8 'If *one*, settling a pillow . . . / . . . should say'. Syntactical continuity is in contrast to the discontinuity of impressions and ideas. The conjunction *And* begins no less than 21 lines, and seven of the uses introduce verse-paragraphs. It is therefore of some importance to study the logical connection of Eliot's transitions. After each of the introductory paragraphs there is the choric interpolation: 'In the room the women come and go / Talking of Michelangelo'. To link the major paragraphs, Eliot employs the rhetorical device of *ploce* (sporadic word repetition), which is more significant than rhyme; it acts as a cohesive force in sustaining the rhythm. *Prufrock* would not be the kind of poem it is without the poet's resources of word play, demonstrated by my use of italics in the passages selected.

The key-word at the beginning of the poem (lines 23–39) is *time*; the word is so insistent that it appears ten times in paragraphs 3 and 4. Georges Poulet in *Studies in Human Time* (Johns Hopkins Press, 1950) shows how tendentious a role time plays in writers who draw on the resources of memory, such as Montaigne, Flaubert, Proust, James and Eliot. Eliot's criticism abounds in phrases such as 'the wisdom of time' and 'the pastness of the past'; and he speaks in his poetry of 'redeeming' time (cf. *Ephesians* V, 16 and *Colossians* IV, 5) of its 'partial ecstasies', and warns us that 'time is no healer'.

So important is repetition in Eliot's verbal monotone that it is worth examining. There are repetitions within the paragraph, and there are echoes that link each paragraph to its successor. Here are some obvious uses of *epanaphora, ploce* and *epiphora* (different manipulations of repeated words):

Paragraph 1 *Let us go* (1, 4) – link-word *evening* (2, 17)
Paragraph 2 *The yellow, that rubs, window-panes* (15, 16) – link-words *yellow smoke* (16) and *its back upon the window-panes* (15, 25)
Paragraph 3 *There will be time* (23, 26, 28)
   face and *meet* (27)
   hundred (32, 33)
   visions (33) –
   link words *there will be time* (28, 37) *decisions, revisions* (33, 48)
Paragraph 4 *Do I dare* (38, 45)

They will say and *thin* (41, 44)
minute (47, 48)
my (40, 42, 43)
hair (40, 41) –
link words, *my* (43, 51) *morning* (42, 50) and *how* (44, 54)

In paragraph 5, there are permutations of words from the group *I have known them all* in lines 49–51, while 52 repeats *dying*, and 54 contains the linking question *how should I presume?* Rhetorical questions of this kind (*erotema*) are a feature of the poem. The reader may trace repetitive patterns of words, phrases and sentences throughout the poem; they are conducive to many antithetical structures, such as 'though I have *wept and fasted, wept and prayed*' (81), to assonances and alliterations too numerous to mention.

Eliot's technique is throughout schematic in word and thought. The following are instances of his proficiency in the devices of rhetoric:

(*a*) Words
  Eclipsis: 111 No! I am not Prince Hamlet, nor was meant to be; / ₐAm an attendant lord
(*b*) Schemes of Thought
  Ecphonesis: 11 *Oh, do not ask*, 'What is it?'
  Synathroismus (Congeries): 115–17 Deferential, glad to be of use, / Politic, cautious, and meticulous; / Full of high sentence, but a bit obtuse;

The tropes are among the most inventive in modern poetry:

Metonymy: 2 evening is *spread out against the sky*; 51 I have *measured out* my life *with coffee spoons*; 85 the *eternal* Footman
Simile: 3 *like a patient etherised upon a table* (this image is a blend of suggestions from Laforgue and Baudelaire)
Personification: 5–6 *muttering* retreats / Of *restless* nights
Hyperbole: 45–6 Do I dare / *Disturb the universe*?
Metaphor: 56 The eyes that *fix you in a formulated phrase*; 60 To *spit out all the butt-ends* of my days; 92 To have *squeezed the universe into a ball* (the last adapted from Marvell's *To His Coy Mistress*).

Eliot's satirical poems usually contain scornful portraits of types

that American society labels 'screwballs'; their oddities are cari-
catured in verbal strokes, daring as they are controversial. What
the highlights signify is left to the interpretation of the individual
reader. The French flavour in these touches was derived from
Baudelaire and his successors, who parodied vague romanticism.
Eliot's symbolist reminiscences and concealed allusions are found
in most paragraphs of *Prufrock*:

8–9 Streets that follow like a *tedious argument | Of insidious intent*

16–17 The yellow smoke . . . | *Licked its tongue into the corners of
the evening*

29–30 And time for all the *works and days of hands | That lift and
drop a question on your plate* (Eliot thinks of Hesiod, Marvell and
Ecclesiastes III, 1–8)

52–3 I know the voices *dying with a dying fall | Beneath the music*
from a farther room (Suggested by Orsino's opening speech
in *Twelfth Night*)

60 *To spit out all the butt-ends* of my days and ways

73–4 I should have been a pair of ragged claws / Scuttling across
the floors of silent seas

82 Though I have seen my head [grown slightly bald] *brought in
upon a platter* (suggested by *Mark* I, 17–28)

105 But as if a magic lantern threw the *nerves in patterns* on a
screen

124–5 I have heard the mermaids singing, each to each. / I do not
think that they will sing to me. (A recollection of Donne's
'Song', combined with an experience of the hero in Homer's
Odyssey)

129 We have lingered in the *chambers of the sea.*

To give rational meaning to such lines in context is not feasible,
nor is the reader invited to try. Their function is to stimulate
feelings of revulsion, approval, surprise or wonder, based on the
sensitive reader's knowledge of life, as well as the breadth of his
reading. Most are *ad hoc* images of an 'interior monologue',
contributing to the mosaic of impressions, and felt to be relevant
to the tone of *Prufrock,* as set by the epigraph. This clue depicts
Guido, imprisoned in flame in the Eighth Chasm of Hell, the
punishment for giving untrustworthy advice to the Pope.

Prufrock is a study in frustration and accidie; the images of the
sea and drowning in the conclusion indicate the willing sub-

mergence of the subjective, and perhaps the a-sexual, personality. It is impossible to say of any poem how much of the experience that prompted it is autobiographical; but it is noteworthy that Eliot, in a document attached to his will, desired that no biographers should be given any encouragement. His reticence is likely to prove a deliberate deterrent in solving the obscurity of some of his poems. Writing of 'death's dream kingdom' in *The Hollow Men,* he confides: 'Let me also wear / Such *deliberate disguises* / . . . / Behaving as the wind behaves'.

Eliot's early poems reveal a spiritual dryness, and the treatment of many themes is seemingly passionless, despite their lyrical form. The poet skilfully depersonalized his experience, in order to transform it to the kind of material suitable for his poetry. Transmogrification was desirable for other reasons: intellectually he lived in the past, but his intention was to adapt his thinking (*eg*, on the religious background of Dante) to the needs of a contemporary generation. As Eliot himself said, 'the great poet . . . in writing himself, writes his time' ('Shakespeare and the Stoicism of Seneca', *Selected Essays*, p. 137). There is an interesting passage in the first chapter of Eliot's *Knowledge and Experience*, which reads:

> The majority of feelings have never succeeded in invading our minds to such an extent as completely to fill it; they have from first to last some objectivity. . . . To say that one part of the mind suffers and another part reflects upon the suffering is perhaps to talk in fictions. But we know that those highly-organized beings who are able to objectify their passions, and as passive spectators to contemplate their joys and torments, are also those who suffer and enjoy the most keenly. . .
>
> Our ordinary speech declares that two people may share the same feeling as well as regard the same object. Yet we persist in believing that about feelings there is something private, that we cannot 'know' them from the outside; although we are compelled to admit that often an observer understands a feeling better than does the person who experiences it. . . So far as feelings are merely felt, they are neither subjective nor objective. (p. 23–4).

In phrases as precise and appropriate as those of Pound's master Flaubert, Eliot in his early poems captured the sordidness and vulgarity, but also the pathos, of *fin-de-siècle* city life. This was a remarkable achievement for a brash New Englander, simultaneously infected and appalled by the decadence of Europe. The memorable shock of a cultured Puritan's reactions would not, however, have been possible without the lucid exposition learnt (as he admits) from his tutor, Harold Joachim, at Oxford, and the innate knack of recognizing the relatively true and the absolutely false in the viewpoints of philosophy.

Eliot was the first English-speaking philosopher to give sensitive expression to illusory experience through poetry; and this may account for the uniqueness of his position in literature. Prufrock can be appreciated as a disillusioned solipsist confronted with the disagreeable realities of a materialistic world, and thoroughly bored with the inanities of tea-parties. Browning had not the academic training to create such a dramatic monologue, whose tropes and schemes of thought convey the character's confused subjectivisms. Professor George Gordon's typical contemporary reaction to Eliot, that he is 'neither English nor American, but a little absurdly French' (see 'Poetry and the Moderns', *The Discipline of Letters*, p. 121) only reveals that academic specialists, too, may live in an enclosed world. *Knowledge and Experience* is an indispensable book; and if Eliot in 1964 said that he did not pretend to understand his own thesis, this was because, as a poet, he had outlived its abstract terminology.

Eliot came to believe that a complex civilization, 'playing upon a refined sensibility', compels the poet to become more 'allusive' and 'indirect' ('The Metaphysical Poets, *Selected Essays,* p. 289). Difficulties in his own poems, beginning with *Prufrock,* do not result from obscurity of expression, but from the allusive and fragmentary development of themes, so diffused in time and reference as to disturb the disciplined consciousness of the reader. The linguistic relations are neither narrative in sequence nor logical, but imagist and rhetorical, using both the latter words in the sense of the functional, not the artificial, employment of figures of speech. These figures give the early poems design, whether they were written in *vers libre* that is not so free, or in a precise stanza form. A memorable dictum from 'The Music of Poetry' (1942) is that 'only a bad poet could welcome free verse as a liberation from form'. Nobody saw more plainly that Eliot that free verse offers no excuse for indifferent writing. *(sp)*

GERONTION
(from *Poems*, 1920)

This poem, composed in London in 1919, was intended by Eliot as an introduction to *The Waste Land*. Ezra Pound, however, believed the association would not be to the advantage of either poem, though both were in a tone of spiritual aridity, here suggested by the key phrases *in a dry month* and *waiting for rain*. The epigraph, 'Thou hast nor youth nor age / But as it were an after dinner sleep / Dreaming of both', comes from the Duke's speech to Claudio in Act III, scene 1, of *Measure for Measure*; and the opening lines of the poem were taken, with slight modification, from a letter in A. C. Benson's life of *Edward FitzGerald* (1905). The *hot gates* of the first paragraph point to Thermopylae, where the Greeks opposed the Persians in 480 BC; but the ostensible reference to Gerontion, as a non-combatant, implies those who did not participate in the First World War. The Greek title *Gerontion* means 'little old man'. Permissive societies are, to him, nothing new; but the latest recurrence springs from the aftermath of war; as a scrutator, he has observed man through two millennia.

The poem consists entirely of the comments and reflections of a *persona*. The poet does not speak in his own voice, but uses the mask figure as a commentator upon life and religion, especially the negative attitudes of unredeemed and superstitious Christians. They, and those who have made the naturalism of sex a religion, are responsible for the world's corruption and desolation, symbolized in the 'decayed house' Gerontion inhabits. The subsidiary theme of 'sterility', indicated by sexual symbolism, is a parallel one, and related to man's loss of faith. The rationalizing voice of the old man seems to be that of a Greek stoic, whose role is passively sceptical. This type (characteristically blind) Gerontion suggests has had a disrupting effect throughout history. The poem should be read preferably in conjunction with Eliot's other critiques of Christian civilization, *The Hippopotamus* and *Mr Eliot's Sunday Morning Service,* in the same volume. The stream-of-consciousness technique owes much to the methods of Proust and Joyce in fiction.

> Here I am, an *old man* in a dry month,
> Being read to by a boy, waiting for rain. . .

My *house* is a decayed *house,*
And the Jew squats on the window sill, the owner, . . .
      I an *old man,*   5
A dull head among windy spaces.

Signs are taken for wonders. 'We would see a *sign!*'
The *word* within a *word,* unable to speak a *word,*
Swaddled with darkness . . .
      I have no ghosts,   10
An *old man* in a draughty *house*
Under a windy knob.

After such knowledge, what forgiveness? *Think now*
History has many cunning passages, contrived corridors
And issues, deceives with *whispering* ambitions,   15
Guides us by vanities. *Think now*
She *gives* when our attention is distracted
And what she *gives, gives* with such supple confusions
That the *giving* famishes the craving. *Gives* too late
What's not *believed* in, or if still *believed,*   20
In memory only, reconsidered passion. *Gives* too soon
Into weak hands, *what's* thought can be dispensed with
Till the refusal propagates a fear. *Think*
Neither fear nor courage saves us. Unnatural vices
Are fathered by our heroism. Virtues   25
Are forced upon us by our impudent crimes.
These tears are shaken from the wrath-bearing tree . . .
      Think at lást
Í *have* nòt máde this shów púrposelessly
And it is nót by ány còncitátion   30
Of the báckward dévils.
Í would méet you upòn this hónestly.
Í that was néar your heárt was remóved therefróm
To lòse beáuty in *térror, térror in* ìnquistítion.
Ì *have lóst* my pássion: whý should I néed to kéep it   35
Since whát is képt múst be adúlteràted?
Ì *have lóst* my síght, sméll, heáring, táste and tóuch:
Hów should I úse them for your clóser cóntact?

These with a thousand small deliberations
Protract the profit of their chilled delirium,   40

Excite the membrane, when the sense has cooled,
With pungent sauces, multiply variety
In a wilderness of mirrors. . .
                              Tenants of the *house,*
Thoughts of a *dry* brain in a *dry* season.   45

When one grasps that *Gerontion* is principally concerned with the
distintegrating effects of humanism, and that the allusions have to
be pursued to their sources, the discontinuous impressions fall
into place. In the order of their appearance, the more important
allusions are:

Signs are taken for wonders and *The word within a word, unable to speak
    a word* (Lancelot Andrewes, Christmas sermon, 1618; based on
    Matthew XII, 38 and *John* I, 1).
Christ the tiger (Blake, *The Tiger,* penultimate stanza, from *Songs of
    Experience*).
In depraved May, dogwood and chestnut, flowering judas (*The Education
    of Henry Adams,* p. 268).
To be eaten, to be divided, to be drunk (A reference to the Christian
    Communion Service).
Vacant shuttles weave the wind (*Job* VII, 6–7).
Multiply variety / *In a wilderness of mirrors* (Jonson, *The Alchemist,*
    1612, II, 1).
whirled / *Beyond the circuit of the shuddering Bear* (Chapman, *Bussy
    D'Ambois* V.4).

There are other echoes in *Gerontion* from Tourneur, *The Revenger's
Tragedy*; Middleton, *The Changeling*; Shakespeare, *The Merchant of
Venice* and *Antony and Cleopatra*. An interesting sidelight appears
in a letter from Dorothy Wellesely to W. B. Yeats, dated July
4, 1936, which reads:

But Eliot, that man isn't modern. He wrings the past dry and
pours the juice down the throats of those who are either too
busy, or too creative to read as much as he does. I believe that
in time to come he will be regarded as an interesting symptom
of a sick and melancholy age. He has written lovely things.
I always ask myself however (being limited in learning) 'Is this
or that cribbed from a Greek, an Indian, a Spaniard, anyone you
like?' He is not perhaps influenced by the past, he being at
pains to tell us so. The question is: *does he crib*?

Eliot should not be regarded as an imitator, who adapts or parodies technical effects. Borrowings are assimilated to his matter and rhythm in a way that suits them to the new setting, as appropriately as to the original. The *tiger* identified with Christ is an extraordinary symbol of God's power. 'May' is a *depraved* month, because it is the time of the crucifixion, and also the spring of the year when sensual beauty induces the spirit to hanker after the flesh. The allegorical personages that conclude this paragraph, Mr Silvero, Hakagawa, Madame de Tornquist and Fräulein von Kulp, represent modern surrogates for religion. The ghostly presences of the Jewish landlord and Judas Iscariot, just hinted at, are significant in Gerontion's dream of the Decline of the West; history's 'cunning passages' and 'contrived corridors' are Dantesque mazes for sinners guided by their 'vanities'. The poet concurs with Adams that history, without a spiritual centre, leads inevitably to chaos. The *wrath-bearing tree* (27) is generally thought to refer to the Tree of the Knowledge of Good and Evil, but may it not look back to the *flowering judas* of an earlier line, and therefore to the hanging of Christ's betrayer? The *backward devils* of line 31 recall the diviners and sorcerers of Dante's *Inferno*.

This broad interpretation of *Gerontion's* purpose provides a meaning at only one level. The condensed syntax and masterly adaptation of Jacobean blank verse to modern needs are the poem's true merits. There is a noticeable transition with the line beginning 'After such knowledge, what forgiveness', where a vigorous infusion of Elizabethan eloquence occurs. Note the inversion of word order (*hyperbaton*), in the sentence Us he devours.

The best analysis of the language of *Gerontion* is J. C. Ransom's in *T. S. Eliot, The Man and his Work* (ed. Allen Tate, Chatto and Windus, 1967). He draws attention to the symphonic structure of the poem, corresponding in miniature to the musical form adopted in *The Waste Land, Ash Wednesday* and *Four Quartets,* which are Eliot's most valued compositions. The five movements have 16, 16, 15, 13 and 15 lines, each with a final coda of two lines, except in the third, which has only one. Ransom observes the wealth of new rhythms that are merged by Eliot's 'unified sensibility'. He likens *Gerontion* to the singing verse of the *Greek Anthology*, with the stresses sounding 'loud and clear'.

Musical form certainly contributes to harmonies that have a distinct Elizabethan ring, as illustrated in lines 28 to 38 of the selection. The beats are varied in number and location; but the pentameter measure never gets out of control. One enjambed line (30) in eleven is a low proportion, the rhythm being completed in the truncated line 31, which has only six syllables. Brisk sentences have an Horatian simplicity of statement and conciseness; the punctuational pauses are nicely calculated for delivery, three being caesural (33, 34, 35). The unique line (37) seems to use more than five primary stresses, but has three internal pauses.

The rhythmical progression shows how closely Eliot had studied the movement of Jacobean dramatic verse, especially Tourneur's and Middleton's. The effects of natural speech are secured partly by trochaic substitution in the dominantly iambic measure, which may be seen in lines 29, 32, 33, 34, 35, 37 and 38; and partly by the use of polysyllabic line terminals: *concitation* (30), *devils* (31), *inquisition* (34), *adulterated* (36), *contact* (38). The same nuance is achieved by the feminine ending in *keep it* (35). Ransom called *purposelessly* (29) 'a grammarian's cacophony, twice compounded of sibilants too difficult to pronounce briefly before the following *l's*'. There are analogies in plenty among the Jacobean dramatists. Eliot regarded their art as 'impure', but considered Tourneur and Middleton to be 'masters of versification'.

Gerontion's musical continuity is inseparable from the meaning of its words. Continuity does not here imply 'smoothness', but coherence arising from intensive care of the phrasing. Sometimes the movement is halted by this intensity; at others, a prosaic patch is introduced to relax the verse. Eliot chose to sectionalize the poem's development into 'movements', in order to secure different rhythmical patterns; the scope of his practice goes far beyond the traditional methods of modulating the individual line. *Gerontion* avoids pastiche by harmonizing a number of disparate techniques.

The poem contains the germ of most of Eliot's future experiments, not the least being incantation, in such lines as 7–8:

> We would see a sign!
> The *word* within a *word*, unable to speak a *word*,
> Swaddled with darkness.

His delight in slow elegiac rhythms of this kind stems from the sermons and prayers of Lancelot Andrewes, who drew his inspiration from the poetic books of the Old Testament, especially *Job*,

Ecclesiastes and the *Psalms*. The *Preces Privatae* of Andrewes, published in an all-English version by Methuen in 1908, abounds in examples of leisurely expanding rhythms, whose art is the parallelism of words, phrases, clauses and ideas. Andrewes so presented his lines as to draw attention to their structural and mnemonic design. In his disposition, time stops were of some liturgical importance. For example, take this prayer on *Penitence*:

> *Deep* calleth unto *deep,*
> the *deep* of our *misery* unto the *deep* of thy *mercy*
> Where sin *abound*ed let grace much more *abound*:
> overcome our *evil* with thy *good*:
> let *thy mercy* rejoice against *thy iustice*
>   in our sins.
>   Yea, o Lord,
>   for above *all things* and before *all things*
>   I believe . . .

In contrast to this acquired respect for ritual, Eliot elected to employ foreign-sounding names, such as *Hakagawa, De Bailhache, Fresca* and *Mrs Cammel,* whose pronunciation might be vague, but for the rhythm of his verse. Charles Grandgent in his book *Dante* suggested that this derives from the Florentine's choice of contemporary public figures, rather than allegorical abstractions, to symbolize the Seven Deadly Sins. In dramatic monologue, concrete examples are much more vivid than abstract names, such as 'Christian' in the narrative prose of *Pilgrim's Progress.*

As usual, a dominant feature of Eliot's structural practice is the use of rhetorical devices:

Tropes:
Metaphor: 6 *A dull head among windy spaces*; 9 *Swaddled with darkness*; 33 I that was *near your heart* was *removed*; 38 How should I use them for your *closer contact*; 40 Protract the *profit of their chilled delirium*; 41 When the sense has *cooled*; 42 *With pungent sauces multiply variety*; 43 a *wilderness of mirrors*; 45 Thoughts of a *dry* brain
Personification: 14 *cunning* passages: 15 *whispering* ambitions; 25 Unnatural vices / Are *fathered* by our heroism; 19 the giving *famishes* the craving; 26 *impudent* crimes
Metonymy: 10 I have *no ghosts*; 14 History has many cunning *passages, contrived corridors*; 27 These tears are shaken from the

wrath-bearing tree; 44 *Tenants* of the house, / Thoughts
Hyperbole: 37 I have lost my sight, smell, hearing, taste and touch (The loss of five senses is incompatible with Gerontion's cynical intelligence).

Schemes of Words

Ploce (sporadic repetition): *old man* (1, 5, 11); *house* (4, 11, 44); *sign* (7 twice); *word* (8 three times); *I have* (10, 29, 35, 37); *Think now* (13, 17); *Gives* (19, 21); *believed* (20 twice); *what's* (20, 22); *Think* (23, 28); *lost* (35, 37); *dry* (45 twice).
Anadiplosis: 18 And what she *gives, gives* with such supple confusions; 34 To lose beauty in *terror, terror* in inquisition
Polyptoton: 19 That the *giving* famishes the craving. *Gives* too late

Schemes of Thought

Erotema (rhetorical question): 13 After such knowledge what forgiveness?; 38 How should I use them for your closer contact?
Hypophora (the question is answered): 35–6 I have lost my passion: why should I need to keep it / *Since what is kept must be adulterated*?

Among the most useful comments on the use of tropes in poetry, is the following by G. T. Wright (*The Poet in the Poem*, University of California Press, 1962, pp. 23–9):

> Inseparable from literature is its use of rhetorical devices, and inseparable from their use is the art of dissimulation ... Of course, there is a sense in which some of these misstatements may be true ... Such uses possess the validation not only of conventional practice but also of a part of the mind which may have as good a right to the term 'truth' as any other part of the mind ... The scientific verifiability of the fact is nothing compared with the poetic rightness of the image. But the two worlds are in conflict ... The form of the poem is superior to the struggle: appearances notwithstanding, order triumphs over anarchy ... Poet and reader meet together at that point of vision from which the meaning of the poem becomes most clear and most comprehensive.

Though a final meaning is seldom assignable to Eliot's poems, the reason is neither loose syntax nor a limited vocabulary.

Obscurity results from the symbolical juxtaposition of impressions, and the interaction of thoughts and emotions. There is but one coinage in *Gerontion,* besides the title; it occurs in the phrase *'juvescence* of the year', where Eliot needed a trisyllabic form of *juvenescence* to find the right nuance of rhythm. Ransom observes that the normal Latin contraction would have been *junescence,* which is paralleled in the comparative *junior* from *juvenior* (p. 146). The word-choice here and elsewhere suggests that Eliot wanted to create a style with an Elizabethan flavour, while modernizing the versification, and giving it what Donald Davie calls 'prosaic strength'.

Both Ransom and B. C. Southam (*A Student's Guide to the Selected Poems of T. S. Eliot,* Faber, 1968, p. 46) are in error in supposing that *concitation* (30) meaning 'rousing', 'stirring up', was an innovation. According to the Oxford English Dictionary the word was coined by Erasmus in the English version of his *Playne and godly exposytion of the commune crede* (1533), and used by Florio in translating Montaigne (1603), as well as by Thomas Stanley in the *History of Philosophy* (1656). The verb *concitate* was a back-formation from the noun in 1574. Eliot must have come across this abstract term in his Elizabethan studies, and revived it. In the same way he resuscitated the obsolete word *merds* ('dung') in the memorable line 'Rocks, moss, stonecrop, iron, *merds',* a Shakespearian or Miltonic collocation of nouns, known to the rhetoricians as *schesis onomaton.* This fifteenth-century borrowing, from Latin *merda,* was another technical term, occurring in Act II, sc. 3 of Jonson's *The Alchemist,* and again in Burton's *Anatomy of Melancholy* (1621). In the powerfully suggestive line 'Spawned in some *estaminet* in Antwerp', the word means a 'café in which smoking is allowed' (Oxford English Dictionary). Southam indicates that the word was 'brought into English by soldiers returning from France and Belgium during the First World War'. But it was used by Thackeray in *Vanity Fair,* and was in fairly common employment in the nineteenth century, both in England and the United States. *Knob* (12), meaning a 'rounded hill', seems to be a dialect word of mid-seventeenth-century vintage, rarely used except in Southern American English (see the examples in OED, p. 737).

Eliot gained two of his principal objectives in *Gerontion*: 'a rhythm close to contemporary speech' and 'a form of verse in which everything can be said which has to be said'. The elements of his innovation are complex; but so are the definitions of poetry, feeling, emotion and sensation in published utterances. Eliot's deliberate eclecticism is paradoxically the measure of his individuality. A few discriminating critics, such as Leonard Unger (*Moments and Patterns*, Minnesota University Press, 1956) have noticed that he owes his characteristic rhythms as much to the early novels of Conrad, as to Laforgue; and Unger makes the important point that it is truer to speak of Eliot's 'voice' than his style.

THE WASTE LAND, 1922

It had not been practicable to discuss the textual history of this poem, until the *Facsimile and Transcript of the Original Drafts* was edited by Mrs Valerie Eliot (Faber, 1971). Her introduction gives a full account of the circumstances that led to Eliot's donation of the manuscripts and typescripts to John Quinn, a New York lawyer and collector, whose heirs later sold the documents, once thought to be lost, to the New York Public Library. Ezra Pound was the person responsible for the short-lived relationship between the poet and his patron, who died in July 1924. Pound also shaped the poem's destiny in a way that Eliot gratefully acknowledged, when he said in 1938 that his friend turned *The Waste Land* 'from a jumble of good and bad passages into a poem'. It appeared in *The Criterion*, London, in October 1922, and in *The Dial,* New York, in November of the same year; from the latter he received a timely award of two thousand dollars, which he generously suggested should go to *il miglior fabbro*. In these terms Eliot dedicated the poem to Pound, quoting Dante's tribute to the Provençal poet, Arnaut Daniel, in Canto XXVI of the *Purgatorio*.

When, thanks to Quinn, *The Waste Land* first appeared as a book in 1922, the New York publishers, Boni and Livewright, asked Eliot for additional matter to fill up the awkward blank pages, and through this contingency the 'notes' appended to the poem, fortunately or unfortunately, saw the light. In captious reviews, Eliot afterwards said, these notes received more attention than the poetry. Eliot wrote in July 1922: 'I only hope the printers are not allowed to bitch the punctuation and the spacing, as that is very important for the sense'.

The bulk of the poem was written during three months' con-
valescence, between October and December 1921, after a breakdown caused by nervous tension and overwork. The first month
Eliot spent at Cliftonville, near Margate, a period of emotional
upset (as the poem records) when he 'could connect nothing with
nothing'. But at a sanatorium in Lausanne, he was so much better
that he could add to some poems composed in the last seven years,
most of the new writing. Returning to England in January 1922,
he stopped over in Paris to seek Pound's advice on the manuscript
of nineteen pages (Pound's statement). The documents edited
nearly fifty years later by Mrs Eliot consisted of 54 leaves (without
notes), divided into two sections, the main text (42 leaves), and
some miscellaneous poems (12 leaves); all was tentatively offered
for inclusion in *The Waste Land,* which Eliot intended should be
elucidated by an epigraph selected from Conrad's *Heart of Darkness.* This material incorporated duplicated lines and fair copies.

When Pound examined the draft, what appealed to him
instantly was the collection's 'cinematographic' technique,
reminding him of the verse of Laforgue's disciple, Jean Cocteau.
As Pound was among the first to write approvingly of James
Joyce, he must have been aware that the technique was also indebted to the rapidly changing focus of *Ulysses,* the early chapters
of which had appeared while Eliot was assistant editor of the
Egoist. Writing on a new edition of *A Portrait of the Artist as a
Young Man* (The *Future,* May 1918) Pound commented on the
author's 'swift alternation of subjective beauty and external
shabbiness . . . Disgust with the sordid (he said) is but another
expression of a sensitiveness to the finer thing'. These observations are as apt for *The Waste Land,* particularly the last scene in 'A
Game of Chess'.

The following is the allocation of lines in the five parts of *The
Waste Land,* as published, showing the extent of the writing in the
original draft in brackets. The facsimile reveals that parts I and II
were in typescript; parts III, IV and V, as well as the miscellaneous poems, were in both manuscript and typescript:

I *The Burial of the Dead* 76 (130); II *A Game of Chess* 97 (98); III *The
Fire Sermon* 138 (193); IV *Death by Water* 10 (93); V *What the
Thunder Said* 112 (117). Totals: 433 (631).
Miscellaneous Poems: *The Death of St Narcissus* (40); *Song* (15);

Exequy (30); *Death of the Duchess* (73); *Elegy* (24); *Dirge* (17); *Those are Pearls that were his Eyes* (5). Total (204).

Not more than 835 lines were, therefore, submitted for Pound's scrutiny, and of these he recommended the excision of about 400. The decision to delete passages was finally made by Eliot himself. One title, 'He do the Police in Different Voices' was at first placed at the head of parts I and II; but the subtitle of the latter, originally 'In the Cage', was changed by Eliot to 'A Game of Chess', from Middleton's play. The original drafts contain a number of marginal comments and suggestions, chiefly by Pound; but there are a few in a different hand which were made by Eliot's first wife.

As the poet accepted Pound's judgement in nearly every instance, it is worth considering the undoubtedly wise principles of condensation. The first considerable passage to be forfeited by Eliot himself contained 54 graphic lines of low comedy in the style of *Ulysses*. The incidents, as Mrs Eliot's editorial notes show (p. 125), recall Eliot's adolescence in Boston. This rambling, reminiscential opening, with interspersed dialogue, is in the colourful language of Sweeney, a local bar-tender. Pound may have felt that this voice was more economically and incisely represented in lines 139–172 of the poem, which end part II, 'A Game of Chess'. But Pound's improvement of the dialect speech, by changing 'Something of that' to '*Somethink o*' that', Eliot resisted: 'I want to avoid trying to show pronunciation by spelling'.

Detailed marginal notes are provided in 'A Game of Chess'. Pound did not appreciate what Eliot had in mind in emulating the Shakespearian passage where Enobarbus describes Cleopatra's majestic image in her barge (*Antony and Cleopatra* II.ii.190). He found the rhythm of line 101 'Filled all the desert with inviolable voice' too 'penty', meaning perhaps that it was too cunningly modulated in the Jacobean iambic pentameter tradition. An archaic construction in line 22 of the draft he considered its 'weakest point'; it contained the subjunctive clause *you had thought* for 'you'd have thought'; this line Eliot finally jettisoned.

Pound was enthusiastic about the second passage that imitated Joyce, beginning 'When Lil's husband was *demobbed*. . .'. The slang participle was his suggestion; for Eliot had written '*coming back out of* the Transport Corps'. His eye immediately detected an anachronism in 'closed *carriage*' for *taxi* (line 61) and Eliot complied by supplying the word *car* (136).

The next long elimination was the first 70 lines of 'The Fire Sermon', in mock-heroic couplets to simulate Pope's *Rape of the Lock*. Eliot was rather partial to this *tour de force*, but Pound objected: 'Pope has done this so well that you cannot do it better; and if you mean this as a burlesque, you had better suppress it, for you cannot parody Pope unless you can write better verse than Pope – and you can't' (Introduction to *Selected Poems of Ezra Pound*, p. xxi). The abandoned lines were replaced by ten new ones, with which part III opens in the published text.

'*Demotic* French' (212) was gratefully accepted, to replace Eliot's less fortunate adjective *abominable*. Another cut (instigated by Pound) consisted of some twenty lines before and after the paragraph commencing 'Unreal City' (207); the draft reveals such hesitation in its many changes, that the sacrifice may have come as a relief. The Highbury lines (292–3) Eliot also considerably reduced.

The Tiresias episode, beginning with line 215, was originally in quatrains, which received Pound's uninhibited censure. Eliot complied by curtailing 68 lines to 42, which appear in the published version as free verse, with an irregular rhyming pattern. Pound's well-grounded reasons were that the verse in quatrains was 'not interesting enough . . . to warrant so much of it'; one line came too easily, another was vaguely indecisive; a third had an inversion of word order 'not warranted by any real *exegiency* (*sic*) of the metre'.

'Death by Water' opened with a passage of 83 lines, in which Eliot relived his youthful sailing adventures off the Dry Salvages; it was too sprawling and personal to be relevant to the apparent theme of *The Waste Land,* namely to reflect the desolation of the modern world through man's loss of faith. To create a private Inferno was undoubtedly Eliot's intention; for Theodore Spencer records his remarkable understatement, that the poem 'was only the relief of a personal . . . grouse against life . . . a piece of rhythmical grumbling'. The sea-faring incidents sacrificed used echoes from Canto XXVI of Dante's *Inferno* which concerned the voyages of Ulysses, as well as from Tennyson's poem of that title. Pound's opinion was that both the opening quatrains and the prosaic free verse were 'bad', and he left only the last ten lines for publication, because Phlebas, the Phoenician, was 'an integral part of the poem'. 'What the Thunder Said' is generally regarded as the best of the five parts, and Pound suggested only a few minor verbal changes.

The 400 lines shorn from *The Waste Land* were never published; Eliot, indeed, hoped that they would never be included in the collected works. Of the miscellaneous poems only *The Death of Saint Narcissus* and *Song to the Opherion* (which should be spelt *Opharion*) appeared in print, the second pseudonymously in *The Tyro*, April 1921. Pound had looked hard at *Exequy* and *Death of the Duchess*, regarding the latter as a dim shadow of *Prufrock*; but he was convinced that *The Waste Land* should stand alone, unencumbered by an appendage of minor poems. His directive was clearly to give the poem greater concentration, and to exclude what would probably be condemned as pastiche. In this plan he succeeded admirably; Eliot knew better than anyone that a sound integration of form and meaning was essential, if so daring a poem were to make any impact upon the reader.

In the thirty-five known allusions of *The Waste Land* there are references to the Bible, the Upanishads, and *Pervigilium Veneris*; and to the works of Ovid, Vergil, St Augustine, Spenser, Shakespeare, Kyd, Chapman, Webster, Middleton, Day, Marvell, Milton, Goldsmith, Froude, Conrad, Joyce, Wagner, Hermann Hesse, Baudelaire, de Nerval, Verlaine, F. H. Bradley, J. L. Weston and J. G. Frazer. There was no especial need for the appended notes, but they do provide the reader with helpful clues to *The Waste Land*'s form and meaning. For instance, (1) 'the plan and a good deal of the incidental symbolism of the poem were suggested by Miss Jessie L. Weston's book on the Grail legend, *From Ritual to Romance*' (Cambridge, 1920); (2) 'Tiresias, although a mere spectator and not indeed a "character", is yet the most important personage in the poem, uniting all the rest'. This blind soothsayer of Thebes, appearing in the *Odyssey* and *Metamorphoses,* is a counterpart of Gerontion in Eliot's earlier poem. In the high dream of the Dantesque visionary, he becomes a mask, merging with other figures, who appear in the narrative from time to time.

It is appropriate that a poem, based upon the Vegetation myth and fertility rites of the anthropologist, should begin with 'The Burial of the Dead', a title taken from the Anglican *Book of Common Prayer*. The opening lines lead one to the heart of the matter:

> April is the cruellest month, breeding
> Lilacs out of the dead land, mixing
> Memory and desire, stirring
> Dull roots with spring rain.

Although he was not yet an orthodox churchman, *The Waste Land* indicates that Eliot was familiar with historic churches of London, and that a growing interest in asceticism foreshadowed a need for religion to solve his psychic and domestic problems. Inscribing a copy of *The Waste Land* to his first wife, he observed that she alone would be able to understand its mysteries. At the time of writing this poem he said he was on the brink of accepting Buddhism; this is supported not only by the titles of the third and fifth parts, headed 'The Fire Sermon' and 'What the Thunder Said', but by their contents. In one of the notes he recalls knowledge of H. C. Warren's *Buddhism in Translation,* from which the third title is derived; the sermon is briefly quoted at the end of Part III. It may be that Eliot's experience of renunciation and atonement was not profound, but they figured significantly in his later poems and plays. Through ascetics like St Augustine he was able to reconcile his Orientalism with Christianity.

One can sense in *The Waste Land* Eliot's commitment to eclectic styles, to accord with the universality of his thinking. The characteristically American bookishness of his tastes creates the impression of a learned poet, a reputation he found embarrassing and tried to live down. When he met a finely turned phrase, he succumbed to its influence, even though in principle he disapproved of its author, as with Tennyson and Yeats. His spare style, with short sentences, he once attributed to composing on a typewriter; but in reality he developed it as a reviewer, who admired the economy of phrase of Pound and Madox Ford, whom he considered the neglected critics of the day. Charles Maurras and his French colleagues on *L'Action Française* taught him that a modern poet's preoccupation ought to be with precision of expression, rather than originality of ideas. Through art, the vulgar and banal could be made distinguished. An example of Eliot's ability to write lucidly, economically, as well as symbolically, is the following, in which he harmonizes disparate experiences:

> *Madame Sosostris*, famous clairvoyante,
> Had a bad cold, nevertheless

Is known to be the wisest woman in Europe,
With a wicked pack of cards. Here, said she,
Is your card, the drowned *Phoenician Sailor*,   5
(Those are pearls that were his eyes. Look!)
Here is Belladonna, the Lady of the Rocks,
The lady of situations.
Here is the *man with three staves,* and here the Wheel
And here is the one-eyed merchant, and this card,   10
Which is blank, is something he carries on his back,
Which I am forbidden to see. I do not find
The *Hanged Man*. Fear death by water.
I see crowds of people, walking round in a ring.
Thank you. If you see dear Mrs. Equitone,   15
Tell her I bring the horoscope myself:
One must be so careful these days.

                              (*The Burial of the Dead,* 43–59)

Besides the allusions to Ariel's song in *The Tempest* and Leonardo
da Vinci's portrait, La Gioconda, there is oblique reference to
rootless persons who put their trust in fortune-tellers and occult
mysteries. The name, Madame Sosostris, was taken from a
similar character in Huxley's *Crome Yellow* (Chap. XXVII),
published in 1921; but the poet may also have indulged in a sly dig
at Madame Blavatsky and Yeats. Clairvoyantes used the Tarot
pack of 78 cards, said to be of Egyptian origin; they figure
widely in fertility rites, as ancient as the *Rig-Veda* (see Chapters III
and VI of Weston's *From Ritual to Romance*). The 'man with three
staves' and the 'Hanged Man' are represented in the Tarot pack;
and probably the latter is in capitals because in legend he was a
demigod whom men had to kill in order that the fertility of the
earth might be restored. The Phoenician Sailor was another such
god; in the late summer an effigy of his head was cast into the sea
at Alexandria, and carried by the currents to Byblos, where it was
'resurrected' to herald the spring of the new year. This cult gives
its name to Part IV of the poem, 'Death by Water'.

Eliot made selective use of the myths of Weston and Frazer,
without adopting their conclusions about the pagan origins and
uses of Christian sacraments. He saw the blight of urban civilization as boredom and *spiritual* deadness. Many of the seemingly
unconnected vignettes, like the above, are aspects of the world's

despair, reflecting his own. The modern tragedy is that the ribald, the outrageous, the immoral are not incompatible, and in realistic literature, depicting the breakdown of society, it is right that they be juxtaposed with the seemly and 'poetical'. Only thus could the meaning and purpose of *The Waste Land* be subsumed in the apparently chaotic form of its presentation. This form contains most kinds of poetry, except the epical. What unites the experiments in technique is a rhythmical continuity, comparable to that of music, which overcomes the semantic hiatus between lyrical verse and satirical or incantatory monologue. The paradox, says F. R. Leavis, is that Eliot is 'both definite and vague at once' (*New Bearings in English Poetry*, Chatto and Windus, 1954, p. 100).

In reading *The Waste Land* it is better to have few preconceptions. The theme of 'regeneration' is too abstract to explain the vivifying symbols and broken images, which are flashbacks to man's past, as it affects the present consciousness of an individual. The work of Freud and Jung was then topical, and showed the psychical implications of 'mixing memory and desire'. F. W. Bateson suggests that Eliot's 'shining fragments', resembling 'cultural bric-a-brac', produce the 'hysterical sublime' (see 'Burbank with a Baedeker, Eliot with a Laforgue', *The Review*, November 1962, pp. 12–15). The truth is that the author had been studying Valéry, and shared his faith in the 'omnipotence of rhythm' and the power of the 'suggestive phrase'. Few of poetry's technicians have been so rational.

Picturing Eliot as a plagiarizing magpie will not do. It is more profitable to dwell on his enlargement of the scope of poetry's language, and to enter the timely caveat that a long poem can succeed only if it admits the prosaic. The aim of Eliot's language is to find a 'sensuous embodiment' for the thought through the feelings; images and symbols have as their main purpose the capturing of a 'vision' that words inevitably stammer to express. To the extent that English could achieve this purpose, Eliot modelled himself on the classical technique of Dante, in which images are concrete, words direct and definite, and the syntax of minimal complexity. Every vignette is intended to exhibit a 'point of view', which Eliot contends is the emotional equivalent of ideas (See 'Kipling Redivivus', *Athenaeum*, 4645, 1919).

Evidence of development in the technique of *The Waste Land* may be discerned in the extract selected for analysis. It induced

Eliot to say, soon after the poem's publication: 'I am now feeling toward a new form and style' (*Letter* to Richard Aldington, November 1, 1922). Within a year he had written to Madox Ford 'There are *I* think about 30 *good* lines in *The Waste Land* . . . The rest is ephemeral . . . They are the . . . lines of the water-dripping song in the last part'. The advance to be noted is the increasing employment of incantatory verse, which he described as word magic that does not sacrifice sense to sound. The melody he extracts from the rhythm comes from the choruses of Milton's *Samson Agonistes*, and from Tennyson and Poe, as well as the Bible.

> There is *not* even *silence* in the *mountains*
> *But dry* sterile thunder without rain
> There is not even *solitude* in the *mountains*
> *But* red sullen faces *sneer* and *snarl*
> From doors of mud*cracked* houses   5
>   *Íf there were wáter*
>
>   *And* nó *róck*
>   *Íf there were róck*
>   *And* álso *wáter*
>   *And wáter*   10
>   *A* spríng
>   *A* póol *among* the *róck*
>   *Íf there were* the *sóund* of *wáter* ónly
>   *Nót* the cicáda
>   *And drý* gráss *sínging*   15
>   *But sóund* of *wáter* òver a *róck*
>   Where the hérmit-thrúsh *síngs* in the píne trées
>   Dríp dróp dríp dróp dróp dróp dróp
>   *Bút there* is nó *wáter* . . .
>
> What is that *sound* high in the air   20
> Murmur of maternal lamentation
> Who are those hooded hordes swarming
> Over endless plains, stumbling in *cracked* earth
> Ringed by the flat horizon only . . .
>
> In this decayed hole *among* the mountains   25
> In the faint moonlight, | the *grass* is *singing*

Over the tumbled graves, | about the *chapel*
There is the empty *chapel*, | only the wind's home.
It has no windows, | and the door swings,
Dry bones can harm no one.   30
Only a cock stood on the rooftree
Co co rico co co rico
In a flash of lighting. | Then a damp gust
Bringing rain

The greater part of 'What the Thunder Said' is lyrical, characterized by a singing tone that is the essence of incantation. One distinguishing mark is the absence of punctuation in all but the last ten narrative lines; here the stops indicate pauses (mostly medial) meaningful for the rhythm. In 34 lines, a mere five are run-on (4, 6, 22, 26, 27). A feature of the song-like lines (6–19), introduced by the unusual indentation before *If there were no water,* is the flexibility of stressed syllables they contain (from one to seven); each is rhythmically linked with the next, yet most are end-stopped. The omission of question marks in lines 20–24 should be noted; there is no need for them, as there is elsewhere in this part, where the rhetorical figure is also *erotema*.

Another characteristic of incantation is the interweaving and repetition of key words (*dry, grass, cracked, rock, mountains, sounds, water*), and of assonantal syllables. The echoing sound that dominates this passage is *-ing*: *spring* (11), *singing* (15, 26) and *sings* (17), swarm*ing* (21), stumbl*ing* (22), *Ringed* (24), *swings* (29), light*ning* (33), *Bringing* (34). The rhetorical devices that Eliot employs most frequently are *epanaphora* and *ploce*; they include the repetition of conjunctions (*But, And* and *If*), the indefinite article, interrogative pronouns, the negative adverb *Not*, and onomatopoeic words such as *Drip, drop,* which represent both the song of the hermit-thrush and the falling of water particles. Most of these functional words are made prominent by their position at the beginning of the line, which gives them both visual and syntactical importance.

An effective practice is to repeat, after a short interval, a complete line, with a single semantically significant word excepted. In lines 1 and 3 such words are *silence* and *solitude*, linked by alliteration, as well as by association with *mountains*. A convincing example of the concrete image occurs in line 4: 'red sullen faces *sneer* and *snarl*', where onomatopoeia is the more effective for the combination of initial consonants. In verse of this kind the variation of long open vowels, as in *water, cicada, pine, bones,* and the use of liquid, nasal and trilled consonants, make for resonance and smoothness. For an example of the latter, consider the Tennysonian line 21: *Murmur of maternal lamentation.* Eliot is a skilful artist in phonetic effects, his use being both deliberate and unobtrusive. Perhaps he aimed in this part at the 'purity and sweetness of tone and exquisite modulation' of the hermit-thrush, which he remarks upon in the notes.

Recognizing the allusions is essential to the meaning of *The Waste Land,* and Eliot may have needed the notes to provide the clues to this part. Line 21 *Murmur of maternal lamentation* recalls the Crucifixion and perhaps Jesus's words in Luke XXIII, 28 'Daughters of Jerusalem, weep not for me'. Lines 22–3 *Who are the hooded hordes swarming | Over endless plains* embody a quotation from Hermann Hesse's *A Glimpse into Chaos,* referring to the recent Bolshevik Revolution. Lines 27–30 introduce the Chapel Perilous of the Quest for the Holy Grail, as described in Chapter XIII of Weston's *From Ritual to Romance.* It was part of the knight's initiation into the lower mysteries to show his courage by withstanding the demons of the haunted chapel, into which he had ventured. Eliot's depiction was influenced by a fifteenth-century Dutch painting by Hieronymus Bosch. Line 31, *Only a cock stood on the rooftree,* may refer to the crowing that heralded Peter's rejection of Jesus during the latter's trial. The words that represent the crowing in line 32 are, for the sake of their sound, in Portuguese. The main thread of 'What the Thunder Said' is the Resurrection, as told in the last chapter of St Luke's Gospel.

Although *The Waste Land* has some technically great poetry, such as the lines cited, and may be considered Eliot's most challenging poem, it is not the most satisfying. The evocative processes and fortuitous shape are puzzling, and the impression gains ground that this is a private poem, to which the reader is denied access, if not by the theory of impersonality, then by a negative biography, hinted at in lines 111–23. Only time can reveal the answer. A searching revaluation of the poem has been made by Ian Hamilton for *Eliot in Perspective* (ed. G. Martin, Macmillan, 1970, pp. 102–111), and these are among his conclusions:

Eliot wanted the poem to be difficult and no doubt conceived of its difficulty as an important aspect of its total meaning ... At the source of [the] confident allusiveness there seems to be a personal despair which he is more interested in disguising than exploring ... The poem's energy is not directed, as it might have been, towards a deepening exploration of the intuitions experienced with the hyacinth girl ... Eliot's technique in *The Waste Land* is to proffer personal disabilities as impersonal talents.

Such objections overlook the probability that a poet is as much influenced by feeling for words, phrases and images, as by his personal experiences with persons, to whose attitudes the poem reacts. Eliot afterwards explained that *The Waste Land* was 'a calculated piece of mosaic ... designed to produce a certain series of poetic effects', and that its final form was, to some extent, accidental. Undoubtedly, such form as the poem possesses, is owing to the technical handling of the verse and the underlying significance of the fertility ritual. The primary feelings exhibited are those of aesthetic value. In the Preface to the 1928 edition of *The Sacred Wood* (first published in 1920) Eliot tried to establish (1) that a poem has its own life, and (2) that this life embodies a vision or an emotional state quite different from that which existed in the mind of the poet.

It is reasonable, upon this evidence, to postulate that *The Waste Land* depicts a clash between the permanent primal consciousness of mankind, and the transient modified man, regarded as the product of a limited education and environment. The pattern of the poem, like that of some music, is a free fantasia of ideas. The critic who wrote (in 'Tradition and the Individual Talent') that 'much learning deadens or perverts poetic sensibility' was unlikely to have placed first in composition the mosaic of erudite allusions. He was strenuously preoccupied with the paradox of versification, which was to be free to capture the nuance of actual conversation, and yet be highly disciplined in its technical structure. A sophisticated verse sense had, catalytically, to fuse the scarcely logical oddments of experience. In the same essay, Eliot put his art in a nutshell:

It is not the 'greatness', the intensity, of the emotions, the components, but the intensity of the artistic process, the pressure, so to speak, under which the fusion takes place, that counts . . . The difference between art and the event is always absolute . . . The poet has not a 'personality' to express but a particular medium . . . in which impressions and experiences combine in peculiar and unexpected ways.

(*The Sacred Wood*, 1928, pp. 55–6)

THE HOLLOW MEN 1925
(from *Poems 1909–1925*)

In this poem Eliot continues the 'new form and style' adumbrated in Part V of *The Waste Land*; the form is lyrical, and the style ritualistic and incantational, employing the usual rhetorical effects of balance and repetition. The allusions are less pointed than they were in the earlier poem; indeed, they are partially re-collected echoes of reading in Dante's *Inferno*, Canto III, and *Paradiso*, Canto XXX, as well as Conrad's *Heart of Darkness*.

Incantation through ritualistic insistence of word and phrase conditions the emotions to a mood of spiritual receptivity. Here are examples from Sections II and III:

II

Eyes I dare not meet in *dreams*
In *death's dream kingdom*
These do not appear:
There, the *eyes* are
Sunlight on a *broken* column
There, is a tree sw*inging*
And voices are
In the *wind's* s*inging*
More distant and *more* solemn
Than *a fading star.*

Let me be *no nearer*
In *death's dream kingdom*
Let me also wear
Such deliberate disguises
Rat's coat, crowskin, crossed staves
In a field
*Behav*ing as the *wind behav*es

173

No nearer –

Not that final meeting
In the twilight *kingdom*

III

This is the *dead land*
This is cactus *land*
Here the stone images
Are raised, *here* they receive
The supplication of a *dead* man's hand
Under the twinkle of *a fading star*.

Is it like this
In *death's* other *kingdom*
Waking alone
At the hour when we are
Trembling with tenderness
Lips that would kiss
Form prayers to *broken* stone.

In this associative kind of writing, it is futile to elicit the poem's meaning through tenuous hints from Shakespeare (*Julius Caesar*), Morris (*The Hollow Land*), Kipling (*The Broken Man* and *Danny Deever*), Valéry (*Le Cimetière Marin*), Dowson (*Non sum qualis eram*) and the Bible (*Lamentations of Jeremiah* and The Lord's Prayer), to name only some of the annotators' speculations. Eliot wrote and published four of the five parts in the *Chapbook,* the *Criterion* and *Dial,* during the latter part of 1924 and early in 1925. Three grouped as *Doris's Dream Songs* may have been planned in a dramatic context (Doris figures again in the 'Sweeney' works); but Eliot changed his mind and welded the poems together by his customary resource in thematic re-organization, altering and adding, limiting punctuation, until he had harmonized the parts by rhythmical affinity.

Eliot tended to conceive his longer poems as musical compositions, differentiating the parts as a composer would the movements of 'sonata form'. But B. C. Southam's conjecture that 'the sections were developed from material left over from *The Waste Land* (*A Student's Guide to the Selected Poems of T. S. Eliot*, p. 135) is out of court, since none of the material used in *The Hollow Men* was in the draft submitted to Ezra Pound in 1922. There are, however, occasional echoes from the third and last parts of *The Waste Land* in *The Hollow Men*, eg, in the similes of lines 8 and 9: As wind in *dry grass* / Or *rats' feet* over broken glass.

Eliot was a poet who did not always link images, as Dante did; their *source* is but partly germane to the significance of the unified poem, which he preferred to treat as a chain of sudden emotive illuminations. The key to *The Hollow Men* is to understand its symbolic relationships. The broad theme is the psychic impotence of the spiritually dead, and it is based on the fertility myths of man's primitive forefathers.

The speaker is one of the 'hollow men', who chant their ritualistic chorus:

> Our dried voices, when
> We whisper together
> Are quiet and meaningless

They are not *lost* / *Violent souls* (15/16), like Kurt in *Heart of Darkness* (mentioned in the epigraph), but remind Eliot of the 'dismal company' in Limbo of the *Inferno* (III), faithful to themselves alone, hopelessly waiting to be ferried across the Acheron. Eliot had been reading the anthropological writings of Sir James Frazer, Jane Harrison, and others; in the *Criterion* of July, 1924, he had reviewed W. J. Perry's *Origin of Magic and Religion*. At the time he was absorbed, as Jung was, in the evolution of primitive instincts from myth to theology, and in their relation to man's unfulfilled desires. The stuffed effigies of Guy Fawkes, central to Part I, recalled to him the straw men of Frazer's *Golden Bough*, which recur as sacrificial representations of the vegetation spirit in pagan fire festivals, the object being to appease the gods presiding over good or ill fortune.

The poem is unquestionably about those who drift in spiritual allegiance, the waverers and the uncommitted; it does not react to avowed agnostics or sinners, like Baudelaire, who perversely cultivate diabolism. The spiritual aridity of negative souls is symbolized by the cactus land of Parts III and V; their desolation and despair are represented by the *broken column* (23), *broken stone* (51) and the *prickly pear* (68), round which the ritualistic dance takes place.

The various 'kingdoms' of death provide recurrent phrases that bind the parts together; but their attributes are most confusing.

Scarcely less so are other linking images, such as *eyes* (14, 19, 22, 52, 53, 62) and *fading* or *dying* or *perpetual stars* (27, 44, 54, 63). Those who see God *with direct eyes* (14) pass to the promised life after death (Dante's *Paradiso*), symbolized as *death's other Kingdom* (14 and 46). Those with averted eyes (*Eyes I dare not meet in dreams*, 19) are empty dreamers; their living death is in *this* world, *death's dream kingdom* (20, 30). Death's *twilight kingdom* (38, 65) is difficult to place; but *twilight* and *fading star* or *dying star* suggest that it is intermediary, and Eliot may be thinking of the moments of truth in the passage of the *tumid river* (60), Lethe or Eunoë (Dante's *Purgatorio,* II), where the memory of righteousness is restored through humility. The final *Kingdom*, never attained because it requires *At-one-ment,* is that of God (77, 91).

Eyes are significant for the symbolism, because no *hollow* person (or man of straw) can shed spiritual influence. Commentators, such as D. E. S. Maxwell and A. F. Cahill, have suggested that the eyes referred to are those of the saints; both *the perpetual star* (63) and the *Multifoliate rose* (64) were associated with the Virgin Mary in *Paradiso,* XXXIII.

Part V was added by Eliot, when he decided to unify the group. Ironically, the *Shadow* that falls across the path to salvation, is personal identity, to which men cling most desperately. Self-gratification halts their decision-making. The idea of, and half-hearted desire for, the religion of Christ (suggested by the snatch from the Lord's Prayer) never become an actuality. The maimed syntax of lines 92–4 suggests the *broken column* of line 23, and Dr Johnson's dictum that 'the road to Hell is paved with good resolutions'.

It is worth observing that, in ancient pagan worship, the sacrifice of the vegetation demigod was connected with the survival of the community, and not with individual salvation. In Eliot's poem the psychology of religion is rather vaguely expressed through the poet's aesthetic emotions; if a criticism may be offered, it is that the denotative intention of the words is obscured by the dreamlike ambiguity of the imagery. Eliot did not emulate Dante's illumining relationship between sound and sense.

The Hollow Men is penned in rhymed free verse, with no ostensible strophic pattern; there are several unrhymed lines and frequent phonic reminiscences. G. N. Leech in *A Linguistic Guide to English Poetry* (Longman, 1969) shows admirably how much modern poetry is indebted to the schemes and tropes of rhetoric, and Eliot is no exception. The schemes, in particular, reinforce patterns of identity and contrast, in a style analogous to the language of music. Eliot employs precise verbal repetition, as well as phonological echoes; the resources of his music would have been impossible without them. There are probably more kinds of verbal and sound repetition than the vocabulary of Renaissance rhetoric can name. The verbal range, though economic, invariably intensifies the vigour of expression.

Three years after publishing *The Hollow Men,* Eliot introduced his selection of the *Poems of Ezra Pound* (Faber, 1928) with an essay that emphasized an important distinction between 'verse as speech' and 'verse as song'. The earlier satirical poems and the dramatic monologues belonged mainly to the former kind; *The Waste Land* was an attempt to reconcile the two voices.

Gerontion, The Waste Land and *The Hollow Men* are homogeneous in tone, their aim being to give artistic unity to poems on the post-war theme of 'disorganization'. Juxtaposed in a single volume, these poems would form a group comparable to the best of Pound's *Cantos.* Possibly, 'shape without form' was what made these Cantos unattractive to the reading public. Eliot's ascendancy over Pound arose partly from a sensitive reticence, and in time from a tighter artistic discipline. It should not be overlooked that Pound himself submitted poems for his friend's critical scrutiny.

The poems Eliot wrote between 1909 and 1925 show abundant lexical virtuosity, and of his word-choice no one has spoken better than Charles Williams in *Poetry at Present* (Clarendon, 1930, pp. 165–173):

> I have seen the *eternal* Footman hold my coat, and
>   snicker

Whether the word 'eternal' here means 'timeless' or 'everlasting' doesn't much matter. Mr Eliot is one of the few poets of whom one might hope that when he said eternal he meant eternal, and not merely immortal.. The word sums up a whole state of being. It is the experience, so common and so detestable, when the whole universe seems to be sniggering at one behind its hand, and at the same time obsequiously assisting the exhibition one is making of oneself... It is the Dweller on the Threshold of the old traditions occupied on his modern business. It is Fear, blatant and ungentlemanly . . .

Mr Eliot's poetic experience of life would seem to be Hell varied by intense poetry . . . It is also, generally, our experience of Mr Eliot's poetry . . . The recognition of his phrases is the recognition of our own experience, and the importation into that experience of some sense of enjoyment. Those mornings when we are

> aware of the damp souls of housemaids
> Sprouting despondently at area gates . . .

It seems as if Mr Eliot reserved his strength for his intellect, especially for the expression of his intellect, and allowed himself otherwise to endure passively the tiresome assaults of the external world. By his mere passivity he infuses in those assaults a weakness. . . .

Reminiscence (which fools call plagiarism, and annotators used to point out drearily and with none of the excitement of delight it should convey) is 'a law, not a privilege', of Mr Eliot's verse. Reminiscence, and even direct quotation . . . So rich now is our inheritance of associations in literature that it is beginning to be difficult to avoid them in creating new . . . We approach a form of poetic life which acts through the earlier myths of verse . . . This new development, if it proceeds, will make poetry a more specialized thing; for the specialist it will become more exciting and intriguing . . . Our knowledge of our contemporary poet will arise from the method with which he deals with those phrases, from his evocation and control of them.

CHAPTER VII

T. S. Eliot (2):
Poems 1926–35

🔊🔊🔊🔊🔊🔊

A useful introduction to Eliot's thinking and writing during the decade following the publication of *The Hollow Men* is to be found in *Essays Ancient and Modern* (Faber, 1936), which reprints, with some pertinent additions, five of the essays that had previously appeared in *For Lancelot Andrewes* (1928). Eliot had written on this learned and eloquent divine in the *Times Literary Supplement* of 23 September 1926; and the essay on Bishop John Bramhall, appeared in *Theology* in July 1927. His interest in seventeenth-century divines and preachers was not unrelated to his regard for the poetry of Donne and Herbert. In the journal *Enemy 1* 'A Note on Poetry and Belief' had appeared in January of the same year.

There had been indications of a change in Eliot's attitude to religion, and consequently to poetry, in part V of *The Waste Land,* though its concern was partly with Buddhism. The immediate cause of his conversion to the Anglican faith was a recurrence of his wife's nervous complaint, which affected his own health. At a centre near Geneva, where they went for treatment, Eliot met Robert Sencourt, who introduced him to Lord Halifax, one of the leaders of the Anglo-Catholic movement in Britain. Into this devout sacramental faith, emanating from the Oxford Movement of the nineteenth century, Eliot was received, with baptism and confirmation, on 29 June 1927. After twenty years of virtual agnosticism, he had accepted the spiritual road of Dante, as well as the English way of life, by becoming a naturalized British subject in the following November.

Regarded simply as a technique of 'musicalized' composition, Eliot's poetry changed in no material way through this conversion. But words so charged with meaning and emotive suggestion, fusing the prosaic and the poetic, would not have been acclaimed for their Mallarmean perfection. Not only the criticism, but the poetry, of Eliot developed 'a definite ethical and theological standpoint'; he sincerely held 'the primacy of the supernatural over the natural life' (see 'Religion and Literature', *op. cit.* p. 108). The feelings in this period are therefore more withdrawn, and the outlook more 'depersonalized'. Poems that convey mystical experience strive unceasingly to achieve an identity between their self-determining form and their subject, between the rhythm and the thought.

A close analysis of the Ariel poems will show that the phrasing serves a dual and simultaneous purpose: to advance the total meaning and to accommodate the metrical structure to it. One of Eliot's most invigorating contributions to poetry was the revival of Christian images and symbols, which the intellectuals among modern poets had thought to be defunct. Such symbols give to the poems a total significance beyond the sense of the phrases or sentences that constitute the lines. In a language study this holistic effect is difficult to convey, except by noting the symbolic relationship of the linear patterns.

Eliot's desire for a style to suit each poem is not uncommon in poets of the first order, though it negates any general conclusions about his methods. A closer contact with the meaning may be made only through a step by step *evaluation* of the text, but the reader is aware that the precise sense of the patterns is indeterminate. It was, no doubt, Eliot's intention that the poem should be *known* through the complex attitudes, rather than its external details. Unless the rhythms are prosaic, the reader is primarily moved by the musical cadence of the words; he must go back to be assured of their referential content.

In the first two Ariel poems, the religious symbols have a traditional power that upholds the sense, without subordinating it to feeling and tone. One is, perhaps unconsciously, moved by the objects the words represent, and it is to Eliot's credit that the doctrinal is never mingled with the poetic.

In prosaic passages meaning is largely determined by the logic of emphasis, which differs for the silent reader from an ideal performance, such as a reading by Eliot himself. Using *voice* in the sense of 'personal style', a young commentator, Elizabeth Gordon, described her reaction to Eliot's mature poetry perceptively:

This voice has the power to express feelings, atmosphere, moments, moods so that they are touchable, tastable. Behind all the poetry it is his voice that gives a kind of tangible thickness to everything. It is impersonal, at the back of the mind, accusing, sad, wondering, yet confident . . .

It is when Mr Eliot is describing something naturally fresh, like a child of nature, that the rising feeling of excitement comes in one. . . (In) 'An old white horse galloped away in the meadow' . . . we get that moment of joy.

(*T. S. Eliot, A Symposium for his Seventieth Birthday,*
Hart-Davis, 1958, p. 113)

In the Ariel poems, lines such as this are repeatedly embedded in the language of every day. The rhythmical aplomb of these exercises in a new style is that of a free-versifier, whose sense of form flows naturally from the narrative or colloquial syntax employed, and creates a pleasing tension between the prose rhythms and the overall metrical pattern. In its compression, Eliot's syntax is simpler than that of any other modern poet. The difficulties that arise result from the impressionistic fragments of thought and inadequate use of stops to signal their relationships; for example, lines 21–3 of *Animula*:

> The pain of living and the drug of dreams
> Curl up the small soul in the window seat
> Behind the *Encyclopaedia Britannica.*

The Ariel poems were originally intended as a series of Christmas offerings, to which Eliot contributed five. No. 35, *Triumphal March,* does not fit into the festive pattern. The monologues *Journey of the Magi, A Song for Simeon* and *Marina* are stages in a poet's spiritual progress, dealing with aspects of rebirth. One of Eliot's historical virtues is that, like Shakespeare, he looks at the past with the eyes of the present.

JOURNEY OF THE MAGI, 1927

Eliot had probably read Yeats's prose study 'The Adoration of the Magi', published in *Mythologies* in 1925; but the traditional source of the narrative monologue is *Matthew* II, 1–11. The *magi* (or 'wise men' of the Scriptures) were ancient Persian priests, skilled in astrology and magic. The speaker in the poem is one who has

accepted belief in the Incarnation, but has not yet shaken off the
sensuous attractions of the past life)(see Jung, *Psychological Types*,
Chapter I). The journey of the Magi was undertaken to verify the
birth of Christ, as prophesied; in reality, it recounts the quest for a
new faith, rejecting the ancient wisdom of man. The hardships
described convey allegorically the travail of Eliot's own conversion (cf. lines 13 and 14 below).

The opening five lines, in quotation marks, are modified words
from Lancelot Andrewes's Nativity Sermon, preached on
Christmas day 1622. The preacher actually used the term *magi*, and
the details of the journey in the succeeding fifteen lines are taken
from an earlier section of his sermon. The last twelve lines (7–18
below) provide a retrospect, from which one is to divine Eliot's
intention in the poem; they, too, are adumbrated in the sermon.
The point made is that an acceptable faith does not depend on
evidence, and should survive the transient doubts that every
proselyte experiences.

The poem is in three paragraphs of unrhymed free verse, in
the manner of *Gerontion*. (The paradox giving it force, that a Birth
imports a Death (of the old spiritual beliefs), is symbolically
introduced in the second paragraph, by juxtaposing proleptically
reminiscences of the Crucifixion. In this paragraph, *three trees on the
low sky*, recall the crosses on Calvary; and the *white horse* in the next
line probably represents the one on which Christ, the Conqueror,
rides in *Revelation* VI.2 and XIX, 11. The poem continues:)

Then we came to a tavern with vine-leaves over the lintel,
Six hands at an open door dic*ing* for pieces of silver,
And feet kick*ing* the empty wine-skins.
But there was no information, *and* so we continued
And arrived at evening, not a moment too soon   5
Find*ing* the place; it was (you may say) satisfactory.

All this was a long time ago, I remember,
And I would do it again, but *set down*
This set down
This: were we led all that way for   10
Birth or *Death*? There was a Birth, certainly,
We had evidence *and* no doubt. I had seen *birth and death*,
But had thought they were different; this *Birth* was
Hard *and* bitter agony for us, like *Death*, our *death*.

We returned to our places, these Kingdoms,   15
But no longer at ease here, in the old dispensation,
With an alien people clutch*ing* their gods.
I should be glad of another *death*.

The personal allusion in line 2: *Six hands at an open door dicing for silver,* reminds the reader of the betrayal of Christ by Judas Iscariot. The poem ends on an ambiguous note; (but the interpretation of the final lines is surely that rebirth through Christ means death to the old paganism. Inevitably the convert becomes a stranger in his own land, patiently anticipating his physical death.)

The style in which this poem is written is modelled on biblical prose of the Tyndale era, with plentiful phrasal coordination, and participial constructions taking the place of clauses. Three of the participial lines are initiated by the preposition *With*:

> *With* the voices *singing* in our ears
> *With* a *running* stream and a water-mill
> *With* an alien people *clutching* their gods

The conjunction *and* is used 23 times, and present participles 18 times in 43 lines, examples of *polysyndeton*, consonance and assonance unequalled in any other poem. Adversative conjunction *But* begins lines 4, 13 and 16. The patterning of the prosaic rhythm is thus largely syntactical, but there are only nine enjambed lines.

The rhetorical figure *litotes* (understatement) should be observed in line 6: *it was (you may say) satisfactory*. This matter-of-factness, immediately preceding the crucial final paragraph, is as though Eliot were saying: 'A convert to a new faith must not expect miraculous changes'. The decisive lines are 8–11:

> And I would do it again, but *set down*
> *This set down*
> *This*: were we led all that way for
> Birth or death?

Here the line division, with its deliberate omission in 9 of a comma after *This,* has a rhetorically archaic effect typical of Eliot at this time. The emphatic repetition of the three words in this line combines two schemes of words, *ploce* and *epimone* (dwelling on a point by repetition).

The curt, deliberate language of lines 7–11 in the final section is an attractive variation in the use of prosaic rhetoric. Its characteristic feature is the abruptness apparent in the short sentences, which are set off against each other, but not syntactically balanced. French critics call this writing *style serré*; precise punctuation is often essential to it. The tight phrasing produces the effect of lively thought.

The clever variation of line-length and stress inhibits the monotony that mars much narrative verse. Stresses vary from seven to two in a line, and unstressed syllables easily outnumber the accented ones. Not a line approximates to blank verse, the nearest being 17 *With an alien people clutching their gods*. The prose rhythm of the verse is aided by the neglect of stressed syllables at the end of lines; only thirteen terminate in stressed or partially stressed syllables.

A SONG FOR SIMEON, 1928

The source of this monologue is *Luke* II, 25–35; another is the Order for Evensong in that section of the *Book of Common Prayer* headed *Nunc Dimittis*, which reads: 'Lorde, now lettest thou thy servaunte departe in peace: according to thy woorde. For myne iyes have sene thy salvacion'.

Simeon, an old man of eighty years, is the speaker in the poem; he believes he has been a good servant of the Lord, and patiently awaits his death, in the days of Caesar Augustus and the Roman occupation of Judaea. The setting is conveyed by reference to *Roman hyacinths* in the first line. In a vision, the Holy Ghost had promised Simeon that he would not die before the advent of Christ, whose birth in Bethlehem is followed ten days later by the visit of his parents to the Holy City. The central passage in the Gospel is that in which Simeon (a latter-day Jeremiah) takes the child in his arms and says 'Mine eyes have seen thy salvation' (verse 30, cf. line 24 of the selection). He then foretells the dire, as well as the good, results for mankind of Christ's coming; as well as the tragedy for Israel, which Eliot describes in line 7 as 'the dead land'.

The 36 lines of the poem are in strophes of 7, 9, 8 and 12 lines of irregular length. Most lines are metrically self-contained, only two being run-on in the whole poem. There is no specific rhyme scheme, and several rhymes are only approximate. Some of the ten unrhymed lines are casually linked by assonance (*eg*, 2/4 *hills / wind*), which also helps to link strophes. Rhyme seems to emphasize the note of prayer and incantation, which is central to the passages selected.

Simeon craves peace, but realizes that Christ's coming brings also a sword; and thus he forecasts the doom and dispersion of his children (strophe 2). This citation is composed of strophes 1, 3 and most of 4:

Lord, the Roman hyacinths are blooming in bowls and
The winter sun creeps by the snow *hills*;
The stubborn season has made stand.
My life is *light,* waiting for the *death wind,*
Like a feather on the back of my hand.   5
Dust in sun*light* and memory in corners
Wait for the *wind* that *chills* towards the dead land . . .

Before the time of cords and scourges and lamentation
Grant us thy peace.
Before the stations of the mountain of desolation,   10
Before the certain hour of maternal sorrow,
Now at this birth season of decease,
Let the Infant, the still *unspeak*ing and *unspoke*n Word,
Grant Israel's consolation
To one who has eighty years and no to-morrow.   15

According to thy word.
They shall praise Thee and suffer in every generation
With glory and derision,
Light upon light, mounting the saints' stair.
Not for me the martyrdom, the ecstasy of thought and   20
    prayer,
Not for me the ultimate vision.
Grant me thy peace . . .
Let thy servant depart,
Having seen thy salvation.

In line 10 *the stations of the mountain of desolation* are those of the Cross on the way to Calvary. The ambiguity of *Now at this birth season of decease* (12) looks back to the ending of *The Journey of the Magi*. *The unspeaking and unspoken Word* alludes to the opening chapter of St John's Gospel, where *Word* (in capitals) symbolizes the Incarnation (or divine principle made flesh). As in the preceding poem, the speaker anticipates sayings and events of the Gospels in lines 16–19. *Light upon light, mounting the saints' stair* (19) is an allusion to the beatification of Christ and his saints. *Salvation* in the final line of the poem probably signifies 'God's mercy'. Eliot takes the words from Scripture; but Simeon does allude to the passion of Christ in line 10, and has pre-vision of the persecution of Christians.

The title-word 'song' is meaningful for technique; the poem is lyrical, not only in its abundant use of alliteration, assonance and sibilant, nasal and liquid consonants, but in the Hebraic way of pious reflection, mingled with prophecy. Replacing the rhetorical pattern of its narrative predecessor, this lamentation employs tropes singularly appropriate, both to the winter season, and to the melancholy of an occupied country; they reflect, moreover, the depressed spirit of the poet. *Prosopopoeia* (or personification) is strongly represented in: The winter sun *creeps* (2), The *stubborn season* has *made stand* (3) and *memory in corners* (6). *My life is light . . . / Like a feather on the back of my hand* (4, 5) employs metaphor and simile respectively; and the symbolic *death wind* (4) is an instance of metonymy.

The last two strophes are schematic, both in balance and repetition; *epanaphora* is illustrated in the recurrence of *Before* at the beginning of lines 8, 10, 11; *epimone* in *Not for me* which introduces lines 20 and 21. *Unspeaking* and *unspoken* in 13 are examples of *polyptoton*.

The final strophe is introduced by the phrase *According to thy word* (16), referring to the testimony of the Gospels; but the line is unorthodoxly isolated by its period. *With glory and derision* (18) is a unique example of metrical and semantic antithesis, reverting to the verbs *praise* and *suffer* in the previous line. There seems to be no syntactical connection between the initial three lines of the strophe and 19 *Light upon light, mounting the saints' stair*; a semantic leap has to be made by the reader, who is perceptive enough to link this line with *glory* in the preceding one. Simeon concludes that these are glories his lease of life will not permit him to share (20–21); in the preceding strophe he prayed that death would release him from misfortunes, especially the agony on the Cross.

The benediction Simeon repeatedly craves is for personal peace, and the last part of the final strophe is transparently a gloss on Eliot's own state of mind. 'Grant *us* thy peace' now becomes 'Grant *me* thy peace'. Through the persona of dramatic monologue he subjectively transformed the objective account of Simeon in the Gospel, expressing the realization that the only peace to be hoped for is death.

The poem has many overtones and several layers of meaning. The reluctance of the weary Simeon, who had conscientiously honoured the old Hebraic pieties, to face the new world of Christianity, with all its probable animosity, is splendidly captured. It also exemplifies Eliot's ability to adjust his sympathy to the conditions of historical time, and to make it relevant to his own. He shrewdly imagined what it would be like to rank as the first Christian, at an age when change is difficult; for Simeon would have been a convert, without Paul's harrowing experience of rebirth or devout knowledge of Redemption.

MARINA, 1930

In *T. S. Eliot, the Design of his Poetry* (Eyre and Spottiswoode, 1950) Elizabeth Drew says that this is the only 'joyous' poem that Eliot wrote. But the epigraph is taken from *Seneca*'s tragedy *Hercules Furens* (line 1138): 'What place is this, what country, what part of the world?' The questions are on the lips of Hercules, when he regains sanity after killing his family, under a spell of madness cast upon him by Juno. But the title *Marina* shows that the germ of the poem came from Shakespeare's *Pericles, Prince of Tyre*, whose daughter was born at sea, and lost upon it, while still a child. The voice in the monologue is that of Pericles, though there are alternate echoes of Hercules in lines 6–13 and 17–19. What Eliot attempts is a new slant to the recognition scene (Act V, scene 1) of the play.

Marina represents the wonder-child, seen in dreams by persons about to experience a *vita nuova* (see Jung's *Psychological Types*, Chapter V). Pericles believed that his daughter was dead, through the treachery of those in whose care she had been left. His life since then had become meaningless, and the miracle of her restoration would have had the impact of a rebirth. The correlation of birth and death in the fantasy mind is real, and Eliot repeatedly used the Jungian situation in poems with a religious orientation. *Marina* offers the spiritual dilemmas that occupied the mind of Dante, and critics have suggested that Beatrice of the *Divina Commedia* is the prototype. Only a year earlier, Eliot had published his study on *Dante* (Faber and Faber, 1929), in the Preface to which he named the Florentine as '*the* master for a poet writing to-day in any language . . . I should not trust the opinion of anyone who pretended to judge modern verse without knowing Homer, Dante and Shakespeare'.

> *What seas what* shores *what* grey rocks and *what* islands
> *What water* lapp*ing* the bow
> And scent of *pine* and the woodthrush *singing through the fog*
> *What* images return
> O my *daughter*.   5
>
> *Those who* sharpen the tooth of the dog, *meaning*
> Death
> *Those who* glitter with the glory of the humm*ing*bird, *meaning*
> Death
> *Those who* sit in the stye of contentment, *meaning*   10
> Death
> *Those who* suffer the ecstasy of the animals, *meaning*
> Death
>
> Are become unsubstantial, reduced by a wind,
> A breath of *pine,* and the *woodsong* fog   15
> By this *grace* dissolved in *place*
>
> *What* is this *face,* less *clear* and *clearer*
> The pulse in the arm, less *strong* and *stronger* —
> Given or lent? more distant than stars and *nearer* than the eye
>
> Whispers and small laughter between leaves and hurry*ing*   20
>   feet
> Under *sleep,* where all the *waters meet*.
>
> Bowsprit *cracked* with ice and paint *cracked* with heat.
> I *made* this, I have forgotten
> And remember.

The rigg*ing* weak and the canvas rotten   25
Between one June and another September.
Made this un*know*ing, half conscious, un*know*n, my *own*.
The garboard strake leaks, the seams need caulking.
This form, this *face*, this *life*
Living to *live* in a world of time beyond *me*; let *me*   30
Resign my *life* for this *life*, my *speech* for that un*spoke*n,
The awakened, *lips* parted, the hope, the new *ships*.

What seas what shores what granite *islands* towards my
     timbers
And *woodthrush* call*ing through the fog*
My *daughter*.   35

The water-lapping movement in the opening lines is rhythmically
evocative. So nostalgic is the scene that a sense of place is postulated, and Eliot supplied some facts, both in the original draft
of the poem and in the preface of 1928. The locality is Rogue
Island, Maine, at the mouth of the New Meadows River, which
he visited in his youth.

From a literary viewpoint, the alternation of reminiscences
from *Hercules Furens* with those from *Pericles* occasioned some
criticism. Eliot probably intended the usual effects of contrast,
by juxtaposing horror with superabundant joy. Pericles is pictured
as a man, like Clarence in *Richard III*, awakening from a melancholy dream; he should be seen as one who has lived through a
private Hell, whether by culpable neglect, or sins of the flesh. It
was mere pride that was the downfall of Hercules.

The ship, described in lines 22–28, however defective, was of
Pericles' own making, and is a symbol of himself, old and broken,
awaiting his end. In his mind's eye the past comes back to him
with all the subjectivity of a vision. Marina's childhood is recalled
in line 20: *Whispers and small laughter between leaves and hurrying feet.*
This may have been suggested by Kipling's short-story *They*. The
image was enduring enough to recur in the minor poem *New
Hampshire*, and in Part I of *Burnt Norton*.

As lines 17–19 show, the awakening senses of Pericles are con-
fused. The contradictory impressions *less clear and clearer | . . . less
strong and stronger | . . . more distant . . . and nearer,* illustrate a
scheme of thought known to the Elizabethan rhetoricians as
synæciosis. Shakespeare uses it to emphasize delusion in *Macbeth.*

In Eliot's poem one is not sure whether rebirth is achieved or envisioned. The *daughter* image of lines 5 and 35 is a symbol of hope; the *new ships* (32) suggest the prospect of a happier next generation.

The Eliot idiolect in *Marina* deserves special attention, because it is the voice of maturity and pervades *Ash Wednesday* and *Four Quartets*. The poem has thirty-five lines and seven paragraphs, varying from two to eleven lines, the rhythm being adapted to the sense of their content. Having no determinable metrical pattern, the paragraphs can hardly be called stanzas. Nor have they perceptible connection, though paragraphs 2 and 3 are linked by grammatical syntax. Organic unity of the parts is, as always, aided by assonance, alliteration and rhetorical schemes of repetition, such as *ploce*. There are only seven rhyming lines: 20/21/22, 23/25, 24/26. But note the haunting effect of internal rhyme and assonance, whenever the tone is incantational, as in lines 15–21 and 27–32.

The only formal paragraph is the second, where *Death*, with its doleful echo, is isolated in alternate lines. The repetitious pattern is classified in rhetoric as *Carmen correlativum*, and the effect in Eliot's use of it is to halt the interlinear rhythm of the couplets. There is, in fact, very little enjambement in the poem, as a whole. *Death* is the punishment of four of the deadly sins, gluttony, pride, sloth, and lust, which figure prominently in Dante's *Purgatorio*. *Those who sharpen the tooth of the dog* (6) has a possible connection with *Psalm* XXII, 20, in the King James Bible.

The powerful association of the sea-world, from which all life emerges, with the dream-world, is reinforced by the musical poise of the verse. Technical terms, such as *garboard strake* (28) do not transfigure it; nor do resonant lines, whose sense is mystifying as the *fog*, disturb the receptive reader, *eg*,

16 the woodsong fog / By this grace dissolved in place
21 Under sleep, were all waters meet
30 Living to live in a world of time beyond me

The chanting effect of many lines is secured by the *-ing* endings of participles and gerunds, and the interplay of long vowels and consonants *l*, *m*, *n*, *r* and *s*. The poem's concluding peace is splendidly conceived in relation to its opening, anticipating the motto of *East Coker*: 'In my beginning is my end'.

An acceptable account of *Marina* might see it as a Dantesque vision of rebirth, whose orderly verbalism echoes the sermons of Lancelot Andrewes. The monody is not intended to have the religious connotations of *Ash Wednesday*, which was completed earlier in the same year. Probably for this reason Eliot substituted *speech* for *word* in line 31 of the original draft; he was unwilling that *word* should carry overtones of meaning relevant to the philosophizing of the first chapter of St John's Gospel. In a note to Chapter II of his *Dante,* Eliot confessed to a difficulty in analyzing his own feelings:

> I cannot, in practice, wholly separate my poetic appreciation from my personal beliefs . . . 'Literary appreciation' is an abstraction, and pure poetry a phantom . . . In creation and enjoyment much always enters which is, from the point of view of 'Art', irrelevant. (pp. 59–60)

ASH WEDNESDAY, 1930

Eliot began to write the poems in this group to mark his conversion to Anglo-Catholicism in 1927. Three titles were published separately, (of which Part II was the first), before the six, entitled *Ash Wednesday*, appeared as a homogeneous work of 184 lines. They all concern aspects of feeling induced by religious experience. The poems were undoubtedly influenced by the Ash-Wednesday sermons delivered by Lancelot Andrewes in 1602 and 1619. This holy day of the Church, coming at the beginning of Lent, involves self-examination and aims at discipline of the soul.

Perhaps the most important impact on the style was Dante's *Divina Commedia,* especially the last three Cantos of the *Purgatorio* and the *Paradiso.* The words *turn* and *stair* in Parts I, III and VI suggest the poem's spiral movement, and so recall the winding mount of Dante's epic. Spring, too, is regarded as a turning point in the year. The orderliness of the verse coincides with the disciplined humility that expands, and does not inhibit, fulfilment of the Christian life.

In *The Waste Land* the poems were unified by what I. A. Richards called 'the accord, contrast and interaction of their emotive effects' (*Principles of Literary Criticism,* 1924, Appendix B, p. 290); in *Ash Wednesday* the movements are variations on the same theme – preparation for the New life. The poems are written in verse paragraphs, rather than stanzas. The convert seems to be addressing his will, for he speaks in tones of prayer and renunciation; the voice of all but the fifth poem is that of the poet himself. The incantational note, resembling the liturgy of the Church, is designed to appeal to the auditory imagination at a deeper level of sensibility than the intellect. The tone of solitary reverence is quite unlike that of Donne, Herbert or Hopkins.

The language of repentance echoes many phrases in the Bible (*Psalms, Ezekiel, Revelation*) and the Prayer Book. Eliot subtly explores the implications of liturgical words, and gives them a richer meaning. But the evocative symbols and allusions are not drawn from the picturesque Christian tradition alone; often the sensuous world is laid under tribute for images that can move the affections. The integration of the sensory and the spiritual worlds makes *Ash Wednesday* a unique, if anachronistic, phenomenon, whose limpid clarity is offset by its allegorical purpose. St John of the Cross provides the ascetic passivity, Dante the dignity of common speech.

With little change in his technique of writing verse, Eliot substituted for secular irony a spiritual austerity that possesses an irony of its own. In sickness, he had never rejected the resources of modern psychology; now he was sublimating human frailty by interceding with a Supernatural Power. The poetry is doubly assuring, first in the technical excellence of its irregular verse, then in the power to convey, without doctrinal bias, the phases of scepticism, dryness and surrender that a convert must experience. Frederick Grubb, who is unsympathetic to Eliot's hermetic writing, admits that the meditations in *Ash Wednesday* 'infuse a new rhythm into devotional poetry' (*A Vison of Reality*, Chatto and Windus, 1965, p. 60). Figurative language is stripped of ornament, and replaced by a schematic recurrence of words, intended to strengthen the will. How can images so concrete tend to obscurity? The answer is that the emotions they represent are essentially private.

PART I, 1928

The poem opens with a translated line of a ballad by Guido Cavalcanti, Dante's friend, who had been exiled from Florence; line 4 repeats line 7 of Shakespeare's Sonnet 29, substituting the word *gift* for *art*. The latter word was felt to be out of keeping with the context of renunciation contemplated in the initial adverbial clauses. Three renunciations are made in a corresponding number of paragraphs. The first bids farewell to worldly ambition, of which *art* is foremost (4 *I no longer strive to strive towards such things*); the second dismisses the *transitory power* of knowledge and the natural sources of inspiration (*trees, springs* etc); the third denies physical beauty, both of feature (that of earthly woman – 21 *I renounce the blessèd face*) and *voice* (22). The latter would include the sound of words. The *blessèd face,* of course, recalls Dante's Beatrice.

Eliot resolved not to go back to his past life, to the pagan world of *The Waste Land*. He abandons *The vanished power of the usual reign* (8), suggesting the vanities of the worldly artist; but occasionally apathy halts the spiritual struggle (6 *Why should the agèd eagle stretch its wings?*). The eagle was a symbol of grace, first through fire, then through baptism (cf *Purgatorio* IX, 19–33). In the Christian bestiaries the eagle renewed its youth by flying dangerously near the sun until its plumes were singed, and then plunged into a cool spring. The myth may have been of considerable age, since it is referred to in *Psalm* CIII, 5, and *Isaiah* XL, 31. The 'agèd eagle' has nothing to do with the decline of the poet; symbolically, the unpurged soul was said to be *old*, the purged man was regarded as born anew. St Paul used 'the *old* man' image in the same sense.

The first steps in self-knowledge are to dispel self-deception. In the first four lines of paragraph 3 Eliot makes a philosophical observation to which he returns in *Four Quartets*, that actualities are really contingencies, due to the intersection of place and time. One must therefore accept past lapses as inevitable (21 *I rejoice that things are as they are*). Resignation does not imply that the springs of action have evaporated; one finds a stillness at the spiritual centre, round which to build a new life. What Eliot 'constructs', in order to rejoice, is the poem itself.

In the second half of the poem the three renunciations are succeeded by three prayers, viz. for mercy, for feelings untrammelled by anxiety, and for divine intercession. As the prayers take the form of communal petitions the first personal pronoun becomes *us* in lines 26, 33, 38–41. The key lines in the requests for grace are:

33 May the judgement not be too heavy upon us
38 Teach us to care and not to care
41 Pray for us now and at the hour of our death

The second of these lines emphasizes the ever-present ambiguity of the spiritual conflict; the last is the familiar invocation of the Catholic Church to the Virgin Mary. The line *Teach us to sit still* (39) was probably suggested by *Isaiah* XXX, 7.

Philip Martin in *Mastery and Mercy* (Oxford, 1957, p. 105) describes the poem as 'an unrhetorical diagnosis of the inner life of a man'; but, in fact, functional use of rhetoric is the principal element in the technique. Contrition and detachment could not have been communicated so effectively without the tropes and schemes that Eliot used with much ritualistic novelty. The most significant of the tropes are, perhaps, oxymoron and paradox, because these suggest the dialectical oppositions of the conflict, *eg,*

9/10 Because I do not hope to know again / The infirm glory of the positive hour
13 The one *veritable transitory* power (intellectually, truth is not transient)
38 Teach us *to care and not to care* (paradox)

In the last example the meanings of *care* are different; the first suggests 'taking infinite pains', the second 'worrying'. Interest in the ambivalence of words derives from Shakespeare and Andrewes, and penetrates the most successful of Eliot's meditative discourses. Thus in 'I no longer *strive* to *strive* towards such things' (5), the first use of the verb connotes 'exhaust myself', the second implies 'hanker after'. In 'Because I *know* I shall not *know*' (12), the meaning is first 'aware of', secondly 'experience'. The verb *turn* has so many metaphorical implications that ingenuity and context alone can supply them.

In 'The *vanished power* of the *usual reign*', metonymy provides a further layer of meaning to that discussed earlier. In classical mythology the *eagle* was a symbol both for imperial might and the sway of justice. A splendid instance of metaphor occurs in 35: 'no longer wings / But merely *vans to beat the air*' (*vans* are the sails of a windmill, here functionless, because the air is 'thoroughly small'). Two lines later the noun *will* is employed metaphorically by being associated with the 'dryness' of the air.

The most memorable of the rhetorical devices is, however, the reverberation of words, phrases and sentences, resembling a composer's variations in music. The adverbial clause *Because I do not hope to turn again* provides the first theme, and it is played upon, with several modifications, in lines 2, 3, 9, 11, 12, 14, 16, 23 and 30. *Because* introduces no less than eleven lines, and *And* six, reminding the reader of the contentious matters 'that with myself I too much discuss / Too much explain' (28–9). This figure, *epanaphora,* is resorted to in many other places, *eg,* 6 and 7, 38 and 39, 40 and 41. But repetitions to reinforce rhythmical pattern are legion, beginning with the omnipresent use of the first personal pronoun *I*:

Ploce: *strive* (5 twice); *know* (9, 12, 16); *time* (16, 18); *place* (17, 19); *actual* (18 twice); *are* (20 twice); *rejoice* (20, 25); *pray* (27, 28); *too much* (28, 29); *done* (32 twice); *wings* (34 twice); *air* (35, 36); *dry* (36, 37), *care* (38 twice);
Pray for us now and at the hour of our death (40, 41) serves as a kind of liturgical response.
Epiphora: *upon us* (26, 33)

Other devices are:
Alliteration and *Assonance*: 15 *There, where* trees *fl*ower, and *springs fl*ow *f*or *there* is nothi*ng*
28 And I *pray* that I *may* forget
39 Teach us to *sit still*
Antithesis: 4 Desiring *this man's gift* and *that man's scope* (parallelism)
8 The *vanished power* of the *usual reign* (syntax)
10 The *infirm glory* of the *positive hour* (syntax)
15 *trees flower* and *springs flow* (syntax)
32 For *what is done, not to be done* again (semantic opposition)
38 Teach us *to care* and *not to care* (semantic opposition)

Schematic devices are thus varied, but all-pervasive; they enable Eliot to dispense with much punctuation, what he retains being mainly metrical.

The rhythm of the verses differs little from that of most devotional prose. Its effect is obtained by decisive, meaningful stresses, as in the following lines:

And práy to Gód to have mércy upón us
And I práy that I máy forgét
Thése mátters that with mysélf I tóo múch discúss
Tóo múch expláin
Becáuse I dó not hópe to túrn agáin
Let thése wórds ánswer
For whát is dóne, | nót to be dóne agáin
May the júdgement nót be tóo héavy upón us (lines 26–33)

It can be seen that the stresses are primary and numerous. The gravity of the language is, indeed, associated with the slow, deliberate rhythm, and strengthened by rhyme on monosyllabic terminals, with *hour* and *power* (10/13) probably in that category. There are a few approximate rhymes, such as *turn* / *mourn* (3/7); the only unrhymed lines (20, 24, 27, 31) are enjambed ones. Most of the lines are metrically self-contained, but not isolated; the rhyme scheme has no determinant but the needs of the free verse. Eliot's technique is seen to be most unobtrusive, but clearly basic to his design.

PART II, 1927

This poem, originally called *Salutation,* is different in conception, and in the rhythmical use of polysyllables; it has an unrhymed litany of contemplation (23 lines) inserted in the predominantly narrative free verse. The desert scene, under a Juniper tree, has allusions to the Bible and Dante, which coalesce. The tree is an allusion to the Old Testament (I *Kings* XIX), recalling the prophet Elijah on Mount Carmel. The poem tells us that repentance means dissolution of the old self and a new birth; it deals incidentally with the restorative power of grace and of communion with the Saints. In this part and the two succeeding, Eliot follows the path of Dante, whose quest through Hell, Purgatory and Heaven was a spiritual progress to a beatified Beatrice.

The first episode, one that troubles most readers, is a Dantesque vision of death, as *spiritual* dissolution; the *physical* terms employed are allegorical. The three white leopards of line 1, possibly suggested by *Jeremiah* V.6 and *Hosea* XIII.7, are aspects of the person addressed, the Virgin Mary; these are goodness, beauty and meditation (8–10). Through reverence for the Virgin, the poet voluntarily relinquishes the old, self-regarding life. The

likeness of the Lady to Beatrice is implied in lines 16–21, probably
the most difficult in the poem to interpret:

> The Lady is withdrawn
> In a *white gown,* to contemplation, in a *white gown.*
> Let the *white*ness of bones *atone to forget*fulness.
> There is no life in them. As I am *forgot*ten
> And would be *forgot*ten, so I would *forget*
> Thus devoted, concentrated in purpose.

The symbolic words are *white* (the colour of fidelity) and *forget*
(a prelude to the soul's purgation). One key to understanding is
the earliest meaning of *atone to* in line 18, namely 'be at one with'.
(The modern usage is not found until the latter half of the sixteenth century.) In context, *atone* is an antonym of *dissemble* (11),
which has a dual significance. The punning sense of Eliot is 'dis-
membered'. In the *Purgatorio* (Canto XXX) Beatrice, too, is *veiled*
(*ie, withdrawn*) from sight, but acts as an intermediary between the
dejected spirit of Dante and God.

The symbolic use of the body-members *legs, heart, liver* and
skull (lines 3 and 4) invites annotation, since in Dante's *Vita
Nuova* they signify 'bodily strength', 'feelings', 'passions' and
'perceptions'. The penitent must sacrifice all four, in the secular
functions of the past. The bones that come to life, and are given
breath for speech by the wind, were suggested by the vision of the
prophet in *Ezekiel* (XXXVII, 1–10). In the original sense of
spirit ('breathing') they are relevant to the death-birth relationship
of the poem; in the event, they sing *the burden of the grasshopper* (24),
which is a recollection of *Ecclesiastes* XII.5. In *the posterity of the
desert and the fruit of the gourd* (13), the allusions are to the desert
fathers and St John of the Cross.

Most of the lyrical interlude looks back to Dante's *Paradiso,*
Cantos XXX to XXXIII. The *Lady of silences* (25) is Beatrice and
at the same time Rosa Mystica, or the Virgin Mary. The saints
in Dante's vision make up the petals of a great Rose, signifying
the Church Triumphant. The *Rose of memory* (28) was Eunoë, and
the *Rose of forgetfulness* (29) Lethe, streams in the Earthly Paradise.
Lines 26–7 and 30–47 of Eliot's lyric are a tissue of paradoxes and
oxymorons, rendered obscure by the absence of punctuation as a
guide to syntax. The passage 35–44 contains apparently dis-
traught ejaculations, which illustrate the clash between the sensual

and the spiritual life. The truth is that the richness of the spiritual life depends on the worth of the penitent's choices. Words, though incapable of resolving ambiguities, may be used to 'organize sensibility'. For instance, lines 32–4, borrowed from Dante, read:

The single Rose / Is now the garden / Where all *loves end*

Here the plural *loves* stands for *earthly* passions, and *end* means 'terminate'. In line 47 (where all *love ends*) singular *love* connotes the *spiritual* kind, (and *ends* means 'finds its resting place'. Twelve of the two-stressed lines of the litany are trochaic in rhythm, giving to the initial word semantic prominence.

The last seven lines (48–54) return to the biblical theme, as follows:

Únder *a* júniper-*trée* the bónes sáng, *scáttered* and shíning
We are glád to be *scáttered,* | wè did líttle góod to *eàch óther,*
Únder *a trée* in the cóol of the dáy, | with the bléssing of sánd,
Forgétting themsélves and *eàch óther,* | *united*
In the quíet of the désert. | *Thís is the lánd* which yé
Shall *divíde* by lót. | And nèither *divísion* nor *únity*
Mátters. | *Thís is the lánd.* | Wé hàve our inhéritance.

The heavily stressed lines have the 'Senecan amble' of seventeenth-century prose and Old Testament verse in English translation. Only three are run-on, and the rhythm is modulated by medial pauses and occasional secondary stresses.

Ploce is the dominating scheme of words. The tropes in the quoted passage are: *the bones sang* (48, metonymy); *the blessing of sand* (50, metaphor). Scriptural use of the plural *ye* (52) marks the reference to *Ezekiel* (XLVIII, 29 and XXXVII, 15–22). The *cool of the day* (50) is an obvious allusion to Eden in *Genesis* III, 8.

The predilection of the critics for this poem is due to its spontaneity and mythological truth. Vision is proved to be a credible medium for poetical ideas, and biblical allegory a viable method of conveying the mysteries of religious psychopathology. When *death* and *birth* are allegorically treated, the poet's gift of words liberates them from the physical connotations of Elizabethan tragedy. The interpenetration of allusions enabled Eliot, here as elsewhere, to concentrate in one time and place, some of the comeliest thoughts of past literature, with all their associated overtones of meaning.

PART III, 1929

The third poem's tone is in contrast to the helplessness of the first part; the penitent begins the upward path, but always with distraction and trepidation. The 24 lines of this part are in three irregularly rhymed strophes of 6, 5 and 10 lines, ending with a coda of three lines, in the form of a prayer. In the original version, a further line was added to the latter: 'And my soul shall be healed'. This was subsequently discarded.

The stair represents spiritual advancement, the turnings being efforts to discipline the will. Eliot has in mind the progress of Dante on the Mount of Purgatory, but he may also be thinking of the mystical ladder of St John of the Cross. What is important is the sense in which the noun *turning* is used in the first line of each strophe. Whereas in part I *turning* meant 'going back', here it implies the 'need to surmount' difficulty and temptation, the latter suggested by the *devil* of line 5. The turnings are in progressive order, but only two stairs are mentioned in the poem, the second and the third; the first is passed over, though in strophes 1 and 2 the poet is obviously looking down upon it. There must be significance in this arrangement, Eliot's purpose apparently being to purge the sins of the past rather than the present. This to some extent differentiates Eliot's conception from Dante's.

Each strophe presents a different kind of temptation. In the first, *The same shape twisted on the banister* (3) refers to the evil already surmounted on the first stair, which is self-delusion through *hope* and *despair* (6). The next turning presents one's own struggle from a higher elevation. *There were no more faces* (9) means the absence of masks or 'deceitful' appearances; but lines 10 and 11 present frightening images of unregenerate evil:

Damp, jaggèd, like an old man's mouth drivelling, beyond
    repair,
Or the *toothed gullet of an agèd shark*

The second simile probably represents 'malice'.

The third stair is that of self-improvement through contrition. As the will ascends, the temptations that linger tend to be aesthetic distractions. These are venial sins; the difficulty, however, is to suppress the memory of their sensuous delights. The impressionistic method of suggesting these pleasures is worth noting:

> At the first turning of the *third stair*
> Was a slotted window bellied like the fig's fruit
> And beyond the hawthorn blossom and a pasture scene
> The broadbacked figure drest in blue and green
> Enchanted the maytime with an antique *flute*.
> *Blown hair* is sweet, *brown hair* over the mouth *blown,*
> Lilac and *brown hair*;
> Distraction, *m*usic of the *flute*, *st*ops and *st*eps of the *m*ind
>   over the *third stair,*
> *Fading, fading*; strength beyond hope and despair
> Climbing the *third stair*.   (lines 12–21)

The *strength* acquired by the will in the final stage of spiritual progress is ultimately *beyond hope and despair* (20). The *broadbacked figure
drest in blue and green* (15) is probably meant to be Pan, enchanting
the maytime with an antique flute (16); the introduction of the liturgical colours *blue* and *green* anticipates their use in the next part of
Ash Wednesday.

These lines remind one more of Marlowe and the Elizabethans,
than of the Pre-Raphaelites, whose influence some critics have
found in them. The verse is cunningly constructed, *eg*, line 19 in
its admirable blend of alliteration and assonance. Lines 12–16
employ a flowing, pictorial style, lines 17–21 an abrupt rhythm, to
reflect the *distraction* and *stops and steps of the mind,* mentioned in 19.
Throughout the strophe, Eliot uses past and present participles
(ten times) with pleasing effect, the most prominent being the
metaphor *bellied* in line 13.

The rhetoric of repetition in this citation has interesting
features. *Blown* at the beginning and end of line 17, disturbs the
normal order of words in the sentence (*hyperbaton*) and at the same
time illustrates the scheme of words known as *epanilepsis*. The
word-play between *blown* and *brown*, involving the change of a
single consonant (lines 17–18), is a device much liked by Eliot,
called *antistoecon*. *Ploce* is illustrated in the repetition of the
following words and phrases: *third stair* (12, 19, 21), *flute* (16, 19),
brown hair (17, 18), *fading* (20 twice).

The final prayer *Lord, I am not worthy ... speak the word only*
(22–4) is part of the confession of humility in the ceremony of the

Mass, echoing the words of the centurion of Capernaum in *Matthew* VIII. 8.

PART IV

Two grammatical features of this poem have semantic import. The first is the ambiguous *Who* at the beginning of lines 1, 2, 7 and 8, used as an indefinite pronoun, meaning 'one who', as in '*who* steals my purse steals trash'. The problem is to determine whether *who* is singular or plural. The second is the absence, for the first time in *Ash Wednesday*, of the first personal pronoun *I*. Eliot describes, in impersonal terms, the possibility of redemption through sanctified womanhood, as in the high dream of Cantos XXVI to XXXIII of Dante's *Purgatorio*. The poet suggests this on pp. 47–50 of his study, *Dante*.

In Canto XXVI, 136–148, Dante meets the spirit of the Provençal poet Arnaut Daniel, whose parting words to him are: 'Be mindful of my sufferings'; *Sovegna vos* (10) recalls this speech. *Eternal dolour* (6) is a reminder of the inscription above the gate of Hell in Canto III of the *Inferno*. It is most likely that Eliot was thinking of Matilda in Cantos 27–8 of the *Purgatorio,* when he wrote the opening line: *Who walked between the violet and the violet*.

The poem, in 29 irregularly rhymed lines, has a strophic division of 8, 3, 3, 7, 3, 3, 1, 1 lines. The strophes have little logical connection, though there is a clear division at line 21. Both parts are sparsely punctuated, especially at the end of lines and strophes. There are two tercets in each half, unlike the terza rima of Dante, because they are irregular in the number of syllables and virtually unrhymed. The poem aptly illustrates Eliot's technical resources of controlled free verse.

In lines 1, 3, 4, 10, 15 and 22, the liturgical colours, violet, green, white, blue, respectively symbolize penitence, hope, purity and heavenly attributes (those of the Virgin Mary). The first strophe suggests the acquiescence of the disciplined soul in seclusion, unconscious of the unhappiness and restlessness of the world. Assuming that *who* is singular, the one who *walks* is imaged as a nun; her *talking of trivial things* (5) indicates that the worldly life and the spiritual are not incompatible, but antithetical. Thus the lady is said to be both '*In ignorance and in knowledge of eternal dolour*' (6). Throughout, images of the physical and

spiritual world are juxtaposed. But blessed with grace, the
religious can withdraw 'to contemplation', and is adjured by St
Paul in *Colossians* IV, 5 and *Ephesians* V, 16 to *Redeem the time*
(18/19, 26).

The garden where the devout sisters *walk* is Eliot's version of
the Earthly Paradise; here harmony does not come from the
fiddles and the flutes (13), but from reconciling activity with peace,
and a lovely environment with spirituality. Paradise is certainly in the
poet's mind in the vision of Beatrice in her beatitude (lines 14–15).

> One who moves in the time between sleep and waking,
>   wearing
> White light *folded,* sheathed about her, *folded.*

The repetition of the attributive participle is noteworthy. The
words *restoring | With a new verse the ancient rhyme* (17/18) un-
doubtedly refer to the hoped-for rejuvenation of the poet's
talents. 'The *unread* vision' of line 20 implies that the *higher dream*
is commonly misunderstood. Dante's pomp and pageantry are not
thought of as vanity in line 21:

> While *jewelled unicorns* draw by the gilded hearse.

Such unicorns are said to have been depicted in a Florentine
engraving of Petrarch's 'Triumph of Chastity.' But Eliot's
recollection was of the triumphal car, drawn by a gryphon, which
carried Beatrice to Paradise in *Purgatorio*, XXIX.

The latter half of the poem provides a graceful solution to the
mystery. The *yews* (23, 28) are symbols of resurrection and immortality; the *word* (27) is the Logos of St John, and the *wind*
(28) symbolizes the spirit of God. Death becomes an enviable
state, and life itself is *an exile,* comparable to that of Dante, who
found both good and bad in it.

> The *s*ílent *s*íster véiled in *wh*íte and *b*lúe
> *B*etwéen the *y*éws, | *b*ehínd the gárden *g*ód,
> Whose *fl*úte is *b*réathless, | *b*ént her héad and *s*ígned | but
>   spóke nó *w*órd
>
> But the *f*óuntain *s*práng úp | and the *b*írd *s*áng dówn
> *R*edéem the tíme, | redéem the *d*réam
> The tóken of the *w*órd unhéard, un*sp*óken

Till the *w*índ *sh*àke a thóusand *wh*íspers from the *yéw*

And àfter thís our éxile   (lînes 22–29)

The *garden god* (23), Priapus, is represented by a statue, so that
naturally the *flute is breathless* (24). *Signed* (24) means 'made an
appropriate gesture of respect'. For Eliot, this was not inconsistent with the paganism of the deity, but another witness to the
reconciliation of two worlds. Perhaps there is significance in the
sign of the cross being made *behind* the statue.

Technically, the rhythm is modulated by control of the vowel
and consonant sounds; the melody is partly achieved by alliteration
of the words beginning with *s, w, b, g, f* and *d*, and the assonance of
lines such as 26–27, which tease the ear by internal rhyme:

> Red*ee*m the time, red*ee*m the dr*ea*m
> The *token* of the word unheard, un*spoken*

These words, with the configuration of prophecy, are designedly
cast in the incantational mould. Lines 22–24: 'The silent sister . . .
signed' are in immaculate blank verse; but the last has supernumerary stresses, and the iambic rhythm is abandoned in lines 25
and 28. Eliot's principle was not to settle long in a conventional
rhythm, lest it should become stereotyped.

The rhetorical scheme of words is predominantly *ploce,* the words
repeated being *yew, spoke, word* and *redeem.* Schemes of thought
are found in the syntactical and semantic antitheses of lines 23 and
25 respectively. The tropes are not many, but purposeful:

Personification: 24 Whose *flute is breathless* (the sense of *breathless*
    is here 'impotent')
Metaphor (with hyperbole): 28 Till the wind *shake a thousand
    whispers* from the yew
Metonymy: 29 after this *our exile* (this phrase comes from the
    prayer *Salve Regina,* addressed to the Virgin Mary).

PART V

A querulous incantation on the Logos in the prelude to the Gospel
of St John (1–9), and a return to the *veiled sister* (20, 24, 29), link
this poem to the preceding one; the whirling words point to a
necessary relation between penitence and the Incarnation of the
Word in Christ. A note of firm declamation marks the rhythm,

with the poet playing upon the homophones *Word, World* and *whirled* in recollection of the Christmas sermon of Lancelot Andrewes in 1611. The sorrows of Christ are echoed in the refrain: *O my people, what have I done unto thee* (10, 28). The source of this is the Lord's rebuke to the backsliders of Israel in *Micah* VI.3.

The poem is a meditation in free verse, its tones reminiscent of the Wisdom books of the Bible – a form Eliot devised by combining Hebrew parallelism with Greek schematic rhetoric. There are four strophes, with 9, 9, 8 and 7 irregularly stressed lines, whose length is determined by the cadence of the words. Rhyme is predominantly internal in the song-like strophes 1 and 2; it is both internal and terminal in the others.

The first strophe reflects despair and even exasperation with words, finding an outlet in *paronomasia* (semantic punning). The lapsing penitent is confused by the worldly and spiritual meanings of *Logos*, eg, 7 *the light shines in darkness* (*John* I, 5). A passage in Reinhold Niebuhr's *The Godly and the Ungodly* (Faber, 1958, pp. 123–37) throws some light on Eliot's situation:

> We live our life in various realms of meaning, which do not quite cohere rationally. Our meanings are surrounded by a penumbra of mystery, which is not penetrated by reason... Sir John Davies, writing in the early seventeenth century, elaborates a persistent theme of the poets in his lines:
>
> 'I know my life's a pain and but a span, I know
>   my sense is mocked in everything;
> And to conclude, I know myself a man which is
>   a proud and yet a wretched thing.'
>
> Biblical faith, or rather the two faiths rooted in the Bible, Judaism and Christianity, engage in the hazardous enterprise of discerning in some events in history a revelatory depth or height, a 'light that shineth in darkness', which are clues to the meaning of history. Christianity goes farther and asserts in the words of the Johannine prologue that all previous revelatory moments are summarized and climaxed in the drama of the suffering Messiah, in the 'Christ event' ...
>
> The faith of the New Testament does not regard the excessive self-regard of men as 'natural'. It insists that the inclination of

men to make themselves their own ends is a corruption of the freedom which makes it necessary to find their end beyond themselves.

The Word that is *unheard, unspoken* (2) refers to the still inarticulate Infant Christ; but it also looks back to line 27 of part IV, and to the *silence* of the veiled sister in 22-4 of that poem. The last two lines of strophe 1 (8-9) recall the turning wheel at the end of Dante's *Paradiso* (Canto XXXIII):

> But yet the *will* roll'd onward, like a wheel
> In even motion, by the *Love* impell'd
> That moves the sun in Heaven and all her stars.

The second strophe is a response to the distraction of the first. *Silence*, at the end of line 11, is a condition of spiritual rebirth. Salvation is not found in any geographical region, but in the heart of the man who faces his situation (18 No place of grace *for those who avoid the face*). This recalls Dante's inability to look at the shining presence of Beatrice in Canto XXX of the *Purgatorio*.

The third strophe records the penitent's self-searching. The convert is like other spiritually unenlightened persons; he has responded to the Word, but not sufficiently; he is yet torn between the spiritual and material worlds. Will the sister in holy orders (an analogue for Beatrice) intercede for the soul of such a man?

In strophe four the theme is man's spiritual hesitancy. Eliot refers to those who affirm emotionally (32 *before the world*) and deny intellectually (*between the rocks*); in the heart the joy of the *garden* (34) is made arid by doubt, symbolized in the *desert | Of drouth*. The metaphor *spitting from the mouth the withered apple-seed* (35) probably represents the act of confession; but the final words can only suggest the temptation in Eden. There is, however, an optimistic note of victory in the final struggle.

The verbal patterning in this part of *Ash Wednesday* reveals a rhetorical virtuosity unequalled in modern poetry:

> *Whére* shall the *wórd* be fóund, | *whére* will the *wórd*
> Resoúnd? | *Nót hére,* | there is *nòt* enough sílence
> *Nót* on the séa or on the íslands, | *nót*
> On the máinlànd, | in the désert or the ráin lànd,
> For *thóse* who *wálk* in dárkness
> Bóth in the dáy *tìme* | and in the níght *tìme*
> The *ríght tìme* | and the *ríght* pláce are *nòt hére*

Nó pláce of gráce for thóse who avóid the fáce
Nó tíme to rejóice for *thóse* who *wálk* among nóise | and dený
    the voíce   (lines 11–19)

In each strophe the rhythm is firmly established by the disposition of strong stresses, and sensitively modulated by internal
pauses. Only two lines (11, 13) are enjambed; five others have
double endings (12, 14–17), whose effect upon the rhythm is to
throw the line into bold relief.

In the strophe quoted, the central line, both positionally and
semantically, is *For those who walk in darkness* (15). It contains the
Johannine metaphor that turns, in the succeeding line, to paradox
(*in the day time*). The strophe is built on the collaborative principles
of antithesis and paradox, assonance and alliteration, making the
fullest use of internal rhymes. Of these *silence | islands* (12/13) and
noise | voice (19) are imperfect.

Ploce is seen in the sporadic repetition of *Where, here, word, not*
(five times), *those, walk, right* and *time* (four times). The other
schemes of words employed are:

Epanilepsis: 13 *Not* on the sea or on the islands, *not*
Epanaphora: 18/19 *No* place of grace for those who avoid the face /
    No time to rejoice

The schemes of thought that illustrate balance are:
Parison (clauses in parallel construction): 11/12 Where shall the
    word be found, where will the word / Resound?
Anthypophora (where a rhetorical point is answered): Where will
    the word / Resound? *Not here, there is not enough silence*
Carmen correlativum (special arrangement of corresponding words):
    14 On *the mainland,* in the desert or on *the rain land*

All this patterning would have been jejune, but for the plangent
music Eliot extracted from it, and the earnest beliefs he put into
it.

PART VI

Freshness and strength, after resolved conflict, are the keynotes
of this poem, which resembles *Marina* in its sea visions and use of
the storehouse of memories. The sea suggests the expansiveness of
God's beneficence, once the soul is liberated from its envelope of
self-regard. The poet's theme is *The dreamcrossed twilight between*

birth and dying (6), and it takes the form of a confession, indicated by the words *Bless me father* in the next line. Hope replaces despair in the final invocation to the Virgin Mary.

The introduction repeats the first three lines of part I, with a significant change: the concessive conjunction *Although* replaces *Because,* revealing that spiritual progress has been made. Then follow three strophes of 7, 9 and 15 lines, rounded by a single-line coda, which is part of a prayer to the Holy Mother. The typographical divisions are visual; for all the sections are linked by syntax or rhyme. The first strophe is rhymed irregularly, the second in couplets. In strophe 3 most lines are usually unrhymed, though 28, 30 and 33 are exceptions, the last of these rhyming with *Thee* in the coda.

Lines 8–22 of the poem should be compared with *Cape Ann* and *The Dry Salvages*:

From the *w*íde *w*índow towàrds the gránite shóre
The *w*híte *s*áils *s*till *fly séaward,* | *séaward flý*ing
Unbróken *w*íngs

And the *lóst* héart *s*tíffens *and* rejóices
In the *lóst l*ílac | *and* the *lóst s*éa vóices
And the wéak spírit *quíckens* to rebél
For the bént gólden-ród | *and* the *lóst* seá sméll
Quíckens to recóver
The crý of quáil | *and* the *w*hírling plóver
And the blínd éye créates
The émpty fórms *betwéen* the ívory gátes
*And s*méll renéws the *s*ált *s*ávour of the *s*ándy eárth

Thís is the *t*íme of *t*énsion | *betwèen* dýing and bírth
The pláce of sólitude | where thrée dréams cróss
Betwéen blúe rócks

This singularly moving passage evokes memories of the New England coast of Eliot's youth. The sea is viewed from the land; the poet feels that he is no longer a part of it, as a sailor isolated on the ocean is. The impression conveyed is that the sea no longer moves him actively, as it did. What he now seeks is grace through penance.

Wavering between the profit and the loss (4) is an image not unworthy of an ex-banker assessing the sacrifices of the new life. The penitent in the second strophe echoes the word *lost,* as though fitfully regretting the loss of physical awareness (lines 11, 12, 14). Such are the fragrant memories of *lilac, golden rod, sea voices, sea smell,* the cries of birds and *the salt savour of the sandy earth* (19). Actually, the better part of his nature rejoices in the forsaken beauty of nature; for he finds, in puritanical rejection, that the new symbols are adequate to express his revitalized faith. The *blind eye* (17) is a symbol for memory; and the *empty forms* it creates are 'worldly distractions'; by *ivory gates* is meant 'false dreams'. The gates of sleep are mentioned at the end of the sixth book of Vergil's *Aeneid.* The *time of tension between dying and birth* (20) is the new life (note the reversal of order), whose struggle is never-ending.

In strophe 3 Eliot's first purpose is to identify the figures that appear in parts 2 and 4 of *Ash Wednesday.* The *veiled* (or *Blessèd*) *sister,* the *spirit of the fountain,* and the *spirit of the garden* (25) are recognized as aspects of *Beatrice* in Dante's *Divina Commedia,* representing both the Church and the Virgin Mary. In a pantheistic vision, Eliot sees them also as *spirit of the river, spirit of the sea* (33). The second yew tree of part IV becomes the voice of prayer (24); the *rocks* (29) are symbols of aridity and destruction. Three supplications all take the form of allusions. *Our peace in His will* (30) echoes *Paradiso* III, 85 (embodying St Paul's teaching in *Ephesians* II, 12–16). In the relevant scene, Beatrice leads Dante to the Moon (symbol of inconstancy), where he talks with Piccarda dei Donati; there she expounds to him the poet's belief in Paradise as 'the identity of the soul's will' and God's:

> His will our peace;
> This is the *sea* whereunto all things fare

Suffer me not to be separated (34) comes from an old prayer *Anima Christi; let my cry come unto Thee* is one of the suffrages of church liturgy.

The rhythm of the passage is nuanced by caesural employment of the internal pauses in lines 12, 14, 16 and 20; modulation of this kind is invariably necessary in a succession of rhyming couplets. It is aided by the alliterative use of words beginning with *w, s, l* and *t,* and four enjambed lines in the second strophe (11, 14, 15, 17). In this strophe there are eight uses of the co-ordinating conjunction *and.* This *polysyndeton* leads, in lines 13 to 16, to obscure syntax, the semantic function of *Quickens to recover* (15) being uncertain.

In Eliot's poetry it is often hard to distinguish metaphor and symbol. *The white sails . . . fly . . . | Unbroken wings* (9/10) and the *lost heart stiffens* (11) are metaphors; but the *lost lilac* (12), the *blind eye* (17), the *ivory gates* (18) and the *blue rocks* (22), as used by Eliot in *Ash Wednesday*, are mainly private symbols. Too frequently, the symbolism adds to the problems of meaning. The reader tends to be concerned with the properties of things symbolized, and not with the purposeful use of the poet's language.

Schemes of thought are prominent. The repetition of *fly, seaward, lost* and *between* constitutes *ploce*.

Ash Wednesday, if not generally regarded as the best of Eliot's poems, was influential in bringing to fruition most of his technical accomplishments. Every facet of his mature art has its roots in the conception of this poem, the most satisfying of his tributes to Dante. But while Dante's theme was the morals and religion of a politically unstable society, Eliot's was the private conscience. His conflict arose from experiences that could not be expunged from memory, while worldly distractions kept intervening. His was not really the mind that could isolate itself in the intellectual world, by embracing the negative philosophy of St John of the Cross, who was also a poet.

The six parts of the poem are contemplative steps in a convert's progress from hopelessness to regeneration and no doubt Eliot achieved, through application to the faith, a remedial release from nervous tension. His reconciliation of faith and reason was not unlike that of Pascal, to whose *Pensées* he wrote an illuminating introduction. Eliot, too, had a sneaking admiration for Montaigne, whose scepticism was not only 'puckish', but obstinate. As Eliot himself made clear:

> Every man who thinks and lives by thought must have his own scepticism, that which stops at the question, that which ends in denial, or that which leads to faith and which is somehow integrated into the faith which transcends it.
>
> (Pascal's *Pensées*, Introd. p. xv)

The problem of Eliot's inability to say something hard and definite in discursive poetry remains. Through the association of images and symbols employed, the reader divines the drift of his discourse. But the poem cannot be assessed from the thoughts propagated; its meaning dawns only when the reasons for the poet's associations are understood. With Eliot, the clues are invariably the allusions to his sources, often casually disclosed in the prose he was engaged on at the time.

To counter the accusation that Eliot is wilfully mystifying, one has to turn to some of the earliest observations on poetry in *The Sacred Wood*. In 'Tradition and the Individual Talent' he wrote that a poem is 'a new thing resulting from the concentration of a very great number of experiences . . . *which does not happen consciously or of deliberation*'; in 'The Perfect Critic' he said: 'The end of the enjoyment of poetry is *pure contemplation from which all the accidents of personal emotion are removed*'. If there is a distinction to be found between the language of the poetry and that of the prose, it is this: that in the former he is sceptical of his knowledge of truth; in the latter he directs us, in very intelligible language, to the path along which he hopes to find it. In the poetry he sees things through a glass, darkly; in the prose he proclaims the truth he hopes will make men free.

The ulterior motive for *Ash Wednesday* was undoubtedly to show that controlled vision, such as Dante's, is still possible through spiritual exercises. Eliot believed, not unjustly, that the pragmatical learning of the past two centuries has deprived men of those ritualistic, repetitive symbols that the heart once understood and received with delight.

In the poems of this period it is therefore necessary to envisage two kinds of experience, the poet's and the reader's. The poet's is presented in evocative symbols or images, with little expectation of intellectual response. The reader's reception is different for different persons, depending on the reactions each has in attempting to interpret the poem. If he cannot, at a first reading, understand it, he may still be emotively affected by the power and skill of the words, in the kind of association he can make.

Even when Eliot's verse contains social criticism, as in the Choruses from *The Rock* (1934), it is subjective; it deals with the feelings that accompany the attitudes, rather than with the attitudes themselves. The monologue style has inexplicable switches from one mode of presentation to another, and these may be disconcerting to the reader, as *Ash Wednesday* has shown.

Eliot is that unique phenomenon, a philosophizing poet. Disparate perceptions of time intrigue him; he asks that we should be conscious 'not only of the pastness of the past, but of its presence'. The concurrence of time and place has, for him, both a personal and practical relevance, upon which he continually reflects:

> All our knowledge brings us nearer to our ignorance,
> All our ignorance brings us nearer to death,
> But nearness to death no nearer to GOD.
> Where is the Life we have lost in living?
> Where is the wisdom we have lost in knowledge?
> Where is the knowledge we have lost in information? ...
>
> The world turns and the world changes,
> But one thing does not change.
> In all of my years, one thing does not change.
> However you disguise it, this thing does not change:
> The perpetual struggle of Good and Evil ...
> The desert is not remote in southern tropics,
> The desert is not only around the corner,
> The desert is squeezed in the tube-train next to you,
> The desert is in the heart of your brother.
> The good man is the builder, if he build what is good ...
>
> In the land of lobelias and tennis flannels
> The rabbit shall burrow and the thorn revisit,
> The nettle shall flourish on the gravel court,
> And the wind shall say: 'Here were decent godless people:
> Their only monument the asphalt road
> And a thousand lost golf balls'.
>
> (Choruses from The Rock, I and III.)

This is social criticism, religiously aimed and immediately intelligible. It had to serve the purposes of a drama that Eliot himself did not write. The modern discontents are treated with irony, in comparing the futility of life in the Unreal City (London) with Dante's Hell. The experiences sinners gather, like the accumulation of their wealth, are mistakenly regarded as valuable in themselves.

But here, as elsewhere, the ringing of changes is so varied that the style defies systematic analysis. The attitudes are *personae,* not because the treatment is impersonal (we have seen that it often is not), but because it is oblique. The only direct writing is in the humorous verse of *Old Possum's Book of Practical Cats* (1939). Eliot wrote approvingly of Ben Jonson's satirical method as, perhaps, the most serviceable in spirit for the incorrigible follies of our time. But *his poetry*, even in satire, is the antithesis of the direct, formalized writing of the English Augustan poets. For similar reasons, classic and romantic fall away, in considering most modern poetry.

CHAPTER VIII

T. S. Eliot (3):
Four Quartets, 1936–42

᠁᠁᠁᠁᠁

I<small>F</small> the Choruses of *The Rock* may be described as Eliot's 'Vanity of Human Wishes', it would not be amiss to compare *Four Quartets* with Lucretius's *De Rerum Natura*, Sir John Davies's *Nosce Teipsum*, Dryden's *Religio Laici* and Pope's *Essay on Man*. The theme is time and history in relation to personal belief. Most of *Burnt Norton* was written during the period of Eliot's residence with Father Eric Cheetham, Vicar of St Stephen's Church, Gloucester Road, of which Eliot became Warden in 1934. The four titles offer an internal allegory, conveyed through meditation, in moving symbolic verse; and it is necessary to recapture their holistic purpose if the thoughts and feelings embodied in the religious experience are to become intelligible. Eliot's caution should always be remembered: an 'approach to the meaning restores the experience / In a different form' (*The Dry Salvages* II, 46–7). There is, unfortunately, no alternative but to divine what the poems are about.

The poems studied in the preceding two chapters reveal that Eliot prefers the traditional or personal symbol to the sensuous metaphor. Symbols are figures of thought, rather than of speech. Eliot's *rose, garden, wheel, rock, sea, fire* and *water* are universal symbols of psychological import; unlike the metaphorical Boston fog, they come from ancient literary and anthropological sources. For Eliot, these are 'objective correlatives'; they fuse meaning with sensation, they help to connect the conscious with the unconscious mind. A reader who looks beyond the artistic purpose of the poems, will not stop at the level of their prose meaning, but aim at the ulterior suggestive significance.

Despite their difficulties, the twenty poems of *Four Quartets* become coherent through their formal structure; they are on the theme of time, not as a physical abstraction, but as a background

213

to spiritual growth; they also show how the flux of time multiplies the problems of verbal communication.

The explication of symbolist poetry has attendant dangers, with which practical critics are familiar. The pattern, as C. A. Bodelsen makes clear in his *Commentary* (Copenhagen University, 1958) is also 'closely involved in Eliot's *theodicy*', and a design in the dimension of time must, necessarily, be fragmentary to the mortal observer. In these poems, Eliot's faith seems to release him from the bondage of time, and enables us, in moments of illumination, to see the whole pattern. Meaninglessness gradually gives place to significance. Eliot's poems are meant to image the truths of existence more cogently than works, such as J. W. Dunne's *The Serial Universe* and *An Experiment with Time,* with which the poet was probably acquainted.

The universal style of *Four Quartets* is an efflorescence that seems to occur in culminating ages, like those of Vergil, Dante, Shakespeare and Eliot. He owed more to Dante than to anyone in the English tradition since the literary revolution of the seventeenth century; and his modernism was able to reach a wide audience, because the spirit of the time was congenial to the rejection of the romantic ideal of poetry.

The poet's interest in words, was, however, Shakespearian in the many levels of response and types of association found in these poems. They are full of esoteric learning. He has done more here than elsewhere to separate the functions of poetry and prose, while recognizing critically the limits of their special appeals. About the levelling of their techniques, especially in the play he had just written, *Murder in the Cathedral*, he was wholly unrepentant. Individual poems in each of the *Four Quartets* are in the colloquial idiom of fireside discourse, perhaps to counter their weight of dialectic. Eliot seems to have shared Poe's contention that a long poem (and particularly a philosophical one) is a contradiction in terms. The homiletic tone of some passages at first seems fitter for the essay than for poetry; for example, *Little Gidding*, III, 10–14:

> Thus, love of a country
> Begins as attachment to our own field of action
> And comes to find that action of little importance
> Though never indifferent.

Useful interpretations are sometimes matters of chance, rather

than deliberation; for instance, lines 35–39 of the first Movement
of *Little Gidding*:

> There are other places
> Which also are the world's end, some at the sea jaws,
> Or over a dark lake, in a desert or a city –
> But this is the nearest, in place and time
> Now and in England.

Bodelsen, after noting that the 'other places' are Iona, Lindisfarne,
Lake Glendalough and the Thebiad – dwelling places of saints –
comments: 'The above would have remained insoluble puzzles
but for the information supplied by Eliot's friend John Hayward
in his notes to Pierre Leyris's translation (*Quatre Quatuors*, p.
149)'. Such allusions, without ascertainable referents, are regarded by impatient critics as brakes on the reader's search for
enlightenment.

In *An Experiment in Criticism* (Cambridge University Press,
1961) C. S. Lewis observes how the increasing 'purification' of
poetry (which dates from *The Waste Land*) has narrowed its
audience to 'arty' dons, intellectuals and practising poets. The
field of poetry is now limited, he thinks, to the things prose
cannot attempt to do; which affects interpretation, since it is not
possible to derive meaning, except in snatches from the poet's
emotive effects. The expositor-critic thus becomes a necessary
intermediary, and his interpretation can never be said to be 'right'
(even by the poet himself), but only 'better' than that of some
other hierophant. The disadvantages of this for posterity are
obvious. In a century it is possible that Eliot's poetry will be a
closed book.

What C. S. Lewis calls 'a trance-like condition', enabling images,
associations and sounds to operate without 'logical and narrative
connection', (p. 97) T. S. Eliot established as one of poetry's
legitimate functions. The incantational verse in *Four Quartets* is
effective, largely because of Eliot's contrapuntal skill and use of
symbols that may mean several things at the same time.

The unity of the twenty poems consists less in their speculations
about time than in the harmony of the faith to which a kind of
signature tune inevitably recalls us. Through the symbols and
rhythms of the poetry, Eliot offers a mystical religion with conviction for readers who know and appreciate the Thomism of

Dante. His individual expression, and ability to assimilate foreign material without pastiche, gives validity to poetry that reflects the intellectual uncertainty of the age.

Eliot patterned the poems, in mood and content, on the lines of musical compositions, whose overtones are discerned in the intricate network of allusions. The conception of *Four Quartets* was, no doubt, adumbrated in a lecture Eliot gave at New Haven in 1933; there he envisaged an ideal that he thought would be worth attempting: 'poetry so transparent that in reading it we are intent on what the poem *points at*, and not the poetry... To get *beyond poetry*, as Beethoven, in his later works, strove to get *beyond music*'.

If *Four Quartets* did not fulfil the aspiration for verbal transparency, it came near to succeeding in Eliot's formal analogy. To borrow an aesthetic idea of Walter Pater, each group 'aspires to the condition of music', and in particular to the sonata form of Beethoven's final quartets. Eliot's personal taste was for the Quartet in A Minor, Opus 132, which has five movements. The relation of *Four Quartets* to the form of chamber music has been fully discussed by H. Howarth in *Notes on Some Figures Behind T. S. Eliot*, (Chatto and Windus, 1965, pp. 277–89). This writer suggests that Eliot culled expressive hints, such as 'Old men ought to be explorers' (*East Coker* V, 31), from J. W. N. Sullivan's book *Beethoven – His Spiritual Evolution*.

The play of verbal instruments in each 'movement' of the poems embodies principles of dialectic, such as reversal and contrast, these being suggested by different voices. *Burnt Norton* serves as a good model. The first movement in blank verse has considerable impact, because it states the principal theme, and then proceeds to another in contradictory terms. The second movement begins with a rhymed lyrical passage, which gives place to a conversational piece usually in free verse, with a personal significance. The third movement delves into and reconciles what has gone before, while the fourth is again songlike in character. The fifth movement attempts a recapitulation in two sections, the first conversational, the second serious and in stricter rhythm. This may sound like a concert-programme, but it indicates that the groups of poems have a designed unity in their apparent variety.

There are four quartets because in medieval belief the universe was composed of the four elements, air, earth, water and fire, which respectively symbolize thought, life, flux of the blood and pure love. In Eliot's conception, the different permutations of these elements illustrate, through nature imagery, the different phases of the *psyche* or soul. In each poem the soul is on trial at different elemental levels. The titles of the groups of poems, which appear in the order of the elements given, represent places of historical or personal interest to the poet.

As usual, Eliot begins the poetic discourse with epigraphs, in this case from Heraclitus, as preserved in Diels's *Fragments from the Pre-Socratics* (page 77, no. 2, and p. 89, No. 60):

(i) 'Though the law of reason is universal, the common herd live as though they possessed a wisdom of their own'.
(ii) 'The way upward and downward are one and the same'.

Both Heraclitus and St John of the Cross make play with the resolution of opposites, and in *The Dry Salvages*, III, Eliot fuses ideas from Hinduism and Buddhism with those of Heraclitus.

Man's consciousness of time takes many forms, but the core of the spiritual conception is found in the *Upanishads* and St Augustine – the liberation of self into a new dimension. Spiritual life makes the world explicit on a new plane, in a way impossible for the determinist, for whom time is what the Greeks style a cyclic phenomenon. St Augustine explained the relationship between physical time and the eternal in his *Confessions* and *The City of God*, and came to the consluion that time was purely psychological. The mystic, through vision, has intimations of immortality, at the intersection of physical time and eternity; thus Dante's dream enabled him to perceive simultaneously, and whole, the fragmentary experiences of life's pilgrimage. *The still point of the turning world* (*Burnt Norton*, II, 16) is older than the Christian tradition, and attainable through withdrawal from the endless turmoil and movement of existence.

It would appear that the drains and tensions of Eliot's domestic and public life compelled him daily to retreat within himself and seek detachment; these poems depict the paradoxes of every believer's situation. As a creative artist, he found that awareness is achieved through concentration on the present moment – something that Aristotle and Kierkegaard, for different reasons, also recommended.

There is evidence of scholastic tightness and precision in

Eliot's language; but in contrast, there is also much bafflement at the imprecision of words. The problem of the poet, seeking order out of chaos, had been voiced before in *The Rock* IX, 21-24:

> Out of the sea of sound the life of music,
> Out of the slimy mud of words, out of the sleet and hail of
> *verbal imprecisions*,
> Approximate thoughts and feelings, words that have taken the
> place of thoughts and feelings,
> There spring the *perfect order of speech*, and the beauty of incantation.

It will be the task of the remaining pages to study this quest for order, and to interpret some of the symbols that make *Four Quartets* meaningful. As Eliot explained in the Introduction to Pascal's *Pensées*, 'even the most exalted mystic must return to the world, and use his reason to employ the results of his experience in daily life'.

Burnt Norton, the only poem of the series written before the Second World War, had its origin in material that was unusable in *Murder in the Cathedral* (1935). Parts I and II do not seem to contain much from this source. All the other poems arose out of war conditions, and were attuned to the spirit of that trying time.

BURNT NORTON, 1936

This title was suggested by a Cotswold manor house near Chipping Campden, which Eliot visited in 1934. The place was deserted when he entered the rose-garden and discovered the empty concrete pool. Probably the motto on the sundial read: 'Redeem the time'. Some children happened to be hiding in the shrubbery, and their merriment won the poet's friendliness.

I

The language of the opening ten lines is in the dogmatic style of scholastic philosophers, who were influenced by the logic of Aristotle. Like Aquinas, who said that even God cannot undo the past, Eliot reconciled Christianity with some beliefs in Hellenic and oriental religion. Throughout he repeats the theme that *all time is eternally present* (4); the corollary, *All time is unredeemable* (5) is found in the unknown philosopher of *Ecclesiastes* III, 15:

That which hath beene, is now: and that which is to be, hath
alreadie beene, and God requireth that which is past.

The introduction is succeeded by a passage of 33 lines in words of
enigmatic clarity. The *rose-garden* (14), a symbol which dates back
to Persian mystical literature, stands in Eliot for the sensuous, for
natural beauty. But to this he opposes the spiritual way, upward as
by Dante's stair to the source of light, or downward as by St
John's Dark Night of the Soul. The first of these alternatives is the
way of the saint, the second that of the sufferer who purges the
dross of temporal life.

By a bridge passage (11–17), Eliot transfers to a world of
reverie and fantasies of the past. *Down the passage which we did not
take | Towards the door we never opened* (12–13) recalls the adventures
of *Alice in Wonderland*, where, according to Louis L. Martz, the
garden symbolizes the heroine's longing for 'spiritual refresh-
ment' (*T. S. Eliot, A Selected Critique,* ed. L. Unger, Rinehart,
1948, p. 448). The *bowl of rose-leaves* (15) is the poet's reservoir of
memories.

In a world of simultaneity, which embodies a symbolic bird,
as in D. H. Lawrence and Maeterlinck, the poet sees graceful
figures, which are ghosts from his forgotten life. *Deception* (22)
suggests that happy memories may delude. For earthly peace is an
illusion; most of us are like the 'closed selves' of F. H. Bradley,
mere recorders of phenomenal details. *Moving without pressure* (24
'disembodied') is a metaphorical way of referring to the fourth
dimension, 'space time'. In the difficult lines that follow (28–32)
the sensuous images cannot be logically elucidated:

> And the únseen eýebéam cróssed, | for the róses
> Had the lóok of flówers that are lóoked at.
> Thére thèy wére | as our gúests, | accépted and accépting.
> So we móved, | and thèy, | in a fórmal páttern,
> Alòng the émpty álley, | ìnto the bóx círcle . . .

The first three lines must imply that a spiritual relation exists
between the beauty of the physical world and human perceptions.
They in line 30 refers to the ghostly figures of the past; the *formal
pattern* (31) stands for culture and discipline of the soul; and the
empty alley (32) implies 'life' as we lead it. *Drained pool | Dry the
pool, dry concrete* (33/4) are appropriate symbols of spiritual aridity.

But the poet does not linger in the drought-land of *The Hollow Men*. The pool *filled with water out of sunlight* (35) is a mirage; but water symbolizes a need for spiritual fulfilment. The *lotos* (36) is a Buddhist image of forgetfulness and fertility, more pragmatic than the rose in the mystic world of Dante. *Heart of light* (37) recalls Dante's *Paradiso* XII, 28, where the pilgrim is taught the Thomist truth that 'knowledge of God precedes love'. In the baffling reference *they were behind us, reflected in the pool* (38), *they*, no doubt, represents the merry children discovered among the leaves; but the secondary meaning is our 'potential selves, behind real selves'.

The last three lines (44–6) function as a musical coda, returning to the theme of the opening lines. Indeed, the thought in the poem is neatly summarized in *What might have been and what has been | Point to one end* (45–6). The end in view is eternal life, and the object of *Burnt Norton* I is to give a fleeting glimpse of its reality.

The poetry has a stately cadence, firmly sustained by strong stresses, and sensitively modulated by internal pauses. There are five contiguous primary stresses in line 28. Notice the unostentatious roles that assonance and *ploce* play in the rhythm of lines 28–32. The essential qualities of this forward-looking poetry are the magic of its music, and the integrating power of its symbols. Although the lines are unrhymed, their infinitely varied movement offers no hint of blank verse. Eliot had been experimenting for some time on a measure, without discernible metrical pattern, that would provide a natural medium for the dialogue of his plays.

II

Burnt Norton shows that Eliot has a taste for epiphanies similar to that of James Joyce in *A Portrait of the Artist as a Young man*. An *epiphany* is a revelation in a moment of time. Having experienced the grace of vision, the believer undergoes a reaction, often negative and meaningless, which is apt to discourage for apparent want of progress. The second movement of *Burnt Norton* therefore appears paradoxical in relation to the first; the human spirit is bogged down in opposing tensions implied by that second epigraph of Heraclitus.

The movement begins with a lyrical strophe of 15 lines, the opening ones being suggested by two sonnets of Mallarmé, *M'introduire dans ton histoire* and *Le tombeau de Charles Baudelaire*.

The mingling of repulsive and elevating experience is borne out by juxtaposing '*Garlic and sapphires* in the mud'. The poem's paradoxical realism is sustained by *The trilling wire in the blood* (3 'the vibrant music of life'), which mollifies *inveterate scars* (4 'wounds of hatred healed by time'), the latter a phrase borrowed from Chapman's translation of Petrarch's second *Penitential Psalm*. Lines 6–15 are symbolic to the point of obscurity. The forces of life assert themselves, but beneath the metaphorical tree of life, old physical patterns continue, activated by the unconscious mind. *Reconciled among the stars* (15) suggests that there is no longer conflict with the spiritual ideal. The *figured leaf* (11) is thought by Grover Smith to be a recollection of line 811 of Tennyson's *In Memoriam*.

The second section has 28 lines of unrhymed free verse, beginning with five long ones, which emphasize stillness, balance, not movement, as essential to peace. The *still point* (16 'axis') of *the turning world* (symbolical wheel of Fortune) is the realization of the new life. From this point of rest, the centre of spirituality, all action worthy of the name begins. *The dance* (17 and 21) has a paradoxical significance; for Aristotle pointed out that movement is the measure of time. In line 22, *I can only say, there we have been: but I cannot say where,* the word *there* (italicized) is important; it signifies a moment of illumination; but its nature is not to be determined by reason, because it is timeless. At the still point the believer attains the love of God. Eliot proceeds, in a mood of detachment, to explain the effects of this upon the spirit (24–36):

The ínner fréedom from the práctical desíre
The *reléase* from áction and súffering, | *reléase* from the ínner
And the óuter compúlsion, | yet surróunded
By a gráce of sénse, | a whíte líght stíll and móving,
Erhébung withoùt mótion, | concentrátion
Withoùt elímination, | bóth a néw wórld
And the óld màde explícit, | ùnderstóod
In the complétion of its *pártial* écstasy,
The resolútion of its *pártial* hórror.
Yèt the encháinment of pást and fúture
Wóven in the wéakness of the chánging bódy,
Protécts mankínd from héaven and damnátion
Which flésh cannót endúre.

German *Erhebung* (27) means 'elevation'; *smokefall* (41) 'evening in the city' is a word coined by Eliot. Lines 31–2 imply that illumination completes the ecstasy that was not wholly realized, and resolves the fear of what was not completely understood. In lines 33–6 the poet suggests that man's physical state, changing in time, is a fortunate bulwark against excess of joy and sorrow. Moderation in all things is indispensable to the spiritual life.

In the coda to this poem (36–43) Eliot clarifies the issue. We are conscious of little in the past or the future (he asserts), for consciousness is not in time. On the other hand, memory operates in the dimension of time only; by its involvement with the past, it restores hope for the future. All temporal considerations are paradoxically overcome by time. Were it not for memory, the *moment* (of illumination) *in the rose-garden* (39) could not have taken place. Thus the garden for Eliot, as for Dante, is the symbol of both kinds of love, profane and sacred; through the moment of ecstasy, the garden initiates the transition from human to divine love.

G. Melchiori in *The Tightrope Walkers* (Routledge and Kegan Paul, 1956) has shown that Eliot's imagery in the first two movements of *Burnt Norton* is indebted to D. H. Lawrence's Preface to *New Poems* (1920) and 'The Shadow in the Rose-Garden', a short story in *The Prussian Officer* (1914).

The verse of the quoted passage can be described as expanded blank verse, in which the unstressed syllables outnumber the stressed ones. There is a larger than usual employment of Latin polysyllables. The primary stresses vary from three to six, and there are four enjambed lines. Throughout the poem the syntax is that of ordinary speech, with little subordination. The rhythm is admirably adapted to the discursive manner, which is modulated by internal pauses and antithesis. *Ploce* and repetitive word-schemes are less in evidence than usual.

Two reasons for the difficulty of interpreting poetry like this are offered by Eliot at the conclusion of *The Use of Poetry and the Use of Criticism* (1933): one, that *personal causes* 'make it impossible for a poet to express himself in any way but an obscure way'; the other, that the author seems to have 'left out something which the reader is used to finding', namely a *meaning* that is not intended to be there. These observations have in mind Eliot's own poems; for he designed a way to be non-explicit, while the poem does its work upon the reader through the tonal expertise of the language. In reading the lyrical opening of *Burnt Norton* II one is aware of a contextually refined mosaic that conflates Jacobean and Mal-larméan 'fragments of musical rhythm', in a way that Eliot made his own. His method resembles that of Coleridge in *Kubla Khan*; it is 'an original way of assembling the most disparate and un-likely material to make a new whole' ('The Frontiers of Criticism', *On Poetry and Poets*, p. 108).

III

The third movement, beginning *Here is a place of disaffection*, speaks of the temporal world of urbanized life, with *its strained time-ridden faces* (11); this setting is in contrast to the peace of the rose-garden and its still point of contemplation. The adverb of place *Here* is dialectically opposed to *there* in line 22 of the second move-ment. The temporal world is restless and obscure – in *a dim light* (3); the poet contrasts two ways open to the convert, the en-lightened path of the saint (the way of knowledge), and the gloomier life of the penitent (the way of ignorance). Using the negative way, that of *darkness to purify the soul | Emptying the sensual with deprivation* (7/8), Eliot wrestles with words to communicate the ineffable experience. Thus in line 10, 'Neither *plenitude* nor *vacancy*. Only a *flicker*', the noun *plenitude* stands for 'the fulness of light', *vacancy* for 'the emptiness of gloom', and *flicker* for 'inter-mittent consciousness'. In the Eliotic line '*Distracted* from *dis-traction* by *distraction*' (12) three different implications are devised for *distract*, the first signifying 'drawn away from', the second *madness*, the third *pleasure*.

As Melchiori has remarked, '*the cold wind |* That blows before and after time' (15/16) is a Whitmanesque symbol of transience (*The Tightrope Walkers*, pp. 97–8). *Eructation* (19), meaning 'violent ejection', is a medical term for 'belching', introduced into the language by Sir Thomas Elyot in *The Castle of Helthe* (1533); it was commonly used as a religious metaphor in the seventeenth century, for instance by Henry More and Andrew Marvell, who are the probable sources of Eliot's borrowing.

Ethel Stephenson in *T. S. Eliot and the Lay Reader* (Fortune Press, 1944, p. 77) likens the poet's method in *Burnt Norton* to an 'ejected yeast ball of fermenting thought'; and she speaks of 'his reasoned search for an interpretative motive behind the necessity of living'. Eliot chose to pursue the negative way of St John of the Cross in *The Dark Night of the Soul* (see II.6.4), which he recalls at the beginning of the second strophe, very reminiscent of *Ash Wednesday* V. *Descend* (25) is the counterpart of *Erhebung* in Part II. But as Heraclitus realized, the goal is one and the same. The world of *perpetual solitude* (26) is described in metaphysical imagery of seventeenth-century divines, using medical and physical terms. Eliot's division of the sense faculties (30–32) follows the Aristotelian pattern. Lines 28–37 read:

> Ìntérnal dárkness, | *dè*privátion
> And *dè*stitútion of àll próperty,
> *Dé*siccàtion of the *wórld* of sénse,
> Evácuàtion of the *wórld* of fáncy,
> Inóperancy of the *wórld* of spírit;
> Thís is the óne *wáy*, | and the óther
> Is the sáme, | nòt in *móvement*
> But absténtion from *móvement*; | while the *wórld móves*
> In áppetency, | on its métalled *wáys*
> Of tíme pást and tíme fúture.

The abstract polysyllables *deprivation, destitution, desiccation, evacuation, inoperancy, abstention* and *appetency* have a curious function in these ten lines. The rhetorical or metrical stress opposes that of natural speech, and the allocation of primary and secondary stresses therefore depends on individual interpretation. This heavy-footed measure seems designed to display the disruptive forces in a world of abstractions. *Desiccation,* which dates from fifteenth century, was an alchemist's term for one of the properties of Fire. *Inoperancy* ('inactivity') is a coinage from Coleridge's use of the positive form *operancy* in 1810, in reference to 'the grace of God'. *Appetency* ('craving') entered the language in the seventeenth century, when it was mostly employed in a religious sense. Contextual shades of meaning abound in Eliot's poetry; thus *property* (29) refers to the 'essential quality' of things; and 'appetency, on *its metalled ways*' resorts to metaphor to suggest the mechanistic nature of contemporary culture.

The incantational verse of this second section is unrhymed, and has three or four strong stresses to the lines, four of which are enjambed. The repetitive words, characteristic of Eliot's liking for *ploce,* are *world, way* and *movement.*

Eliot's suggestion in this movement is that modern city life is directionless, lacking the spiritual centrality of the past. It makes for unwholesome living and religious apathy. The 'descent' of the third movement is imaged as a journey by underground railway. Thus men are appropriately likened to *bits of paper, whirled by the cold wind / That blows before and after* (15/16). Existentialist thinking is reflected in the language, which connects Eliot with the theological reasoning of St Augustine and Søren Kierkegaard. Eliot's theme in *Burnt Norton,* like that of Lawrence in *New Poems,* implies that the 'eternal now', symbolized by the moving train, is ever present. Time is psychical, rather than objective. In the flux of life we are conscious only of motion and gradual change; the past lives in memory, the future in expectation.

IV

This movement is a lyric of ten lines, only the third being unrhymed. The brevity of lines 5 and 6 is adapted to the rhyme scheme; the emotive word of the poem *Chill* constitutes the single syllable of the latter line. Arrangements like this have been increasingly employed in modern poetry. All but lines 1, 2 and 5 are run-on. The stresses vary from one in line 5, to six in line 9, and one finds subtle modulation of the secondary stresses and internal pauses in lines 3, 4, 8 and 9.

Because this is a hymn to the Creator, the rhythm is joyous in communion with nature, as well as with the divine. The natural and easeful tone illustrates Eliot's use of the auditory imagination.

> Tíme and the béll have búried the dáy,
> The bláck clóud cárries the sún awáy.
> *Wíll* the súnflòwer túrn to *us,* | *wìll* the clématis
> Stráy dòwn, | bénd to *us;* | téndril and spráy
> Clútch and clíng?
> Chill
> Fíngers of yéw be cúrled
> *Dówn* on *us?* | Àfter the kíngfisher's wíng
> Has ánswered *líght* to *líght,* | and is sílent, | the *líght* is *stíll*
> At the *stíll* point of the *túrn*ing wórld.

Eliot's feeling for the relationship of words is characteristic of his mature period. There is a sensibility for rightness, which is musical rather than onomatopoeic. The keynotes are the rhetorical use of rhyme, the flexibility of rhythm, and the blend of lively and impressionistic words, as in lines 6 to 9. Eliot studied the art of complete rhythm that spans the verse paragraph, which in this case is the whole poem. The rhythm of this movement exemplifies the skilful manipulation of repetitive elements:

Alliteration: of plosive consonants *t*, *b*, *c* (and *cl*), as well as sibilant *s*

Ploce: *sun* (2, 3), *will* (3 twice), *turn* (3, 10), *us* (3, 4, 8), *down* (4, 8), *light* (9 three times), *still* (9, 10)

Every line, except the last, contains *prosopopoeia* (personification), while the heart of the poem is expressed in *erotema,* the rhetorical questions in lines 3–5 and 6–8.

The symbolism of this monody is paramount; inevitably the reader requires significance for the symbols, so that the author's intention becomes meaningful. The *time* is nightfall, and the *bell* is curfew; *buried* conjures up death, represented by the *black cloud* (2) that extinguishes the light of life. The *sunflower* and (blue) *clematis* (3) are chosen as flowers that aspire to the sun, and so symbolize Christ and the Virgin Mary. The problem on which the convert seeks assurance, is this: are believers reborn, through God's grace, or is death (*Chill | Fingers of yew*, 5/6) the end? In short, his doubt is the promise of immortality and eternity, of which the long-living yew-tree is the symbol. To this perplexity no one receives an answer. The *kingfisher's wing*, a symbol of illumination, is the questioner's flash of *light* (9); this word *light* occurs three times, and was probably suggested to Eliot by lines 24–6 of *Paradiso,* Canto XII, in which the important words are italicized:

> *Light* upon *light* serene and joyous, all
>
> By one *mind* *moved*, and at one moment, *came*
> To *rest*, as when the will that moves the eyes
> Together shuts or opens both of them.

The poem ends with the thought that 'illumination' *is still | At the still point of the turning world*. This is the axis of rest to which impotent man, distracted by the varying forces of compulsion, has to come, if questioning is not to strangle his life.

The tale of Alcyone, which is the source of the kingfisher's classical name, is told in Ovid's *Metamorphoses,* Book XI. This bird was said to await the *calm seas* of the winter solstice, in which to breed.

The poet is concerned in all final movements of the Quartets with the formal principles of his art, and the means of communicating them. Poetry is more closely allied to music than to the plastic arts, and Eliot's point of departure is Aristotle's concept of music as relationships in time (*Physics* II.3). He had studied Aristotle with Joachim at Oxford. Aristotle held that music, besides being useful for relaxation, had a cathartic effect upon the disturbed soul; it is a popular misconception that music corresponds to no reality but its own formal structure. But art is temporal, not eternal – what perpetuates it is the pattern that corresponds to Plato's 'divine idea'. The *Chinese jar* that *Moves perpetually in its stillness* (6/7), perhaps, as Grover Smith suggests, in the modern sense of its molecular motion, enjoys a certain eternity in the perfection of its form. *Words after speech, reach | Into the silence* (3/4) refers to Aristotle's theory in the *Metaphysics* of *entelechy*, whereby the 'end product', in its completed condition, is seen as the fruit of the artist's *energeia*.

Co-existence (9) has an Aristotelian significance, also to be found in the *Metaphysics,* where God, the Unmoved Mover is shown to be both the first and the final cause. This doctrine Eliot has in mind in lines 9–13:

> Or say that the end precedes the beginning,
> And the end and the beginning were always there
> Before the beginning and after the end.
> And all is always now.

Words in poetry are more vulnerable to abuse than notes in music; Eliot observes that they abound in inadequacies of connotation, morally and aesthetically. This is the gist of what he conveys in lines 13–22. Words are under severe strains because of their multi-purposes, and the writer's temptation to use them illegitimately. They lose their minted clarity, they become strident, *Scolding, mocking or merely chattering* (18). Used idly, they end in disorder and confusion.

This critique is couched in both theological and figurative language, the latter employing the most concrete terms. The doctrinal use of *Word* (19), with a capital letter, indicates its significance: 'the creative principle and divine order'. *Desert,* in the same line, refers to the conditions of life the poet finds about him. The *temptation* of line 20 recalls that suffered by the desert father in Flaubert's *La Tentation de Saint Antoine*. *The crying shadow in the funeral dance* (21) is said by John Hayward to have originated in lines 5–9, Book XXIV of the *Odyssey,* where Hermes rounds up the ghosts of the dead suitors in Hades. The source of the *disconsolate chimera* (22) was the mythical female monster slain by Bellerophon, a personification for the Lycian volcano, which was surrounded by desolate country. In Eliot's context, the phrase is a symbol for 'tragic unintelligibility'.

The seventeen lines of the second section have a more lyrical note, and return to the earlier themes of *Burnt Norton,* with the object of synthesis. In a congenial rhythm the disquisition on art is concluded (lines 23–32):

> The détail of the páttern is *móvement,*
> As in the fígure of the tén stáirs.
> *Desíre itsélf* is *móvement*
> Nót in *itsélf desír*able;
> Lóve is *itsélf* un*móv*ing,
> Ónly the cáuse and énd of *móvement,*
> *Tím*eless, and ùn*desír*ing
> Excépt in the áspect of *tíme*
> Cáught in the fórm of lìmitátion
> Betwèen ún-*bèing* and *béing.*

These lines are short and end-stopped, needing no internal pauses. The stresses are decisive, to match the confident incantational note of the poem's consummation. *Ploce* repeats the dominant words: *movement, desire, itself, time* and *being.* With the exception of the emphatic pronoun *itself,* all these words have metaphysical significance.

The only symbolic reference is to *the figure of the ten stairs* (24). Eliot substituted the word *stairs* for *steps,* in referring to the ladder of love of St John of the Cross in Chapters 17 to 19 of *The Dark Night of the Soul.* The ladder, whereby the believer learns discipline, has ten steps on which the Soul painstakingly ascends to union with God. Eliot told Ethel Stephenson that the *figure* on the stairs recalls the mystical Bride, personifying the Soul.

The subject of these lines is taken from Aristotle's *Metaphysics* and *De Anima.* The synthesis involves no less than the reconciling of antitheses: *Desire* (25) and *Love* (27), *movement* (28) and the *un-moving* (27), *time* (30) and the *timeless* (29), *being* and *un-being* (32). In these manifestations one can discern the grouping of first causes and final causes. According to Aristotle, in whose thinking Eliot finds a sympathetic chord, both causes are united in the presence of God. For Aristotle's theology was closely related to his unique ideas about motion and the Unmoved Mover. Motion, he argued, is the means whereby potentialities (Eliot's *pattern*) become actualities. God's presence (the principle of goodness) moves the universe, just as desire moves men. He inspires form in existing matter and His presence creates and preserves order, even in the basic elements which Greek philosophers like Heraclitus postulated. A work of art, for Aristotle, was an incarnation *in time* of form in matter; it might acquire an individuality of its own, *out of time,* just as a person would.

Lines 33–9 correspond to the musical coda, and restore the dominant images of the first movement, *the shaft of sunlight, the dust* on the rose-bowl, *the hidden laughter / Of children,* and the *quick* darting movements of birds, symbols of sudden illumination. Such moments are divine potentialities in those whose quest is Love.

Burnt Norton may be described as a poem about the need for grace through humility; it embodies an experienced moment of joy, perhaps several, without the terms of doctrinal religion. The element represented is *air,* which connotes the spiritual processes and the restorative power of memory. In following Dante, whose intelligence was grounded in Thomist philosophy, this Quartet reviews the Aristotelian conflict of the real and the ideal, and ends with the suggestion that the conflict does not really exist.

If *form* is the kind of 'inspiration' a poet should acknowledge, Eliot reminds us that it entails a 'subsequent process of deliberate, conscious, arduous labour' (Introduction to Paul Valéry's *The Art of Poetry,* Routledge and Kegan Paul, 1958, p. xii). Two pages later, on the theory that poetry should be assimilated to music, Eliot adds:

Music itself may be conceived as a striving towards an un-attainable timelessness; and if the other arts may be thought of as yearning for duration, so Music may be thought of as yearning for the stillness of painting or sculpture.

EAST COKER, 1940

Eliot's supposed ancestors had lived in the village of East Coker, Somerset, since the fifteenth century, one being Sir Thomas Elyot, author of *The Boke Named the Governour* (1531), who was a high churchman and royalist, as well as a Neo-Platonist. Eliot, who visisted East Coker in 1937, felt some cultural affinities with him, and designed this Quartet to take cognizance of man's relation to history. It is therefore more personal than its predecessor. The element represented is earth, and the theme is man as natural being involved in time.

Mary Stuart's motto, *En ma fin est mon commencement*, recurs in *East Coker,* as a *leitmotif* to dispel determinism. Physically, man's end is death; but philosophically, awareness of it may give a purpose to life. Alluding disapprovingly to Bergson's *Creative Evolution*, the poet takes the *flux* of time as his dominant image. A cyclic view of civilization in history postulates a pattern of events and a rhythm; and Eliot, as usual, chooses quietude and peace. He depicts East Coker on a restful summer's afternoon, or in a breathless morning silence. He suggests the rhythm of seasons, which bears some resemblance to the mystic's way of perfection. Seasonal expectancy is more satisfying than a physical sense of time, which is oppressive and confining. Earth is heavy and weighs man down, but the spiritual life enables the believer to overcome this inertia.

In the first movement Eliot selects the ancestral home and the village dance as symbols of cyclic movement in history. *Houses live and die* (9) is the theme of the first section in a basic four-beat line, unrhymed, which Eliot devised as the staple for *The Family Reunion*. Images, such as the *loosened pane* (11) and the *tattered arras* (13), contribute to the picture of age and decay. Even the family motto *Tace et Fac* (Be silent and act), as old as Heraclitus, confirms the impression that movement in time is unproductive and disintegrating.

The vignette of the third section is the ghostly medieval dance of the villagers round a midsummer *bonfire* (which continued to be spelt *bone-fire* until 1760). Dancing around this was a primitive rite later adapted to the celebrating of Christian saints; it may have suggested the allegorical paintings of the 'dance of death'. Two sources are merged in this picture of East Coker: Friedrich

Gerstäcker's German novel, *Germelshausen*, 1862 (translated into English as *The Strange Village*, 1878); and his forebear's *Boke Named the Governour*, Book I, Chapter 21, from which Eliot borrowed lines 28–33, in the original spelling. As usual, he adapted the borrowings to his needs.

In the novel, the irrepressible folk of the hamlet indulge in a dance of *mirth*, which ends in the grave; but ghosts renew the festival each year. In Elyot's *Governour*, the author devotes six chapters to dancing, as among the 'commendable exercises, and pastimes, not repugnant to virtue'. Every movement is treated symbolically, as though it were the instrument of dignity through moderation, the ideal he advocates in the partnership of the sexes. Elyot does not employ the poet's adjective *commodious* (30), but the noun, in describing 'the dignitie and *commoditie*' of marriage; the sense of this abstract noun is 'a fitting condition'.

Into his free verse Eliot introduces some highly schematic lines, such as 36–9 describing the country dancers:

> *Lift*ing heavy *feet* in *c*lumsy shoes,
> *Earth feet*, loam *feet*, *lift*ed in *c*ountry *mirth*
> *Mirth* of those *l*ong since under *earth*
> Nourishing the *c*orn.

This is unobtrusive illustration of *ploce*, assonance, alliteration and *anadiplosis* (the contiguous repetition of *mirth* in adjoining clauses).

In the second movement of fifty lines, two poems, different in treatment, present related themes. The second, which is prosaic, begins by describing its lyrical predecessor as *not very satisfactory / A periphrastic study in a worn-out poetical fashion* (18/19). The explanation seems to be that the first eight lines parody the romantic vagueness of Swinburne, in poems such as *Before the Mirror*, which uses *snowdrops, roses, thunder, snow*, as images of the November season. In Eliot's lyric the season is unseasonable, and the cyclic pattern appears to have broken down, with chaos portending the end of the world. One should note the irregular rhyme scheme and the use of approximate rhyme such as *doing / spring* (1/2).

Lines 9–17 contain images of war (9/10), accompanying disturbances in the heavens, which the poet expresses in the symbolic jargon of astrology. This might have been suggested by Cowley's second *Anacreontique,* lines 9–12. Metaphysical conceit is evident in *Comets weep and Leonids fly* (13), *Leonids* being meteors that appear in November, once in a generation. The *vortex* bringing *destructive fire* (15/16) was foretold by Heraclitus; the first symbolizes the life of passion, while the *ice-cap* (17) represents 'death'.

The *intolerable wrestle | With words and meanings* (20/21), which produces obscure poetry, is replaced by a less pretentious language in lines 22–48. The anticipated *serenity* (24) of age the poet now realizes is a falsification; hoped-for wisdom never comes. The *quiet-voiced elders* (26, Renaissance thinkers like Sir Thomas Elyot), never discovered that progress is an illusion. All is flux, as Heraclitus saw. The eternal *Now* darkens our concept of the past; therefore we are perpetually in the *dark wood* (40) which Eliot quotes from Dante's *Inferno.*

In lines 29–31 Eliot discredits the mounting knowledge of the physical world, to which the Renaissance ideal has led. Not this, but humility, is the true wisdom. Man's way through life is a *terra incognita*; Dante was among the few who perceived that the dangers of the journey are as nothing to the onset of pride.

The revived word *hebetude* (28), meaning 'blunting', 'lethargy', 'dulness', seems to have passed from the language in the nineteenth century. *Grimpen* (41), which Eliot employs as a common noun, is the name of a bog on Dartmoor, the Grimpen Mire, *mise en scène* of Conan Doyle's novel *The Hound of the Baskervilles.*

In the third movement Eliot asks whether civilization, as we know it, is valid; man's knowledge of space-time and the expanding universe only makes darkness more obscure. The tone of the poem is that of the *Rock* choruses. Line 12, however, introduces the philosophy of the negative way, taught by St John of the Cross, who said that the faculties should be trained to work passively, not actively. *I said to my soul, be still, and let the dark come upon you | Which shall be the darkness of God* (12/13) is developed into a prayer-like meditation in lines 23–28. The suggestion may have come from A. E. Housman's *The Shropshire Lad,* poem XLVIII, which begins 'Be still, my soul, be still, the arms you bear are brittle'. But the ultimate source is earlier. For the negative way arose, not from the Bible's teaching, but from the Christian Neo-Platonists of the sixth century; it is found in Dante's *Paradiso,* and in *The Cloud of Unknowing,* an anonymous English mystical treatise of the fourteenth century. By that time the *soul,* which in the Old Testament signified the 'life principle', had been given by philosophers three different functions, the vegetative, sensitive and rational. Theologians, however, regarded it only as 'spiritual'. St John of the Cross wrote in the sixteenth century:

> The fitting disposition for union with God is not that the soul should understand, feel, taste or imagine anything on the subject of the nature of God, or any other thing whatever, but should remain in that pureness and love which is perfect resignation and complete detachment from all things for God alone.

Eliot is conscious of the paradox in every man's situation, and expresses it succinctly in *East Coker* III, 28:
    the *darkness* shall be the *light,* and the *stillness* the *dancing.*
Here *darkness* means 'despair', the stepping-stone to rebirth; and *stillness* implies 'access to creative activity', of which the rhythm of *dancing,* as Sir John Davies demonstrated in *Orchestra,* is the physical symbol.

The second section contains brief directives for the way of self-denial, which are borrowed from the paradoxical rules in *The Ascent of Mount Carmel,* Book I, Chapter 13. Paradox often arises from the different meanings that can be assigned to words, such as *are, know* and *possess* (36/38/40). *Soul* is a particularly ambiguous word. As Aldous Huxley observed in *The Perennial Philosophy* (Chatto and Windus, 1946) 'Obscurely and unconsciously wise, our language confirms the findings of the mystics and proclaims the essential badness of division' (p. 17).

In this movement the first exhortation to the soul (12) is separated from the second (23) by three extended similes, illustrating spiritual darkness, mental vacancy and unconscious consciousness, the terms of comparison being a theatre, an underground train and the operating table. These Miltonic or Vergilian emulations occupy ten lines (13–22), some very long; but they are effective, despite their disjunctive character. Occasionally, Eliot inserts recollections from the past in *Burnt Norton,* eg, *The laughter in the garden* (31) in order to link *East Coker* to it. Such, in general, are the poetical lines 29–33, where he indulges in a Miltonic inversion in 'The wild *thyme unseen*' (30), which is most unusual.

Movement IV of *East Coker* is a Good Friday hymn on the theme of Redemption, resembling, in its rigid stanza form and firm rhythm, the Latin poems of the Middle Ages, to which W. P. Ker drew attention in Chapter III of *English Literature: Mediaeval* (1912). To treat the Passion as an allegory in the metaphysical style of Donne and Marvell, using medical terms, was an original conception. But little attention has been given to the influence of Valéry upon the form and imagery. In his Introduction to Valéry's *The Art of Poetry*, Eliot quotes this critic's ideal of the modern poet:

> He is a cool scientist, almost an algebraist, in the service of a subtle dreamer... He will take care not to hurl on paper everything whispered to him in fortunate moments by the Muse of Free Association. On the contrary, everything he has imagined, felt, dreamed, and planned will be passed through a sieve, weighed, filtered, subjected to *form,* and condensed as much as possible so as to gain in power what it loses in length (p. xviii).

Valéry also discusses his own procedure in composition:

> Before making any deep examination of the content, I take a look at the language; I generally proceed like a surgeon who sterilizes his hands and prepares the area to be operated on. This I call *cleaning up the verbal situation* (p. xxi).

Eliot approved of Valéry's insistence that the poet should exercise himself on rhyming stanza forms of some difficulty, in order to overcome self-imposed limitations. As he himself expressed it: 'Form and content must come to terms... it is only the poet who has developed this sense of fitness who is qualified to attempt "free verse"' (p. xiii).

The poem consists of five stanzas of five lines each, in iambic measure, with the rhyme scheme ababb. The norm is a four-stressed line, but there is more rhythmical freedom in the last two lines than in the first three. Only three of the lines are enjambed (3, 13, 28), the rhymes being strong, masculine and true, with the exception of the last, *blood | good.*

The poem recalls some of the horror of the Second World War, and its symbolism has the clarity of application that Eliot found in Marvell's *Dialogue between the Soul and Body,* an obvious source. Other suggestions came from *The Dark Night of the Soul* II, 16, and Pascal's *Pensées,* 354–5 and 552. The *wounded surgeon* symbolizes Christ; the *dying nurse* (7) the Church; *Adam's curse* (9) Original Sin; the *ruined millionaire* (12) Adam; and the *fever* (17) earthly love. The poem abounds in metaphysical paradoxes, such as *Our only health is our disease* (6), where the last word implies *dis-ease,* 'the acceptance of unhappiness'.

Because the poem is an experiment in the serious wit of metaphysical language by a modern poet, the tropes, the paradoxes and the conceits are worth examining:

1/2 the steel / That *questions* (personification)

2 *distempered part* (metaphor). This represents the 'ailing individual', lacking a proper relation to the wholeness of God

4 The *sharp compassion* of the healer's art (oxymoron). Literally, *compassion* means 'suffering with'

5 Resolving the enigma of the fever chart (conceit); *fever chart* (metonymy)

10 our *sickness* must grow worse (metaphor; *sickness*='spiritual unrest')

12 the *ruined millionaire* (metonymy; his *endowment* is Original Sin)

14 Die of the *absolute paternal care* (metonymy; *ie,* 'by estrangement from Fatherly protection')

16 The *chill* ascends (metaphor; *ie,* 'the disease')

17 The fever *sings in mental wires* (metaphor, recalling *The trilling wire in the blood, Burnt Norton,* II, 3)

18 If to be *warmed,* then I must *freeze* (metaphor and paradox)

19 in *frigid purgatorial fires* (oxymoron)

20 the flame is *roses,* and the smoke is *briars* (metaphor; the italicized words represent 'light' and 'darkness', which co-exist)

21/2 The dripping blood our only *drink* / The bloody flesh our only *food* (metonymy; the reference is to the Eucharist, a symbolic way of salvation).

In the last line of the poem *that* refers to loss of humility. Eliot believes, with the metaphysical poets, that true Christianity is mental discipline, involved with dogma. Easter Friday, he argues, is 'Good' in the sense that Christ died for us; yet modern man, preferring a physical and autonomous concept of life, believes that secular philosophies are valid for his salvation.

Eliot's theme in the first eighteen lines of movement V is the management and elusive quality of words; the struggle to subdue them, which he calls a *raid on the inarticulate* (8), resembles the endless battle to retain a foothold in North Africa in 1940. Consequently, he finds appropriate language in war imagery: *shabby equipment* (9), *Undisciplined squads* (11), *strength and submission* (12), *the fight to recover what has been lost* (15). By implication, he describes the vague feelings and imprecise emotions that precede a poet's self-discipline and dedication. An aspiring writer battles to maintain his ground, not to outdo others.

The second Section (19–38) is a synthesis of the preceding movements:

Hóme is where one stárts fròm. | As we grów ólder
The wórld becomes stránger, | the páttern mòre cómplicated
Of déad and líving. | Nót the inténse *móment*
Ísolated, | with nó befóre and áfter,
But a *lífetìme* búrning in évery *móment*
And nót the *lífetìme* of óne mán ónly
But of óld stónes that cánnot be decíphered.
There is a *tíme* for the *évening under* stár*lìght*,
A tíme for the *évening under* lámp*lìght*
(The *évening* with the phótogràph álbum).
Lóve is mòst néarly itsélf
When *hére* and nów céase to *mátter*.
Óld mén óught to be explórers
Hére and thére dòes nòt *mátter*
We mùst be *stíll* and *stíll* móving
Ìnto anóther inténsity
For a fúrther *únion*, | a déeper comm*únion*
Through the dárk cóld | and the émpty desolátion,
The wáve *crý*, | the wínd *crý*, | the vást wáters
Of the pétrel and the pórpoise. | In my énd is my begínning.

Eliot is back in the verse language of drama, in which the greater part of *Four Quartets* is cast. What he offers is evocation of sometimes powerful and often ironical contrasts, made through symbols that well up from the unconscious memory, in an unconnected way. *The pattern . . . | Of dead and living* (20|21) means, of course, 'the meaning of life and death'. The life of an artist is not a succession of intense moments. From a temporal viewpoint, we are all involved in the continuity of history, even our ancestors whose gravestones stand undecipherable in the churchyard (25). Like Dante, Eliot pictures life as an exploration, something like that of Ulysses, but a journey of the soul, *Through the dark cold and the empty desolation* (36). This line appears to express Eliot's view of the present as a doomed epoch. How could a Christian retain a foothold in a world concentrating its energies on destruction? He considered it tragic, though not purposeless, that every man has to discover truth for himself, as every artist has to re-learn the techniques of his predecessors. The final sentence *In my end is my beginning* inverts the order of the opening motto of *Burnt Norton*; the reason for this is to be found in the succeeding poems.

It is worth noting how *ploce* lights upon the words most loaded with meaning: *old, moment, lifetime, evening, light, matter, still, union, cry*. The rhythm is sensitively modulated, either by shortened lines, or by varying the internal pauses.

The tendency of Eliot's thinking in *East Coker* is to discard evolution as a mechanical, and to replace it as a spiritual conception, whereby one lives in hope of a turning point that faith inevitably will bring. The kind of evolution to be welcomed involves overcoming limitations, avoiding the static attitudes and rejecting ineffectual credos for new ones. Eliot shares the doctrine of Heraclitus, that every moment which spells an end also promises a beginning.

THE DRY SALVAGES, 1941

The cyclic view of time as succession and decay is not the only phenomenon in Eliot's conception of history. His plan in the *Four Quartets* is to fit the individual and the family into the picture of change; *home is where one starts from*, and *The evening with the photograph album* is a powerful reinforcer of the historical memory.

The Dry Salvages is a reminiscential poem, which nostalgically relives the American scene of the poet's youth. The element that dominates the first movement is water; consequently the rhythms have a fluid, if prosaic, beauty to match the twin symbols of river and sea. The relation between these more than geographical features, and Eliot's vision of the timelessness of spiritual life, is more convincingly worked out than in either of the preceding poems, because the modern mind, educated in geography and anthropology, better understands the atavistic nature of these symbols. In Eliot's first poem the river and the sea also represent the climatic cycle by which the earth is watered and life sustained.

The *strong brown god* (2) is the River Mississippi, where Eliot was born; the sea recalls the Atlantic coast near Cape Ann, where the poet spent much of his boyhood. Only one generation before, St Louis had been a frontier town, where the inhabitants were in close touch with a primitive race of Indians; and Eliot evokes the kind of feeling towards his river that Conrad did for the Congo in *Heart of Darkness*. The Mississippi also recalls the river of Heraclitus, whose ceaseless flow resembles personal history and the effluxion of time.

The sea, on the other hand, adds a further dimension and is multifarious; it is the deep to which all temporal rivers contribute. A symbol of man's Darwinian origin, it is also a means of his destruction. The relation of river to sea is that of microcosm (biological time) to macrocosm (historic time), of personal to universal, the latter involving the lifetime of many men and countless generations. The biological aspects of the symbols do not escape notice. The river represents the circulation of the blood (the dark current of racial experience), whereas the sea (Bergson's 'life force') is the flux of time on which man is afloat. Time, like the sea, is described in the second movement as the destroyer, but also the preserver.

In his backward glance Eliot was probably influenced by Shelley's *Ode to the West Wind* (the penultimate stanza), and by Whitman, whom Donald Davie thinks he was parodying in the first movement (see 'T. S. Eliot: The end of an era', *The Twentieth Century*, April 1956, pp. 350–362). Although Eliot spoke of some of Whitman's romantic Americanisms as 'clap-trap', he must have been affected at an impressionable age. Davie points to *worshippers of the machine* (10) as a likely echo. The prophetic note and the mannerisms of syntax are what Eliot chiefly parodies, though there is evidence enough that he unconsciously revived phrases (see S. Musgrove, *T. S. Eliot and Walt Whitman*, New Zealand University Press, 1952, pp. 24–34, 65–74).

The symbolism of the language is sometimes put to most delicate use, as in 24–26:

> The sea has many voices,
> Many gods and many voices.
> The salt is on the briar rose,
> The fog is in the fir trees.

The poet's suggestion, that the sea is more powerful than the river, implies that the life-surge is greater than man's elemental nature. The meeting of the sea and the land is both a *menace and caress* (29).

The final section of the first movement (26–48) employs haunting images of sound, as well as two American marine terms: *rote* (30, 'the roaring of sea or surf'), and *groaner* (32, 'an automatically sounding buoy'). The tolling of the warning bell for shipping (35, 48) sounds like a call to prayer, but it is equally a summons to eternity.

The first 36 lines of movement two are in the sestina form, six-lined stanzas of no clearly defined metre. There is no rhyme within the stanza, but each line-ending rhymes with the corresponding terminal word of the succeeding stanza. All rhymes are feminine, either disyllabic or trisyllabic. Stanzas 1 and 4 ask questions, to which 2/3 and 5/6 provide answers. The first three stanzas are unspecific, the last three particular, on the theme of *the fishermen sailing* (19). The mariner is a symbol of the purposeful life; if he has hardships, they make the struggle meaningful.

Eliot in this poem is not concerned with his own, but with all human experience. The sestina form has a gentle music that corresponds to the motion of the sea, as felt by a boat. The *calamitous annunciation* (6) is the 'news of disaster'. What the poet suggests in the second stanza is that personal events bear no relation to anything beyond themselves; our brittle faith ends in disillusionment. But, equally, imaginary destinations of the future have no meaning, until realized. A typical example of Eliotic paradox is 33: (There is no end . . .) / To the *movement* of *pain* that is *painless* and *motionless* (the sense of which is 'There is no end to the feeling of grief that has no *physical* pain, but inhibits movement'). Death is the end of all things.

The second half of the movement (37–75) is a philosophical disquisition on 'time past', written in a style that is virtually prose.
Here are lines 37–41:

It séems, as óne becòmes ólder,
That the pást has anóther páttern, and céases to bè a *mére
séquence* —
Or éven devélopment: *the látter* a *pártial fállacy*
Encóuraged by *sùperficial nótions* of evolútion,
Which *becómes, in the pópular mínd, a méans* of disówning the
pást.

This passage is prosaic for three reasons: (1) There is a dis-
proportionate number of unstressed and half-stressed syllables.
Frequently, the determination of primary stresses is speculative;
indeed, they often fall on insignificant words, such as the colourless
verb *seems*, the indefinite pronouns *one* and *another,* the down-
toner adjective *mere,* the modifying adverb *even,* the drab substantive use of *latter.* The lines have a limp rhythmical structure.
(2) The syntax is both diffuse and crabbed; before *development*,
there is a concatenation of co-ordinated statements and a loose
afterthought. A single adverbial clause is placed too early to bring
relief. After *development*, there is a succession of qualifying make-
shifts, only one taking the form of a relative clause. (3) The style
is strewn with clichés, familiar to the school and boardroom, *eg,*
a *mere* sequence; the *latter*; a *partial* fallacy; *superficial notions*;
becomes, in the popular mind, a means.

Eliot disagreed with Valéry's distinction between poetry and
prose, in which he suggested that poetry bears the same relation to
prose as dancing does to walking (or running). Valéry amplified
this by arguing that prose is *instrumental,* its purpose being to convey meaning, impart information and direct action; once prose
communication is achieved, the means are dismissed. But poetry,
like dancing, it is an end in itself. A poem exists 'for its own sake',
and should be so *enjoyed*, not looking *through* the words, but *at*
them.

Eliot thought this an oversimplification. In the Introduction to
Valéry's *Art of Poetry*, he justified his practice of mingling the two
media (pp. xvi–xvii):

We can distinguish between prose and verse, and between verse
and poetry; but the moment the intermediate term *verse* is

suppressed, I do not believe that any distinction between prose and poetry is meaningful . . .

The farther the idiom, vocabulary, and syntax of poetry depart from those of prose, the more artificial the language of poetry will become . . . so artificial as no longer to be able to convey living feeling and living thought. Speech on every level, from that of the least educated to that of the most cultivated, changes from generation to generation; and the *norm* for a poet's language is the way his contemporaries talk. In assimilating poetry to music, Valéry has, it seems to me, failed to insist upon its relation to speech.

In the opening lines of the third movement Eliot wonders whether Krishna, the charioteer and incarnation of the god Vishnu, would have agreed that eternity is ever-present. Krishna's message to Arjuna (Everyman) in the *Bhagavad-Gita* arose out of a war situation, and was therefore relevant to Eliot's theme. In brief, he advised the Prince to consecrate the action of the moment, by refusing to consider the end, and giving undivided attention to the means.

Eliot had interested himself in oriental philosophy since his graduate years at Harvard and was bound to re-think the Indian religions, which are based upon the myth and poetry of the *Rig-Veda*, and their culmination in the *Upanishads*. Their value to him was that they teach insights whose validity is not dependent upon place of origin or on historical time. *Samsara,* 'the stream of existence', differs very little from the flux of Heraclitus; and the dilemma of man's self-ignorance is given the same attention in the optimistic *Upanishads,* as in the pessimistic analysis of St Augustine. What Eliot could not reconcile were the different theistic principles of unity and dualism, and the absence of dogma in Indian religions.

Both Buddhism, which arose out of the wisdom of the *Upanishads,* and early Christianity, placed a high value on asceticism and illumination. A Buddha may be regarded as a rational Messiah, but the Avatars (Incarnations) are not unique. Christopher Isherwood on pp. 8–9 of *Vedanta for the Western World* (Allen and Unwin, 1948) has described the possibility of mystical union (*samadhi*) for modern man; but he shares Eliot's difficulty of communicating the experience in words. Rabindranath Tagore once showed how misleading Indian philosophy appears when translated into the Hebrao-Hellenic terms of occidental languages.

In lines 3–8 Eliot shows the consequences of the Christian mystic's belief that 'eternity is ever-present'. Regrets and longing for what is not, in no way differ. The poet rejects the consolation that 'Time is a healer' (8), and offers the retort of Heraclitus that the same person is no longer being treated. The changes that time effects are illustrated in images of journeys by train or ocean liner (9–45), which symbolize the fluctuating *now*. In 14, 26 and 39 the forward-looking journey is parodied in Whitmanesque exhortations. The 'forward-ness' is seen to be an illusion, like material progress.

History, in Eliot's reasoning, is a time continuum that has little to do with the eternal pattern, beyond intersecting it at the Incarnation, a word that is only once used in *Four Quartets, Dry Salvages*, V, 32. The purpose of the references to the *Bhagavad-Gita* is to introduce the idea that the soul undergoes infinite changes, when it lacks detachment; that knowledge, spiritual dedication and good work should co-operate in attaining life's goals. As Christianity implies belief in a Second Coming, its concept of history should be enlarged to accept other incarnations, as potential avatars.

The fourth movement is a dirge of three unrhymed stanzas, of five lines each, composed in the rhythm of church liturgy. The Lady addressed is *Stella Maris,* the Virgin Mary, protectress of seamen. She stands on a promontory where land and sea meet, and is besought to intercede on behalf of lost souls. The *fish* of line 3 recalls the early Christian symbol. But the prayer has a war significance, too, for the times were dangerous for men on the sea. *Jonah* is referred to in *the dark throat which will not reject them* (13), remembering his thanks to God: 'yet hast Thou brought up my life from corruption, O Lord'. Line 14 is taken from St Bernard's prayer to the Virgin, *Paradiso*, XXXIII, 1. The *angelus* (15) is the bell that calls the faithful to thanksgiving for Redemption. The purpose of these symbols is to call the reader back to Eliot's theme, the temporal and the eternal.

Movement V has 50 lines, undivided, though there are three related phases of thought, the last formulated in shorter lines than the other two. The whole is in free, unrhymed verse. Lines 1–17 are a diatribe on the surrogates for religion. In modern life, the curious are less occupied with the present than the past and future; with the spirit world, psycho-analysis, horoscopes and palmistry, and with drugs that induce extrasensory perception. To emphasize the fatuity of these blind-alleys, Eliot unearths cant phrases, such as *haruspicate* (3, 'to foretell the future by examining animal entrails' – a practice of Etruscan soothsayers), and *scry* (3, 'to indulge in crystal-gazing'). The sea monster of line 2 is a vague prehistoric reptile.

All those who pry into the past or future for 'signs' by which to enliven their temporal existence are triflers, who have never known what is essential *sub specie aeternitatis – The point of inter-section of the timeless | With time* (18/19). In lines 17–32 Eliot, resorting to little imagery, makes clear the conception of eternity, which he shared with St Augustine and Søren Kierkegaard; it is characterized by A. G. George as a 'religious-existential theory' (See *T. S. Eliot: His Mind and Art*, Asia Publishing House, 1962, pp. 67–72). Eternity is reflected in time only at a moment of revelation, which invites union with the Supreme Being. Full apprehension is the privilege of the saint, bestowed through *a lifetime's death in love, | Ardour and selflessness and self-surrender* (21/22). For the lesser man, awareness of the moment is fitful (*unattended . . . | . . . in and out of time*); but it is nevertheless balm to the spirit (*you are the music | While the music lasts*), because it is the mark of non-attachment. The meaning of Incarnation for ordinary mortals is not Christ's visible presence, but the *half understood hint* (32) of His love, acquired through religious discipline. The 'moment in the rose-garden' was, for Eliot, such an illumination; but there were other *hints and guesses* (29), such as the odour of *wild thyme unseen* (26), which recalls *East Coker* III, 30. The experience is not apparently of a different order from Word-worth's; but pantheists see it as an inspiration rather than a visitation.

The concluding sixteen lines (35–50) point to the preceding movement, revealing the significance of Krishna's advice on action and causation:

> Here the past and future
> Are conquered, and reconciled,
> Where action were otherwise movement

Of that which is only moved
And has in it no source of movement –
Driven by *dæmonic, chthonic*
Powers. And right action is freedom
From past and future also.
For most of us, this is the aim
Never here to be realised;
Who are only undefeated
Because we have gone on trying;
We, content at the last
If *our temporal reversion nourish*
(Not too far from the yew-tree)
The life of significant soil.

Temporal reversion (48) is a legal metaphor whimsically employed to
suggest the necessary return of the body to the soil from which it
sprang. Assonance, as a rhetorical device, should not be over-
looked in 7/8 *riddle | fiddle*, 11 *womb, or tomb*, 40 *dæmonic, chthonic*.

The welcome clarity of *The Dry Salvages* is the result of its more
positive clues and philosophic argument. Eliot, the politico-
moral observer, is commenting on misdirected activity, in a less
declamatory tone than that of the Choruses of *The Rock*.

LITTLE GIDDING, 1942

The title of this Quartet is the name of the village in Huntingdon-
shire where Nicholas Ferrar, a deacon of the Anglican Church,
founded a religious group in 1626, consisting of his mother and
his brother's and brother-in-law's families. It was the last experiment of its kind in the Anglican Church. Because the community
had Catholic leanings, it became an inspiration for the Anglo-
Catholic movement two hundred years later. Cromwell dis-
banded the community during the Civil War in 1647, and his
forces destroyed the chapel, which was restored in the nineteenth
century, and is now the parish church of the village. It was visited
by Eliot in 1936, on the shortest day of the year.

Good works made Little Gidding a place of dedication, and an
admirable description of the life there is contained in J. H.
Shorthouse's *John Inglesant* (1881), chapter IV. Eliot's interest in
the movement was historical, for Charles I (the *broken king* of line
26) is said to have taken refuge in Little Gidding after the defeat at

Naseby (June 1645). The spirit of the last Quartet is therefore one of meditation and religious observance; but the results of historical action are also evaluated. The poems attempt to re-capture the mystical preoccupations of Christian thinkers in the first half of the seventeenth century, as reflected in the devotional poetry of Herbert, Vaughan, Crashaw and Traherne. These poets believed that the soul of man and of nations may be re-deemed through a life of selflessness and love.

In the first movement Eliot's arrival on a *Midwinter spring* after-noon indicates that it was a freakish day of bright sunshine, with the warmth of the sun reflected from the frost and ice. This he likens to the *pentecostal fire* (10) of *Acts* II.3, which reminds us that the element represented in *Little Gidding* is *fire*. The word is men-tioned three times in the first movement (4, 10, 51); and *pente-costal fire*, which stands for the Holy Ghost that descended upon Christ's apostles, is the dominant image of this group of poems. Pentecost is the Whitsun festival, seven weeks after Easter; and snow on the hedgerows in December would resemble the spring blossom of Whitsuntide. The seasons are thus out of tune, because for the spiritual man they are *not in time's covenant* (14), ie, 'timeless'. Not only is time *suspended* (3), but history is frozen for our scrutiny. *The unimaginable | Zero summer* (19/20) represents eternal blessedness, when time becomes intelligible. *The soul's sap quivers* (12), because illuminated by the blinding light of grace.

The second section (20–39) pictures Charles the Martyr arriving at Little Gidding at night-time after the battle. By then Ferrar had been dead nearly ten years. Those who visit religious places on pilgrimage, or with no particular aim, are apt to be disappointed. Eliot thinks of the dwelling places of five saints, Columba, Cuthbert, Kevin, and the two Anthonys, of the Thebiad and Padua (35–9); but Little Gidding happens to be the nearest to London (forgetting Canterbury). In lines 39–53 he remarks that visitors with guide-books often come for the wrong purpose. These are places of worship, for which reason he defines the meaning of prayer (46–8). Mystical communion with saints is referred to in lines 50–1: *communication | Of the dead is tongued with fire beyond the language of the living*. But the wording of the last line again looks back to *Acts* II, 3. In *the intersection of the timeless moment* (52), the poet recalls Kierkegaard's pronouncement: 'Christ is the intersection of Time and Eternity'.

The second movement (longest in *Four Quartets*) opens with a poem of three stanzas, having four rhymed couplets in each, and incorporating Heraclitus's observations on the replacement of elements. Dust is associated with air in this scheme. Each stanza illustrates a different form of frustration, and the first suggests that human desire (*burnt roses*) and effort (*house*) are futile. *Hope and despair* (7) are regarded as the extreme points of emotion.

The second stanza, with a number of criss-cross allusions, is concerned with the barrenness of nature and the *vanity of toil* (14). Images of aridity are vivid, *eg, The parched eviscerate soil | Gapes . . . | Laughs without mirth*; *drouth* (9) is associated with fire.

The third stanza treats symbolically the destruction of the church, not only physically, as by bombing-raids on English cities. *Deride* (19) is a powerful personification; by acting together as destructive agents, water and fire 'make a mockery of' the Eucharist (*sacrifice*), which can no longer be solemnized on the ruined altar. *The marred foundations . . . | Of sanctuary and choir* suggest also the ruins of Little Gidding Chapel.

The next section consists of 72 lines (25–96) in *terza rima*, which differs from Dante's cantos in being unrhymed. This part is personal, and 'hallucinates' Eliot's experience as an air-raid warden during 1940. Before the all-clear signal, he imagines an encounter with another poet. The suggestion for this ghost is the figure of Brunetto Latini in Dante's *Inferno*, Canto XV, which promotes the sombre mood and metre of Eliot's poetry. This man was a scholar and Dante's neighbour, with whom he renewed acquaintance among the violators of nature in Hell. In 'What Dante means to me' (*To Criticize the Critic*, Faber, 1965, pp. 128–9) Eliot provides an instructive account of his intention in this movement, 'to present to the mind of the reader a parallel, by means of contrast':

I borrowed and adapted freely only a few phrases – because I was *imitating*. My first problem was to find an approximation to the *terza rima* without rhyming. English is less copiously provided with rhyming words than Italian; and those rhymes we have are in a way more emphatic. The rhyming words call too much attention to themselves . . . I therefore adopted, for my purpose, a simple alternation of unrhymed masculine and feminine terminations, as the nearest way of giving the light effect of the rhyme in Italian... I am always worried in anticipation, by the inevitable shifts and twists which I know the translator will be obliged to make, in order to fit Dante's words into English rhyme...

This section of a poem – not the length of one canto of the Divine Comedy – cost me far more time and trouble and vexation than any passage of the same length that I have ever written. It was not simply that I was limited to the Dantesque type of imagery, simile and figure of speech. It was chiefly that in this very bare and austere style, in which every word has to be 'functional', the slighest vagueness or imprecision is immediately noticeable. The language has to be very direct; the line, and the single word, must be completely disciplined to the purpose of the whole; and, when you are using simple words and simple phrases, any repetition of the most common idiom, or of the most frequently needed word, becomes a glaring blemish.

The last paragraph conveniently explains how Eliot's method differs from Dante's. His normal verse style is neither austere, direct nor simple; rather, it emphasizes, by repetition, 'the most frequently needed word'. It was Shelley's individualistic imitation of Dante in *The Triumph of Life* that aroused Eliot's admiration.

It cannot be said that Eliot's blank verse experiment in *terza rima* is metrically satisfying to a student of Dante; but loss of rhyme is sometimes compensated by dexterity in the use of devices, such as weak participial endings *-ing* and *-ed*, medially and at the end of lines. Note the paradoxical oxymorons of lines 26–7:

Near the *ending* of *interminable* night
At the *recurrent end* of the *unending* (cf. 33 *loitering* and *hurried*)

The periphrastic image of *the dark dove with the flickering tongue* (28) represents enemy aircraft, and the *metal leaves* of lines 30 and 34 foliage scorched by fire.

Misunderstandings aroused by the ghostly newcomer in line 33 are due to his composite nature, sometimes speaking in the voice of the poet himself (cf. line 44). This is a symbolist mask, owing something to the example of Mallarmé. The phrase *To purify the dialect of the tribe* (74) was culled from this poet's *Le Tombeau d'Edgar Poe*.

After line 45 Eliot is involved in both question and answer, as in the dream-world of *Divina Commedia*. In lines 65–6 the poet from another world remarks that the thoughts of each generation are meaningless to the next. *Peregrine* (68, 'alien', 'wandering') has been little used since the nineteenth century, except in a technical sense; Eliot's poetical inversion in *the spirit unappeased and peregrine* tends to escape notice, because of the unusual medium of the language. The periphrasis for 'died', *When I left my body on a distant shore* (72) was probably suggested by Vergil's *Aeneid*, VI.314.

Richard Ellmann in *Eminent Domain* (Oxford University Press, 1967, pp. 94–5) reminds us that Eliot had Yeats in mind in lines 76–93, intending them as a belated tribute to the poet, who had died three years earlier. This is kindly inference, but there may be substance in the following lines (76–84 and 91–3):

> 'Lét me disclóse the gífts resérved for áge
>   To sét a crówn upòn your lifetìme's éffort.
> First, | the cóld fríction of expíring sénse
> Withòut enchántment, | óffering nò prómise
>   But bítter tástelessness of shádow frúit
>   As bódy and sóul begín to fáll asúnder.
> Sécond, | the cónscious ímpotence of ráge
>   At húman fólly, | and the láceràtion
>   Of laúghter at what céases to amúse . . .
> From wróng to wróng the exásperàted spírit
>   Procéeds, | unléss restóred by thàt refíning fire
>   Where yòu mùst móve in méasure, | like a dáncer.'

This reveals a nice perception of the Irish poet's artistic struggle, so different from Eliot's. The lines are not strictly *terza rima,* but sensitively modulated blank verse, with alternating feminine endings. The pauses are in varied positions, and usually in the middle of a foot. Three of the lines have trochaic inversion in the first foot, and there are several substitutions within the line. This verse is unlike *terza rima,* because only the first of the four stanzas is syntactically linked with the succeeding one. In the search for Dantesque simplicity, Eliot here denies himself the repetitions of schematic rhetoric, and concentrates on tropes such as metaphor, which is in nearly every line. *Expiring* (78) is used in its original sense of 'exhaling'; *refining fire* (92) is the symbol of God's love, and recalls the line on Arnaut Daniel at the end of *Purgatorio*, XXVI.

Movement III is of the first importance in understanding the purpose of *Four Quartets*. Eliot begins with a brief meditation on Krishna's advice to Arjuna concerning non-attachment (1–16). The quality of life depends on a man's relationship to the world, which may take three forms (3–5):

Attachment to self and to things and to persons, *detachment From self* and from things and from persons; and growing between them *indifference*
Which resembles the others as *death* resembles life

Death in life (or indifference) is an *unflowering* (6) condition between the poles of blind action and enlightened passivity.

Memory is man's instrument for *liberation* (7/8). Eliot suggests that one may be enslaved to *the future as well as the past* (9/10), and the remedy is to expand one's concept of *love beyond desire* (9). The principal use of memory is to review objectively one's past life and relate it to *history*; this brings freedom from the *servitude* (3) imposed upon one's thinking about the past. Love of country is involved with love of self, beginning *as attachment to our own field of action* (11); but true patriotism (history as freedom) discovers that personal involvement is *of little importance* (12). The *faces and places* (15) that the self cared for then *become renewed, transfigured, in another pattern* (16). It was Buddha who first taught that *Karma* ('causal sequence in time') binds a man, until he is freed by 'dying to' the temporal self.

In lines 17–19 Eliot borrows a quotation from the fourteenth-century mystic, Dame Julian of Norwich, author of *Revelations of Divine Love* (1373–93). She was an anchoress of no education, born about 1342, who recorded sixteen revelations, whose meaning was divinely imparted. As she was often in physical pain, the sins she repented were probably the result of *accidie*. She considered prayer to be of two kinds: *beseeching* (acquiescence) and *beholding* (self-surrender). She sought for an explanation of God's reasons for permitting sin in the world. In *Revelation* XIII Jesus, in a vision, vouchsafed the answer that Eliot modifies in lines 17–19:

Synne is *behovabil*, but al shal be wel & al shal be wel & al manner of thing shal be wele.

The italicized word means 'useful', 'advantageous', and *behovable* remained in use until the end of the sixteenth century; but *behovely*, the earlier and commoner form of the adjective, occurs in Robert Mannyng of Brunne, Chaucer and Gower. Sin is said to be *behovely* because it exacts faith, and is rewarded by compassion. Eliot's purpose is to show that, although often suffering results from sin, it is not without its use as a means to salvation.

In line 20 Eliot returns to the fate of Little Gidding in the seventeenth century. Its devotees were people who sacrificed themselves for a cause (25). The three protagonists who died on the scaffold were Charles I, Archbishop Laud and Strafford (27). Among the *few who died forgotten | In other places* (28/9) were the poet, Richard Crashaw, exiled in France. The *One who died blind and quiet* (30) was Milton; *the spectre of a Rose* (35) symbolizes the lost Royalist cause. The *antique drum* (38) is unlikely to represent the militant Roundheads, but the entire Civil War. It is the proper course of historical detachment not to take sides with either cause; for (says Eliot) time has united the opponents *in the strife which divided them* (25); they *accept the constitution of silence* (41), and the *symbol* of their heroic sacrifice is *perfected in death* (46).

As a coda to this memorable passage, Eliot speaks of *the purification of the motive | In the ground of our beseeching* (49/50). This comes from Dame Julian of Norwich's Fourteenth 'Shewing' or Revelation. In response to her quest for the meaning of Prayer, the Lord appeared and said, 'I am Ground of thy beseeching'; she explains that *beseeching* 'is a true, gracious, lasting will of the soul'. In the thirteenth century the word *ground* began to be employed by mystics in the sense of 'foundation' or 'bottom', especially of the *heart*.

The fourth movement is a formal lyric of two seven-lined stanzas on the symbolic theme of Pentecost, rhyming ababacc. This is the only poem in which Eliot used regular four-beat iambics. It is full of pessimistic paradox, and different in spirit from Herbert's metaphysical poems. Only a modernist would have used the image of the *dove,* not for peace, but for attacking war-planes. The *choice of pyre or pyre* (6) offers the alternative of Hell or Purgatory. The two *fires* of line 7 stand for self-love and purification, for being and becoming. Love has an *unfamiliar Name* (9), because it is linked with suffering, especially from those who wield the instruments of war. *The intolerable shirt of flame* (11) is that of Nessus, the centaur, given to Deianira, the wife of Hercules; it caused him to die, as a demigod, upon a pyre that he himself had built. This poem purports to say that men die to live, and that they do so only through divine love.

Speaking of ambiguity, Eliot in several places mentions the poet's gift of squeezing the utmost meaning out of words. Three of these are of importance in this passage: the noun *discharge* (4), and the verbs *devised* (8) and *suspire* (13). *Discharge* has legal overtones and implies both 'the firing of a weapon' and 'unburdening the soul'. *Devise* once signified 'separate, divide', and then acquired the sense of 'invent'. Intransitive *suspire* had the primary meaning of 'breathe', but was also used figuratively in the sense of 'long for'.

Movement V consists of two parts, bridged by line 25. 'Words and poetry' is the theme of the first part, beginning with the metaphysics of finite and infinite being. A poem is like life; it is a succession of moving moments. Its plotting is not, however, linear, because all beginnings are involved with ends. The paradox of creation is, therefore, that the start is made with an ultimate end in mind. For instance, in a sentence that feels right, the phrases have a structural end determined by the initial choices. The function of an *epitaph* (12), 'an inscription on a tomb', is to commemorate an individual's fulfilment of existence. Eliot's comments on writing in lines 5–10 have the mark of disciplined order, recognized by classicists from Horace to Flaubert.

In lines 12–24 emphasis shifts to man's activity and history. As each poem is an epitaph, so every action leads by devious paths to the grave, where the testimonies of life are undecipherable. We do not find in the churchyard the aspiring humanism of Gray's *Elegy*, though the dead are an inseparable part of the living tradition. Eliot's comparison of the *rose* and *yew-tree* (19) is not to contrast *intensity* with *duration*, but to suggest that in the scale of perfection they carry equal weight. Why bemoan the sadness of mutability? What it reveals is a *pattern / Of timeless moments* (21/22). History is a 'becoming' all the time, wherever men congregate.

As the poet visualizes the story of Little Gidding, the *pattern* of events gives it meaning; men have faith in the pattern, because life would else be meaningless. In the sentence *A people without a history | Is not redeemed from time* (20/21) Eliot implies that an un-cultured people is not exempt from the destiny of the pattern their way of life entails. But what history does is to take the national ethos out of time, and view it in the aspect of eternity.

The bridge-line *With the drawing of this Love and the voice of this Calling* (25) comes from the second chapter of *The Cloud of Unknowing*. The fourteenth-century author is unknown, but the essence of this mystic's teaching is humility and love. He believed that 'a good will is the substance of all perfection'. By *Calling*, he meant 'the kindling of desire' for God's love.

In lines 26–46 Eliot draws together the threads of his meditation, and cites lines from all the earlier Quartets. The effect of this is to show that detachment, understanding and love are valuable potentitalities. They cannot be perceived intellectually, however, because their worth is experienced emotionally. The experience is vouchsafed through *A condition of complete simplicity | (Costing not less than everything)* (40/41).

The justice of Eliot's analogy with musical expression becomes obvious in *Little Gidding*. In *Four Quartets* communication is the major difficulty, and it is inevitable that the poems should be as capable of many interpretations as chamber music is. 'The poetry does not matter' (*East Coker* II.21) must not be taken literally. Nothing was more important to Eliot than his art; but he was a poet eternally conscious of the limitations of his medium.

Time is a speculative aspect of all mystical religions. In *Burnt Norton* Eliot looks into the past; in *East Coker* he relates the past to the present, and in *The Dry Salvages* he relates the present to the future; while *Little Gidding* considers the individual's place in history. The instruments of faith are, respectively, memory, tradition, hope and love. Only Eliot could have thought this material viable for poetry, and Eliot alone could have triumphed over the transformational difficulties. He agreed with Pascal that there 'was evidence for and against the existence of God; but that if a man kept his mind in suspense about it, he could not live a rich and active life' (W. B. Yeats's *Wheels and Butterflies*). The range of Eliot's psychic experience helped him to transcend private ills and to identify personal problems with the malaise of society, whose cultural decline he dated from 1926 (see *Criterion*, January 1939).

Eliot was a tentative and cautious explorer, whose puritan background and philosophic training did not confine his researches to the Christian creeds. But this very diversity made it difficult to formulate his religious thinking; his prose articles invariably defend ecclesiastical practice, and the place of the church in the social and cultural order. Religious poetry had never succeeded in English, and Eliot realized that it could only be made palatable in small doses. To avoid tedium, the poems in *Ash Wednesday* and *Four Quartets* had to be diversified in form, but united in a common thematic aim.

To reconcile a thinker of urban culture and wide intellectual interests with the negative way of a Christian ascetic is the uneasy association a critic has to accept. Many writers who approve Eliot as an artist question the efficacy of his mystical withdrawal. David Ward, offers a typical comment in *T. S. Eliot: Between Two Worlds* (Routledge and Kegan Paul, 1973, pp. 248–9):

> There is a strange insecurity in Eliot's retreat into the consolations of the hermit. Paul's magnificent hymn of praise to love admits of no doubt at all of its nature, or of the possibility that, love being real, it could be 'love of the wrong thing.' In Paul's account of the matter love exalts all other virtues, purifies all other virtues, comprehends all other virtues: 'Love never faileth'; but Eliot fears the expansiveness, the generosity of Paul's claim, its joyful enthusiasm ...
>
> To encapsulate a remembered ecstasy and anticipate a transfiguring fulfilment is to put all the rest of life in brackets, exchange the inevitably repeated errors of maturation for one long grey parenthesis ... Perhaps the claimed relationship with St John of the Cross is not entirely legitimate.

But John of the Cross was a poet, and mystical ideas were in the air, especially in Western America, when Aldous Huxley published *Ends and Means* in 1937. At first, Eliot dismissed Huxley and Lawrence as characteristic products of the disintegration of Protestantism; but later he accepted, with caution, Huxley's conviction that 'we live on the border-line between two worlds, the temporal and the eternal, the physical-vital-human and the divine' (*The Perennial Philosophy*, Chatto and Windus, 1946).

The citations from Heraclitus at the head of *Burnt Norton* show that Eliot was well acquainted with the early Greek philosophers.

Heraclitus was a mystic, and so were Pythagoras and Parmenides, who were actively teaching in the sixth century BC, contemporary with Buddha. In *From Religion to Philosophy* (Arnold, 1912), F. M. Cornford traced the descent of the mystical tradition, from the religion of Dionysus, through the Orphic and Pythagorean reforms, to the *Phaedo* and *Timaeus* of Plato. Many ideas concerning the wheel of human destiny, re-incarnation and rebirth came to the Ionian Greeks from the East, via the Persian mystics; the Greek god *Zeus*, (*Zen*, 'Life' or 'God') was addressed by the poet, Pindar, as the son of *Chronos* (Time) and *Rhea* (Flux), the motive powers in the philosophy of Heraclitus. Chinese Buddhism had its *Tao* (the Way), corresponding to Indian *Dharma* (principle of life) and Greek *Dike* (righteousness). Aristotle wrote in *De Anima* that Heraclitus took *Psyche* (the soul or 'capacity of awareness') as his first principle, identifying it with vapour, the least corporeal thing in the endless flux (energy). The only constant in this world of ceaseless change was the *Logos* (the Spirit of Harmony or Justice) which was regarded as the measure of all things. The *Logos* is the means whereby opposites are reconciled, such as death and re-birth; without it the cycle of regeneration was thought impossible.

The relevance of these beliefs to language was perceived by the Greeks and discussed by Plato in *Cratylus*. Cornford explains the Pythagorean reformation in terms quite appropriate to Eliot's position in *Four Quartets*:

> The 'truth' which mysticism guards is a thing which can only be learnt by being experienced (*pathein mathein*); it is funda-mentally, not an intellectual, but an emotional experience – that invasive, flooding sense of oneness, of reunion and communion with the life of the world, which the mystical temperaments of all ages seem to have in common, no matter in what theological terms they may happen to construe it after-wards. Being an emotional, non-rational state, it is indescrib-able, and incommunicable save by suggestion. To induce that state, by the stimulus of collective excitement and all the pageantry of dramatic ceremonial, is the aim of mystic ritual. The 'truth' can only come to those who submit themselves to these influences, because it is a thing to be immediately felt, not conveyed by dogmatic instruction. For that reason only – a

very sufficient one – 'mysteries' are reserved to the initiate, who have undergone 'purification', and so put themselves into a state of mind which fits them for the consummate experience. (Op. cit. pp. 198–9)

The philosopher who proposed the two orders of physical time and eternity, denied by Hobbes in the seventeenth century, was Plato. The Greek word *chronos* appears in *Revelation* X, 6 'there should be *time* no longer'; but New Testament Greek has no word for *eternity*. Adjectival and adverbial translations, such as *eternal* and *forever*, usually have the sense of 'everlasting'. The belief that 'God is eternity' arose from the Christian mystics; and the inspired idea that the Incarnation is the intersection of human time with eternity is derived from St Augustine's *City of God*. Hobbes's denial was based on the argument that time and change are fundamental to man's conception of reality.

If religion, as Eliot admits, needs to adapt itself to the conditions of the time, that it may continue to be believed in, the negative way of the mystic is hardly likely to be practicable in our time. 'The still point of the turning world' is not in the religion of Christ and St Paul, whose faith is grounded in redemption through constancy, hope and love.

Most critics of Eliot's language have accepted the inevitable obligation to interpret his intentions. His poetry, defended by prose of Bradleyan clarity, has been too influential in development not to take it seriously. Yet the obscurity remains, and the success of the prosaic elements is the most unaccountable. Was the obfuscation deliberate or incidental? Critics are unlikely to decide until a biography, the collected letters, and the ungathered prose, are available; these may justify the suggestion that *Four Quartets* is a 'religious autobiography'.

Eliot maintained that certain kinds of illness are favourable to literary creation, and *The Waste Land* was written under such conditions. Its mosaic of borrowings and daring non-sequiturs became exciting for readers to explicate. Not only did Eliot enjoy the results of this challenge, but he encouraged the notion of an 'invisible' poet, who prefers to remain inscrutable in his work.

This is one explanation; but there are more tenable reasons for Eliot's obscurity. The fragmentation of images and ideas became a stylistic norm for handling the complex procedures necessary to his French taste for symbolism. Pound convinced him that this was inevitable to break the deadlock of exhausted conventions. Semantic puzzles result from the bonding of fragments, without adequate syntactical boundaries. Though the welter of modern conceits is disciplined by the old rhetorical balance, and by extraordinary phrasal economy, there are passages of marginal status where it is hard to distinguish parody from genuine conviction.

Eliot's longer and distinguished poems, *The Waste Land, Ash Wednesday* and *Burnt Norton,* consisted of isolated compositions, dealing with existential states of mind rather than points of view; they did not lend themselves to logical exegesis. Many erroneous speculations about the poems had to be countered by private correspondence. The earnestness of Eliot's prose encouraged these speculations, as sensible readers were satisfied that the author had a valuable message for his generation. That being so, interpretation and meaning were essential for understanding and enjoyment.

Nevertheless, Eliot's poems were responsible for a shift of emphasis from meaning to technique. The concentrated yet enigmatic language produces an effect that is partly unconscious, because it is deliberately emotive. The symbolist technique does not arouse any expectation of a logical pattern.

The poetic style of Eliot is therefore different in complexity from that of the great English poets who preceded him – Shakespeare, Donne, Milton, Pope, Wordsworth. Metaphysical though it may be, it seldom resembles the duologue style of Donne, who addressed God and his lady with respective eloquence and irony. There is nothing comparable in English with Eliot's rapid transitions of *persona* from priest to logician, from anthropologist to philosopher. The extinction of personality is not signally demonstrated in his poetry; it has the Eliot mannerism in nearly every line. The tradition he extols is of content; in form he was more experimental than any predecessor or contemporary that mattered.

Though the basic rhythm of English poetry is the iambic, Eliot's good ear enabled him to exploit trisyllables and trochaic modulation more successfully than any other English poet since Shelley. He owed this facility to his reading of the Hebrew poets in biblical translation, and to the cadences of the *Book of Common Prayer.* His control of free verse, whether in irregular rhyme or blank verse, shows the nicest judgement in determining the length of lines. He invented new and memorable rhythms and did not, like Yeats, expand the possibilities of existing forms. His contribution was the re-instatement of Old English falling rhythms, in which some of the most memorable lines are expressed:

> I have measured out my life with coffee spoons
> I will show you fear in a handfull of dust
> Not with a bang but a whimper
> Wavering between the profit and the loss
> human kind / Cannot bear very much reality

Besides enlarging the scope of figures in Renaissance rhetoric, Eliot was an acknowledged master in weaving schematic insistence through balance and repetition. His knowledge of the European tradition on which Dante built, and his reading of Elizabethan and Jacobean dramatists persuaded him that the structural advantages of rhetoric are still operative, and that poetry without it would be lamed and unattractive.

Eliot kept his equilibrium in the midst of adulation and occasional scorn. He became a conscientious and deliberate artist, aware of the technical problems involved in all he undertook. His plays were all experiments in expression as well as ideas. *Murder in the Cathedral* was a medieval tragic morality, written in the idiom and verse of *Everyman*. In *The Family Reunion* he determined to treat contemporary life in verse for the commercial theatre, and to enter successfully into competition with prose drama. Here he carried contemporary speech rhythms a step further, and remained faithful to this seemingly prosaic verse in all his later poetry. *The Cocktail Party* and *The Confidential Clerk* revealed increasing flexibility in the medium, and an alarming denial of the usual graces of poetry. The difference between the style of *The Waste Land* and that of the verse dramatist is that the first was written in Eliot's 'own voice', the plays for unkown actors performing to unpredictable audiences.

The least successful of the plays on the stage was *The Confidential Clerk*; yet it is a lively and polished comedy. Its economy of expression is as near classical perfection as a modern writer could hope for. Eliot seldom wrote in verse such clear, cogent and intelligible English; it does its work at the unconscious level, which is all that Eliot desired of it. There is no escaping the impression that the play owed something to Wilde's *The Importance of being Earnest,* though it has in its denouement nothing so farcical as the handbag left at Victoria Station. Paradox of a spiritual, heart-searching kind permeates the play; Eliot seems to have agreed with Congreve that nature hates to be forced.

For some tastes the verse of the later plays is too deflated, the plots too flimsy, incredible and confusing. Eliot knew his limitations as well as he knew London and the middle-aged roués in fashionable drawing-rooms. Behind the façade of the frustrated confidential clerk, from Prufrock to Mr Eggerson, we see Eliot himself, and the heart of the withdrawn scholar, like Montaigne or Voltaire, who cultivates his metaphorical garden.

After *Murder in the Cathedral,* more verse and less poetry appeared in the plays; but the predominantly falling rhythm continued to flow naturally from the emphatically stressed syllables of significant words, producing a movement quite unlike that of blank verse. The drawbacks of the later verse are the diminished projective power, and the scholastic tone, that makes the existential debates much less dramatic than the ritual language of *Murder in the Cathedral.*

Eliot's New England education and acquaintance with American literature had lasting effects upon his modernism; yet he said his impact on the language of poetry was re-creative, rather than revolutionary. In 'American Literature and Language' (*To Criticize the Critic,* Faber, 1965, p. 59) he wrote:

> I think it is just to say that the pioneers of twentieth century poetry were more conspicuously the Americans than the English, both in number and in quality ... So far as my observation goes, I should say ... of contemporary verse, that the most dangerous tendency of American versifiers is towards eccentricity and formlessness ...

The American streak in Eliot produced a Mencken-like impulse to think anti-socially. He left America dissatisfied with the uncritical apotheosis of the common man, but never quite shed his inheritance. The severe critical attitudes were compensations for a timid introvert, and Lionel Trilling diagnosed the desired impersonality of such authors astutely: 'The more a writer takes pains with his work to remove it from the personal and subjective, the more ... he will express his true unconscious'. (*Art and Neurosis,* Secker and Warburg, 1961, p. 169). The Manichean world of Eliot's time-kept, Unreal City seems to have had its origins in St Louis and Boston.

Eliot's Sweeney (a degraded image of man) in *Fragment of an Agon,* is, like Burbank, an atavistic revival of Eliot's youth. The original is said to have been a Bostonian pugilist, of Irish extraction, who gave the young student boxing lessons, and afterwards became a bar-tender. Herbert Howarth in *Notes on Some Figures behind T. S. Eliot* (Chatto and Windus, 1965, pp. 123–4) says that the Sweeney 'talk' *eg,* 'We're *gona* stay and we're *gona* go / And somebody's *gotta* pay the rent' probably burlesqued the musical comedies of the Hasty Pudding Club at Harvard University. The Jamesian lady who offers tea to friends in *Portrait of a Lady* typifies the 'five-foot-shelf culture' of New England pseudo-intellectuals. Eliot was determined to make poetry out of his casual experiences with vulgarians as well as superior intelligences; but the patter of *Sweeney Agonistes* is the most stylized of all his experiments. Howarth describes it as 'the poetry of comic animosity' (*op. cit.* p. 337).

CHAPTER IX

W. H. Auden (1):
Poems 1927–47

𝕾𝕾𝕾𝕾𝕾𝕾

FEW English poets of this century have drawn more intellectual sustenance from their times than Wystan Hugh Auden, who was born in York, the son of a doctor, on 21 February 1907. Soon after his birth the family migrated to Birmingham, where Dr Auden became Medical Officer and University Professor of Public Health. At Gresham School, Holt, Auden's interests were in biology and music, and he later cultivated a special taste for the operas of Mozart and Verdi. He was at Christ Church College, Oxford, from 1925 to 1928, and enjoyed the personal and literary friendship of Stephen Spender, whose account of their relationship in *World Within World* (Hamish Hamilton, 1951) observes Auden's nascent talent for a 'clipped, clear-cut, icy quality' in poetry (p. 51).

The mind of this young poet was analytical almost from infancy, and his memory for abstract learning, as well as for the poetry he liked, was prodigious. An early clinical direction in his writing came from Freudian psychology, in which he thought to discover a road to self-knowledge and detachment. Although Auden advanced the cause of liberal socialism for a decade, independent judgement was his strongest characteristic; throughout his life he refused enslavement to any pattern of consistency. The group of young political writers to which he belonged had its origins in Oxford, and became known as the 'poets of the nineteen-thirties', with Auden as their unquestionable leader. Spender, Day Lewis and MacNeice were allies, all with different shades of left-wing opinion, and a single desire to rescue Europe from rising authoritarian factions. Writing in *Oxford Poetry*, 1927, Auden said: 'Our youth should be a period of spiritual discipline, not a self-justifying dogma' (Spender, *op. cit.*, p. 57).

The formative influences on Auden's poetry were Hardy, Eliot, Byron, Pope, Goethe and Shakespeare. The inequality of his verse can be traced to the inveterate habit of experimenting in different styles, without penetrating below the surface texture. After his departure for America in January 1939, Auden became severely self-critical of his earlier poems, and altered or suppressed many that anthologists insisted were characteristic of the man. His conversion to Anglo-Catholicism introduced fewer changes into his mode of life than Eliot's, since the family creed had always been High Anglican; for Auden, however, it brought disenchantment with the political causes of the nineteen-thirties. Though there appeared some loss of intellectual sharpness in the poetry, there was a gain in craftsmanship, noticeable in the handling of stanza forms.

Auden was a born teacher, with an immense capacity for stimulating receptive minds. Throughout his career the discipline pursued was of mind and body rather than of art. After thirty he read less in poetry and criticism, and more books that would keep him abreast of the world, or shape his destiny in it. In 'The Poet and the City' he gives unmistakable evidence of the writing he favoured:

> The characteristic style of 'Modern' poetry is an intimate tone of voice, the speech of one person addressing one person, not a large audience; whenever a modern poet raises his voice he sounds phony. And its characteristic hero is ... the man or woman in any walk of life who, despite all the impersonal pressures of modern society, manages to acquire and preserve a face of his own.
>
> *(The Dyer's Hand,* Faber 1963, p. 84)

Auden's *obiter dicta* on reading and writing are largely of this kind; they provide the best introduction to a study of his poetry. For him, the most valuable literature is that which can be read in different ways. His judgements, as wholesomely charged with common sense as Dr Johnson's, read like potted wisdom or the sayings of La Rochefoucauld, *eg,* 'The poet is the father of his poem; its mother is a language' (*op. cit.,* p. 22).

But Auden's taste was for German, rather than French, literature; and this Nordic tendency explains much that differentiates his style from Eliot's. He tolerated scholarly criticism more for its quotations than its comments; he disapproved of criticism that attacks worthless books, unless the writing corrupts the language.

The integrity of language is essential because it is not a medium reserved for the craft of writing alone, as paint is for painters.

Auden regarded some kinds of experiments as therapeutic, for instance those that enable the writer, by building up 'antibodies', to rid himself of affected ways of feeling and thinking, not authentic to his talents. The essay on 'Writing' in *The Dyer's Hand* is specially relevant to some of the poetry written before 1939. He speaks of personality traits every poet should be aware of, if he is to avoid themes that offer no potentiality of truth in a poetic sense; for no poet can be sincere, who is not emotionally involved in the ideas and beliefs he represents. The reader, however, does not need to share the writer's beliefs in order to enjoy the poem.

Auden, in his criticism, is deeply concerned with the relationship of a poet's integrity to his social conscience. Authenticity, not originality, is the desired end; indeed, the danger of *avant-garde* art is its 'solipsist subjectivity'. If the terms classic and romantic no longer have meaning for modern literature, Auden's alternatives, the aristocratic and democratic principles, respectively defend poetry from 'barbaric vagueness' and 'decadent triviality'. The style of his judicial utterances is much given to vigorous expletives, and the matter-of-fact tone is often extended to poems. It gives a didactic flavour to the writing, which hardened with maturity.

Auden was aware of the need for a 'consistent *oeuvre*' in a modern poet's development, but his output has less homogeneity than that of Yeats or Eliot. The reasons for this will appear in analysis; but an initial generalization may be hazarded: he does not share their feeling for universal symbols, or for a close affinity between poetry and music. His approach to all writing is pragmatic, honest and down-to-earth; for the genuineness of each art depends on technical mastery of its peculiar technique. Auden contends for the equal utility of poetry and prose in the lucid expression of ideas, and therefore commends Pope's *Essay on Man* for its 'Cartesian' clarity.

The modern poet is, for Auden, a man speaking to himself, not a dialectician, like Pope, who interanimates ideas. Some critics see Auden's intellectualism as a quixotic quest for a pattern of living that he knew poetry was inadequate to supply. A moralist needs order; and most artists of the time were in the unpropitious condition of living in a disintegrating urban and industrial society. Moreover, Auden's early dedication to science had had the unfortunate effect of undermining his trust in the significance of sensory experience. This, he concluded, was a loss all moderns must endure, and a cause of the subjectivity of their work. Haunted by the transience of life's values, the artist invariably feared that his compositions might prove ephemeral, and doubted whether a successful poem would again be achieved. The cultural tradition Eliot appraised seemed obsolescent, and it had become increasingly difficult for a poet like Auden to find the authentic note that he admired in the work of Robert Frost.

From his study of Freud, Auden acquired the habit of appealing to an internal Censor. In *Making, Knowing and Judging* (1956), his inaugural address as Professor of Poetry at Oxford, he asks the self-revealing question: How much does a poet 'conceal from himself'? (*The Dyer's Hand*, p. 51). The bugbear of the modern poet is inability to test his work for idiosyncrasy and lapses of taste. Having found himself, the poet is ironically warned by the Censor not to repeat his achievement. He must never relax in keeping 'a sharper look out for obsessive rhythms, tics of expression, privately numinous words' (p. 52).

As a result of Auden's censorious conscience, *The Collected Shorter Poems* (Faber, 1945) was remarkable for the revisions, partial eliminations and rejections already mentioned. Several poems are found to have different titles in the English and American editions; and Auden paid small regard to the chronological sequence of poems, when editing this collection. Establishing the canon of his poems is consequently proving a long and unenviable task. The reasons for modification were partly aesthetic, and partly the outcome of the shifting ground of Auden's politics, philosophy and religion. He seems to have abandoned the Marxian philosophy in 1937, and to have chosen a more humanistic viewpoint. The neo-Augustinian idea of a *Just City*, founded upon religion, first appeared in *Spain* (1937) and *New Year Letter* (1940).

The result of numerous personal tensions in Auden's poetry is its ambiguity of intention. The emotional irreconcilables had their root in the poet's isolation and self-exile; the ambiguity of intention arose from difficulty in reconciling religion with scientific rationalism. In poetry he was soon to distinguish the primary and secondary imagination as spiritual or sacred in the first case, and cerebral or social in the other. Auden was fully aware of his divided personality and part of his design in revising and re-shuffling the poems was to eliminate the more obvious incongruities. The youthful sense of fun, the 'fencing wit of an informal style' that exposes humbug, possess more liveliness for his wide public than the chameleon-like speculations that spring from omnivorous reading. The undoubted virtue of Auden's poetry is its scope and range of vocabulary, which are wider than those of any other modern poet. But with all his inventiveness, he did not evolve the characteristically Audenesque idiom his poetry required for universality. The different definitions and offices of *love* alone would fill a chapter in a biography, yet none leaves much room for optimism.

Auden has been compared to Byron in the facile and immature ideology of some early writings, and to Kierkegaard in the complexity of his later existentialism. What is Byronic is the tone of burlesque that tends to rhetorical gesture, and the mind that synthesizes borrowed ideas, without feeling them experientially. The *Letter to Lord Byron* (1936), although in rhyme royal and not the *ottava rima* of *Don Juan*, captures the Juanesque rhythm of run-on verses and multiple rhymes, with fanciful wit and more cynical circumspection than Byron's:

> In setting up my brass plate as a critic,
>   I make no claim to certain diagnosis,
> I'm more intuitive than analytic,
>   I offer thought in homoeopathic doses
>   (But someone may get better in the process).
> I don't pretend to reasoning like Pritchard's
> Or the logomachy of I. A. Richards.

Auden remained loyal to Marx's reasoning, but not to his conclusions; similarly, he was faithful to Freud's methods, but not to his insights, especially concerning things of the spirit. After 1940, he lost the cultishness with his class interests, and renounced egotism for a becoming humility. If, in the change, he sacrificed conviction, he gained something in sensitivity and capacity for contemplation. Like 'Ironic Kierkegaard', his pessimism turned to the psychological causes of the sickness of spirit, the mistrust, which affects man under the pressures of mass society:

> Whichever way we turn, we see
> Man captured by his liberty . . .

Time makes old formulas look strange,
Our properties and symbols change,
But round the freedom of the Will
Our disagreements centre still
                    (*New Year Letter*, 1940, Part III)

The future of Auden is therefore likely to be faced with a similar dilemma to Eliot's; for it has aroused antagonism from liberal intellectuals, who prefer the young poet's unflinching addiction to shock and bewilderment, the unimpeachable tokens of a writer's modernity. When, in the dignified valedictory *At the Grave of Henry James* (1941), Auden complained of the 'Resentful muttering Mass', vilifying 'the landscape of Distinction' with 'its vague incitement', the responsive group of early readers recoiled with amazement, and were largely untouched by his final moving appeal:

            Master of nuance and scruple,
    Pray for me and for all writers, living or dead:
        Because there are many whose works
    Are in better taste than their lives, because there is no end
    To the vanity of our calling, make intercession
        For the treason of all clerks.

Auden seems to have been unaffected by the American brand of English that he heard for over twenty years. Even the vigorous slang which obtrudes in quite serious poems, such as *New Year Letter*, belongs more frequently to the background of his youth than the country of his adoption. He uses it for strong contrasts, and for the light relief of phrases unusually overloaded with meaning. The long, discursive poem, addressed to Elizabeth Mayer, is in octosyllabic couplets, and needed the kind of diversion Auden was keen to supply. In Part II, he is talking of the Devil's 'polysyllabic oratory':

            All vague idealistic art
            That *coddles* the uneasy heart
            Is *up his alley*, and *his pigeon*
            The *woozier* species of religion,
            Even a novel, play or song,
            If loud, lugubrious and long . . .

The verb *coddle*, first employed by Jonson in *Every Man in his Humour*, is an expressive colloquial word, which in Auden suggests both senses, 'to warm gently' and 'to pamper'. The other italicized words are slang uses, of which only *woozy* ('confused') appears to be of American origin.

Verbally, Auden is 'on the ball', and relishes the racy effect of a popular slogan. In line 44 of his early poem *Consider* occurs the music-hall tag *It is later than you think*. Perhaps Auden was its originator. In *New Year Letter* Part I, line 13, he uses the phrase *wishful thinking*, doubtless echoing German *das Wunschdenken* (See Simeon Potter, *Changing English*, André Deutsch 1975, p. 67). Incidentally, another political slogan, *the winds of change*, credited to Harold Macmillan, was the coinage of D. H. Lawrence in his poem *The Difference*.

Auden's credential for an aspiring poet was that he be 'a lover of language', and for his own better instruction he possessed and used the twelve-volume edition of the greater Oxford Dictionary. He incorporates, with more delight than pedantry, words borrowed from German, French, Latin and Greek sources, in that order of preference. Etymology and the evolution of meanings enthralled him, and sensitive use of the formal, entertaining and expressive functions of words was among the principal pleasures of writing poetry. In 'Symposium' (*Kenyon Review*, XXVI, 1964, pp. 207–8) he wrote:

> I want every poem I write to be a hymn in praise of the English language: hence my fascination with certain speech-rhythms which can only occur in an uninflected language rich in mono-syllables, my fondness for peculiar words with no equivalents in other tongues, and my deliberate avoidance of that kind of visual imagery which has no basis in verbal experience and can therefore be translated without loss.

This may have been the ideal of the Auden who had arrived; it was not the primary objective of the proselytizing poet who returned from Germany a year after graduating at Oxford. Few poems better illustrate the anonymity and the limitations of the young Auden's language than the sonnet in oddly-rhymed coup-lets, numbered XXX in the volume of 1930:

> *Sir, no man's enemy*, forgiving all
> But *will his negative inversion, be prodigal*:

Send to us power and light, a sovereign touch
Curing the intolerable neural itch,
The *exhaustion of weaning*, the liar's *quinsy*,   5
And the *distortions of ingrown virginity*.
Prohibit sharply the rehearsed response
And gradually correct the coward's stance;
Cover in time with beams those in retreat
That, *spotted*, they turn though the reverse were great   10
Publish each healer that in city lives
Or country houses at the end of drives;
Harrow the house of the dead; look shining at
New styles of architecture, a change of heart.

Phrases and words have been italicized, where they point to the poem's obscurity, which is partly due to the paucity of the punctuation.

The syntax of the opening couplet is insoluble, until (after reading a similar sonnet of G. M. Hopkins, poem 74), one realizes that the personage addressed as *Sir* is the Deity, that *will* (2) is a noun, and that *be prodigal* (perhaps an unconscious recollection of *Venus and Adonis*, line 755) is an imperative of request. The appositional phrase *no man's enemy* (1) is a clue to the significance of the possessive *his* in line 2. *His negative inversion* is another appositional phrase, relevant to man's *will*, a faculty which Auden by implication rebukes for moral obstinacy.

When one has unravelled this initial syntactical difficulty, in the knowledge that Auden's terms and images are theological, lines 1-4 are made intelligible. But the verbal condensation imposed by the sonnet's spatial limitations introduced further obscurities. *The exhaustion of weaning* (5) is a blurred phrase, implying the figurative sense of 'alienation' or 'deprivation' in the use of the verbal noun. *Quinsy* (5, 'inflammation of the tonsils') and *virginity* (6) are ill-assorted rhyme words, whose reference is to the evils of life. The first probably has in mind the 'lie in the throat'; the second suggests a metaphorical malformation, presumably the 'twisting of truth'.

Lines 9-10 contain images of war; the *beams* one takes for those of searchlights revealing the position of retiring forces. *Spotted* (10) has the ambiguous meanings of 'detected' and 'defiled by cowardice'. The figurative language of the last four lines is off-centre, but the intention is to warn back-sliders, wherever they live. The irrelevance of *country houses at the end of drives* (12) must be an excuse for the metaphor *New styles of architecture* (14), a metaphysical conceit for 'change of heart'.

This kind of obscurity has diminished the readers of modern poetry, and justifies the generalized criticism of W. E. Baker (*Syntax in English Poetry*, 1870–1930, p. 158):

> Not only do modern poets exercise liberty in their ordering and disordering of sentence elements, they often disregard the usual grammatical meaning of individual words. They do not feel bound to make syntax consonant with morphology; they use adjectives, prepositions or adverbs as subjects of sentences; and nouns as adverbs or adjectives. The language permits a degree of such flexibility, but many poets otherwise dissimilar go far beyond precedent in their disrespect for grammatical categories.

THE WANDERER
(from *Poems*, second edition 1933)

This poem was first published in *New Signatures* (1932), without its present title, and described as a 'Chorus'. In the American edition of the *Collected Poetry* it is flippantly called 'Something is Bound to Happen'. The poem, in its collocation of phrases, recalls the Old English elegy of *The Wanderer*, but the impressive opening was undoubtedly suggested by *Sawles Warde*, a Middle English prose homily of the first half of the thirteenth century.

Auden, whose family was of Icelandic origin, was first attracted to medieval English at Oxford, where he heard J. R. R. Tolkien recite *Beowulf* and Nevill Coghill read Langland and Chaucer; poems of homage to these scholars appear in *About the House* (1966) and *City Without Walls* (1969).

In *Sawles Warde* the unknown religious author adapted chapters of the fourth book (in Latin) of *De Anima* by Hugh of St Victor. The allegorical figures of the homily are a household, consisting of Wit (the husband), Will (the wife), four daughters representing the cardinal virtues, and five servants who symbolize man's senses. In this woman-dominated family, the husband is humbled, and leaves home. Then a visitor, Love of Life, appears and endeavours to restore order, that the 'treasure' of the house (Soul) should not be lost. The first line of Auden's poem was borrowed, with modifications, from the Christian advice of this visitor:

Dóom is dárk | and déeper than any sèa-díngle.
Upon what man it fall
In spring, day-wishing flowers appearing,
ᴧÁvalanche slíding, | whíte snów fromᴧróck-fáce,
That he should leave his house,   5
No cloud-soft hand can hold him, restraint by women;
But ever that man goes
Through place-keepers, *through* forest trees,
A *stránger* | to *strángers* | over úndrìed séa,
Houses for fishes, suffocating water,   10
Or lonely onᴧfell asᴧchat,
By pot-holed becks
A *bird* stone-haunting, an unquiet *bird*.

Thereᴧhéad fálls fórward, | fatígued at évening,
And dreams of home,   15
*W*áving from *w*índow, | spréad of *w*élcome,
Kissing ofᴧwife underᴧsingle sheet;
But waking sees
Bird-flocks nameless to him, throughᴧdoorway voices
Of new men making another love.   20

Save him from hostile capture,
Fromᴧsudden tiger's spring atᴧcorner;
Protect his *house*,
His anxious *house* whereᴧdays are counted
Fromᴧthunderbolt protect,   25
From gradual ruin spreading like a stain;
Converting number from vague to certain,
Bring joy, *bring*ᴧday of his returning,
Lúcky with dáy appróaching, | withᴧléaning dáwn.

The emphasis in Auden's poem is entirely different from that in *Sawles Warde*, since the poem only hints at family discord (5–6, 15–17, 23–26). The poet's interest is to reflect the nostalgic images a lonely man would entertain, when closely associated with his natural environment. This sympathy is expressed through alliterative figures and compounds, similar to those of the Anglo-Saxon *Wanderer*; Auden again used the figured baroque style in *The Age of Anxiety* (1948).

Of the 29 lines only six (1, 4, 9, 14, 16 and 29) have the alliterative bonding of staves, coupled with caesura, as in Old English verse, and generally with falling rhythm. There are nine short lines for variation, but none has the alliterative characteristics of Anglo-Saxon verse. Elsewhere the alliteration is sporadic; but the poem is remarkable for its echoes of internal rhyme and assonance, especially of the syllable -*ing*, which appears twenty times, fourteen in present-participial endings, and the rest in *dingle, evening, single, spring, bring* (twice). *Ploce* occurs in lines 8, 9, 13, 23–4 and 28, the repeated words being *through, stranger, bird, house* and *bring*.

The Anglo-Saxon elegiac tone is sustained largely by the use of word-compounding, sometimes descriptive, elsewhere figurative:

Descriptive: sea-dingle (1), *rock-face* (4), *pot-holed* (12), *Bird-flocks* (19).
Figurative: day-wishing flowers (3 – personification), *cloud-soft* hand (6 – metaphor), Through *place-keepers* (8 – metonymy, the meaning being 'home-dwellers'), A bird *stone-haunting* (13 – metaphor).

The diction cunningly suggests pathos that accompanies loss, melancholy and desolation *eg, Doom, dark, fall, sliding, rock-face, restraint, stranger, suffocating, lonely on fell, pot-holed becks, unquiet, head falls forward fatigued, dreams of home, nameless, hostile capture, tiger's spring, anxious, days are counted, thunderbolt, ruin spreading like a stain, from vague to certain.* 'Love, language, loneliness and fear' (*New Year Letter*, 1940, line 4) are the principle themes of Auden's poetry.

The Wanderer is composed of impressionistic strokes, with a syntax that affords little logical connection. The economy of the phrasing, as in 2 Upon *what* man it *fall* (subjunctive), is characteristic of the Anglo-Saxon models it resembles, and is partly secured by the omission of articles. At least fifteen are missing, by modern standards (*eg,* 11 Or lonely on˄fell as˄chat, 19 through˄ doorway voices / Of new men). Modern poets complain that both articles are a trial to the free-versifier because of their frequency, and Auden learnt to dispense with many of them, whenever he wished to tighten the diction. Another device used for condensation was the absolute participial phrase, *eg,*

3–4 day-wishing flowers appearing, / Avalanche sliding
13 A bird stone-haunting

Among the poetic nuances Auden revived was inversion of the
normal order of words; there was nothing unusual about this in
early inflected languages, *eg*:

7 But *ever* that man goes
25 *From thunderbolt* protect

It should be noted that short lines such as these are often enjambed
with the succeeding long ones, whereas the latter (except 19) are
self-contained.

No Christian morality is discernible in Auden's poem, as in the
Anglo-Saxon *Wanderer*; but the pessimism of the *peregrinus* or
exile is hopefully dispelled by the final invocation for mercy.
In the earliest Old English poetry this would have been addressed
to Fate (*Wyrd*). Auden's poem is an intricate reverie in the pagan
style, where *dōm* does mean 'doom' rather than 'judgement'.
Sea-dingle was actually a euphemism for the *abyss*, introduced by
the Middle English author of *Sawles Warde*.

MAY WITH ITS LIGHT BEHAVING
(*Look Stranger*, XVI, 1936)

This poem was first published in *The Listener*, 15 May 1935. The
thirty-one poems in *Look Stranger* were numbered, but not titled,
and the book was dedicated to Erika Mann, daughter of Thomas
Mann, whom Auden married in the year of the volume's publication. According to M. K. Spears (*The Poetry of W. H. Auden*,
Oxford University Press, 1963, p. 76), the poet had never met
Miss Mann, but married 'in order to provide her with a passport'.

Apart from the *Epilogue*, in which Auden reviews the great
explorers, humanitarians, psychologists and novelists who had
moved him, all the poems in *Look Stranger* are lyrics, including
four sonnets, in which the influence of Rilke is apparent. At this
period Auden disciplined himself to experiment with the technique
of traditional forms, and the stanzaic structure of his verse
frequently called for rhyme of the approximate kind.

May with its light behaving is at first sight a metrically simple spring song, but there are complexities of thought and subtleties not to be grasped by perusing the poem in isolation. The whole volume reflects the mind of a poet, at twenty-eight, still maturing, yet questioning loyalties and political affiliations.

XVI

May with its light behaving
Stirs vessel, eye, and limb;
The singular and sad
Are willing to recover,
And to the swan-delighting river   5
The careless picnics come,
The living white and red.

The dead remote and hooded
In their enclosures rest; but we
From the vague woods have broken,   10
Forests where children meet
And the white angel-vampires flit;
We stand with shaded eye,
The dangerous apple taken.

The real world lies before us;   15
Animal motions of the young,
The common wish for death,
The pleasured and the haunted;
The dying master sinks tormented
In the admirers' ring,   20
The unjust walk the earth.

And love that makes impatient
The tortoise and the roe, and lays
The blonde beside the dark,
Urges upon our blood,   25
Before the evil and the good
How insufficient is
The endearment and the look.

The verse pattern of the seven-line stanza is iambic trimeter, modulated with occasional four-beat lines, as in 12, 15 and 19.

Ease of movement depends largely on the interplay of the liquid, nasal, trilled and sibilant consonants (*l, m, n, r, s*), and on the Audenesque rhymes. The first line in each stanza has no rhyming fellow, and the other six are matched only approximately, the rhyme-pattern being abcddbc, which is individual. The unequal quality of the rhymes is worth noting:

Stanza 1: 2/6 *limb | come*, 3/7 *sad | red*, 4/5 *recover | river*
Stanza 2: 2/6 *we | eye*, 3/7 *broken | taken*, 4/5 *meet | flit*
Stanza 3: 2/6 *young | ring*, 3/7 *death | earth*, 4/5 *haunted | tormented*
Stanza 4: 2/6 *lays | is*, 3/7 *dark | look*, 4/5 *blood | good*

The first (unrhymed) line always prefers a feminine ending, and two of the remaining three double terminals occur in the middle pair of the stanza (lines 4 and 5). The off-rhymes are adroit in their effects, and alliteration (lines 3 and 6) is restrained. A dominating note of the first three stanzas is the use of attributive, predicative or modal present- and past-participles, with echoing inflexions *-ing, -ed* and *-en* (see lines 4, 5, 7, 8, 10, 13, 14, 18 and 19).

In the lyrical poems of Auden the choice of epithets repays study. *Light* behaving (1), *singular* and *sad* (3 – substantival uses), *swan-delighting* river (5), *careless* picnics (6), The *living white* and *red* (7), The dead *remote and hooded* (8 – note inversion), *vague* woods (10), *white angel*-vampires (12), *shaded* eye (13), *dangerous* apple (14), *red* world (15), *Animal* motions (16), *common* wish (17), The *pleasured* and the *haunted* (18 – substantival uses), *dying* master (19), *impatient |* The tortoise and the roe (22/3 – inversion), The *blonde* beside the *dark* (24 – substantival uses), How *insufficient* is | The endearment and the look (27/8). Only *living, white, red, common, dying* and *insufficient* appeal to the reader as conventional; yet they are the precisest in context. In most instances symbolic use of adjectives is the clue to their sense in the poem.

The words *light* (*ie*, 'uninhibited') *behaving* suggest a figurative meaning of *vessel* (perhaps 'sexual power'), cf. the phrases *weaker vessel, blood-vessel*. Freudian ambiguity continues in lines 3 and 4, where *singular* and *sad* refer to psyches that are maladjusted; hence the phrase *willing to recover* (4). In line 5 the sensuous and poetic image of the *swan-delighting river* is ambivalent in the objective or subjective relationship that the compound epithet bears to the noun. Empson might enquire whether the river delights the swans, or the swans are delightful on the river. Again, the adjective *careless* (6) may refer to picnics enjoyed 'without care' or to the residual litter. These ambiguities denote aspects of neurosis. In *Look Stranger* and other of Auden's earlier poems, the colours *white* and *red* (7) are symbols of the Fascist and Communist causes, the white hawk representing the helmeted airman of *Consider this and in our time* (*Poems*, 1930, XXIX). This innocent-looking stanza therefore embodies illnesses of the modern human's condition.

In stanza 2 the *remote* dead are past generations, blinkered by superstitions (8/9, *hooded | In their enclosures*). The vague *woods* (3) from which *we* (9), *ie*, the poets of the 1930 ethos, have emerged, are beliefs in supernatural powers; these remain as the refuge of the immature, peopled by mythological fantasies (12, *angel-vampires*). The *shaded eye* (13) of the mature individual may have particular reference to Auden's practice of drawing the curtains, and working by artificial light, protected by a journalist's eye-shade. The *dangerous apple* (14) is the fruit of the biblical Tree of Knowledge of good and evil.

Stanza 3 contains scraps of reading in Freudian psychology, which Auden once thought was the key to the real world (15); hence the references to *Animal motions* (16) and *The common wish for death* (17). Psychoanalysis claimed that everyone was the victim of some form of neurosis. *The pleasured and the haunted* (18) are hedonists and those who have guilt complexes. The characteristically vague allusion *The dying master sinks tormented | In the admirers' ring* (19/20) is an Audenesque touch, which cannot refer to Freud, who was still alive in 1935; the reference is to an artist, such as D. H. Lawrence, whose reputation tends to be tarnished by the adulation of misunderstanding admirers. Maturity brings concomitant awareness of the world's injustice.

Stanza 4 compares personal love with the physical coupling of animals. Man, with consciousness of evil and good, is not merely a creature of impulse; he has freedom of choice; but his self-knowledge has the disadvantage of repressing natural impulses. Love as romantic allurement (28, *the endearment and the look*) is seen by the mature to be inadequate. Auden thus ends on a note of disillusion; his mind is divided not only on the value of Freudian psychology, but on Marxian politics, in both of which he had sought liberation.

LAY YOUR SLEEPING HEAD
(from *Another Time*, 1940, Part I, XVIII)

Another Time contains three Parts, 'People and Places', 'Lighter Poems' and 'Occasional Poems'; this personal lyric belongs to Part I. The poem first appeared in *New Writing*, Spring, 1937, and was later called *Lullaby* in the author's *Penguin Selection* of his poems (1958). This title would apply to the rhythm, rather than the theme, since the song celebrates 'a night of love'. Though the piece has often been anthologized, there is no adequate analysis of it.

Lay your sleeping head, my love,
Human on my faithless arm;
Time and fevers burn away
Individual beauty from
Thoughtful children, and the grave   5
Proves the child ephemeral:
But in my arms till break of day
Let the living creature lie,
Mortal, guilty, but to me
The entirely beautiful.   10

Soul and body have no bounds:
To lovers as they lie upon
Her tolerant enchanted slope
In their ordinary swoon,
Grave the vision Venus sends   15
Of supernatural sympathy,
Universal love and hope;
While an abstract insight wakes
Among the glaciers and the rocks
The hermit's sensual ecstasy.   20

Certainty, fidelity
On the stroke of midnight pass
Like vibrations of a bell
And fashionable madmen raise
Their pedantic boring cry: 25
Every farthing of the cost,
All the dreaded cards foretell,
Shall be paid, but from this night

Not a whisper, not a thought,
Not a kiss nor look be lost.   30

Beauty, midnight, vision dies:
Let the winds of dawn that blow
Softly round your dreaming head
Such a day of sweetness show
Eye and knocking heart may bless,   35
Find the mortal world enough;
Noons of dryness see you fed
By the involuntary powers,
Nights of insult let you pass
Watched by every human love.   40

The song has four ten-line stanzas, with a trochaic tetrameter pattern, modulated by iambics in lines 7, 12, 13, 16, 19, 20 and 24. The rhyme scheme is abcbadceed, but only seven of the rhyming pairs are true ones (3/7, 13/17, 16/20, 23/27, 26/30, 32/34, 33/37); there is thus a decided preference for approximate rhyme. Enjambement occurs at the end of lines 3, 4, 5, 7, 9, 12, 15, 32, 37; in the chosen measure it is necessary to ensure the rhythmical movement of the phrasing, which contains more monosyllables than usual with Auden (139 in a total of 201 words, with five completely monosyllabic lines). The terminal stress of lines 4 and 12 falls on prepositions *from* and *upon*. Nearly all terminals are monosyllables, the outstanding exceptions being *ephemeral* / *beautiful* (6/10), *sympathy* / *ecstasy* (16/20), where Auden indulges the rhetorical licence of rhyming on unstressed final syllables, characteristic of English Renaissance poets.

There is a strong metaphysical flavour in *Soul and body have no bounds* (11). The Jacobean language often involves devices reminiscent of Donne or Marvell. Epithets are sensitively chosen, and are sometimes in inverted order: *Human* on my *faithless* arm (2); the child *ephemeral* (6); Let the living creature lie, / *Mortal* (9); *Grave* the vision (15); Eye and *knocking* heart may bless (35); By *the involuntary* powers (38, involving the Elizabethan licence of elision). Auden rarely cultivates the sensuous image drawn from nature. His analysis of love takes the form of empirical commentary, and the epithets are mainly human and social. But there are exceptions in stanza 2; for instance *enchanted* (13), *supernatural* (16), *sensual* (20). The traditional tone of love-songs is discernible in the theme of mutability, with the suggestion that passion and beauty are fleeting.

Nevertheless there are typically Audenesque breaks with tradition, tending to a flamboyant note irreconcilable with the setting. One notable mark of Auden's invention is to create a tension between qualifier and noun:

13/14 *Her tolerant enchanted slope* / In their *ordinary swoon* (in which the force of the possessive *Her* is arguable);

18/19 an *abstract insight* wakes / Among the glaciers and the rocks / The *hermits sensual ecstasy*

24/27 And *fashionable madmen* raise / Their *pedantic boring cry* / Every farthing of the cost, / All the *dreaded cards* foretell (There is a touch of insincerity here).

In keeping with abstract reflections on the universal and particular, Auden makes moderate use of Elizabethan figures of rhetoric:

Tropes
Personification: 2 *faithless* arm; 35 knocking heart *may bless*; 18 *an abstract instinct wakes*
Metaphor: 13 Her *tolerant enchanted slope*, 37 *Noons of dryness* see you fed
Simile: 23 Like vibrations of a bell

Schemes of Words
Ploce: 29/30 *Not* a whisper, *not* a thought, / *Not* a kiss (also *parison*)
Parison (or *parallelism*): 37 and 39 *Noons of dryness* . . . / . . . / *Nights of insult*

The lyric exhibits both the strength and weakness of Auden's art. Technically, the happiest stanza is the first; the least satisfactory is the third, because of its straining for effect, from line 25. The reader is left uncertain whether Auden means that physical and spiritual love should be regarded as complementary.

HEAVY DATE
(from *Another Time*, Part II, 1940)

Strange are love's mutations:
Thus, the early poem

Of the flesh sub rosa
   Has been known to grow
Now and then into the   5
Amor intellectu-
-alis of Spinoza;
   How we do not know. . . .

Love has no position,
Love's a way of living,   10
One kind of relation
   Possible between
Any things or persons
Given one condition,
The one sine qua non   15
   Being mutual need.

Through it we discover
An essential secret
Called by some Salvation
   And by some Success;   20
Crying for the moon is
Naughtiness and envy,
We can only love what-
   -ever we possess.

I believed for years that   25
Love was the conjunction
Of two oppositions;
   That was all untrue;
Every young man fears that
He is not worth loving: 30
Bless you, darling, I have
   Found myself in you. . . .

When two lovers meet, then
There's an end of writing
Thought and Analytics: 35
   Lovers, like the dead,
In their loves are equal;
Sophomores and peasants,
Poets and their critics
   Are the same in bed.   40

This is an extract from the full poem of 112 lines, which stands at the head of the 'Occasional' group in the second Part of *Another Time*. It has fourteen eight-line stanzas in trochaic trimeter, rhyming on the strong beat of the fourth and eighth lines, the rhymes being catalectic (with the metrical weak syllable truncated). Auden sensibly avoids the monotony of feminine rhymes, in favour of sporadic assonance on stressed syllables, as in lines 3, 4, 7, 8: rosa, known, grow, Spinoza, know. The verses being short, a high percentage of monosyllabic lines occurs. There is much syntactical enjambement, and some sportive line-division, as in 6/7 and 23/4. The measure chosen is suitable for light verse; but Auden jauntily exploits it for reflections on love, as a private and social phenomenon.

Auden contended in the Introduction to the *Oxford Book of Light Verse*, which he edited in 1938, that a playful technique in verse may be serious in content, provided society is 'united in its religious faith and its view of the universe' (p. x). This could hardly be said of the 'rendevouz' Auden depicts in New York, at the end of the nineteen-thirties. Although he commends Burns and Byron as romantic exponents of light verse, what Auden attempts in *Heavy Date* is best characterized in his own terms, 'simple, clear . . . gay . . . and adult' *vers de société*, having for its subject-matter 'the experiences of the poet as an ordinary human being' (Introd. pp. ix and xx).

The patter-like tone of Auden's verse is in keeping with the title, the poem being about an assignation for the purpose of amorous encounter. The thoughts range widely, but the stanzas quoted (8 and 11–14) are adequate to illustrate what is germane to the light-hearted conception of *love* as Eros. Save for *Amor intellectualis* (6/7), the language is engagingly luminous.

Spinoza in Part V of the *Ethics*, 'On the Power of the Understanding', discussed the love of knowing the good, and believed that he supplied a Euclidean proof of the identity of God with this high aspiration. Auden's propositions are more pragmatic: physical love may lead, by unknowable ways, to Spinoza's divine goodness, but on the earthly plane love is merely a relationship between persons that arises from mutual needs. One can only love what one is likely to be able to possess, and love as a union of opposites is an illusion. Because it is all-consuming, love defies logical analysis; it is the greatest leveller of social distinctions.

This biological premise Spinoza does not effectually counter in previous sections on 'The Origin and Nature of the Emotions' and 'Of Human Bondage'. Auden takes the anthropologist's standpoint, citing Malinowski, Rivers and Benedict, and stresses the uniqueness of each individual's situation, its possible weakness and desperation. In anticipation of the event, the lover is capable only of 'random thinking'; and this is all *Heavy Date* intends to communicate. The *ad hoc* pleading of the social scientist is inevitably barren of figurative language. Auden, like Swift and Byron, chose the light-verse form as an expedient to entertain readers.

ALONSO TO FERDINAND
(from 'The Sea and the Mirror', *For the Time Being*, 1947)

The Sea and the Mirror is a pseudo-dramatic allegory, in which the mirror that reflects nature is the symbol of art; Auden treats, in particular, of the aesthetic magic of Prospero. The subtitle of this group of poems is, consequently: 'A Commentary on Shakespeare's *The Tempest*'. The work was conceived by Auden between 1942 and 1944, and performed at Oxford as recently as May 1968. The central figures are Prospero, Ariel and Caliban, and the varied series of dramatic monologues is both reminiscential and forward-looking.

Alonso to Ferdinand, a poem in 96 lines, appears in chapter II, devoted to the Supporting Cast, *sotto voce*. It first appeared in *Partisan Review*, September–October, 1943. Only the last 36 lines are used in this analysis:

> How narrow the space, how slight the chance
> For civil pattern and importance
> Between the watery vagueness and
> The triviality of the sand,
> How soon the lively trip is over   5
> From loose craving to sharp aversion,
> Aimless jelly to paralyzed bone:
> At the end of each successful day
> Remember that the fire and the ice
> Are never more than one step away   10
> From the temperate city; it is
> But a moment to either.

But should you fail to keep your kingdom
And, like your father before you, come
Where thought accuses and feeling mocks,   15
Believe your pain: praise the scorching rocks
For their desiccation of your lust,
Thank the bitter treatment of the tide
For its dissolution of your pride,
That the whirlwind may arrange your will   20
And the deluge release it to find
The spring in the desert, the fruitful
Island in the sea, where flesh and mind
Are delivered from mistrust.

Blue the sky beyond her humming sail   25
As I sit today by our ship's rail
Watching exuberant porpoises
Escort us homeward and writing this
For you to open when I am gone:
Read it, Ferdinand, with the blessing   30
Of Alonso, your father, once King
Of Naples, now ready to welcome
Death, but rejoicing in a new love,
A new peace, having heard the solemn
Music strike and seen the statue move   35
To forgive our illusion.

The dominant metre is the iambic three- or four-stressed line of nine syllables, with frequent trisyllabic-foot modulation. Each stanza contains twelve lines, but ends with one of only seven syllables. This invented form has a complex rhyme-scheme aabbcddefefc, in which a substantial proportion of the rhymes is approximate (*eg*, 1/2 *chance* / impor*tance*) or off-beat (*eg*, 25/7 *welcome* / *solemn*). This poem is claimed to be Auden's first experiment with syllabic verse, and great trouble was taken, as is shown by the survival of half-a-dozen manuscript versions. Auden's mature, disciplined style succeeded, where others might have failed. The tone is epistolary and informal, the movement flexible and dignified, nearly half the lines being enjambed.

As line 29 indicates, Alonso's letter to his son was not intended to be read until after the father's death. It is cast in figurative language, permeated by the symbols of sea and desert, which stand for the sensual and the spiritual life, respectively. The letter contains advice, not only on the duties and responsibilities of a ruler, for whom 'The Way of Justice is a tightrope', but on the dangers of kingly office. Alonso stresses the need for order, and acceptance of secular events; his message to Ferdinand is that he should resolve, by studied self-possession, the inevitable anxieties of a monarch. The drama in his speech is potential, rather than actual.

The ceremonial, measured tread of the verse is in accord with the metaphorical language and personification. Auden, under the stimulus of Shakespeare, gives freer rein to the powers of his imagination. Few metaphors are more characteristic of the poet's development in his American period than *watery vagueness* (3), *triviality of sand* (4), *the whirlwind may arrange your will* (20). Resourceful lexical ingenuity is evident in the prosopopoeia of *Aimless jelly to paralyzed bone* (7), *fire and ice | Are never more than one step away* (9/10), *thought accuses* and *feeling mocks* (15).

Auden was 'fascinated by (the) drab mortality' of existence. What interested him in *The Sea and the Mirror* was the transformation of individuals through a ripened understanding of the psychology of human relations. The thought behind these timeless poems is anti-romantic, often paradoxical, because their purpose is disenchantment. No faith is feasible in an art that mirrors chaos; any progress in religion is unthinkable without order perceived, and evil accepted.

In *The Sea and the Mirror* Auden came near to realizing Arnold's dictum that 'poetry is a criticism of life'. The serious talkers in his critique of *The Tempest* suffer from a sense of Audenesque isolation, not unlike Kierkegaard's account of the human lot of despair and anxiety. By extending his protagonists' lives into the next phase of their fictitious existence, Auden envisages a Jamesian return to reality; but the disillusioned Prospero no longer functions as a controlling deity. In this dilemma, a new wisdom, born of necessity, appears less flattering to Prospero than to Caliban, whose grandiose monologue in poetic prose is the focal disquisition of Auden's vision.

For the Time Being also contains speeches and themes, based on the Bible, in the *Christmas Oratorio* (or Morality) which gives the book its title. These are parables of an intellectual profoundly moved by the existential distinction between Being and Becoming. Man's primal duty, Auden suggests, is to accept life with all its imperfections, while acknowledging that wisdom of this world holds little hope of salvation.

Auden read critically more science than most poets, and he was liberal in his literary taste and prosodic ingenuity; in every new volume there were worthwhile surprises for readers. His place is among those who freely invent, emulate and modify, without regarding technical perfection as their principal aim. As he developed, he regretted the immature social and political opinions of the early poems, but was unable to sacrifice the ebullient rhetoric that disfigured the design of his polemical work.

At first Auden wrote to please or impress friends and colleagues, like Isherwood, or his publisher, Faber, for whom Eliot was the principal poetry adviser. Nearly all the books of verse were dedicated to admirers of Auden's lively, but unruly, gifts. Torn between applied science, poetry and philosophy, it was long before he overcame a suspicion that the aesthete or pure poet, who takes himself seriously, uses his art to escape from the realities of life.

Two principal directions are observable in accounting for the divided nature of Auden's poetic personality. The *personae* he adopted to explore attitudes to art and life were almost unlimited, but a dichotomy accounts for the major inconsistencies. He wanted, by experiment, to contribute his mite to the English poetic tradition; at the same time, verbal curiosity and the urge to entertain attracted him to comic verse. In the 'thirties Auden was engaged in an endless struggle to unify, harmonize or reconcile opposing talents, which were producing discordant poems. In cynical mood, he gravely distrusted the power of serious art to change the world.

The comic and satirical vein descended by a narrow line from Butler's *Hudibras*, Prior's *Alma*, Swift's *On the Death of Dr Swift* and Byron's *Don Juan*. In the spirit of Byron, Auden depicted the seemingly frivolous *persona* of his ambition. John Bradford and Thomas Cottam were religious martyrs of the sixteenth century, at Cambridge and Oxford respectively.

> I want a form that's large enough to swim in,
>   And talk on any subject that I choose,

From natural scenery to men and women,
   Myself, the arts, the European news . . .

'The fascination of what's difficult',
   The wish to do what one's not done before,
Is, I hope proper to *Quicunque Vult*,
   The proper card to show at Heaven's door . . .

   The most I ask is leave to share a pew
   With Bradford or with Cottam, that will do:
To pasture my few silly sheep with Dyer
And picnic on the lower slopes with Prior.
   (*Letter to Lord Byron*, Part I, lines 134–7, 155–8, 165–8)

Auden's muse of nonsense, modelled on the lines of Lewis Carroll, Edward Lear and Hilaire Belloc, was not so prolific.

The moralist in Auden developed more slowly, and arose partly from the bourgeois intellectual's interest in Marx and Freud. He indulged in interminable debates with his *alter ego*, unconcerned by confusing leaps of tone, which are damaging to formal art. Not until he went to live in New York did Auden succeed in disentangling the superficial omniscience of this dichotomy. Obduracy began to recede with his reading of Kierkegaard's *Sickness unto Death* and Reinhold Niebuhr's *The Nature and Destiny of Man*; both books loosened the hold of Freudianism on his mind, and induced him to accept Protestant Christianity. His faith in Marxism was undermined by Arnold Toynbee's *Study of History*. Ten years after the publication of *Dog Beneath the Skin* (1935), Auden, revising his poems for the American collected edition, could no longer tolerate early flights of eloquence, and even devalued poems like *The Wanderer* by giving them frivolous titles. The congenial eccentric depicted in Isherwood's *Lions and Shadows* (Hogarth, 1938) was soon, with irresistible verbal energy, to debunk even what he enjoyed – the foolishness of man's pretensions.

Auden's linguistic behaviour was undoubtedly affected by changes in his beliefs and ideas. A mordant wit replaced the mocking slang and jolly buffoonery of such works as *The Orators* (1932); like a neo-classicist, he revealed a new delight in forceful words from many sources. Auden, the religious poet, is to be read between the lines of his *New Year Letter*:

Hell is the being of the lie
That we become if we deny
The laws of consciousness and claim
Becoming and Being are the same . . .
Bewildered, how can I divine
Which is my true Socratic Sign,
Which of these calls to conscience is
For me the *casus fœderis*, [Latin 'occasion for agreement']
From all the tasks submitted, choose
The *athlon* I must not refuse? [Greek 'prize']
A particle, I must not yield
To particles who claim the field,
Nor trust the demagogue who raves,
A quantum speaking for the waves, [Physics, a reference to
quantum mechanics]
Nor worship blindly the ornate
Grandezza of the Sovereign State . . . [Italian 'greatness']
In politics the Fall of Man
From natural liberty began
When, loving power of sloth, he came
Like BURKE to think them both the same.

(Part III, lines 65–8, 150–161, 230–3)

The style of this bears slight resemblance to poems in the Augustan tradition; but Auden no longer argued that art and life are mutually exclusive. Indeed, the conflicting *personae* of the past now curtsey to each other approvingly in the same poem. But both masks designedly conceal Auden the man, whose humility and zest for life won the respect of his friends.

With the appearance in New York of *Another Time* (1940), American critics began to number Auden among the masters of the 'middle style', appraising his diction as ample, but mannered. The middle style is said to encourage only a moderate use of figures, and to represent the language of an educated person who prefers the familiar phrase to the grand or elegant. Auden's mature style has this merit, and more; it is modern in juxtaposing incongruous elements, and in using prosaic rhythms. Like Eliot's, the free verse of Auden is not formless, because stresses are strongly defined.

If Auden prefers the 'cotton frock' to the poet's 'singing robes'

(*Letter to Lord Byron*, Part III, 57–9), he was never one to concur in the apotheosis of the Average Man, whose clichés debase colloquial language for poetry. His dissenting voice can be heard in the speeches of the Narrator and Fugal Chorus of his oratorio, *For the Time Being*.

CHAPTER X

W. H. Auden (2):
Poems 1948–72

🔳🔳🔳🔳🔳🔳

AFTER seven years in the United States, Auden became an American citizen, and travelled from one lecturing assignment to another, in colleges and universities. The result was that his output of verse diminished, while the prose increased. The more challenging of the writing in this period is to be found in the critical works, such as *The Enchafed Flood* (1950), *The Dyer's Hand* (1963) and *Secondary Worlds* (1968), the latter being the first of the T. S. Eliot Memorial Lectures. From 1956, part of Auden's interest was writing or revising English libretti for operas, such as *The Magic Flute* and Igor Stravinsky's *The Rake's Progress* (1962).

When the war ended, Auden spent a part of each year in Europe, first on the island of Ischia, near Naples, and from 1957 at Kirchstetten, in Southern Austria, where he acquired a house. He died in Vienna on 28 September 1973. The poems written in New York and elsewhere were less concerned with politics and collective society, and more with the individual's attainment of self-knowledge. Packed as they are with metaphysical comment and observation, they tend to be longer and more complex. For Auden's copiousness needed elbow-room; he had more to say than Eliot, but less skill and economy in saying it.

Though still a town-poet, the later Auden reflects frequently, and in long elegiac lines, on man and his environment. *Nones* (1951) and *The Shield of Achilles* (1955) contain some of his best free-verse bucolics, both reminiscential and personal; the tone is more Cowper's than Shenstone's:

> When I try to imagine a faultless love
> Or the life to come, what I hear is the murmur
> Of underground streams, what I see is a limestone landscape
> (*In Praise of Limestone*, *Horizon*, July 1948; *Nones*, 1951)

This four-to-five-beat line has a movement strongly influenced by Yeats and Rilke, whom Auden admired.

That Auden speaks with the voice of his age can be gathered from the encyclopaedic diversity of his themes, public and private; there is hardly a topic which he was not willing to essay. Consequently, there is no discernible pattern in his later work, except the mosaics of quotable lines that critics choose. Auden tried to offset this disadvantage by improved techniques of versification and greater humaneness in his point of view.

The tone of the poems is relaxed and leisurely, the argument meandering and abstract. The cause is longer sentences, and a tendency to depersonalize the language, as though he were composing an essay. Indeed, many items are deceptively set in prose, whose rhythm is indistinguishable from verse. For example:

In my Éden we have a féw béam-éngines, sáddle- | tánk locomótives, óvershòt wáterwhéels | and óther béautiful píeces of óbsolete máchinery | to pláy with: In his Néw Jerúsalem èven chéfs | wìll be cucúmber-cóol machíne mínders.

(*Shield of Achilles, Vespers*, p. 75)

This excerpt consists of five lines of five-stressed free verse. Compare it with the epigraph of *Homage to Clio*:

Búllróarers cannot kéep up the ánnual ráin,
The wáter-táble of a ònce gréen chámpaign
Sínks, will kèep òn sínking: but whý compláin? – Agàinst ódds,
Méthods of drý fárming may stìll prodúce gráin.

This is an amusing parable on the drying-up of the poet's creative energy. But note the superfluous foot in the third line; the prosaic rhythm is not averted by the rhymes in *-ain*.

The informality of Auden's later style seems to his critics overcultivated, and there are even places where it sounds unreal. In stanza forms he dislikes formality, and he makes little attempt to clarify meaning through the resolution of technical difficulties, as other poets do. Nor does he invite the reader to share his feelings, the poems being born of ideas, rather than of moods. The images are random and cerebral, where they need to be integral to the poet's message. Auden, though unsympathetic to modern society,

holds to the romantic myth that it is none the less morally significant. He is like Lawrence's young tortoise:

> Wandering in the slow triumph of his own existence,
> Ringing the soundless bell of his presence in chaos.

(*Tortoise Family Connections, Complete Poems*, Vol II, pp. 87–8)

One result of incomplete realization of the idea, is neglect of
holistic structure, accentuated by syntactical short-circuiting, and
use of words in specialized senses, unfamiliar to the reader. As
Auden's liveliness and acuteness of mind lessened, the poem's
didactic intent lost subtlety and tended to obscurity, as in *Dame
Kind* (*Homage to Clio*, pp. 55–7):

> Steatopygous, sow-dugged
>   and owl-headed,
> To Whom – Whom else? – the first innocent blood
>   was formerly shed
> By a chinned mammal that hard times
>   had turned carnivore,
> From Whom his first promiscuous orgy
>   begged a downpour
> To speed the body-building cereals
>   of a warmer age:
> Now who put *us*, we should like to know,
>   in *Her* menage?
>   . . .
>
> Even there, as your blushes invoke its Guardian
>   (whose true invokeable
> Name is singular for each true heart
>   and false to tell)
> To sacre your courtship ritual so
>   it deserve a music
> More solemn than the he-hawing
>   of a salesman's limerick,
> Do a bow to the Coarse Old Party that wrought you
>   an alderliefest
> Of the same verbose and sentient kidney,
>   grateful not least

A good deal of this imagist poem is a gabble of words, which
demands the introductory notes, entitled *Dichtung und Wahrheit*:

The 'symboliste' attempt to make poetry as intransitive as music can get no further than the narcissistic reflexive – 'I love Myself'; the attempt to make poetry as objective as painting can get no further than the single comparison 'A is like B' . . . No 'imagist' poem can be more than a few words long.

So long as he speaks of the deeds of others, a poet has no difficulty in deciding what style of speech to adopt . . . But how is he to speak truthfully of lovers? Love has no deed of its own: it has to borrow the act of kind which, in itself, is not a deed but a form of behaviour . . .

The most difficult problem in personal knowledge, whether of oneself or of others, is the problem of guessing when to think as a historian and when to think as an anthropologist . . .

This poem I wished to write was to have expressed exactly what I mean when I think the words *I love You*, but I cannot exactly know what I mean; it was to have been self-evidently true, but words cannot verify themselves . . . If I were writing a novel in which both of us were characters, I know exactly how I should greet you at the station:—*adoration in the eye*; *on the tongue banter and bawdry.*

This *jeu-d'esprit* illustrates the blend of self-criticism, irony and frivolity that distinguish Auden's poetry. He regretted that the American public took him so seriously. This caveat is necessary in assessing the gnomic paradoxes of Auden's criticism, for instance, in the article on Yeats: 'In poetry as in life . . . the duty of the present is neither to copy nor to deny the past, but to resurrect it' ('Yeats as an Example', *Kenyon Review* X, Spring 1948).

The more Auden taught, the more didactic his poetics became. While he is seldom dogmatic, he enjoys throwing down ideological challenges, such as:

I am one of those/Who feel a Christian ought to write in Prose,/ For poetry is Magic – born in sin. (Epigraph to *Homage to Clio*, Part II, p. 52).

His critical pronouncements, especially in verse, tend to be 'off the cuff', like those of D. H. Lawrence, and are posed without any discernible set of standards or code of literary principles.

THE MANAGERS
(from *Nones*, 1951)

The earliest edition of *Nones* was published by Random House,

New York; *The Managers* had, however, appeared in England in
Horizon, November 1948, to which Auden contributed regularly.
The poem is a splendid example of Auden's unembittered social
criticism and distaste for bureaucracy.

> In the bád òld dáys it was nót so bád:
>   The tóp of the ládder
> Was an amúsing pláce to sít; | succéss
>   Mèant qúite a lót – | léisure
> And húge méals, | mòre pálaces fílled with móre   5
>   Objects, | boóks, | gírls, | hórses
> Than one would éver get roúnd to, | and to bè
>   Cárried úphíll while séeing
> Óthers wálk. | To rúle was a pléasure whèn
>   One wróte a déath-séntence   10
> On the báck of the Áce of Spádes | and pláyed òn
>   With a néw déck. | Hónours
> Are nót so phýsical or jólly nów,
>   For the spécies of Pówers
> We are úsed to are nót like thát. | Coùld óne of thèm   15
>   Be saíd to resémble
> The Trágic Héro, | the Platónic Saínt,
>   Or would ány paínter
> Portráy one rísing triúmphant from a láke
>   On a dólphin, | náked,   20
> Protécted by an umbrélla of chérubs? | Càn
>   They so múch as mánage
> To behàve like génuine Caésars | when alóne
>   Or drínking with crónies,
> To lèt their háir dòwn and be fránk abóut   25
>   The wórld? | It is doúbtful.
> The lást wórd on hòw we may líve or díe
>   Résts todáy with such quíet
> Mén, | wórking tòo hárd in róoms that are tòo bíg,
>   Redúcing to fígures   30
> Whàt is the mátter, | whàt is to be dóne.

The poem is in free verse, with alternate long and short lines, the
first generally containing five stresses, and the second either two
or three. Auden's use of skaldic rhyme is a tribute to his forebears,
the Scandinavian bards. Every second line ends with a trochaic

foot, and rhymes with its predecessor only on the first (stressed) syllable, *eg, bad | ladder* (1/2). The rhythm of the lines is decisive, because the strong and half-stressed syllables together nearly match the unstressed ones; but what sustains the rhythm's interest for the ear is the subtle variation of the internal pauses. The syntax is so arranged as to make the pauses occupy many feasible positions within the line.

The style is expository, and the rhythmical cycles are nicely adjusted to the compound-complex sentence-structure, in which the force of main and subordinate clauses is balanced. Except for the short antithetical noun clauses in line 31, subordination is adverbial; but there is variation in the use of participial phrases: 19 *rising triumphant from a lake*, 21 *Protected by an umbrella of cherubs*, 29 *working too hard*, 30 *reducing to figures*.

The Managers well exemplifies the controlled middle style, of which Auden thought Dryden to be the father in English poetry. The lexical tone of this style is struck immediately in homely terms: 1 *bad old days*, 2 *top of the ladder*, 4 *meant quite a lot*, 5 *huge meals*, 7 *one would ever get round to*, 13 Honours | Are not so . . . *jolly*, 21 an *umbrella* of cherubs, 24 *drinking with cronies*, 25 *let their hair down*, 27 *The last word* on how we may live, 29 rooms that are too *big*.

In colloquial language of this kind, the problem of meaning scarcely arises. 'The bad old days were not so bad', argues Auden, because the a-moral, callous wielders of power, whether Caesars or other potentates, possessed distinctive personalities, and were often the collectors of books and *objets d'art*; there was a dignity in their eccentric pleasures and non-utilitarian enjoyment of life (lines 1–12). In short, the giants of the past had a tragic dimension that the business magnate of today lacks. No painter could conceive of Managers in mythological or Renaissance settings. They are featureless, depersonalized types, inarticulate about the world they inhabit; yet they are in responsible positions, and determine, by their faith in statistics, the conditions by which men live and die (lines 12–31).

In addition to rhythm, pause and skaldic rhyme, rhetoric aids the steady and lucid march of the phrasing. The language is so restrained in tone that the reader is apt to overlook the figures:

Tropes
Metaphor: 21 Protected by an *umbrella* of cherubs

Metonymy: 25 *To let their hair down* and be frank
    30 *Reducing to figures* / What is the matter (*ie*, solving by
    arithmetic)

Schemes of Words
Ploce: 1 In the *bad* old days, it was not so *bad*
    31 *What is* the matter, *what is* to be done
Asyndeton (absence of conjunctions): 6 Objects, books, girls, horses
Parison: 31 *What is the matter, what is to be done* (also metrical
    antithesis)

Schemes of Thought
Erotema (rhetorical questions): 15–21 Could one of them / Be
    said . . . cherubs?
Hypophora (the speaker answers his own question): 21–6 Can
    they so much . . . doubtful.

As may be observed in line 31, the same form of words may represent more than one figure of rhetoric.

SEXT
(from *The Shield of Achilles*, 1955)

As though to discountenance the critics, *Sext*, with its formal
lucidity, demonstrates that free verse, in a plain style, may have
considerable merits. This obviously Laurentian poem is the third
of the *Horae Canonicae* in Part III of *The Shield of Achilles*, which
received the National Book Award in 1956. In the poems on the
Canonical Hours Auden reflects on the problem of sin and
redemption. As God made man in his own image, so the poet
endeavours to create, without necessarily yielding to the law of
nature. 'The Virgin and the Dynamo', an essay in *The Dyer's Hand*,
was written to explain *Prime*, the first poem in *Horae Canonicae*, but
is relevant to them all. Only the first section of *Sext* is here used
for analysis.

> You néed not sée what sómeone is dóing
> to knów if it is his vocátion,
>
> you have ónly to wátch his éyes:

a cóok mixing a saúce, a súrgeon
máking a prímary incísion,
a clérk compléting a bíll of láding,
wear the sáme rápt expréssion,
forgétting themsélves in a fúnction.
How béautiful it ís,
that éye-on-the-óbject lóok.
To ignóre the appétitive góddesses,
to desért the formídable shrínes
of Rhéa, Aphrodíte, Démeter, Diána,
to práy instèad to St Phócas,
St Bárbara, Sàn Saturníno,
or whoéver one's pátron ís,
that òne may be wórthy of their mýstery,
whát a prodígious stép to have táken.
There shòuld be mónuments, there shòuld be ódes,
to the námeless héroes who tòok it fírst,
to the fírst fláker of fíints
who forgót his dínner,
the fírst colléctor of séa-shélls
to remaín célibate.
Whére should we bé but for thém?
Féral stíll, un-hoúsetràined, stíll
wándering through fórests withoùt
a cónsonant to our námes,
slaves of Dáme Kínd, lácking
áll nótion of a city
and, at thís nón, for thís deáth,
thère would be nó ágents.

The poem consists of four paragraphs, each having its own
rhythmical unity. The lines are grouped in unrhymed couplets,
which seem arbitrary, but are semantically controlled by punctuation and syntax. It should be noted that there are six participial
phrases (4, 5, 6, 8, 27, 29), and five infinitival ones (11, 12, 14, 18,
24). The rhetorical structure is important to the poem's easy
intelligibility. The length of lines is inconstant, as is the number
of stresses, which varies from four to two. Smoothness is secured
by assonance and alliteration, and continuity by occasional
enjambement, as in lines 1, 4, 12, 23, 26, 27, 29 and 30.

Of the 187 words of the section, 44 are borrowings from French, Latin or Greek (including the proper names in lines 13–15) – a high percentage. The most striking in context are *appetitive* (11, 'possessing desire') and *Feral* (26, 'wild', 'untamed').

The first paragraph (1–8) considers the artist's or scientist's complete absorption in his work. Fulfilling his function in a society, he contributes to its civilization.

The second paragraph comments on the artist's ability to resist the pursuits and attractions of nature: fertility (*Rhea*, mother of Earth), love of the sea (*Aphrodite*), agriculture (*Demeter*), hunting (*Diana*). The dedicated craftsman will even neglect religious duties, such as prayers to saints. St Phocas of Sinope was a disciple of Christ and patron of Greek sailors, who was martyred during the reign of Emperor Trajan. St Barbara, martyred in 235 AD, was the saint who protected artillerymen, miners and travellers from blasts and thunderstorms. San Saturnino may refer to the patron of Toulouse, who was martyred in the third century AD. As line 16 shows, the names of the saints have no bearing on Auden's line of thinking. *Mystery* (17) has the obsolete meaning of 'occupation'; but there seems also to be a punning reference to the word's other original sense 'religious rites', *eg*, the *mysteries* of Eleusis (Demeter).

Paragraph 3 suggests that the first unknown artists/scientists who forsook nature and religion for their work should be honoured by monuments and poems; Auden singles out the maker of stone tools and the conchologist. There are humorous touches in the second line of each couplet: the stone-age man *who forgot his dinner* (22), and the zoologist who remained *celibate* (24).

The last paragraph continues in this spirit, with the amusing coinage *un-housetrained* (26), and 'without/a *consonant* to our names', that is, without any titles at all, not even Mr. The poet reminds the reader that without art and science, which are 'primarily spiritual activities', men would still be forest-dwellers, slaves to nature, as animals are (a kind of death for which no agent is necessary). They would lack all cultural amenities of city life.

Each of the three parts of *Sext* ends by incorporating the phrase 'at this *noon*', which is the canonical time of day represented by the title. Auden has tried in *Sext* to embody the orderliness and concentration the poem extols; the place of rhetoric in the scheme is therefore important. Here are some of the figures:

Tropes
Metaphor: 7 *wear the same rapt expression*
  10 that *eye-on-the-object* look
Metonymy: 28 without / a *consonant* to our names
Personification: 29 slaves of *Dame Kind* (*ie*, Nature)

Schemes of Words
Ploce (sporadic repetition): *To* (beginning of 11, 12, 14, 18, 20, 21,
  22, 24); *first* (20, 21, 23); *still* (26, twice)
Parison: 20 There *should be* monuments, *there should be* odes
  31 *at this noon, for this death*
Alliteration: 8 *f*orgetting themselves in a *f*unction
  21/2 to the *f*irst *f*laker of *f*lints / who *f*orgot

WORDS
(from *Homage to Clio*, 1960)

Auden wrote two sonnet sequences, *In Time of War* (1939) and
Quest (1941); they appeared first in *Journey to a War* and *The
Double Man*, respectively. The first contained 27 sonnets of different
rhyming patterns, mostly written while travelling to China with
Christopher Isherwood. The *Quest* series was a mixed group of 19
sonnets (four irregular) and a poem of 21 lines (*The Cross-roads*).

The sonnet form was too succinct and circumscribed to suit
Auden's talents in most moods. The *Quest* series was the more
experimental, but also the more derivative, since it sometimes
adopted the symbols, tone and language of Franz Kafka and
Rainer Maria Rilke.

Words is one of the poet's occasional sonnets in a mixed form,
the octave being Shakespearian in pattern, the sestet Italianate.
The rhyme scheme is ababababcdccdc.

> A séntence úttered makes a wórld appéar
> Where áll thìngs háppen | as it sáys they dó;
> We doúbt the spéaker, | nòt the tóngue we héar:
> Wórds have nó wórd for wórds that are nót trúe.
>
> Syntáctically, | thoùgh, | it mùst be cléar;   5
> One cánnot chánge the súbject hálf-wày throúgh,
> Nor álter ténses to appéase the eár:
> Arcádian táles are hárd-lúck stóries tóo.

But shòuld we wánt to góssip áll the tíme,
Were fáct not fíction for ùs at its bést,   10
Or fínd a chárm in sýllables that rhýme,

Were nòt our fáte by vérbal chánce expréssed,
As rústics in a ríng-dànce pántomìme
The Kníght at sòme lóne cróss-ròads of his quést?

The language is technically in the sonnet's tradition, since the
intricate modulation of rhythm depends largely on the disposition
of primary and secondary stresses; but internal pauses are wanting
in the sestet. Both quatrains end in lines of sustained dignity by
admitting six stresses to the decasyllabic measure.

Semantically, the sonnet falls into three parts. The first quatrain
argues that the language of a poet creates a world which cannot
be untrue, even if the speaker lacks credibility; because one cannot
challenge the truth of words by other words.

The key to meaning (adds quatrain 2) is clear syntax and unity
of theme. It is inexcusable to appeal to the ear at the expense
of grammatical accuracy. Even mythology has its realism; the
Arcadian shepherds, living in idyllic contentment, sometimes told
sad tales or 'hard-luck stories'–another Audenesque humorous
touch.

Difficulties in interpreting the sestet lie partly in the use of
subjunctive *Were* at the beginning of lines 10 and 12, and recognizing that *pantomime* at the end of 13 is a verb. Auden seems in the
sestet to pose a number of shorter questions in a lengthy one:
Should we require idle talk all the time? Would not facts provide
us with a better kind of fiction? Should we choose the magic of
poetic language? Would not our destiny be better expressed in
the spontaneous language (12, *verbal chance*) of prose? Watch the
shepherds, as they mimic, in their impromptu country dances, the
Pilgrim who is uncertain of his way.

It is typical of Auden that the sense of so simply executed a
poem should elude the reader. The reason may be the unusual
compression to which Auden was compelled by the sonnet form.
Of the 109 words in it, only 18 have more than one syllable, and
four are compounds. There are but two rhetorical figures: *ploce*
in line 4, and simile in lines 13/14.

In 'The Virgin and the Dynamo' (*The Dyer's Hand*, p. 68)
Auden wrote: 'We may be and frequently are mistaken as to the

meaning or the value of a poem, but the cause of our mistake lies in our own ignorance or self-deception, not in the poem itself'.

Perhaps *Words* illustrates this point. The structure and the intention of the last seven lines are to most interpreters ambiguous.

EPITHALAMIUM
(from *City Without Walls*, 1969)

This unorthodox marriage-song could have been written by no poet but Auden; it was intended to celebrate the wedding of a relative, Rita Auden, to Peter Mudford, on 15 May 1965. From the technical language and sportive circumlocution, one or both of the parties may have been botanist or zoologist.

> Áll͜ fólk-táles meán by énding
> with a Státe Márriage,
> feást and fírewòrks, | we wísh yóu,
> Péter and Ríta,
> twó ídiosỳncrasies   5
> who ópt in this háwthorn mónth
> to cómmon your líves.
>
> A díffy undertáking,
> for to ús, | whose dréams
> are ódourless, | whàt is réal   10
> séems a bit smélly:
> stróng nérves are an advántage,
> an áccurate wríst-wàtch tóo
> can bè a gréat hélp.
>
> May Vénus, | to whòse capríce   15
> àll blóod must búxom,
> tàke súch a shíne to you bóth
> thát, | by her gífting,
> your pálpable súbstances
> may ré-ify those delíghts   20
> thèy are purvéyed for:
>
> cóol Hýmen from Jéalousy's
> tératoid phántasms,
> súlks, | compétitive heádàches,
> and Príde's mónològue   25

that wón't lísten | but demánds
tàutológical échoes,
éver refráin you.

As génders, | márried or nót,
who sháre with áll flésh   30
a léft-hánded twíst, | your chóice
remínds us to thánk
Mr̀s Náture for dóing
(our úgly lóoks are our ówn)
the hándsome bý us.   35

We are bétter búilt to lást
than tígers, | our skíns
dòn't leák like the cíliates,
our éars can detéct
quárter-tónes, | éven our móst   40
myópic have góod enoúgh
vísion for coúrtship:

and hów uncánny it ìs
we're hére to sáy so,
that lífe should have gót to ùs   45
úp thróugh the Cíty's
destrúction láyers | áfter
survíving the inhúman
Pérmian púrges.

Seven of the nine stanzas appear in this extract, which is characteristic of the later free verse. The seven-line, rhymeless stanzas
are designedly varied in rhythmical pattern; capitals introduce only
the initial lines. This may be taken as an indication of short
prosaic paragraphs; but so strongly stressed are the lines that they
pass as verse. The modulation is in syntactical pauses, with
occasional alliteration and assonance (2 *f*east and *f*ireworks, 3
Peter and *Rita*).

The song is rich in rhetorical devices and Audenesque col-
loquialisms. Among the latter are: 8 *diffy* (a contraction of
'difficult'), 11 a *bit smelly*, 17 *shine* ('liking'), 26 *won't*, 33/35 *doing* /
... / *the handsome by* us ('treating us most generously'), 38 *don't*, 44
we're.

The beginning of the poem is baffling, until *eclipsis* is noticed in the first line – the relative *that* is omitted after *All*. Presumably for a private reason, bride and bridegroom are wished the kind of fairy-tale union associated with state occasions and pyrotechnic displays. By metonymy, the pair are styled *idiosyncrasies* in line 5, and *genders* in line 29.

The substitution of one part of speech for another (*enallage*) is comparatively frequent:

6 this *hawthorn* month (metaphor, 'May')

7 to *common* your lives (adjective as verb, 'unite')

16 whose caprice / all blood must *buxom* (adjective as verb, 'enliven')

18 by her *gifting* (for *giving*, noun as gerund)

41 even our most / *myopic* have good enough / vision (adjective as noun)

A feature of the poem is the unique, sometimes eccentric, coupling of epithet and substantive. On occasion, this, too, involves a figure of speech:

10 whose *dreams* / are *odourless* (personification)

11 *what is real* / seems a bit *smelly* (personification)

22 *cool Hymen* (personification, with a suggestion of paradox)

23 Jealousy's / *teratoid phantasms,* / sulks (personification, with a note of polysyllabic fervour. *Teratoid* means 'monstrous', a derivative of Greek *teras* 'monster')

24 *competitive headaches* (euphemism, for 'petty squabbles')

27 *tautological echoes* (metaphor)

31 *left-handed twist* (metaphor, 'sinister irregularity')

38 *our skins* / don't leak *like ciliates* (simile. *Ciliates* are protozoa of the class *ciliata*, having copious *cilia* 'eyelashes')

49 *Permian purges* (metaphor, 'losses incurred during the later Stone Age')

A syntactical licence worth observing is the transitive use of the verb *refrain* in line 28.

In line 8 *A diffy undertaking* has in mind the state of marriage; hence the admonition *strong nerves are an advantage* (12). *An accurate wrist-watch* (13) supplies an *innuendo* for 'punctuality'.

Comic verse of a personal private kind bulks large in Auden's last three volumes of poetry.

A BAD NIGHT
(from *Epistle to a Godson*, 1972)

This poem is subtitled 'A lexical exercise', and as such appears to emulate Lewis Carroll in *Through the Looking Glass*, Chapter VI. The curious assortment of words is not, however, invented, but mainly dialectal.

> In his dréam zéalous
> To attáin his hóme,
> But ensórcelling pówers
> Have contórted spáce,
> Ódded the wáy: 5
> Instéad of a fácile
> Fíve-mínute trót,
> Fár he must hírple,
> Clúmsied by cóld,
> Búffeted óften   10
> By blóuts of háil
> Or pírries of ráin,
> On stólchy páths
> Over glúnch clóuds,
> Where infréquent shépherds,   15
> Slóomy of fáce,
> Snúdge of spírit,
> Snoáchy of spéech,
> With scáddle dógs
> Ténd a few scráwny   20
> Cág-mág sheép.

Of the 21 dimeter lines, only two (7 and 21) have three stresses, involving initial spondees. Five lines (1, 3, 6, 10 and 20) are enjambed for syntactical purposes.

Fun with words is of three kinds:

(a) Rareties
3 *ensorcell* (bewitch) from O. French *ensorceler*. Cited from Wyatt (1541) in Puttenham's *Arte of English Poesie*. Only two other instances occur in the Oxford English Dictionary, from Meredith, *Shaving of Shagpat* (1855) and Burton's *Arabian Nights* (1886).

11 *blout* (sudden windy downpour), thought to be of Scandinavian origin. Examples in Oxford English Dictionary are confined to the period 1786–1827.

(b) Dialect words

8 *hirple* (hobble, walk at a crawling pace) Scots and Northern English, possibly from Greek *herpein*.

12 *pirrie* (blast or squall), an onomatopoec dialect word, first found in East Anglia. The Oxford English Dictionary cites examples from the fifteenth to the nineteenth centuries.

13 *stolchy* (dirty), a spelling variant of *stoachy*, the latter commonly used as a verb (*stoach*) in Sussex and the Chilterns (18th and 19th centuries) and by Kipling in *Rewards and Fairies* (1910).

14 *glunch* (gloomy-looking) A Scots word found in Ramsay, Burns and Scott. First cited in The Oxford English Dictionary in 1719, and apparently still current.

16 *Sloomy* (dull, spiritless), a dialect word from Old English *sluma* (sluggish), used by Clare and Tennyson (as a northern form) in the nineteenth century.

17 *Snudge* (miserly), a dialect word once in literary use, as a noun or verb, by Ascham, Harvey, Dekker and Prior. Many examples in the Oxford English Dictionary.

18 *Snoachy* (nasal, snuffling). The usual dialect form is the participle *snoaching*. The verb has been in use in Southern England since the fourteenth century.

19 *scaddle* (wild, troublesome, thievish), a dialect adjective employed both in Northern and South-eastern England since the fifteenth century.

21 *Cag-mag* (unwholesome), a dialectal and vulgar word, used also substantivally, since the eighteenth century.

(c) Vicarious employment of parts of speech (enallage)

5 *Odded* (adjective as verb). Auden's active and transitive use is unique, but Thomas Morley in his *Introduction to Practicall Musicke* (1597) employed the past participle passively.

9 *Clumsied* (adjective used as verb). There was a Middle English verb *clumsen* 'to become numb with cold', apparently of Norse origin. In Isaiah XXXV, 3 Wyclif had: Commforte ye the *clumsid* (*ie*, 'bereft of feeling'). The English adjective *clumsy* is from this source, but did not enter the literary language until about 1600, in Philemon Holland's translation of Livy. It was

ridiculed by Ben Jonson in *Poetaster* Act V, Scene 1: *'clumsie chilblain'd judgment'*.

This poem has little merit, except as an amusing parergon in creating opportunities for little-known words.

STARK BEWÖLKT
(from *Epistle to a Godson*, 1972)

The mastery Auden attained over unrhymed free verse in his later poems is sometimes equalled by facility in alliterative measures, as illustrated in this poem. He was able to use the most prosaic themes and language, and yet provide some of the formal graces poetry requires.

I'm no phótophìl who búrns
his bódy brówn on beáches:
fóolish I fínd this fáshion
of módern súrf-rìding mán.
Let plánts by áll mèans sún-báthe,   5
it hélps them to máke their méals:
expósure, | thòugh, | to últra-
víolet vápids the bráin,
bíds us be stódge and stúpid.
Stíll, | sáfe in some shéltered sháde,   10
or wátching through a wíndow,
an ágeing mále, | I demánd
to sèe a smíling súmmer,
a ský bríght and whólly blúe,
save for a drífting cloúdlet   15
like a dóllop of whípped créam.
Thís yéar áll is unthúswise:
Ó whý so glúm, | weáther-gód?

Dáy after dáy we wáken
to be scólded by a scówl,   20
vénomous and vindíctive,
a flát frówning Fríday fáce,
hórrid as a háng-òver,
and meán as wèll: | if you múst
sò disarráy the heávens,   25
at leást you might lèt them ráin.

What Auden has done in *Stark bewölkt* is to isolate expanded hemistichs, resembling those of Middle-English alliterative verse, as separate lines with strong stresses; then to divide the 72 lines of the poem into four paragraphs.

In the above passage some half-dozen lines are semantically enjambed. There are five lines in which the alliterating staves are missing (1, 5, 15, 16, 25), but one of these is supplied with assonance: I'm no *pho*tophil. The ear is constantly teased with similarities of sound; the play is with the plosives *p* and *b*, as well as liquids, nasals and sibilants.

Lexical abundance is a tribute to Auden's philological interests, and the comic resourcefulness to which he turned when the former vigour of phrase was on the wane, *eg*, 7/8 exposure, though, to *ultra- / violet vapids* the brain; 22/3 *a flat frowning Friday face /* horrid *as a hang-over*. Even the rhetorical inversion of line 3 *foolish I find this fashion*; the simile 16 *a drifting cloudlet /* like a *dollop of whipped cream*; and the coinage 17 *unthuswise*, have an enjoyable quaintness.

Photophil (1) 'loving the light', reminds one of Auden's insatiable thirst for biological knowledge. Lines 1–5 delight in the paradox of humans who act botanically and plants who behave humanly (*sun-bathe*); these are happier thoughts than the trite personal metaphors '*a smiling summer*' (13) and '*scolded by a scowl*' (20).

Of the two instances of *enallage*, *vapids* (8 – adjective used as verb) and *stodge* (9 – noun used as adjective), the latter is the more effective, because a better metaphor. *Stodge* is a thick gruel, or watery solid, therefore a 'non-descript' kind of sustenance.

Stark bewölkt is an amusing Ode to the Weather-God, not unbecoming to 'a man of letters / Who writes, or hopes to, for his betters'; who dislikes 'Manichean pornography'; who blames the Generation Gap on 'old or young/Who will not learn their Mother-Tongue' (*Doggerel by a Senior Citizen, ibid*, p. 37). Auden's last volume, though not uniform in tone, was decidedly for the New Generation.

The comic vein in Auden's poetry was irrepressible; intrusive and sometimes disturbing in the earlier work, controlled and better integrated as his style developed. It was twenty years before he discovered ways of exploiting the ironic possibilities of words. Though Auden became disillusioned with the role of romantic anarchist, he did not tire of the mask of entertainer; in America he assumed the mantle of witty commentator and purveyor of paradox.

The Aristotelian gambit of multiple definition was one instinctive habit of Auden's verbal behaviour. In prose, he tended to define scientifically, sometimes dogmatically; in verse, he preferred an equivocal or extremist method, as a means of revealing the incongruous by association. Verbalism was important, in matter or manner, in speaking or reflecting, whatever the mask that Auden adopted; he was ever on the alert to mimic or mock absurdity.

Byron was Auden's master in one essential aspect of comic writing, defined as 'the way in which the mind wanders from one thought to another', the inconsequential 'description of things in motion' (*Don Juan, The Dyer's Hand*, pp. 386–406). Here are some pertinent observations from a perceptive critique:

> Byron's poetry is the most striking example I know in literary history of the creative role which poetic form can play ... He did not realize the poetic possibilities of the mock-heroic ottava-rima until he read Frere's *The Monks and the Giants*. Take away the poems he wrote in this style and metre, *Beppo, The Vision of Judgment, Don Juan*, and what is left of lasting value? ... Byron was really a comedian, not a satirist ...
>
> In English, unlike Italian, the majority of double or triple rhymes are comic. ... The comic verse of poets like Canning, Frere, Hood, Praed, Barham, and Lear was a new departure in English poetry ... Indeed, before them, the only poets I can think of who used it intentionally and frequently were Skelton and Samuel Butler. ...
>
> Comic rhymes provide opportunities for the interpolated comment and conversational aside, and Byron developed this deliberate looseness of manner to the full ... If, on the other hand, what the poet has to say requires several short sentences, the arrangement of the rhymes allows him to pause at any point he likes without the stanza breaking up into fragments, for his separate statements will always be linked by a rhyme ...
>
> What had been Byron's defect as a serious poet, his lack of reverence for words, was a virtue for the comic poet. Serious poetry requires that the poet treat words as if they were persons, but comic poetry demands that he treat them as things and few,

if any, English poets have rivalled Byron's ability to put words through the hoops. . . .

No man is perpetually in a passion and those states in which he is amused and amusing, detached and irreverent, if less important, are no less human.

The assumption of more than one mask in the same poem may have been responsible for the disfavour of Auden's style with some of his early critics. If a poem has more than one message, it taxes a reader who seeks a point of view; he cannot reconcile conflicting elements of seriousness and frivolity. Auden was at first accounted a high-spirited, temperamental poet of inchoate parables, unaware of his self-contradictions. But this estimate passed with the publication of *New Year Letter*, *For the Time Being* and *The Shield of Achilles*. In *The Truest Poetry is the Most Feigning*, from the last of these volumes, Auden's tongue-in-cheek flyting resembles the Epistles of Horace, and is unequivocally a debunking of the romantic approach:

> poets are not celibate divines;
> Had Dante said so, who would read his lines?
> Be subtle, various, ornamental, clever,
> And do not listen to those critics ever
> Whose crude provincial gullets crave in books
> Plain cooking made still plainer by plain cooks . . .
> No metaphor, remember, can express
> A real historical unhappiness;
> Your tears have value if they make us gay;
> *O Happy Grief!* is all sad verse can say . . .
> Poets are suspect with the New Regime,
> Stick at your desk and hold your panic in . . .
> The self-made creature who himself unmakes,
> The only creature ever made who fakes,
> With no more nature in his loving smile
> Than in his theories of a natural style,
> What but tall tales, the luck of verbal playing,
> Can trick his lying nature into saying
> That love, or truth in any serious sense,
> Like orthodoxy, is a reticence.

Auden's change of face begins, one suspects, with the rhetorical deflation of Prospero by Caliban in *The Sea and the Mirror*. The public seems to have been made aware that the poet was not, perhaps, inconsistent in himself, but judging a grotesque world, like that of Carroll's *Through the Looking Glass,* in which the Average Man resembles a creature of chaos. There is no mistaking an Auden revolution in the following quotations:

(*a*) Since of themselves all men are without merit, all are ironically assisted to their comic bewilderment by the Grace of God.

(*The Meditation of Simeon, For the Time Being,* p. 110)

(*b*) If a poet meets an illiterate peasant, they may not be able to say much to each other, but if they both meet a public official, they share the same feeling of suspicion . . . Whatever the cultural differences between them, they both sniff in any official world the smell of an unreality in which persons are treated as statistics.

('The Poet and the City', *The Dyer's Hand,* p. 88)

In context, both Everyman and Bureaucrat are figures of fun, the latter the more sinister, because of his office. Auden had no wish to be a provocative Byron or a menacing Swift, but to find a niche as a laughing physician uncovering the evils others do not perceive, or will not acknowledge. Whether society is sick unto death or merely neurotic is of no moment. The poet, in his later phase, sufficiently distanced himself from it, to burlesque ironically the oddities of a world where 'Euclid's geometry / And Newton's mechanics account for our Experience'.

That Auden chose allegory to deflate science, politics and theology, not to mention his fallen self, is understandable. Medieval bestiaries, Beatrix Potter and Marianne Moore were among his favourite reading; they all used animals as allegorical emblems for passions, desires and foolish behaviour, as well as for metaphorical comparisons. With Auden, allegory is a strategy of approach, principally to aid the 'detached irreverence', which he associates with Byron, in *A Life of a That-There Poet.* His imagination did not work fruitfully until he schematized faculties and emotions in such a way that actions and reactions could be rationally explained. In the affairs of men, proof was the rock to which Auden's faith was anchored. He defined allegory as 'a form of rhetoric, a device for making the abstract concrete' (*Poets of the English Language,* vol. IV, 1950, Introduction, p. xix).

Nearly all Auden's successful poems begin with a concrete conception. The originality of his style resides in its positive power to parody heroics (with no disrespect to the dramatic traditions) and an inhibiting tendency in evaluating sentiment. When, finally, he reached a balanced position as a moralist, he came to regard humanity with serene bemusement. Reading Søren Kierkegaard's *Sickness unto Death* helped him to harmonize the early opposing temperaments, to accept life, with detachment, as an inevitable tragicomedy.

It is difficult to pin down Auden's style by any worthwhile technical analysis; he rejected the 'overpersonal' manner, and cultivated the several voices of the *personae* in his creations. Among his praiseworthy achievements was an attempt to catalyse the scientific thinking of his time in psychology, biology and anthropology, and to render it amenable to the service of poetry. In 'The Virgin and the Dynamo' he handles the function of a poet much as a behaviourist would an experiment:

It is impossible, I believe, for any poet, while he is writing a poem, to observe with complete accuracy what is going on, to define with any certainty how much of the final result is due to subconscious activity over which he has no control, and how much is due to conscious artifice . . . *Some* degree of conscious participation by the poet is necessary, *some* element of craft is always present . . . But no poet can know what his poem is going to be like until he has written it.

The element of craftsmanship in poetry is obscured by the fact that all men are taught to speak and most to read and write, while very few men are taught to draw or paint or write music. Every poet, however, in addition to the everyday linguistic training he receives, requires a training in the poetic use of language . . .

A poem is a natural organism, not an inorganic thing. For example, it is rhythmical. The temporal recurrences of rhythm are never identical, as the metrical notation would seem to suggest. Rhythm is to time what symmetry is to space . . .

Meaning and being are identical. A poem might be called a pseudo-person. Like a person, it is unique and addresses the reader personally. On the other hand, like a natural being and unlike a historical person, it cannot lie . . .

The nature of the final poetic order is the outcome of a dialectical struggle between the recollected occasions of feeling and the verbal system ...

A poem is beautiful or ugly to the degree that it succeeds or fails in reconciling contradictory feelings in an order of mutual propriety.

(*The Dyer's Hand*, pp. 67–71)

No enthusiasm enlivens the passing reference to art as 'beautiful or ugly'; for Auden is a relativist, and many of his analogies between art and science seem whimsical, as this from 'Balaam and his Ass' (*ibid* p. 133):

Imagination cannot distinguish the possible from the impossible; to it the impossible is a species of the genus possible, not another genus.

The style of Auden does not lend itself to wit as repartee, but there is an audacious tendency to epigram, and he is skilled in cultivating flatness of diction to express the banal. Reticence, with Auden, does not extend to withholding likes and dislikes; but the personal frankness is quite disarming. He revels, above all, in the lexical resources of the English language, without much extravagance in the way of neologisms, and he relishes its potential of new compounds for poetry.

The noteworthy features of Auden's verse lines, whether long or short, are flexibility of rhythm and colloquial tone. There is much artifice in this, as he would not have denied; for he held that the nature of art is but partly conscious, and that accident and the tradition of the language play a major part in the final product.

A poet has to woo, not only his own Muse but also Dame Philology, and, for the beginner, the latter is the more important. As a rule, the sign that a beginner has a genuine original talent is that he is more interested in playing with words than in saying something original; his attitude is that of the old lady, quoted by E. M. Forster – 'How can I know what I think till I see what I say?' It is only later, when he has wooed and won Dame Philology, that he can give his entire devotion to his Muse.

(*The Dyer's Hand*, Prologue, 'Writing', p. 22)

It would be wrong to suppose that Auden's speech rhythms are generally prosaic; he is the most versatile experimenter in stanza forms, yet not averse to tweaking the nose of the poetic tradition, and its aesthetic solemnity. Like Eliot's, the Auden voice has distinct characteristics, some of which it may be worthwhile to enumerate:

1) The speech rhythm, unmistakably educated, has the tang of verisimilitude.
2) The tone is masculine, with the note of a middle-class intellectual, and a tendency to slang to avoid commonplaceness.
3) The verse is syllable-conscious, and limits unstressed elements in the line to a point that embarrasses syntax.
4) Auden has a higher percentage of approximate and off-beat rhymes than has any other contemporary poet of standing. He is not, like Byron, Swift and Butler, an exponent of multiple rhyme.
5) The punctuation is syntactical rather than metrical, and sometimes unorthodox, as in reviving the Elizabethan colon as a time-stop.
6) The argument is voluble, the praise sparing, the choice of adjectives original.

Twentieth-century literature would have been the poorer without Auden's quest for a new enlightenment. He was a transmitter of ideas, rather than an original thinker, but his were not ideas easy to formulate as material for poetry. His search for suitable media was indefatigable, and his success by no means negligible. He was against any authoritarian standpoint that imposes Christian sanctions on weaker brethren; but he could see that men have too many limitations to make their dreams of progress possible.

Auden's achievement was that he took the conventions of poetry current in the nineteenth century out of the aesthetic dimension, and put them into a social context, from which they will not soon be dislodged. The place of the individual in society will henceforward be significant only as the organism itself is healthy; and the forces that impinge on mass culture do not make the future look promising. Auden admired and had read Bertolt Brecht, but thought his doctrine of alienation negative. He saw the present situation very much as Kierkegaard described it in the Appendix to *The Sickness unto Death*: 'The entirely unsocratic trait of modern philosophy is that it wants to make itself and us believe that it is Christianity.'

CHAPTER XI

New Lines, Dylan Thomas, and Conclusions

𒀭𒀭𒀭𒀭𒀭𒀭

IN the last chapter of his *Science and Poetry* (Oxford University Press, 1950) Douglas Bush remarked on the 'paradoxical situation that the *poetical* Victorians had a popular audience', whereas 'the *colloquial* moderns have not' (p. 142). One reason advanced is 'the quality of our civilization'; another, that the poets of today tend 'to write for one another and for the critics who have rationalized their retreat'. Auden admitted that he began writing poetry less to please himself than his friends; Eliot defended the retreat of the poet into a laager where only the discriminating could follow. The extent of the 'fit audience, though few' depends on an acquired taste and the power of a new language to communicate with its diminishing body of admirers.

Pound was the leader of the modern cult of indirection, which places responsibility for understanding upon the reader; but Eliot and Auden were the poets who most aided its unexpected development. Free verse remains the principal contribution of American literature to English culture, and is comparable to the influence of Gershwin and Bernstein on music. The three writers who are the subject of this study could hardly be more unlike in tone and execution. Though their poems agree in avoiding explicit statement, in their handling of symbol and metaphor, and control of language and syntax, each writer has the signs of a distinct personality, revealed in the texture and rhythm of the verse.

Yeats appears to have found his first inspiration in the homes and society of artists, but most of the younger poets were products of the old universities, trained in the linguistic psychology of I. A. Richards, who taught that 'thoughts are the servants of our interests', that 'words are ambiguous'; 'it is never what a poem *says* that matters, but what it *is*'; and that 'the poet's style is the direct outcome of the way in which his interests are organized'

(*Science and Poetry*, Kegan Paul, 1935, pp. 19, 28, 31, 44). There were few phrases that occurred more frequently in criticism of poetry than 'organic form', that which is adapted to the needs of a poem's context. The general theory explains that a poem is shaped by an inner necessity that controls the development of its outward form. In a good poem the maker adapts means to purpose; his medium is permitted to distort, but not to obliterate the pattern, which is invariably reconciled with the poetic tradition. In Eliot's words, 'The detail of the pattern is movement'.

Another article of faith, propounded by Ezra Pound and T. E. Hulme, was the need for 'concreteness'; language had to present the living object, not the abstract process. Auden's discarded acts are concretely described in

> torn gloves, rusted kettles,
> Abandoned branchlines, worn lop-sided
> Grindstones buried in nettles.

For the more recent student of poetic language, a fruitful appraisal of modernist aims is to be found in Donald Davie's *Articulate Energy* (Routledge and Kegan Paul, 1955). This critic sees the principal outcome of the Symbolist Movement as a change in the poet's attitude to syntax, meaning the significant arrangement of words. Symbolism begins, he says, 'with a distaste of abstract terms'; most good poets manipulate syntax as a means to articulation and harmonious relationships. Davie argues that the syntax of such dislocated verse as Pound writes in the *Cantos* is not strictly linguistic, but musical, because its unity resides in the 'all-embracing artifice of rhythm'.

Davie's account of the development of English poetic syntax since the sixteenth century distinguishes five kinds: subjective, dramatic, objective, musical and mathematical (p. 67). A subjective syntax he finds in language that adheres to forms of thought and grammar; it may be found in the poetry of Wordsworth and Coleridge, matching 'the audible rhythms of their versification' (p. 75). The appeal of dramatic syntax is primarily to the ear through accompanying imagery and rhythm; it is hardly a syntax in the grammatical sense. The objective class functions by fidelity to a form of action; the syntax is determined by a sense of fitness, as in the balanced epigrammatic couplets of Pope. The remaining categories of syntax are still too vague to be honoured by the name. The difficulty in accepting Davie's thesis is that the criteria, though useful in evaluating gobbets, are of doubtful validity in judging the tenor of a whole work. The word *syntax* can be used with etymological propriety only for the order of arrangement, or for the symbolic relations of words that extend the subtleties of thought. In the latter function syntax overlaps with rhetorical schemes.

Donald Davie sees Yeats as a symbolist of a different order from Eliot and the French school. For instance, Yeats offered guidelines to the significance of symbols, and was so intent that the identity of *personae* should not be missed as to ensure that the structure of sentences seldom required clarification. From this aspect, the verse of Yeats is far from *free*. One of Davie's illuminating conclusions is worth citing:

> There are in language systems of articulation other than syntax. There is, in particular, the articulation indicated by the 'figures auricular' of the old rhetoric-books, the relations that words strike up among themselves by similarities of sound or written appearance, relations known to us as metre, quantity, alliteration, assonance, rhyme. If we are to trust words to do our thinking for us . . . we must trust them when they make this sort of pattern, no less than when they make the patterns we call syntactical. (*Op. cit.*, p. 138).

When Yeats determined to become a poet, he was an archromantic, though a perplexed one. His art was concerned to express his own feelings, and the disappointments of a poet who was conscious of a limiting egotism ('Myself must I remake / Till I am Timon and Lear'). To escape from such an aesthetic cocoon, Yeats launched into Irish mythology; but his methods and ideas remained his own; he had by laborious self-immolation to learn the virtues of domesticity, as Auden did later, and to invent a language to embody their poetic significance. *Embody* suggests the kind of compromise every poet needs to make, between his private values and the public or traditional scheme of things. When a critic described Yeats's mature language as 'public', he was gratified with the compliment. As early as 1900, in an essay on 'The Symbolism of Poetry', he had written:

> Understanding that the laws of art . . . are the hidden laws of

> the world, can alone bind the imagination ... Organic rhythms ... are the *embodiment* of the imagination that neither desires nor hates, because it has done with time.

Yeats found himself as a poet, when he learnt to set down intimate thoughts without heightening or embroidering them; for by this re-thinking the poet inevitably distorts genuine emotions. To temper enthusiasm with unselfregarding realism seemed to him the course for a modern poet, and science should come to his aid. Yeats chose a pseudo-science or transcendental philosophy, which he unashamedly styled 'magic'; he respected it much as Auden did Freudian psychology. It was a system by which he could objectify his experience, while fitting into it world history and life after death. It provided an appropriate psychology, because it was based on a conflict of opposing forces, reconciling scientific determinism with freedom of will. Whatever its credibility for others, Yeats was satisfied with the fruitfulness of his *Vision* (1926) for the enrichment of the imagination.

The case-history of Yeats was necessary to show that poetry, while it is affected by the truths of science, does not use language in that kind of way. His experience confirmed that the problems of communication are not solved by determining what words can or can not be made to do. Their function is as much to conceal by extension, as to clarify by intension, of meaning. The symbolism of language rests very precariously on the logic of representation, and the fitness and power of words to endure has to be tested by their expressive quality. For literature, truth is inherent in expression, not in phenomena. In *Science and Poetry* I. A. Richards therefore argued that science, while it systematizes, 'can tell us nothing about the nature of things in any *ultimate* sense'. But an important way in which science *may* impinge on literature is through its attitude of impersonality. In *An Anatomy of Inspiration*, Rosamond Harding offers a neat semantic antithesis: 'While the scientist creates a discovery, an artist discovers a creation'.

The function of a private philosophy is not to change society, but to unify an individual's responses to the world. Yeats's *anima mundi* was such a concept, used to transfigure his attitudes, for instance to personal ambition and public violence. Like Auden, he came to accept evil as a condition of spiritual growth; self-expression can then be directed to positive ends. Yeats was encouraged by the idea of re-incarnation to believe that history might recur re-vitalized, under less disastrous conditions. In an incautious moment T. S. Eliot described Yeats's supernatural world as a 'sophisticated lower mythology summoned ... to supply the fading pulse of poetry'. A more charitable account would have ascribed it to the absence of a humanist education. The symbols of Yeats's ideas he himself spoke of as medieval talismans, entangling 'in complex colours and forms, a part of the Divine essence'. He used symbols as purifiers of emotions and passions, to which he entrusted his secret personality. His blood, he hoped, had 'not passed through any huckster's loin'.

T. S. Eliot's early poetry was more objective, external to himself with a cold detachment that bespeaks neurosis of the spirit, rather than of the mind. His initial experience and emotions seemed more limited, but his knowledge of art was profound. A certain mark of this is that he wastes no words in securing effects; there are fewer lines of his that a technical critic would wish retrenched. The nuances of speech and invented rhythms sound inevitable, even when they are innovations. The simplicity of his three-stress free-verse line is a source of flexibility that never tires, and enjoys a facility in dramatic monologue that Browning mostly lacked.

The earlier exercises in wry social comment revealed a familiar Jamesian superiority, peculiar to the American abroad; but the tone mellowed with Eliot's greater experience of Europe, and his responsibilities as a writer and editor. The Sweeney-Bleistein period was the least happy; it was marred by an intended ostentatious vulgarity and the quest for portentous polysyllables (*juvescence concitation, defunctive, protrusive, daguerreotypes, polyphloprogenitive, superfetation, piaculative*), symptoms of the gymnastic gimmick, rather than of metrical wit. It is misleading to claim this style as colloquial; moreover, such a *tour-de-force* as the latter half of *A Game of Chess* is a cinematic imitation of the Cockney dialect. As G. S. Fraser has suggested, it was the rhythm of *Prufrock* that created the illusion of conversation (*Vision and Rhetoric*, Faber 1959, p. 122).

If *Prufrock* and *The Waste Land* established Eliot as the leading exponent of free verse, *Ash Wednesday* and *Murder in the Cathedral* earned for him the reputation of a genuine poet. He discovered a natural vein of flowing ritual in choric verse, with a social as well as a religious significance, and this gift he could apparently muster at will. Though he valued the traditions, not only of English literature, but of all Europe, he is the least derivative of modern poets, including Pound, whose influential direction after *Mauberley* was in translation and adaptation.

Overcoming his initial rootlessness, Eliot produced poems of place and personal situation as refined and dignified as any that flowed from the pen of Yeats. His scholarship became him, and he found that the discipline of stanzas was not indispensable to the form of his poems, provided the length did not exceed about two hundred lines. Skill in varying the rhythm to suit the tone and content is evident in the way he incorporated citations from other poems, without disrupting the movement of his own. Although the content of Eliot's poems is more fragmented than in those of Yeats or Auden, unity of conception and treatment make them appear harmonious, development being modelled on the art of the musical composer. He differs from Auden in seldom posing or solving questions. Secular or religious, the mature poems are expressed with a sober control of the emotions.

These marks of a classical style are, however, different from the familiar aspects of Augustanism. Art is, for Eliot, the imposing of order upon a confusion of experiences. He shares, with Auden, a sympathy with existentialism; it supersedes the exhausted tendencies in literature to idealism or realism. What Eliot sought to discipline was philosophical dualism, on the ground that it distorts the vision of experience. He fulfils many desiderata of the philosophical poet, whom Coleridge awaited in English literature; the ordering of his mind and the catholicity of his taste were more secure than Arnold's. Time will probably show that Eliot's stature as a critic added much to his significance as a poet.

Yeats, Eliot and Auden were equally concerned with the complex human condition, and the poetry reflects their different approaches. Yeats was contemplative, Eliot dramatic (with the objectivity of classical tragedy not Shakespeare's), Auden pragmatic. The term 'objective correlative' was an admirable motive for the species of monologue at which Eliot excelled. His religious duties were 'accepted and accepting', providing the only order in which the mind could repose.

Eliot's acquiescence in the Augustinian concept of time in *Four Quartets*, *sub specie aeternatis* (as it essentially is) was not merely the consequence of his Anglo-Catholic faith. He may have found earlier support for it in Bergson's idea of memory as a stream-like continuum. Most poets regard time as a 'unique present', constantly observable; any notion of duration they seem to treat metaphorically, *eg*, 'Time, like an ever-rolling stream' in Isaac Watts's popular hymn. In theory, time should be bounded by the life of the universe or of man himself, and therefore *finite*, *ie*, the opposite of *eternity*.

Dissociation has a role in Eliot's classicism, as counterpart to his holistic theory of art. Not only are men dissociated from their milieu, but their responses are regarded as 'undisciplined squads of emotion'. Below the level of daily experience is the rationalizing consciousness, which weighs, compares and judges, as a stage-manager would direct the drama of life, without any creative part in it. The psyche of the artist is, for Eliot, below this level of consciousness; it is the unknown power that co-ordinates and evokes the appropriate emotions through images, phrases, symbols and ideas. The creative purpose of art is the making of harmonious wholes; and if Eliot is right, this explains the perfection of *Marina*, and some movements of *Burnt Norton* and *Little Gidding*.

At first sight, Auden's appears to be a case of dual personality; for he regarded the world with as much seriousness as Arnold, Yeats or Eliot. What he doubted was the efficacy of poetry, or any other art, to change the conditions of life. His earliest inclination was to side with the fabulists, laughers and mockers, such as Firbank, Beatrix Potter, Byron and Edward Lear. But there was no earnestness in this banter, and he was compelled by the depression of the nineteen-thirties and his interest in science and depth psychology to take a politico-moral line. This was didactic and social at first, because Auden was a natural teacher. In poetry he found the metier wherein accumulated knowledge and ambition could assert themselves without pedantry. The success of *Look Stranger* confirmed a talent for serious verse more traditional in form than what his Oxford colleagues, Spender and Day Lewis, were writing.

The distinguishing marks of Auden's poetry are its metrical dexterity and ambivalence of tone. The poems abound in un-guarded leaps of thought, revealing a whimsical attitude of mind, without the witty insincerity that plagued the writing of Wilde. Auden's sometimes ponderous wit may be exceedingly complex, especially when he loads it with obscure allusions; the reader tends to be deflated by the irrelevance of some of the fun.

As a psychologist in verse, Auden intrigues by his searching analysis of human behaviour; an urge to inspect the errant psyche infects the most wistful of his lyrics. Portrait poems assess the value of a variety of thinkers in a revealing way, for Auden developed a knack of caricaturing the idiosyncrasies of public intellectuals. Yet in spite of Freudian psychology, he adheres to the old-fashioned dichotomy of heart and head.

No modern poet committed himself to so many definitions as Auden; a nut of epigrammatic knowledge was a frequent opening gambit. An insistent theme in social poems is the inadequacy of man's theories to cope with practical biological problems; throughout the English period, man in society remained the staple of Auden's cynical circumspections. Tolerance and wiser counsels prevailed only when the poet returned to religion, and could exchange confidences with friends like Reinhold Niebuhr, or with a circle of music-lovers in New York.

There is something engagingly conciliatory in Auden's later poetry; the humorous twists that restrain his insatiable intellectual curiosity; the innocent pleasure in exercising forgotten words; the muscularity, the technical ease in handling difficult media. Sometimes he overlays the graces with a show of cleverness; but this is one of his masks. When Auden is completely sincere, one detects in the tone of the language an underlying gentleness and humility. Observations, even of landscape, take on a symbolic significance, as though he aimed to be a sophisticated William Blake. Where Blake chooses a limpid epithet, Auden chooses an opaque metallic one, more in keeping with the harshness of the time. His adjectives are a study in themselves; here are some examples from his formative period, the 1930 collections: *secretive* as plants; the / *Fumbled* and *unsatisfactory* embrace before hurting; the *tigerish* blazer and the *dove-like* shoe; From the *conservative* dark / Into the *ethical* life, / The *dense* commuters come. The words themselves are common, but the collocations are unusual.

In his *Poetry since 1939* (Longmans, 1946) Stephen Spender called attention to Auden's 'gift of improvization', and 'mastery of idiom'. The surprising turn of phrase is remarkable in a reader who devoured works of reference as readily as improving literature. His retentive memory seems to have been rich in novelties, on which he could fall back to avoid the danger of repeating himself. But with all these intellectual endowments, the flair for inevitability too often eluded him in phrasing. There is a lack of purposive direction, leaving the impression that Auden wrote for a faceless audience that was unlikely to be roused.

The leading poets of the nineteen-thirties had liberal or socialist sympathies, but were, in theory only, a literary group united in their ideologies. As poets, Auden, Spender and Day Lewis were individualists who went their own way; they did not meet socially, as a trio, until 1947 in Venice. The political hegemony that opponents alleged was largely due to the appearance of their poems together in *New Signatures*, edited by Michael Roberts in 1932. More influential in suggesting a 1930 movement was the magazine *New Verse*, edited by Geoffrey Grigson, a double number of which was devoted to Auden in November 1937, acknowledging this poet's pre-eminence at the early age of thirty. In this number Dylan Thomas (1914–53) described Auden as 'a wide and deep poet, . . . a flusher of melancholies'.

Thomas mingled laughter and despair more irresponsibly than Auden. One may assess his attitude to words by examining his stock of comic eccentricities: 'the *maximless gawky*, the dear and the *daft* and the droll, the *runcible* Booby, . . . the *barmy* old Adam . . . confronted, as social beings, by the *delt* and the *peeve* and the *minge* and the bully, the *maniac new Atom*' ('A Dearth of Comic Writers', *Quite Early One Morning*, Dent, 1954, p. 122).

In popular recognition Thomas seems to have superseded Auden early in the nineteen-forties; but it is not on this account that he needs to be recalled in an estimate of modern poetry. If he is to be regarded as a symbolist poet, it must be as a Cymric Celt who trusted in what he called 'the accident of magic'. The symbols are not, like Eliot's, universal, but private, and by critical standards, irrational. Speaking of his methods, with typical candour, as 'daft', he nevertheless thought he was making 'a contribution to reality'. ('On Poetry', *op. cit.*, p. 169).

Dylan Thomas's 'Notes on the Art of Poetry' (1951) are the best introduction to his writing, whether in verse or prose:

> I wanted to write poetry in the beginning because I had fallen in love with words . . . What the words stood for, symbolized, or meant, was of very secondary importance. What mattered

was the *sound* of them as I heard them for the first time . . . And these words were, to me, as the notes of bells, the sounds of musical instruments, the noises of wind, sea, and rain, the rattle of milkcarts, the clopping of hooves on cobbles, the fingering of branches on a window pane, might be to someone, deaf from birth, who has miraculously found his hearing.

That was the time of innocence; words burst upon me, unencumbered by trivial or portentous association; words were their spring-like selves, fresh with Eden's dew, as they flew out of the air. They made their own original associations as they sprang and shone . . . What I like to do is to treat words as a craftsman does his wood or stone or what-have-you, to hew, carve, mould, coil, polish and plane them into patterns, sequences, sculptures, fugues of sound expressing some lyrical impulse, some spiritual doubt or conviction, some dimly-realised truth I must try to reach and realise . . .

My first, and greatest, liberty was that of being able to read everything and anything I cared to. I read indiscriminately, and with my eyes hanging out. I could never have dreamt that there were such goings-on in the world between the covers of books, such sand-storms and ice-blasts of words, such slashing of humbug . . .

Let me say that the things that first made me love language and want to work *in* it and *for* it were nursery rhymes and folk tales, the Scottish Ballads, a few lines of hymns, the most famous Bible stories and the rhythms of the Bible, Blake's *Songs of Innocence* . . . The Bible I had, of course, known from very early youth; the great rhythms had rolled over me from the Welsh pulpits; and I read, for myself, from Job and Ecclesiastes; and the story of the New Testament is part of my life. But I have never sat down and studied the Bible, never consciously echoed its language . . .

I am a painstaking, conscientious, involved and devious craftsman in words, however unsuccessful the result so often appears, and to whatever wrong uses I may apply my technical paraphernalia. I use everything and anything to make my poems work and move in the direction I want them to . . . Poets have got to enjoy themselves sometimes, and the twisting and con-volutions of words, the inventions and contrivances, are all part of the joy . . .

I do not mind from where the images of a poem are dragged up; drag them up, if you like, from the nethermost sea of the hidden self; but, before they reach paper, they must go through all the rational processes of the intellect . . . One of the arts of the poet is to make comprehensible and articulate what might emerge from subconscious sources; one of the great main uses of the intellect is to *select*, from the amorphous mass of sub-conscious images, those that will best further his imaginative purpose . . .

The joy and function of poetry is, and was, the celebration of man, which is also the celebration of God.

Like Prospero's, the robe of magic is assumed with consummate power; and the humorous self-depreciation disarms, because it reveals the poet's awareness of the tricksy rhetoric of his craft. Part of the magic lies in self-generating images, accumulated and set in order with varying measures of success.

The earlier Thomas exploited to the full the linguistic licences of which W. E. Baker complained. Grammatical signals are unreliable, and Thomas blurs the relationship between literary and colloquial speech, as Auden does. The explication of esoteric symbols is feasible only through re-construction of the associative chain by which the limping sense operates. Thomas also blurs the literary psychologist's distinction between subjective and objective imagery. Whatever the scope of his imagination, its object is invariably himself. In the poem *From love's first fever to her plague*, a poem of his early period, Thomas seeks to objectify the process of composition, but the words *flesh, brain, will* and *my tongue* confirm that his mind is on his own sensations. The images alone are italicized in this citation:

> And from the *first declension* of the flesh
> I learnt man's tongue, to *twist the shapes of thoughts*
> Into *the stony idiom of the brain*,
> To *shade and knit anew the patch of words*
> Left by the dead who, in their moonless acre,
> Need no word's warmth . . .
>
> I learnt the *verbs of will*, and had my secret;
> The *code of night tapped on my tongue*;
> What had been one was *many sounding minded.*

The obscurity of Thomas's diction results from the oddness of his symbolic representation. He said in *Explorations* 4 (Toronto, 1955): 'I thought it enough to leave an impression of sound and feeling and let the meaning seep in later'. His methods involve the following devices:

Words: new coinages; freak compounds; unusual functional liberties; intriguing periphrases.

Sounds: alliteration and assonance, the latter off-set by occasional dissonance.

Tropes: images contradict each other, and extend the ambiguities of syntax.

Schemes: ubiquitous punning and *enallage* (the vicarious use of the parts of speech)

Thomas himself advised literal interpretation, and critics like Edith Sitwell, who attempted to paraphrase, were proved wide of the mark, by Thomas's own explanation. A characteristic example is the first half of *In Memory of Ann Jones* (*The Map of Love*, 1939), in which the obscure references are italicized:

> After the funeral, *mule praises*, brays,
> Windshake of *sailshaped* ears, *muffle-toed* tap
> Tap happily of one peg in the thick
> Grave's foot, *blinds down* the lids, the *teeth in black*,
> The *spittled* eyes, the *salt ponds* in the sleeves,   5
> Morning smack of the spade that wakes up sleep,
> Shakes a desolate boy who *slits his throat*
> In the dark of the coffin and *sheds dry leaves*,
> That *breaks one bone to light with a judgment clout*,
> After the feast of *tear-stuffed time* and thistles   10
> In a room with a stuffed fox and a stale fern,
> I stand, for this memorial's sake, alone
> In the *snivelling hours* with dead, humped Ann
> Whose *hooded, fountain heart once fell in puddles*
> Round the parched worlds of Wales and *drowned* each sun 15

It is obvious that the obscurity arises partly from Thomas's failure to distinguish literal description from tropes, such as *tear-stuffed time* (10, metaphor) and *snivelling hours* (13, personification). The poem suffers from emotive epithet-congestion, the purpose being to make every worked-up phrase evocative.

Ann Jones was Dylan's aunt, and is described in the first sketch of *Portrait of the Artist as a Young Dog* (1940) as 'a little, brown-skinned, toothless, hunchbacked woman with a cracked, sing-song voice' (p. 14). The Welshness of this human tribute is palpable in its graveside magniloquence. Surrealism was in the air, and the first five lines were penned under its influence. They arrest momentum, until the true realism is reached in the monosyllabic line 6, with its homely personification:

> Morning smack of the spade that wakes up sleep.

There is little coherence in the images of lines 5/6: *blinds down the lids, teeth in black, spittled eyes* and *salt ponds in the sleeve*, which may depict the state of the mourners or the disabilities of Ann's 'seventy years'. *A desolate boy who slits his* throat / . . . *and sheds dry leaves* (7/8) refers to Thomas himself, and is a fair example of warring images. There is something incongruous in the '*hooded* . . . *heart*' that '*once fell in puddles*' (14); mixed metaphor like this comes from the habit of excogitating phrases in isolation.

The picture consists merely of graphic strokes. Syntax does not explain the grammatical function of *Windshake of sailshaped ears* (2), a phrase which, like *mule praises* (1) and *Morning smack* (6), is unaccompanied by any article. The reader, having puzzled over the antecedent of the relative clause *That breaks one bone to light with a judgment clout* (9), and found it in *spade* (6), is still in a maze over the sense of *break one bone to light*.

Nature affected Thomas earthily, and the images in the poems are sensuous, rather than profound. In his mature style (*Deaths and Entrances*, 1946), when much of the verbiage was purged away, he could write with attractive simplicity, *eg, Poem in October*:

> My birthday began with the water-
> Birds and the birds of the winged trees flying my name
> Above the farms and the white horses
> And I rose
> In rainy autumn   5
> And walked abroad in a shower of all my days.
> High tide and the heron dived when I took the road
> Over the border
> And the gates
> Of the town closed as the town awoke.   10

A springful of larks in a rolling
Cloud and the roadside bushes brimming with whistling
Blackbirds and the sun of October
Summery
On the hill's shoulder,   15
Here were fond climates and sweet singers suddenly
Come in the morning where I wandered and listened
To the rain wringing
Wind blow cold
In the wood faraway under me.   20

What strikes the reader is the inadequacy of the punctuation,
particularly at the end of lines 3, 8 and 15. Thirteen of the twenty
lines are enjambed, and compound-complex sentences (there are
only four) are much longer than they were in the early poems.
High tide (7) is really a condensed clause, and must be so understood, as it cannot be the subject of *dived*.

The only figures are metaphor and personification in lines 2, 11,
12, 15, 16 and 18, and *ploce* in lines 2 and 10. The ten-line stanzas
need no rhyme, as they are organized by the rhythm and alliteration on letters w, b, f, r, t, s and c. The nostalgic poems composed
in Wales during the Second World War are reminiscent of Vaughan
and Wordsworth, and reveal a control of language which Thomas
had rarely before exercised.

Dylan Thomas, who died in 1953, was not involved in the reaction
to the poetry of Eliot and Auden of the nineteen-fifties. The
principles underlying the desire for change were chiefly (a) the
elimination of obscurity, (b) return to the order of stanzaic verse,
and (c) a desire to wean English poetry from the American influence
that began with Pound. A group of nine poets, known as 'the
Movement' were brought together in the anthology *New Lines*,
edited by Robert Conquest in 1956; six were academics and two
university librarians. The most encouraging poetry of this coterie
came from Philip Larkin and Thom Gunn; the others established
themselves principally as critics or writers of fiction. The attitude
of the Movement, set out in the Introduction, claimed to be
'empirical', citing George Orwell's exemplification of the term.
The editor was troubled by the 'subjective moods' and 'social
pressures' of the poets of the thirties, and the 'debilitating theory

that poetry *must* be metaphorical'. This point has received some enlargement from Donald Davie.

The New Poetry, another anthology selected and introduced by A. Alvarez (Penguin 1962, revised 1966) offered a more convincing account of the development of English poetry after 1950, when Auden and Eliot were still writing. Alvarez explained that the motivation of the reaction was largely negative. The role of free verse had been to open new areas of experience by making fresh techniques available. The merit of his preface is that he distinguished Auden's modernity (a matter principally of up-to-date idiom) from Eliot's originality, a strong sense of form conditioned by metaphysical and religious traditions. The talents of the Movement (argued this editor) had been a blend of intelligent competence and English gentility, pieties that produced a 'unity of flatness', attributable either to the philosophy of the Welfare State or to the stratum of society from which most of the new poets came.

In most value judgements, the worth of a poem is assessed by its intention, tone and execution, as well as its sense. These aspects are subsumed under the four heads to which this study has been committed, and it is convenient to retain them in the summary of conclusions. The creative imagination is not, however, divisible; the interanimation of various aspects and functions is essential to the holistic theory of art that modern poetry favours. Linguistic science has, furthermore, introduced into analytical criticism many new considerations, such as the continuum of sounds and syllables that speech entails, and it shows that some conventions are matters of convenience, rather than phonetically tenable.

FORM

Formal categories in poetry arise from the desire of writers to arrange their language in patterns, which invariably conditions the choice and arrangement of words. Thus form may not be dissociated from lexical considerations or syntax. Modern poets have encouraged innovation by departing from the concepts of traditional grammar, when occasion arises, in devising their structural units. The principle reason for this has been the wish to moderate tendencies to poetic unreality, by using prose or natural speech rhythms. The best poets have continued to practice traditional stanza forms for their disciplinary benefits; but more frequently they arrange units of form in near-rhymed strophes. The alternative to such irregular groupings is the verse paragraph, which Eliot uses in *The Waste Land*. Both the language and the method of grouping are usually adapted to the poet's purpose; the form is then said to be organic or imposed.

In modern poetry the tenor of a work is not frequently homogeneous, and 'style', as a critical term, is being constantly replaced by 'language'. The form of a poem is naturally determined by the degree of its linguistic complexity. For instance, the sentences of a discursive or prose rhythm tend to be longer than those of colloquial speech. The context of conversation is also less coherent in transitions from one thought to another. Incantational verse, which is a feature of modern poetry, thrives on verbal iteration and other rhetorical effects, and such poetry is better adapted to a free choric form, as in *Ash Wednesday*. A known metrical form is not essential to the art of counterpoint, since the practice in free verse is to modulate the stress rhythm against the syntax, a device that may be called for by situations of emotional stress.

Eliot and Pound have undoubtedly gained their point, that while good poetry needs form of a kind, writing may be the better for *reforming* conventions; because the value of a sound tradition is its potentiality to develop taste. Taste is probably improved less by large-scale formal intuitions, than by textural details, which are psychologically important.

RHYTHM

The relaxed tone of free verse has added immeasurably to the resources of rhythm, even where strophic forms are favoured. To accompany greater flexibility, more liberty is demanded in what the grammarian regards as normal syntax. The change has been brought about by the poet's preference for colloquial or matter-of-fact language, even in poems of reflection. But poetry of serious intent cannot be wholly, or even mainly, in the conversational manner; and the tonal transitions found in *The Waste Land* can produce clashes unnerving to the reader, as Auden too discovered. In *Making, Knowing and Judging* (1956) he wrote:

I am . . . thankful that my first Master [Thomas Hardy] did not write in free verse or I might have been tempted to believe that free verse is easier to write than stricter forms, whereas I now know it is infinitely more difficult (p. 10).

Modern verse relies no less than the poetry of preceding centuries on auditory effects, such as alliteration, assonance, consonance and onomatopoeia. In the absence of terminal rhyme and the other expectations of stanza forms, these effects become more significant, yet their bearing on the rhythm of a poem tends to be overlooked. Equally relevant is the position of internal pauses, yet poets such as Auden and Dylan Thomas are notoriously negligent in supplying the punctuation necessary for effective interpretation.

Foot division has become irrelevant to the modern poet. An important aspect of rhythm, however, is linear sequence and natural stress evaluation. Stress contrasts have prosodic value, and are of considerable help in interpretation. Desire for contrast is one motive of rhythmical variation; and the ground for rejecting traditional prosody in free verse is that it limits the kinds of variation a poet can make. As rhythm has a musical basis, it has been proved unwise to impose natural speech variations too often upon the dominant accentual pattern. The grammatical continuum secured by enjambement may be, and often is, different from the rhythmical sequence.

It is quite misleading to discredit the intentions of the thoughtful poet, especially in technical matters. Only into the ultimate form an idea takes does the element of accident enter. Perhaps Vernon Watkins was echoing Dylan Thomas, when he wrote in *Yeats in Dublin*:

> The intellect is impotent
> Labouring in the dark,
> For a poem is always
> A piece of luck.

MEANING

The widening range of themes in modern poetry has increased the possibilities of metaphor and symbol, and this is a principal difficulty in arriving at the plain sense of a poem. Moreover, the light and shade of secondary meaning is crucial to the understanding of a poet's intention. Because a word in poetry may embody simultaneously many lexical associations, ambiguity is a perplexity that may not be unintentional. On the other hand, irony, by intent equivocal, needs to be void of ambiguity, if its purpose is not to be lost.

According to Donald Davie's *Purity of Diction in English Verse* (Chatto and Windus, 1952, p. 92) poems written in the symbolist tradition encourage dislocation of syntax. To trouble the tenuous and fugitive with conventions of syntax offends the symbolist's regard for concision and concreteness. Syntax is not as fundamental to language as sounds and tones are, he explains. The modern man's dilemma is 'speech atomized', and Davie doubts whether poetry will ever return to the orthodoxy of eighteenth-century syntax, whose aim was coherence.

If classical rhetoric recognized oxymoron and paradox as legitimate eccentricities of communication, and the metaphysicals practised 'conceits' or far-fetched comparisons, why should other verbal oddities not be tolerated? This introduces the problems of interpreting figurative language, and why it is indispensable to poetry. Though the content of poetry is words, what it communicates is not merely their literal sense. Poetry is inherent in the *manner* of the saying, the associations of words raised by sounds and rhythmical relationships, and in the transience or permanence of the images they evoke. The language of poetry, in short, is a blend of the real and the fanciful. Conceits have multiplied in modern poetry through the advent of science; but the Elizabethan variety survives in modern poets like Dylan Thomas and de la Mare, who regard it as a mythopoeic privilege. Of whatever kind, conceits cannot be taken literally, because the words employed belong to the linguistic class known as *deviations*.

No poem can tolerate obscurity *ad libitum*. The sound-poet or surrealist, even if he is Dylan Thomas, is invariably a passing fashion. Yeats's 'ghostly voice' of poetry is not metre, but meaning, provided the term stands for 'significant form', not the prose sense of the words.

RHETORIC

Modern criticism is bedevilled by a grave misunderstanding of the place of rhetoric in poetry since Elizabethan times. Even the Romans were accused by Louis MacNeice of swimming 'gracefully around in rhetoric like fish in an aquarium tank' (*The Strings are False*, 1965, p. 145). Only Michael Roberts, among poets, recognized that 'the auditory rhetoric of poetry is dictated, not by its own rules, but by the central impulse of the poem' (*The Faber Book of Modern Verse*, 1936, p. 32).

Continuing reliance upon rhetorical principles by modern poets has been demonstrated in this study, and the compositional practice is not grasped by mastering a list of technical terms and applications. Rhetoric began as an aid to orderly and persuasive communication – but it has become far more, as G. N. Leech has shown in his admirable book *A Linguistic Guide to English Poetry* (Longman, 1969). Rhetoric is preoccupied not only with eloquence, but with the apparatus of style, with such things as heightening and understatement, with parallelism and repetition, with double meaning and punning, with the whole range of tropes and images; and it has added a large number of words to the critical vocabulary of many languages.

The subject is especially useful in describing the manner in which words are structured, apart from grammar, to secure desired effects. Alliteration in Hopkins and Thomas, assonance and repetition in Eliot, are linked with their stress patterning in most illuminating ways. When Dylan Thomas used the phrase 'all the *sun* long', he did so for contextual reasons, not mere novelty. These reasons it is the task of the critic of language to uncover, and to explain in what way metaphor gains potency from word-collocation.

A powerful assault on the sensibilities of readers is the aim of rhetorical method, and it illuminates the complexity of schematic language in an objective way. A link is formed between poetic content and aesthetic form. In the words of de Quincey, such knowledge ranks style 'amongst the fine arts'. Yeats, Eliot and Auden, in different ways, visualized language and literature as a contributory stream to the general pattern of culture.

Bibliography

ꗈꗈꗈꗈꗈꗈ

TEXTS

W. B. Yeats, *Collected Poems*, Macmillan, 1952
  Variorum Edition of the Poems, Macmillan, 1957
T. S. Eliot, *Complete Poems and Plays*, Faber, 1969
  The Waste Land, facsimile and transcript of the original drafts (ed. V. Eliot), Faber, 1971
W. H. Auden, *Collected Poetry*, Random House, 1945
  Collected Shorter Poems, 1930–44, Faber, 1950
  Collected Shorter Poems, 1927–57, Faber, 1966
  About the House, Faber, 1966
  Collected Longer Poems, Faber, 1968
  City Without Walls, Faber, 1969
  Epistle to a Godson, Faber, 1972
The Oxford Book of Modern Verse, 1892–1935, ed. W. B. Yeats, Clarendon, 1936
The Faber Book of Modern Verse, ed. M. Roberts, 1936
A Little Treasury of Modern Poetry, ed. O. Williams, Routledge and Kegan Paul, 1947
New Lines, ed. R. Conquest, Macmillan, 1957
Poems of the Mid-Century, ed. J. Holloway, Harrap, 1957
The New Poetry, ed. A. Alvarez, Penguin, 1962 (revised 1966)
Poetry of the Thirties, ed. R. Skelton, Penguin, 1964
The Mid-Century: English Poetry, 1940–60, ed. D. Wright, Penguin, 1965
Dante Alighieri, *Vita Nuova*, Dent, 1930
  The Divine Comedy (trans. D. Sayers), 3 vols, Penguin, 1949–62
R. Browning, *Complete Poetical Works*, ed. A. Birrell and F. G. Kenyon, 2 vols, Murray, 1945
Walt Whitman, *Leaves of Grass*, Dent, 1957
D. Martin, *Sextette*, Scholartis Press, 1928
A. C. Swinburne, *Collected Poetical Works*, 2 vols, Heinemann, 1927
G. Meredith, *Selected Poems*, ed. G. Hough, Oxford University Press, 1962
T. Hardy, *Collected Poems*, Macmillan, 1930
G. M. Hopkins, *Poems*, ed. W. H. Gardner and N. H. Mackenzie, Oxford University Press, (4th ed.) 1967

E. Pound, *Selected Poems*, ed. T. S. Eliot, Faber, 1935
D. H. Lawrence, *Complete Poems*, 3 vols, Heinemann, 1957
C. Day Lewis, *Collected Poems*, Cape, 1954
L. MacNeice, *Collected Poems*, Faber, 1949
S. Spender, *Collected Poems*, Faber, 1955
Dylan Thomas, *Collected Poems, 1934–52*, Dent, 1952

PROSE SOURCES

W. B. Yeats, *Letters on Poetry to Dorothy Wellesley*, Oxford University Press, 1940
    Letters, ed. A. Wade, Hart-Davis, 1954
    A Vision, Macmillan, 1925
    Autobiographies, Macmillan, 1955
    Mythologies, Macmillan, 1958
    Essays and Introductions, Macmillan, 1961
    Explorations, Macmillan, 1962
    Memoirs, ed. D. Donoghue, Macmillan, 1972
T. S. Eliot, *Dante*, Faber, 1929
    Selected Essays, Faber, 1932
    The Use of Poetry and the Use of Criticism, Faber, 1933
    The Sacred Wood, Methuen, 1934
    Elizabethan Essays, Faber, 1934
    After Strange Gods, Faber, 1934
    Essays Ancient and Modern, Faber, 1936
    On Poetry and Poets, Faber, 1957
    Knowledge and Experience in the Philosophy of F. H. Bradley, Faber, 1964
    To Criticize the Critic, Faber, 1965
W. H. Auden, *The Dyer's Hand*, Faber, 1948
    Selected Essays, Faber, 1964
    Secondary Worlds, Faber, 1968
D. H. Lawrence, *Studies in Classical American Literature*, Secker, 1924
    Selected Literary Criticism, ed. A. Beal, Heinemann, 1955
R. Bridges, *Collected Essays and Papers*, Oxford University Press, 1930
E. Pound, *Literary Essays*, ed. T. S. Eliot, Faber, 1954
C. Day Lewis, *The Poetic Image*, Cape, 1947
C. Isherwood, *Lions and Shadows*, Hogarth, 1938
L. MacNeice, *Modern Poetry*, Oxford University Press, 1938
S. Spender, *The Making of a Poem*, Hamilton, 1955
Dylan Thomas, *Portrait of the Artist as a Young Dog*, Dent, 1940
    Quite Early One Morning, Dent, 1954
Marianne Moore, *Predilections*, Faber, 1956
Modern Poets on Modern Poetry, ed. J. Scully, Fontana, 1966

CRITICAL STUDIES OF THE POETS

A. N. Jeffares, *W. B. Yeats, Man and Poet*, Routledge and Kegan Paul, 1949
　A Commentary on the Collected Poems of W. B. Yeats, Stanford University Press, 1968
　The Circus Animals, Macmillan, 1970
　Profiles in Literature: W. B. Yeats, Routledge and Kegan Paul, 1971
D. A. Stauffer, *The Golden Nightingale*, Macmillan, 1949
V. Koch, *W. B. Yeats, The Tragic Phase*, Routledge and Kegan Paul, 1951
T. Parkinson, *W. B. Yeats, Self-Critic*, California University Press, 1951
　W. B. Yeats, The Later Poetry, California University Press, 1964
R. Ellmann, *The Identity of Yeats*, Faber, 1954
　Eminent Domain, Oxford University Press, 1967
J. Unterecker, *A Reader's Guide to W. B. Yeats*, Thames and Hudson, 1959
P. Ure, *Yeats*, Oliver and Boyd, 1963
J. Stallworthy, *Between the Lines*, Clarendon, 1963
T. R. Henn, *The Lonely Tower*, Methuen, 1965
F. Lentricchia, *The Gaiety of Language*, California University Press, 1968
M. Perloff, *Rhyme and Meaning in the Poetry of Yeats*, Mouton, 1970
T. McGreevy, *T. S. Eliot*, Chatto and Windus, 1931
F. O. Matthiessen, *The Achievement of T. S. Eliot*, Oxford University Press, 1935
E. M. Stephenson, *T. S. Eliot and the Lay Reader*, Fortune, 1944
R. Preston, *Four Quartets Rehearsed*, Sheed and Ward, 1946
K. Smidt, *Poetry and Belief in the Work of T. S. Eliot*, Oslo, 1949
H. Gardner, *The Art of T. S. Eliot*, Cresset Press, 1949
E. Drew, *T. S. Eliot, The Design of his Poetry*, Eyre and Spottiswoode, 1950
Grover Smith, *T. S. Eliot's Poetry and Plays*, Chicago University Press, 1950
M. C. Bradbrook, *T. S. Eliot*, Longman, 1950
R. H. Robbins, *The T. S. Eliot Myth*, Schuman, New York, 1951
S. Musgrove, *T. S. Eliot and Walt Whitman*, New Zealand University Press, 1952
D. E. S. Maxwell, *The Poetry of T. S. Eliot*, Routledge and Kegan Paul, 1952
G. Williamson, *A Reader's Guide to T. S. Eliot*, Noonday, New York, 1953
(Anonymous), *On the Four Quartets of T. S. Eliot*, Stuart, 1953
L. Unger, *T. S. Eliot, Moments and Patterns*, Minnesota University Press, 1956
P. M. Martin, *Mastery and Mercy*, Oxford University Press, 1957

C. S. Bodelsen, *T. S. Eliot's Four Quartets*, Copenhagen University Press, 1958

H. Kenner, *The Invisible Poet: T. S. Eliot*, Allen, 1960

S. Bergsten, *Time and Eternity*, Lund, 1960

S. Lucy, *T. S. Eliot and the Idea of Tradition*, Cohen and West, 1960

A. G. George, *T. S. Eliot, His Mind and Art*, Asia Publishing House, 1962

Northrop Frye, *T. S. Eliot*, Oliver and Boyd, 1963

Fei-Pai-Lu, *T. S. Eliot, The Dialectal Structure of his Theory of Poetry*, Chicago University Press, 1966

B. C. Southam, *A Student's Guide to Selected Poems of T. S. Eliot*, Faber, 1968

H. Williams, *T. S. Eliot, The Waste Land*, Arnold, 1968

H. Howarth, *Notes on Some Figures Behind T. S. Eliot*, Chatto and Windus, 1965

W. T. Levy and V. Scherle, *Affectionately, T. S. Eliot*, Dent, 1968

R. Sencourt. *T, S. Eliot, A Memoir*, Garstone, 1971

B. Bergonzi, *T. S. Eliot*, Macmillan, 1972

D. S. Ward, *T. S. Eliot Between Two Worlds*, Routledge and Kegan Paul, 1973

R. Hoggart, *Auden, An Introductory Essay*, Chatto and Windus, 1951

W. H. Auden, Longman, 1961

J. W. Beach, *The Making of the Auden Canon*, Minnesota University Press, 1957

M. K. Spears, *The Poetry of W. H. Auden*, Oxford University Press, New York, 1963

B. Everett, *Auden*, Oliver and Boyd, 1964

J. G. Blair, *The Poetic Art of W. H. Auden*, Princeton University Press, 1965

H. Greenberg, *Quest of the Necessary*, Harvard University Press, 1968

J. Repolge, *Auden's Poetry*, Methuen, 1969

J. Fuller, *A Reader's Guide to W. H. Auden*, Thames and Hudson, 1970

D. Davison, *W. H. Auden*, Evans, 1970

F. Duchene, *The Case of the Helmeted Airman*, Chatto and Windus, 1972

R. Johnson, *Man's Place*, Cornell University Press, 1973

E. Olson, *The Poetry of Dylan Thomas*, Chicago University Press, 1954

CRITICAL SYMPOSIA ON THE POETS

G. M. Hopkins, The Kenyon Critics, Dobson, 1949

The Permanence of Yeats, ed. J. Hall and M. Steinmann, Macmillan, 1950

An Honoured Guest, ed. D. Donoghue and J. R. Mulryne, Arnold, 1965

W. B. Yeats, 1865–1965, ed. D. E. S. Maxwell and S. B. Bushriu, Ibadan University Press, 1965

Yeats, Last Poems, ed. J. Stallworthy, 1968

W. B. Yeats, ed. W. H. Pritchard, Penguin, 1972

T. S. Eliot, A Study of his Writings by Several Hands, ed. B. Rajan, Dobson, 1947

T. S. Eliot, A Selected Critique, ed. L. Unger, Rinehart, New York, 1948

T. S. Eliot, ed. R. March and Tambimuttu, Poetry London, 1948

T. S. Eliot, A Symposium for his Seventieth Birthday, ed. N. Braybrooke, Hart-Davis, 1958

T. S. Eliot, A Collection of Critical Essays, ed. H. Kenner, Prentice-Hall, 1962

T. S. Eliot, The Man and his Work, ed. A. Tate, Chatto and Windus, 1966

Eliot in Perspective, ed. G. Martin, Macmillan, 1970

Critics on Eliot, ed. S. Sullivan, Allen and Unwin, 1973

Eliot in His Time, ed. A. W. Litz, Princeton University Press, 1973

Auden: A Collection of Critical Essays, ed. M. K. Spears, Prentice-Hall, 1964

GENERAL CRITICISM

A. Symons, *The Symbolist Movement in Literature*, Dutton, New York, 1919

E. Wilson, *Axel's Castle*, Scribner, 1931

C. M. Bowra, *The Heritage of Symbolism*, Macmillan, 1947

E. Starkie, *From Gautier to Eliot*, Hutchinson, 1960

Scrutinies, ed. E. Rickword, Wishart, 1928

L. Riding and R. Graves, *A Survey of Modernist Poetry*, Heinemann, 1929

C. Williams, *Poetry at Present*, Clarendon Press, 1930

F. Swinnerton, *The Georgian Literary Scene*, Dent, 1938

R. Tuve, *Elizabethan and Metaphysical Imagery*, Chicago University Press, 1947

J. L. Lowes, *Convention and Revolt in Poetry*, Constable, 1930

G. Hughes, *Imagism and the Imagists*, Oxford University Press, 1931

I. A. Richards, *Science and Poetry*, Kegan Paul, Trench and Trubner, 1935

D. Bush, *Science and English Poetry*, Oxford University Press, New York, 1950

S. Spender, *The Destructive Element*, Cape, 1935

Poetry Since 1939, Longman, 1946

D. Daiches, *Poetry and the Modern World*, Chicago University Press, 1940

Writers on Writing, ed. W. Allen, Phoenix House, 1948

D. Davie, *Purity of Diction in English Verse*, Chatto and Windus, 1952

Articulate Energy, Routledge and Kegan Paul, 1955

K. Nott, *The Emperor's Clothes*, Heinemann, 1953

Bibliography

H. Read, *Form in Modern Poetry*, Vision, 1953
The True Voice of Feeling, Faber, 1953
F. R. Leavis, *New Bearings in English Poetry*, Chatto and Windus, 1954
B. Groom, *The Diction of Poetry from Spenser to Bridges*, Toronto University Press, 1955
Interpretations, ed. J. Wain, Routledge and Kegan Paul, 1955
P. Valery, *The Art of Poetry* (Collected Works III), Routledge and Kegan Paul, 1958
Contemporary American Poetry, ed. H. Namerov, Voice of America Forum, N.D.
M. Schlauch, *Modern English and American Poetry*, Watts, 1956
G. Melchiori, *The Tight-Rope Walkers*, Routledge and Kegan Paul, 1956
G. Hough, *The Last Romantics*, Duckworth, 1949
Image and Experience, Duckworth, 1960
F. Kermode, *Romantic Image*, Routledge and Kegan Paul, 1957
J. Bayley, *The Romantic Survival*, Constable, 1957
J. Wain, *Preliminary Essays*, Macmillan, 1957
Essays on Literature and Ideas, 1963
J. Press, *The Chequered Shade*, Oxford University Press, 1958
Rule and Energy, Oxford University Press, 1963
A Map of Modern English Verse, Oxford University Press, 1969
G. S. Fraser, *Vision and Rhetoric*, Faber, 1959
The Modern Writer and His World, Pelican, 1964
Metre, Rhyme and Free Verse, Methuen, 1970
J. E. Duncan, *The Revival of Metaphysical Poetry*, 1800 to the Present, Minnesota University Press, 1959
A. Thwaite, *Contemporary English Poetry*, Heinemann, 1959
The Poem itself, ed. S. Burnshaw, Pelican, 1960
G. T. Wright, *The Poet in the Poem*, California University Press, 1962
D. Holbrook, *Llareggub Revisited*, Bowes and Bowes, 1962
F. Grubb, *A Vision of Reality*, Chatto and Windus, 1965
J. H. Miller, *Poets of Reality*, Harvard University Press, 1966
The Poet Speaks, ed. P. Orr, Routledge and Kegan Paul, 1966
E. W. Schneider, *The Dragon in the Gate*, California University Press, 1968
T. Hawkes, *Metaphor*, Methuen, 1972

LITERARY SURVEYS

G. Bullough, *The Trend of Modern Poetry*, Oliver and Boyd, 1949
J. Isaacs, *The Background of Modern Poetry*, Bell, 1951
V. de S. Pinto, *Crisis in Modern Poetry, 1880–1940*, Hutchinson, 1951
The Modern Age, ed. B. Ford, Pelican, 1963

Bibliography

BIBLIOGRAPHIES

A. Wade, *A Bibliography of the Writings of W. B. Yeats*, Hart-Davis, 1958
D. Gallup, *T. S. Eliot Bibliography*, Faber, 1952
B. C. Bloomfield and E. Mendelson, *W. H. Auden, A Bibliography 1924–69*, Virginia University Press, 1972

RHETORIC AND STYLE

I. A. Richards, *The Philosophy of Rhetoric*, Oxford University Press, 1936
G. Whalley, *Poetic Process*, Routledge and Kegan Paul, 1953
J. Miles, *Eras and Modes in English Poetry*, California University Press, 1957
Style in Language, ed. T. A. Sebeok, MIT Press, 1960
W. Nowottny, *The Language Poets Use*, Athlone Press, 1962
Essays on Style and Language, ed. R. Fowler, Routledge and Kegan Paul, 1966
Essays on the Language of Literature, ed. S. Chatman and S. R. Levin, Houghton Mifflin, 1967
W. R. Veeder, *W. B. Yeats, The Rhetoric of Repetition*, California University Press, 1968
P. Dixon, *Rhetoric*, Methuen, 1971

LINGUISTICS AND SEMANTICS

N. E. Enkvist, J. Spencer and M. Gregory: *Linguistics and Style*, Oxford University Press, 1964
S. Ullmann, *Language and Style*, Blackwell, 1964
S. Potter, *Modern Linguistics*, 2nd ed., Deutsch, 1967
W. E. Baker, *Syntax in English Poetry*, California University Press, 1967
G. N. Leech, *A Linguistic Guide to English Poetry*, Longman, 1969
A. E. Darbyshire, *A Grammar of Style*, Deutsch, 1971

PROSODY

Egerton Smith, *Principles of English Metre*, Oxford University Press, 1923
J. R. Kreuzer, *Elements of Poetry*, Macmillan, New York, 1955
S. Chatman, *A Theory of Meter*, Mouton, 1965
K. Shapiro and R. Beum, *A Prosody Handbook*, Harper and Row, 1965
The Structure of Verse, ed. H. Goss, Fawcett Publications, 1966
G. S. Fraser, *Metre, Rhyme and Free Verse*, Methuen, 1970

DICTIONARIES AND HANDBOOKS

Dictionary of World Literary Terms, ed. J. T. Shipley, Allen and Unwin, 1955

Bibliography

L. A. Sonnino, *A Handbook to Sixteenth Century Rhetoric*, Routledge and Kegan Paul, 1968

R. A. Lanham, *A Handlist of Rhetorical Terms*, California University Press, 1969

A Dictionary of Modern Critical Terms, ed. R. Fowler, Routledge and Kegan Paul, 1973

SPECIAL STUDIES

J. L. Weston, *From Ritual to Romance*, Cambridge University Press, 1920

J. G. Frazer, *Adonis*, Watts, 1932

R. de Gourmont, *Decadence*, Allen and Unwin, 1930

C. Mauron, *Aesthetics and Psychology*, Hogarth, 1935

A. Huxley, *The Perennial Philosophy*, Chatto and Windus, 1946

Vedanta for the Western World, ed. C. Isherwood, Allen and Unwin, 1948

RELIGION

B. Pascal, *Pensées* (trans. W. F. Trotter, intro. T. S. Eliot), Dent, 1931

(Anonymous) *The Cloud of Unknowing*, ed. E. Underhill, Watkins, 1934

John of the Cross, *Works*, 3 vols, London, 1934–5

Julian of Norwich, *Revelations of Divine Love*, ed. G. Warrock, Methuen, 1945

R. Niebuhr, *The Godly and the Ungodly*, Faber, 1949

JOURNALS

M. W. Bloomfield, '"Doom is Dark and Deeper than any Sea-Dingle", W. H. Auden and Sawles Warde', *Modern Language Notes* 63 (1948) pp 548–52

M. Hamburger, 'The Unity of Eliot's Poetry', *The Review* 4, November 1962, pp 16–27

K. Wright, 'Rhetorical Repetition in T. S. Eliot', *Review of English Studies*, 6. 2 (1965), pp. 93–100

Index

⟨decorative rule⟩

Latin or Greek terms borrowed from classical rhetoric are printed in italic and marked (rhet.); anglicized terms currently in use are printed in roman type.

Words that appear, *passim*, such as *imagery, meaning, metre, movement, rhetoric, rhyme, rhythm, syntax* are not included, except in special applications.

Index

* There are two spellings, in *The Countess Kathleen and Various Legends and Lyrics 1892*, and 'Countess Cathleen' of *Poems 1895*.

R4